The Literary Guide and Companion to

SOUTHERN ENGLAND

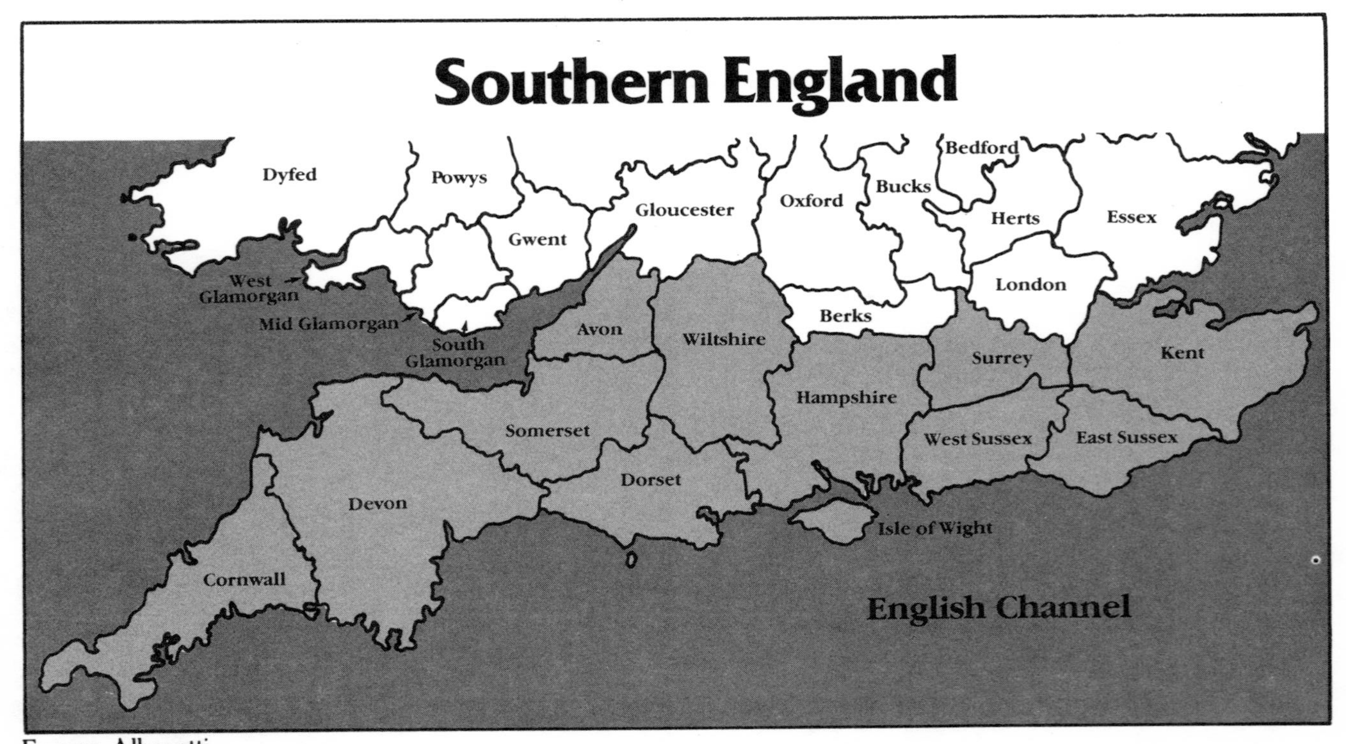

Eugene Albonetti

The Literary Guide
and Companion to

SOUTHERN ENGLAND

Robert M. Cooper

OHIO UNIVERSITY PRESS
ATHENS, OHIO. LONDON .

Library of Congress Cataloging in Publication Data

Cooper, Robert M.
The literary guide and companion to southern England.

Includes index.
1. Literary landmarks—England. 2. Authors, English—Homes and haunts. 3. England in literature. 4. England—Description and travel—1971- —Guidebooks. I. Title. II. Title: Southern England.
PR109.C6 1985 914.22'04858 84-25409
ISBN 0-8214-0790-2

Second printing and first paperback edition, 1985.

TO POLLY

For in every sense, it is her book, too.

CONTENTS

Maps

Photographs

Acknowledgements

Of courtesy, it is much less
Than courage of heart or holiness,
Yet in my walks it seems to me
That the Grace of God is in courtesy.
Hilaire Belloc, *Courtesy*

To the many who showed us courtesy, our grateful thanks— and especially to the following who, setting aside their privacy, opened to us doors not generally open:

Mr. Anthony Brown
Bury House Staff
Father Cassady
The N. A. Chisondale-Marshes
Frederick and Anyon Cook
Mr. Charles Eustace
Mr. A. C. Harrison
Mr. John Holland
Mrs. Dorothy Howell
Jim and Vere Jesty
The Peter Lowrys
The M. G. W. G. Mackeys
Moor Park College
The J. C. Papes
Mrs. Piper
The C. R. Reynolds
The George F. Yateses

***

Bookjacket Portrait by Murray Riss
Map Artwork by Mark Ledgerwood

PREFACE

This book was written for the person who unabashedly loves travel, loves England, and loves English literature. In short, for somebody remarkably like the person I was some years ago when I began to plan my first trip to Britain and looked for just such a book—in vain. I've been looking for it almost yearly since.

You can go batting about England if you like without any guide at all, of course, or with a shopping list of the usual tourist "musts." But you'll waste much time on things you'll find you didn't really care to see, and miss so much you would have loved if you'd only known it was there. Like Gads Hill in Kent, for instance. It's easy to roll right by it on your way from London to Canterbury, unaware you're right where Falstaff accosted his two (four? seven? eleven?) rogues in buckram suits. Unaware, too, that at the same time you are also passing the very house where Dickens wrote books like *A Tale of Two Cities* and *Great Expectations,* and Hans Christian Andersen came for a fortnight visit, drank up all Dickens's whiskey, and stayed six weeks.

Similarly, in Canterbury itself, you'd naturally see the Cathedral and the northwest transept where Becket was hacked to death. You might even realize that the life-size brass figure under the "Miracle Windows" is that of Edward the Black Prince, who had the bad judgment to die before his father, leading to such subsequent unpleasantries as the deposition of his own son Richard and the War of the Roses (and ultimately, it's true, to such delights as Shakespeare's *Richard II* and *Henry IV*).

But chances are you wouldn't know that if you enter the city from the northwest, you can pass through the same gate that Chaucer's pilgrims used . . . you can visit the school that Marlowe and Somerset Maugham (and David Copperfield and Philip Carey) attended . . . follow the route where the hapless Henry II bloodied his feet doing penance for Becket's death . . . and drop by the church that houses all that was salvaged of the author of *Utopia,* Sir Thomas More, after his execution. (His head is buried there.)

The pages that follow also seek to answer basic questions of the kind I so often felt on my literary jaunts to England. Such as:

1. **If I go to such-and-such, what else of literary interest is there nearby?** Well, if it's Canterbury, there are Maugham's boyhood home in Whitstable; Rossetti's grave in Birchington (which pleases the rector not at

all); Joseph Conrad's house in Bishopsbourne (he's buried in Canterbury); Margate, where Keats worked in spasmodic fits at Book II of *Endymion;* and Broadstairs, with the house and cliff where Dickens's Betsey Trotwood tried to fend off those pesky donkeys.

2. **What's the most interesting route to take from such-and-such to so-and-so?** If you're in Brighton, say, and want to get to Portsmouth, turn to the maps and text in the West Sussex and Hampshire sections, and they'll show you how in just those forty-five miles you can see places associated with, among others, Byron (and a pretty girl masquerading as a boy) and Becky Sharp (her honeymoon hotel) . . . Kipling and *Kim* . . . Lewis Carroll, Waugh, and Galsworthy . . . Blake (where he saw Milton in the garden) . . . Keats (*Eve of St. Agnes*) . . . and Dickens and H. G. Wells (how to be miserable in Portsmouth). Meredith even lied about Portsmouth.

3. **What of interest happened in this street (this building, this room) I'm in?** Round that Royal Crescent in Bath, Mr. Dowler, in *Pickwick Papers,* chased Mr. Winkle with a carving knife . . . these Abbey ruins at Titchfield may well have sheltered Shakespeare a time or two . . . that beach at Bude witnessed a monumental pratfall by Alfred Lord Tennyson . . . and in that garden back of Lamb House, Rye, Henry James rebuked his eminent brother William for climbing a ladder to peek at G. K. Chesterton—a tiff adjudicated by H. G. Wells.

4. **How do you find such-and-such a place—Lamb House, for instance?** Whether you come into Rye on the A 259 or the A 268, continue on either until you can turn off on Wish Ward Street. Then turn again onto Mermaid Street, then very shortly right on to West Street—and there it is!

5. **What is the best way—i.e., the shortest, quickest, most efficient—to cover a town that has a number of literary sites?** For such I've included a route tour: for Rye, and Bournemouth, and Canterbury, and Rochester, and Winchester, and many more. The Bath section even has its own marked map.

6. **Are there any places of literary interest where I can get a meal, or a pint of half and half, or even stay overnight?** Yes indeed—many! How about having that half and half where Jane Austen had beef steak and a boiled fowl, but no oyster sauce, or where Blake's scuffle with a drunken soldier led to his trial for treason? How about a pub lunch where Longfellow wrote a poem commemorating a drink of water, or at Daphne du Maurier's Jamaica Inn? And how about staying overnight where Wordsworth and Coleridge began hatching out the idea for *Lyrical Ballads,* or in Tennyson's very own home? You'll find them not only in the general index, but also in a separate listing at the end of the index.

Each step of the way, I've tried to be as informative, as accurate, and as up-to-date as was humanly possible, while trying to produce a book tht would serve for years to come. But underlying it all has been what ought to be fundamental to any trip: FUN. I hope you'll find this book fun to plan with, fun to use as you go, fun to recollect with. And above all, fun to read.

It certainly was fun to write.

Robert M. Cooper

KENT

Kent

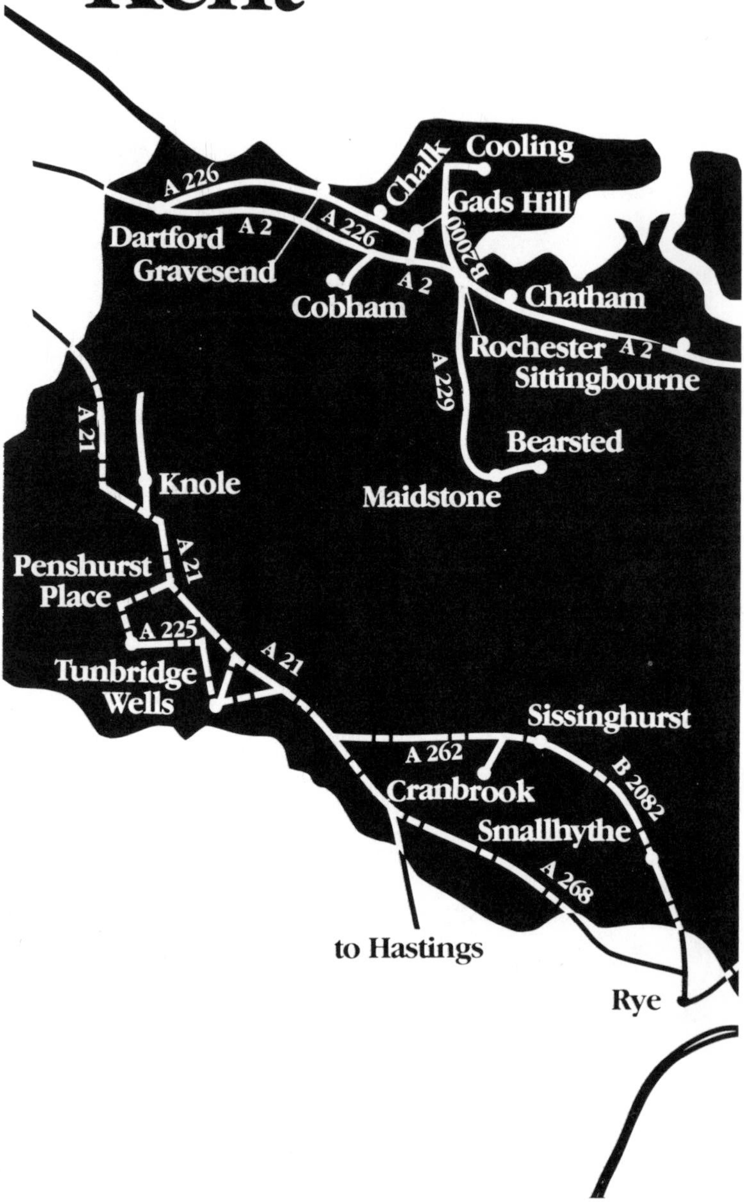

Cooling
Chalk
Gads Hill
A 226
Dartford
A 2
A 226
Gravesend
B 2000
A 2
Cobham
Chatham
Rochester
A 2
Sittingbourne
A 229
A 21
Bearsted
Knole
Maidstone
A 21
Penshurst
Place
A 225
A 21
Tunbridge
Wells
Sissinghurst
A 262
B 2082
Cranbrook
Smallhythe
A 268
to Hastings
Rye

1. The Road to Rochester and On to Canterbury

2. Along the North Sea and Ramsgate to Rye: Along the Dover Strait

3. Showplaces of Kent

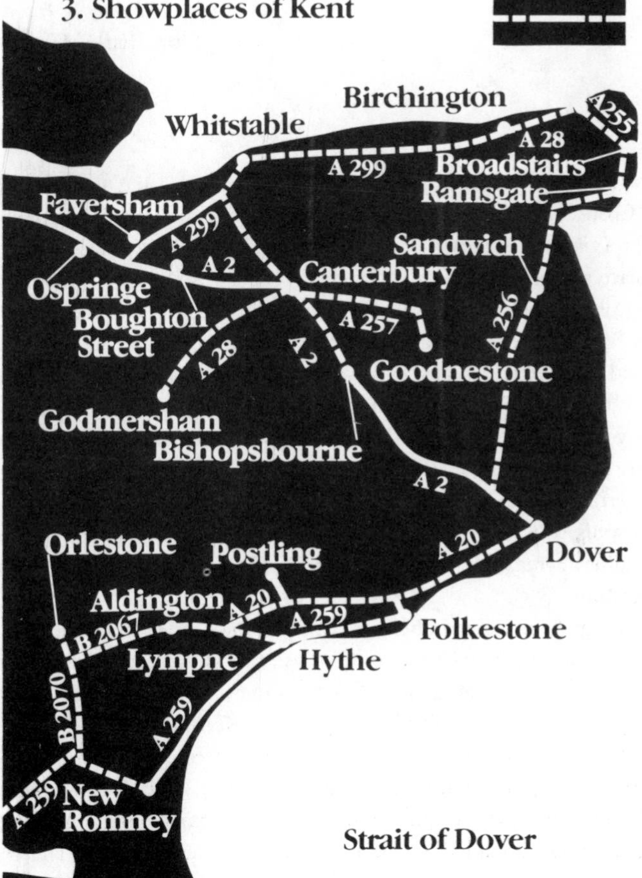

"Kent, sir—Everybody knows Kent—apples, cherries, hops, and women."

Mr. Jingle in *Pickwick Papers*,
by Charles Dickens

And writers, Mr. Jingle might have added, writers. Writers so various as Geoffrey Chaucer and Charles Dickens, epitomes of the writing Englishman, and Joseph Conrad, that darkly brooding son of Poland, alike found Kent a goodly place to live.

Indeed, it's a good thing that ghosts don't take up space, else the specters of literary figures, real and fictional, that throng the highways and byways of Kent would leave little room for the living creatures of today. It's fascinating to conjure up pairs of ghosts right this minute running into each other somewhere along the road from London to Dover. Think of Jane Austen encountering Betsey Trotwood. Or Falstaff reeling (down hill, of course) after his Gads Hill fiasco—and bumping into the Wife of Bath. Or those two fatherless waifs, Pip of *Great Expectations* and H. G. Wells's Kipps, getting together somewhere between Rochester and Folkestone to compare notes on apprenticeship.

All this is quite as it should be. For Kent is at once the seat of some of our earliest Germanic origins, the cradle of English Christianity, and the inspiration of the work that proved in glorious fashion that our vernacular was indeed capable of great literature. Traditionally, Kent was the first part of England taken over by invading Teutonic marauders (remember Hengest and Horsa the Jutes in the mid-fifth century?). In size, today's Kent is not strikingly different from its dimensions as an Anglo-Saxon kingdom: about 1,500 square miles bounded on the north by the Thames Estuary and the North Sea, on the east by the North Sea and the Strait of Dover, on the southwest by East Sussex, and on the west by Surrey.

A hundred and fifty years after Hengest, another Kentish king, one Aethelbert, must have agreeably surprised Augustine when the missionary waded ashore at the Isle of Thanet in 597 A.D., armed only with the dubious protection of Pope Gregory the Great's distant blessings. For Aethelbert not only gave the Roman a friendly welcome, but allowed him to set up shop in Canterbury, giving it an advantage York has yet to catch up with. Nearly 800 years after St. Augustine, of course, Geoffrey Chaucer spun a series of tales ostensibly told by a group of pilgrims going to worship at that same Canterbury—and thereby proved, once and for all, that the descendants of the Angles and the Saxons were best to stick to their own tongue, not Latin or French, for their own literature. (Chaucer himself had a rather good thing going for him in Kent. In 1385 he was made justice of peace for Kent; and the next year he was elected one of the two knights of the shire.)

Speaking of Chaucer, an excellent way to launch yourself on a pilgrimage, whether actual or armchair, to the literary shrines of England would be to follow the trail of *his* pilgrims through Kent, the "hooly blisful martir for to seke." You'll be following the present A 2 if you do. (There's an M 2 expressway to Canterbury, too, but take the A 2.) If today you can't dawdle along at a "*Canterbury* gallop," as did the pilgrims—i.e., at a "canter" or an amble—at least you don't need to roar down an expressway at 70 mph, mowing down the ghosts as you go.

You can pick up the A 2 in London, if you like, across the river in Southwark, where Chaucer himself started at The Tabard (it's gone, but The George, almost as old and very like it, is still there, and still inviting). Or you can leave London to the east and cross the river via the Dartford tunnel, which, though wondrously efficient, was hardly designed to get you in the mood for things ancient and literary.

In any event, you can pick up Kent and your exploration of its literary heritage at the county line: at Dartford.

1. THE ROAD TO ROCHESTER

Dartford to Gads Hill

Dartford Today Dartford is one of those dreary extrusions that any modern megalopolis spews out in all directions. But Dartford was not ever thus, and it does have a literary association or two. Chaucer's pilgrims reached here their first night, after refreshing their horses at the watering of St. Thomas. And Jane Austen stayed at least twice at the George and Bull Inn in the High Street (now the Royal Victoria and Bull), where you can still get a cup of coffee if you like, or a pint of bitter if you remember to get there during pub hours. In 1789, on their way home from visiting her brother in Godmersham Park, near Canterbury, Jane and her parents took rooms up two flights of stairs, and had mixed luck with their food: beef steak and a boiled fowl, but no oyster sauce. However, Jane reported cheerfully that her mother had been "refreshed by a comfortable dinner, and now seems quite stout."

Even before dinner, Jane's good humor had been sorely tested. Shortly after their arrival, her writing and dressing boxes were accidentally packed into a chaise bound for Gravesend and on to the West Indies, with—as Jane put it, her tongue in cheek, "all my worldly wealth, 7£." But a mad chase overtook the carriage, "and in half hour's time I had the pleasure of being as rich as ever."

Ten years later Jane found herself once more in Dartford, bound for Godmersham. Things hadn't improved much: "we went to the Bull, the same inn at which we breakfasted in that said journey, and on the present occasion had about the same bad butter."* No wonder Jane remembered Dartford.

On their second morning, as they left Dartford, Chaucer's pilgrims had a choice of two routes to Strood and the crossing of the Medway River into Rochester—a choice one still faces. The "straight" way was, and is, to continue along the Roman-built road then and now called Watling Street (it remains "Watling Street" all the way to Dover!), today's A 2 highway. As is expected of a Roman road, it is almost relentlessly straight, efficient, and monotonous. With all the time in the world, however, Harry Bailly and his charges may well have taken the route (now the A 226) that swings to the left outside Dartford and passes through Gravesend, Chalk and Higham before reaching Strood. It is slightly longer, but for us more interesting—and far richer in historical and literary associations, from Dickens and an American Indian "princess" to a roistering fifteenth-century knight.

Gravesend Seven miles west of Dartford along the A 226, Gravesend is now an on-the-grubby-side city of about 60,000 people. Historically, it owed its importance to its position on the Thames. Here boats waited for the tide to come up to London twenty-two miles away. Here was the first place incoming ships could supplement depleted stores of fresh food and water, and the last that outbound vessels could do the same. For centuries, the port afforded eminent visitors their first official view of England. As long ago as 1522, Henry VIII met Emperor Charles V here to escort him on a state procession by water to London, and later in the century Elizabeth I established Gravesend as the point where the Corporation of London should welcome in state distinguished foreigners coming to see her.

For many Englishmen, too, distinguished or otherwise, Gravesend was a first, or last, view of home. It was here, for instance, that there stepped

*Jane places this as "fourteen years ago," which would mean either she also stopped at the Bull in 1794—or her memory for dates was hardly flawless.

ashore one September day in 1814 as odd a *ménage à trois* as the literary world has seen: twenty-one-year-old Percy Bysshe Shelley, yet to publish a poem of any consequence; his seventeen-year-old mistress (he already had a wife and two children), Mary Wollstonecraft Godwin (future author of *Frankenstein*), whose father was the radical writer and atheist William Godwin; and Mary's stepsister Claire "Jane" Clairmont, who had joined Mary in eloping from the father they shared. (Claire was later to bear Byron's illegitimate daughter Allegra.) The trio had arrived from a wild trip on the continent without a penny or a care. What's more, they had even talked the ship captain into trusting them for their fare home.

A more touching scene at Gravesend involved Keats, whose devoted friend, sometime nurse (and collaborator) Charles Brown, left England in May 1820 for a trip abroad. As a tribute to their friendship, Keats accompanied him to Gravesend in a smack, both knowing that Keats was a dying man. They never saw each other again. Nine months later Keats was dead.

On a lighter note was the parting of Dante Gabriel Rossetti and Holman Hunt from their comrade in the Pre-Raphaelite Movement, the sculptor Thomas Woolner, and some cronies in July of 1852. (Although they didn't realize it at the time, this was a signal that the movement was already breaking up.) Woolner, discouraged by his lack of artistic success, had decided to chuck it all for the instant riches of Australia's booming gold fields. Rossetti reports on the would-be adventurers with gleeful cynicism and more than a touch of prophetic truth: [they are] "plentifully stocked with corduroys, sou'westers, jerseys, fire-arms and belts full of little bags to hold the expected nuggets." In less than two years, Woolner was back to sculpturing.

Among the saddest stories connected with Gravesend, perhaps, is that of a poor little American Indian, hailed by Jacobean England as a "princess": Pocahontas. She is not strictly a literary figure in her own right, but as the occasion for a number of stories, poems, and books, she surely is worth a brief detour to St. George's church while passing through the city. For here, of all unlikely places, she is buried.

She had left Jamestown in April of 1616 with her English husband, John Rolfe, and their two-year-old son Thomas. After a bittersweet stay in London, they set sail for home in mid-March of 1617. But by the time their ship reached Gravesend, it was clear that she was too ill to continue. It was already too late. She died almost immediately and was buried March 21. It may be, as the more romantic chroniclers have it, that Pocahontas was lionized during her London stay. If so, whoever recorded her death in St. George's registry was not impressed—at least not to the point of accuracy: "March 21, 1617. Rebecca Wrolfe wyffe of Thomas [sic] Wrolfe, a Virginia lady borne, was buried in the chauncell." You can see a photographic copy of this on the church wall.

And, alas, today there's no record of just where in the chancel she lies. But a memorial tablet was put in the chancel in 1896, memorial windows were presented by the Colonial Dames of America in 1914, and in the churchyard a duplicate of her Jamestown statue looks lovely against the sky. St. George's also has the so-called "Gravesend Portrait" of Pocahontas, which suggests she was hardly a beauty—but its reliability is little enhanced by the fact that she is shown wearing eighteenth-century clothing.

Noting Capt. John Smith's less than tumultuous welcome to England to the girl who reputedly saved his life, romantics would like to think that Pocahontas died of a broken heart. It is more likely the cause was tuberculosis, not the least of civilization's gifts to the noble savage. Anyway, as you leave the prosaic portals of St. George's, marveling at the vagaries of fortune that brought a savage chieftain's daughter here to die, ponder something even odder: one of her descendants wound up as the wife of Woodrow Wilson.

Chalk As the A 226 takes you eastward out of Gravesend, there is nothing to indicate you are entering Dickens Country, or even that on its outskirts, you are passing through Chalk. Yet Dickens, in 1836, spent the honeymoon of his ill-fated marriage to Catherine Hogarth here; and, so the natives say, Joe Gargery's forge in *Great Expectations* was here, too. If so, it has, like the honeymoon cottage, long since gone.

Gads Hill

Today Gads Hill (no apostrophe) is an insignificant rise in the land a little more than half way along the eight miles of the A 226 that stretch from Gravesend to Rochester. But in Shakespeare's day it was famous and feared, and justly so. For there lurked the "gads"—roving ("gadding") bands who plundered the travelers going to and from London. It was partly to protect themselves against such that the Canterbury pilgrims were glad to travel as a group.

In Part One of *Henry IV* Shakespeare presents, in Falstaff and his multiplying men in buckram ("Oh, monstrous; Eleven buckram men grown out of two!"), an immortal takeoff of such a gang in action. Often enough, the thieves worked in cahoots with ostlers and tapsters at the inns along the way. Thus they were tipped off as to likely prospects, and, with Falstaff's friend Gadshill (an all too obviously named character), Shakespeare shows this:

The scene is Rochester, an innyard, and Gadshill is talking to the chamberlain (i.e., the man in charge of the inn's bedrooms).

Chamb: There's a franklin [rich farmer] in the wild of Kent hath brought three hundred marks with him in gold. I heard him tell it to one of his company last night at supper. . . . They are up already, and call for eggs and butter. They will away presently.

Gads: Sirrah, if they meet not with Saint Nicholas' clerks [patron saint of thieves], I'll give them this neck.

After a bit of banter, Gadshill heeds the chamberlain's warning that the quarry will soon be under way, but not before promising the informer his reward: "Give me thy hand. Thou shalt have a share in our purchase, as I am a true man."

Among those well aware of Falstaff's connection with Gads Hill was Charles Dickens, and he had special reason to relish it. For after he became wealthy, he made it *his* hill in a poignant realization of a childhood dream. When he was five, his family moved to nearby Chatham, and on their walks father and son would often pass the impressive house on the hill known as "Gads Hill Place." When the boy said he'd like to own it one day, Mr. Dickens replied with sublime disregard for his own ne'er-do-well ways: "If you were to be persevering and were to work hard, you might some day come to live in it." It took him forty years to do it, but by 1860 Dickens was writing a friend: "This is Falstaff's own Gads Hill, and I live on top of it. My house," he added, "is one I was extraordinarily fond of when a child."

And Dickens made a point of reminding visitors of the connection. As a guest descended the staircase to breakfast, he saw on the first floor landing, on an illuminated plaque: "This House, GADS HILL PLACE, stands on the summit of Shakespeare's Gads Hill, ever memorable for its association with Sr. John Falstaff in his noble fancy. *But, my lads, tomorrow morning, by four o'clock, early at Gads Hill! There are pilgrims going to Canterbury with rich offerings and traders riding to London with fat purses; I have vizards for you all; you have horses for yourselves.*"

Even today, with the additions Dickens made, Gads Hill Place is not what one would call a grand house. Rather, it has the simple elegance of the Georgian era (it was built about 1780), the rosy glow of its brick set off by bay windows that run up the front of both storeys and flank a neat white-porticoed entrance. A white-painted cupola graces the roof. Builder of the house was a rags-to-riches hero worthy of a Dickens novel.

He was a man named Stephens, ostler at one of the inns in Chatham, who, very prudently, married the landlord's daughter. He went on to make a good deal of money on his own, and actually rose to be mayor of Rochester—even though to the end of his days he spelled that exalted office "m-a-r-e."

Dickens bought the house in March of 1856 for £1,790, but it was occupied by the vicar of Higham, who took his own time about vacating. It was June of 1856 before Dickens could move in. He chose a snug ground floor room as his study, and from there—in part at least—beginning with *A Tale of Two Cities,* flowed a steady stream of novels and stories. For years, however, he also maintained his London house in Tavistock Square. And from 1865 on, when the weather was good, he wrote in a miniature Swiss chalet, a pretty little two-room building two storeys high, with a fretted balcony and a narrow outside staircase. The chalet had been given to him by his friend, the actor Charles Fechter. It was in the chalet's upper room that Charles Dickens wrote his last words, for *Edwin Drood,* the day before his death.

What is now the A 226 ran right through the Gads Hill property, and since Dickens had placed the chalet across the road, he built a tunnel of goodly proportions to get to it in comfort and safety. (The tunnel still runs under the highway; the chalet itself can be seen at Eastgate Museum in Rochester.) But the tunnel was only one of the many changes Dickens continued to make at Gads Hill until the day he died. In fact, when in 1870 he jokingly protested that the conservatory he was adding was positively his last improvement, he little realized how true he spoke: it was finished one week before he died.

An addition that took heed of Dickens's hardly suppressed yearning to be an actor was the west wing. Below one window the wall was hinged to swing away, so that when the window was raised, an opening was provided for him to make a dramatic entrance for his readings to assembled friends and neighbors. The billiard room—made from the old breakfast parlor—also showed his ingenuity. Since it was a bit on the small side, he had the lower walls tiled so that a cue stick too enthusiastically drawn back wouldn't bang through the plaster.

Looking much as it does in the famous painting "The Empty Chair," done the day after his death, Dickens's study today is especially worth seeing, not only because some of his best work was done there, but also because it is an engaging demonstration of his sly whimsicality. The door is lined with dummy books, so that when it is closed it looks as if it is simply a continuation of the bookshelf-lined walls. And one can have as much fun reading the titles Dickens devised for these pseudo-books as he must have had creating them: *Cats Lives* (in nine volumes) . . . *Five Minutes in China* (in three) . . . *History of the Middling Ages* . . . *Wisdom of Our Ancestors* (including volumes on *Superstitions, The Block, The Stake,* and *Dirt*) . . . and *History of a Short Chancery Suit* (in more than twenty volumes).

Gregarious as Dickens was, it wasn't surprising that Gads Hill Place played host to many a distinguished visitor. But none was more bizarre than Hans Christian Andersen, who arrived June 11, 1857, before Dickens had fairly moved in. They were extremely fond of each other—Andersen had just dedicated his latest novel, *To Be, or Not to Be,* to Dickens—but he often proved a trial and a puzzle. Once he turned up limping badly, "suffering from corns that had ripened in two hours," Dickens said wryly, explaining: "satisfied that the cabman was bent on robbery and murder, he had put his watch and money into his boots—together with a Bradshaw, a pocket-book, a pair of scissors, a penknife, a book or two, a few letters of introduction, and some other miscellaneous property."*

A frequent guest was the writer Wilkie Collins, a pioneer of the detective story, who was there when Andersen arrived and described how, when Dickens advanced to greet his visitor, his right hand outstretched, the Dane clasped it warmly to his heart just as the dinner bell rang. All efforts to free himself having failed, Collins reports, Dickens "was marched into the dining room in full view of his servants and guests, with his hand sentimentally imprisoned in his foreign visitor's waistcoat."

Andersen followed this up by downing most of Dickens's ample dinner supply of whiskey single-handedly, and, when dinner was through, calling for a huge tumbler full of gin and sherry. But the climax came next morning, when he took over the living room, rang the bell, and called loudly for the "son of the house." And when a bewildered twenty-year-old Charley Dickens, who just happened to be home, showed up, Andersen demanded "Shave me." An old Danish custom, it seems. He was supposed to stay a fortnight, and stayed six weeks. No wonder that when he finally left, Dickens rushed into Andersen's bedroom and stuck a card on his dressing table mirror, reading "Hans Christian Andersen slept in this room for five weeks—which seemed in the family AGES."

It was in the dining room at Gads Hill Place that Dickens was fatally stricken. He had spent the day (June 8, 1870) working in the chalet on the sixth installment of *Edwin Drood.* Suddenly, at dinner, he was seized with a stroke and dropped from his chair. Too ill to be moved, he was placed on a couch brought in from the living room, and here he died next day. (The couch can now be seen at the Dickens Birthplace Museum in Portsmouth.)

The easiest way to spot Gads Hill Place today on your way from Gravesend to Rochester is to look for the Falstaff Inn on the left. It is (and was) directly across the street from Dickens's house, and he often used it to house his overflow guests. When asked whether it wasn't rather awkward having a pub just across the street, Dickens would reply: "Oh no, not at all. I always know

---

*Dickens places the incident in London, with the cab taking Andersen from the City to Dickens's Tavistock House. But Wilkie Collins, who witnessed it, says it happened at Gads Hill, the cab presumably coming from the Rochester station.

where to find my men." The fact was, when he boasted about Gads Hill Place he included the inn: "To crown all, the sign of the Sir John Falstaff is over the way, and I used to look at it as a wonderful mansion (which God knows it is not) when I was a very odd little child with the first faint shadows of all my books in my head—I suppose."

Gads Hill Place is now a private day school for girls up to the age of sixteen and is not routinely open to the public. But the directors have a keen sense of responsibility for this historic house, and the would-be visitor who writes in advance for an appointment* and displays something more than a mere gawker's curiosity has a fair chance of being invited to come have a look.

Cooling and Cobham

Cooling About five miles north of Rochester and six miles northwest of Gads Hill, over the B 2000 on a narrow pavement, more lane than highway, is a spot—hardly enough to be called a village, though it was one in Dickens's day—with a churchyard, marshes and, nearby, the ruins of a fourteenth-century castle. This is Cooling.

In the churchyard, thirteen stones mark the graves of the hapless offspring of a family named Comfort, who all died within one short three-year period. This was the bleak picture that, in *Great Expectations,* gave rise to Pip's "five little lozenges, each about a foot and a half long, which were arranged in a neat row . . . and were sacred to the memory of five little brothers of mine—who gave up trying to get a living exceedingly early in that universal struggle."

And standing in the churchyard, especially if you get there near dusk of a raw afternoon, with the outlying marshes turning into a "dark flat wilderness," it is easy enough to hear the terrible voice of the convict, Abel Magwitch, starting up from among the graves and crying to Pip, "keep still, you little devil, or I'll cut your throat!"

Down the road are the ruins of a castle with an interesting link to Shakespeare. For this was once the home of a valiant captain and a hardy gentleman called Sir John Oldcastle, Lord Cobham, an early fifteenth-century Lollard who was declared a heretic in 1414, and three years later had the misfortune of being "hung and burnt hanging." He turns up, badly miscast, as one of the Prince of Wales's disreputable cronies in a wretched sixteenth-century play, *The Famous Victories of Henry the Fifth,* and, borrowing from that play in his first version of *Henry IV,* Shakespeare similarly called his fat knight "Oldcastle." But responding to pressure from the contemporary

---

*Gads Hill Place, Higham-by-Rochester, Kent

holder of the name, he renamed his character Sir John Falstaff. Anyway, the Oldcastle ruins are there in Cooling for you to see, if you're all that fond of ruins—and there *is* a fourteenth-century gatehouse.

Cobham A little over a mile off the A 2 (south on B 2009), four miles west of Rochester, is the village of Cobham, named for the family of Cooling's Oldcastle. The boy Dickens often walked with his father through Cobham Woods and past Cobham Hall, and he remembered the experience most pleasantly in *Pickwick Papers:* "A delightful walk it was . . . through a deep and shady wood, cooled by the light wind which gently rustled the thick foliage." From this, one "emerged upon an open park, with an ancient hall displaying the quaint and picturesque architecture of Elizabeth's time."

Here occurred one of the more sensational murders of Dickens's day, involving a promising twenty-six-year-old painter named Richard Dadd. He'd been known to act oddly, denouncing his patron—and the Pope—as devils, for instance. Still, no one thought him actually insane until August 28, 1843, when he suddenly and quite brutally murdered his own father. Dadd fled to France, but was soon brought back to London and confined in the famous Bethlehem ("Bedlam") Hospital—where he calmly went on painting. The crime seems to have impressed Dickens. He made a point of showing his visitors, when they reached the park, the very spot where Dadd père fell.

A happier Cobham stop for Dickens's guests was the old "Leather Bottle Inn," which the American Longfellow recalled from his stay with Dickens in 1842. It is to Cobham and The Leather Bottle that Dickens has the disconsolate Tracy Tupman retreat, again in *Pickwick Papers,* wryly noting "for a misanthrope's choice, this is one of the prettiest and most desirable places of residence I ever met with." And it still is, even though fire in the 1880's plus the routine ravages of time occasioned considerable redoing of the building, especially the outside, which now has a quaint Tudor-looking half-timbered air about it instead of the plain no-nonsense front of Dickens's day. But as you step inside this "clean and commodious village ale-house," duck under the low wooden beams, and step along the worn stone floor down the very long and narrow corridor, you can almost feel the ghost of Mr. Pickwick silently joining in the search for his missing partner, and follow where he passed through "a door at the end of the passage, and . . . entered a long, low-roofed room, furnished with a large number of high-backed chairs."

It's actually something of a jolt to return to the twentieth century, and to realize that Mr. Tupman's not really there, waiting to be talked into rejoining the Pickwick party. But you can console yourself with a first- rate meal, and pause to examine, on the walls everywhere, what may well be the most extensive collection of pictures, cartoons, illustrations, photographs, and other Dickensiana outside a museum.

A truly worthwhile stop, The Leather Bottle.

Rochester

> An ancient city Cloisterham, and no meeting dwelling-place for anyone with hankerings after the noisy world. A monotonous, silent city, deriving an earthy flavour throughout from the Cathedral crypt, and so abounding in vestiges of monastic graves that the Cloisterham children grow small salad in the dust of abbots and abbesses, and make dirt-pies of nuns and friars.
>
> from *Edwin Drood,* by Charles Dickens

Dickens's "Cloisterham" is, of course, Rochester—which is also his Mudfog in *The Mudfog Papers,* and (with Chatham) the Dullborough of *The Uncommercial Traveller.* It is also Rochester in its own right in *Pickwick Papers, David Copperfield,* and *Great Expectations.* The true Dickens fanatic can spend a week blissfully in Rochester, and linger for more.

But he would hardly find it a "monotonous, silent city." Rather, he is likely to agree enthusiastically with *Pickwick Papers's* Mr. Jingle:

> Ah! fine place—glorious pile—frowning walls—tottering arches—dark nooks—crumbling stair-cases—Old Cathedral, too—earthy smell—pilgrim's feet worn away the old steps—little Saxon doors—confessionals like money-takers' boxes at theatres—queer customers those monks—Popes, and Lord Treasurers. And all sorts of fellows with great red faces, and broken noses, turning up every day—buff jerkins, too—match-locks—Sarcophagus—fine place—old legends, too—strange stories: capital.

Rochester has literary interest other than that connected with Dickens. Chaucer's pilgrims passed it on their second day. Shakespeare's Gadshill, in *Henry IV, I,* gets that tip for the Gads Hill robbery from the chamberlain of a Rochester inn. Pepys boasted of making the ride from London in under four hours, and celebrated: "went into the Cherry Garden [of Restoration House] and here met a pretty young woman and did kiss her."

Few cities in England, however, belong so wholly to one writer as Rochester does to Dickens. And the best way to make his Rochester your own is to stop at the Tourist Information Centre, get a copy of its excellent "A

Walk Around the City," and get going. The walk is level and easy and, since the sites of major interest are concentrated in a relatively small area, not too time-consuming.

On leaving the Centre, one can begin by turning up the High Street to the right. Just before the bridge, on the right hand side of the street, is a large dullish building surmounted by a cupola with a ship weather vane. This is the Guildhall, built in 1687. The weather vane is a 1780 afterthought. In *Great Expectations* it figures as the Town Hall where Pip was bound apprentice to Joe Gargery: "The Hall was a queer place, I thought, with higher pews in it than a church."

To celebrate the occasion, Mrs. Joe insists that Mr. Pumblechook, the Hubbles, and Mr. Wopsle join the Gargerys at the Blue Boar inn—paid for out of Pip's twenty-five guineas "windfall." It is to the Blue Boar, too, that Pip comes to stay overnight when he returns, years later, to see Estella. Model for the Blue Boar, in actuality, was the Royal Victoria and Bull, which you'll find (No. 16–19) directly across the street from the Guildhall—still doing business as "The Bull."

Dickens had already used this hotel in *Pickwick Papers,* introducing it via Mr. Jingle, who, when asked if he stayed there, replied: "Not I—but you'd better—Good house—nice beds—Wright's next house, dear—half-a-crown in the bill, if you look at the waiter." Mr. Jingle, you may remember, goes on to have a glorious evening in the hotel's ballroom in the "borrowed plumage" he removes from the sleeping Winkle.

The ballroom, "a long room, with crimson-covered benches and wax candles in glass chandeliers," still exists. But the so-called "Queen's Bedroom," where Victoria stayed both the year before she became queen and the year after her coronation (hence the *Royal* Victoria and Bull), lost its identity in the hotel's modernization of 1961. But a substantial souvenir of its past glory survives. For it was also Dickens's favorite room, and its big brass bed in which he often slept can now be seen at Bleak House in Broadstairs.

While waiting for his breakfast at the Bull, Mr. Pickwick takes a breather on the Rochester Bridge a few yards away, and enjoys the view with, on the left, the "ruined wall, broken in many places," and behind it "the ancient Castle, its towers roofless, and its massive walls crumbling away, but telling us proudly of its old might and strength, as when, seven hundred years ago, it rang with the clash of arms, or resounded with the noise of feasting and revelry." Dickens had always hoped to be buried in the graveyard in the castle moat. It is a friendly sort of a castle, especially to those dispirited by the normal castle's preference for inaccessible heights. And if you must climb, there's a fine view from the battlements, reached by a steep spiral staircase within the Keep's walls.

At the foot of the road that runs past the castle into the High Street, you'll find the fifteenth-century College Gate, original of the "old stone gate-house crossing the [Cathedral] Close, with an arched thoroughfare passing beneath it," where lived the darkly scheming Mr. Jasper of *Edwin Drood.* Passing through its arch from the High Street on the way to the Cathedral itself, you can still look back and see the gatehouse's two windows, "the one looking [toward the Close], and the one looking down into the High Street," betwixt which, with some concern, the Dean, Mr. Crisparkle, and Mr. Tope viewed Jasper's "own solitary shadow" as he drew his curtains.

Carry on, as the English say, through the Close to the Cathedral. It's still much as Mr. Jingle said it was. The earthy smell is noticeable the minute you open the door; the pilgrim-worn old steps are even more so after nearly 150 years' additional use; and the little Saxon doors are low enough to make you unconsciously stoop, even when you don't have to. You won't find the "confessionals like money-takers' boxes at theatres," however. According to the Cathedral librarian, there were no confessionals there, as popularly understood, in Dickens's day. He thinks that the author must have been referring to the box-pews which were a feature of the Cathedral then. They were removed in the 1870's; and today no trace of them remains, but the library has two pictures of them.

It's a workaday Cathedral, one that in no way puts on airs or attempts to overawe, and seems peculiarly suitable for Rochester. Yet Dickens clearly loved it, and found its north graveyard a fruitful hunting ground for names of characters. (It's fun to spend a few minutes trying to see how many you can spot.) Indeed, he came close to being buried in the Cathedral's St. Mary's Chapel when his family, after he died in 1870, found that the graveyard in Rochester Castle Moat had been closed to further burials. At the last minute, although a grave had already been prepared in the chapel, they consented to his interment in the Poet's Corner at Westminster Abbey.

The Cathedral does have a memorial to Dickens, a brass plate placed in the south transept by his executors to forever connect him and both his earliest and latest years and associations with Rochester. Fittingly, the memorial is directly below one to Richard Watts, a long-ago Rochesterian who gave rise to Dickens's "Seven Poor Travellers." Watts was a sixteenth-century self-made man who left money to befriend six poor travellers. In his story, Dickens himself becomes the seventh.

Watts's Charity, as it is called, built to carry out his bequest, is reached by returning to the High Street and going a few doors beyond the Tourist Centre. Its little galleried Elizabethan bedrooms are worth seeing, and a memorial stone in the street-side wall delightfully tells the story. It reads:

> For six poor travellers who not being rogues or proctors [professional beggars] may receive gratis for one night lodging and entertainment and four pence each.

It goes on grandly to say that

> In testimony of his munificence, in honour of his memory,

and as an inducement for others to follow his example,

> the charitable trustees of this city and borough caused this stone to be renewed and transcribed AD 1865.

Further down the High Street (Nos. 150–154), past Maidstone Road, are "Mr. Pumblechook's premises . . . of a peppercorny and farinaceous character."* High up in this handsome black and white Tudor house, even higher than its four storeys, slept young Pip "in an attic," as he puts it, "with a sloping roof, which was so low in the corner where the bedstead was, that I calculated the tiles as being within a foot of my eyelashes." If you stand across the street and look sharp you can just see the window of Pip's little room, butting out from the roof that slopes down between two gables.

In *Edwin Drood,* the same house reappears as the home of "the purest Jackass in Cloisterham," Mr. Thomas Sapsea, Auctioneer. Dickens describes it as standing "in the High Street, over against the Nuns' House," and "about the period of the Nuns' house, irregularly modernized here and there, as steadily deteriorating generations found, more and more, that they preferred air and light to Fever and the Plague." The Nuns' House, he said, was a "venerable brick edifice," with a brass plate "flashing forth the legend: 'Seminary for Young Ladies. Miss Twinkleton.' " The two houses were, and are, diagonally across the street from each other, the Nuns' House being in actuality Eastgate House, now housing the City Museum. Its exhibits run a haphazard gamut from Indian arrowheads to an early TV set, and its Dickens relics, aside from a few rather good photos, are on the pathetic side. But it's free, and in the back yard you can see the Swiss chalet from Gads Hill, in which Dickens wrote, among other things, *Great Expectations* and *Our Mutual Friend.*

A very brief retracing of your steps back up the High Street and a turn to the left up Maidstone Road will take you to Restoration House, so named because Charles II stayed there in 1660 on his way to reclaim England's throne for the Stuarts. (And it is the same house where, seven years later, Pepys stole his kiss from the pretty wench.) This was the house Dickens used for the "Satis House" of Miss Havisham in *Great Expectations,* "which was of old brick, and dismal, and had a great many bars to it." The windows had bars

---

*Or so the natives say of this and many another "original" of a Dickens fictional house, both here and elsewhere. At any rate, such houses usually are sufficiently "look-alikes" to be satisfactory.

(they still do) because when the house was built, Rochester was a walled city, and the house was outside the walls. Its land no longer runs all the way down to the High Street, as it did in Miss Havisham's day, and its thirty or so rooms are now elegantly maintained by its private owners as their home. But its E-shaped exterior remains much as Dickens described it.

Facing Restoration House is the beginning of "The Vines"—the monks' vineyard of *Edwin Drood,* and in *Great Expectations* the priory garden Pip passes through, with "the nooks of ruin where the old monks had once their refectories and gardens, and where the strong walls were now pressed into the service of humble sheds and stables."

On Monday, June 6, 1870, Dickens spent his last day in Rochester. He had walked over from his Gads Hill Place in Higham accompanied by his dogs, and first was seen leaning on the fence in front of Restoration House, examining it carefully. Later on, he passed slowly by the Cathedral. Two days later he wrote in the last page of *Edwin Drood* he was to achieve:

> Changes of glorious light from moving boughs, songs of birds, scents from gardens, woods and fields . . . penetrate the cathedral, subdue its earthly odour, and preach of the Resurrection and the Life. The cold stone tombs of centuries ago grow warm; and flocks of brightness dart into the sternest marble corners of the building, fluttering there like wings.

Dickens loved Rochester.

2. ON TO CANTERBURY

Chatham

Dickens may or may not have been joking when he insisted he never could tell where Rochester ended and Chatham began, but even so, the modern motorist going east along the A 2 would have to agree. Chatham is continuous to the east with Rochester, and shares with it the right bank of the Medway River. Dickens, in *The Uncommercial Traveller,* lumps them indifferently as "Dullborough Town."

But the two houses in which Dickens lived between the ages of five and eleven, undoubtedly the happiest of his early years, were in Chatham. John Dickens, "The Prodigal Father" as the novelist was to call him, was a minor clerk in the Navy Pay Office, made peripatetic by an improvident purse. He had already shunted his family from house to house and from Portsmouth to London before, in 1817, he got a promotion of sorts to Chatham. There, for a while, they settled in a rather decent house at No. 2 (now No. 11) Ordinance

Terrace. But then, in 1821, came a dip in the drearily familiar Dickens roller coaster way of living, and they moved to the smaller, cramped "house on the Brook" in St. Mary's Place. For a while Charles went to school at Mr. Giles's in Clover Lane. These Chatham years were almost the only normal ones the young Dickens was to know, and he remembered them fondly.

He remembered the Mitre Inn where at evening parties he would sometimes be hoisted to a table as an impromptu stage to sing sea chanties, and where "I was cried over by my rosy little sister, because I had acquired a black eye in a fight." This was the same Mitre Inn where he boarded the London-bound coach, "Blue-Eyed Maid," in 1822 when the family's fortunes took an even more disastrous dip, and they had to give up Chatham altogether.

He remembered, too, the Chatham dockyard which Pepys had visited on official Navy business and where his own father was employed. He devoted a whole chapter to it in *The Uncommercial Traveller,* describing "the creeking little jetty . . . gaunt high-water marks and low-water marks, and the broken causeway, and the broken bank, and the broken stakes and piles leaning forward as if they were vain of their appearance." And he confessed: "running water is favourable to day-dreams, and a strong tidal river [i.e., the Medway] is the best of running water for mine." You can, by the way, still daydream along the Medway, and the Royal Navy offers a free tour of the dockyards three times a day. But both Dickens's houses, as well as Mr. Giles's, the Mitre, and his favored Clarence Hotel are gone.

Despite the derisive tag of "Dullborough," Chatham-Rochester lingered lovingly in his memory, and he records the familiar pangs of childhood revisited. The railroad station, he found, "had swallowed up the playing field; the town had shrunk fearfully since I was a child there." And what had happened to the glamorous Lucy Green, who in their childhood games had come all the way from "England" (actually the second house in the terrace) to ransom him from the dungeons of Seringapatam in "India"? Surely the lovely Lucy couldn't have changed into the fat-faced wife of Dr. Joe Specks? But alas, in those dear but distant days, Dickens had been a boy of ten or so, Miss Green, perhaps a year younger. And the dungeons of Seringapatam had been only a pile of hay, however fragrant.

The Chatham echoes in his fiction in no way rival those from Rochester. But the dockyards did influence scenes in *A Tale of Two Cities,* the Pickwick Club attends military maneuvers at the Great Lines, and the fields near the Ft. Pitt Naval Hospital are the site of Mr. Winkle's anticipated duel with Dr. Slammer. And there is that memorable passage when David Copperfield, footsore and weary on his flight to Aunt Betsey Trotwood in Dover, "toiled into Chatham" late at night, sensing in the blackness "a mere dream of chalk, and drawbridges, and mastless ships in a muddy river." He creeps at last upon a sort of grass-grown battery overhanging a lane, and lies down near a cannon—"happy in the society of [a] sentry's footsteps."

In *Edwin Drood,* the Mitre doubles as "The Crozier," that "hotel of a most retiring disposition," where the mysterious Dick Datchery puts up. In *Dombey and Son,* William Giles serves as the model for Paul Dombey's teacher, Mr. Feeder, B. A., "who was in the habit of shaving his head for coolness, and had nothing but little bristles on it."

Maidstone—Allington—Bearsted—Wateringbury

Maidstone (**MED**-stun)

> I have discovered that the seven miles between Maidstone and Rochester is one of the most beautiful walks in England.
>
> Charles Dickens

Maidstone is still seven miles southeast of Rochester, but one reaches it now along the unexceptional A 229; and if you're heading for Canterbury, it's hardly an "absolute must" detour, unless: a) you're wild about William Hazlitt; or b) you'd like to do a bit of really recherché literary-geographical name dropping when you get back home.

Hazlitt was born in Maidstone in 1778 in Rose Yard, Mitre Lane, near his father's Unitarian Chapel, but the house no longer exists. There is a museum in St. Faith's Street, however, in the sixteenth-century Chillington Manor House, that has an assortment of Hazlitt relics representing commendable industry on the part of the city fathers—especially since Hazlitt left Maidstone at age two.

As for the name dropping, there are several places in Maidstone's immediate vicinity worth a casual (but determined) aside should the occasion ever arise, to wit: Allington, Bearsted, Wateringbury, and Boxley.

Allington On the northwest edge of Maidstone, off the M 20, is Allington. Sir Thomas Wyatt was born at Allington Castle in 1503. He is noted for introducing, with Surrey, the sonnet into England, but he may well have considered even more of an achievement his ability to survive the friendship of Henry VIII.

Bearsted On the eastern edge of Maidstone, on the A 20, Bearsted is where for two months, in 1921, in the Bell House at the end of the green,

Sinclair Lewis worked away at *Babbitt.* There is no indication he was influenced by the local Colonel Blimps.

Wateringbury Wateringbury lies five miles southwest of Maidstone, on the A 26. Here, in 1931, George Orwell and two tramps spent eighteen days picking hops. Orwell described the experience in his essay, "Hop Picking," and later made use of it in a novel, *A Clergyman's Daughter* (1935).

Boxley—Sittingbourne—Ospringe

Boxley Two miles north of Maidstone, Boxley is on a narrow, unnumbered road. Tennyson's family moved here in 1841 to be near their friend Edmund Lushington, who a year later married the poet's sister Cecilia, a marriage which was celebrated in the marriage song that forms the epilogue to *In Memoriam.*

Both the scenery of "Aylmer's Field" and the setting for "The Princess" derive from Lushington's Park House grounds, and at Boxley Tennyson worked at preparing his poems for the 1842 edition that made his reputation, revising and polishing poems from his 1832 collection, among them "Lady of Shalott," "Palace of Art," and "Lotus Eaters," and writing such new ones as "Ulysses" and "Locksley Hall."

Sittingbourne This town on the A 2, almost equidistant (about fifteen miles each way) between Rochester and Canterbury, is forty miles or so east-southeast of London, and since Chaucer's pilgrims passed through it toward the end of their second day, they seem to have been averaging a bit more than twenty miles a day. It boasts the fifth-century Tong "Castle," a be-moated mound of no literary interest save that it is supposed to have been built by Hengest, who—when Vortigern promised him as much land as an oxhide could encompass—outslicked him by cutting the hide into strips before marking out the boundaries.

A literary figure who was not impressed with Sittingbourne was Jane Austen, who passed through it frequently on her visits to her brother Edward in Godmersham. Typical was her comment in a letter of June 15, 1808, describing a brief stop at The George Inn: "a few minutes, of course, did for Sittingbourne."

Ospringe A hamlet just off the A 2 (to the south) six miles east of Sittingbourne, Ospringe was a regular stop for pilgrims on their way to Becket's shrine. Here Chaucer's group probably stayed on their second night, assuring themselves of a comfortable, mid-day arrival in Canterbury, nine miles to the east, on the morrow.

Faversham—Boughton Street—Harbledown

Faversham A very short detour to the north, right after Ospringe (and eight miles to the west of Canterbury), takes you to Faversham. Holinshed's *Chronicles* records its most sensational crime, the murder of its mayor, Richard Arden, in 1550/51, by his persevering wife and her lover, who after many tries finally managed to prove the truth of "if at first . . ." for which success they were duly executed. The story forms the stuff of the Elizabethan play, *The Tragedy of Mr. Arden of Feversham.* Fortunately, the argument that Shakespeare wrote it is wholly refutable.

Boughton Street This is the village, five miles further along the A 2 (and four miles west of Canterbury), where, on their last morning, after leaving Ospringe, Chaucer's pilgrims overtake the canon in the Prologue to the "Canon's Yeoman's Tale":

> Er we hadde riden fully fyve mile,
> At Boghton under Blee us gan atake
> A man that clothed was in clothes blake.

"Under Blee," which is repeated in the *Canterbury Tales'* mention of Harbledown (see next item), means that the village was in the Blean wood.

Harbledown By the time they got to hear the "Manciple's Tale," the Canterbury pilgrims were practically on the outskirts of their goal and may already have caught their first exciting glimpse of the Cathedral itself. For, as the prologue to this tale indicates, they had reached Harbledown, a village on the hill (and the A 2) immediately to Canterbury's west:

> Woot ye not where there stant a litel town
> Which that ycleped [called] is Bobbe-up-and-down,
> Under the Blee, in Caunterbury weye?

Bobbe-up-and-down is Harbledown. The next stop was Canterbury itself.

Canterbury

> It is the bounden duty of every English-speaking man and woman to visit Canterbury at least twice in their lives.
>
> Rt. Rev. Frederick Temple

Visit twice? Well, the speaker was a former headmaster of Rugby who wound up Archishop of—you guessed it!—Canterbury (1896–1902). But Chaucer avers that, even in his day, people made a point of flocking there from all over:

> And specially from every shires ende
> Of Engelond to Caunterbury they wende.

The city's motto is: "Ave Mater Angliae"—Hail, Mother of England. In many ways this is a valid, if less than modest, boast. For centuries the Cathedral has been known as the Mother Church of England. And before that, the city was the base from which St. Augustine and his colleagues, in A.D. 597, spread out to convert the Pagans. And before that, Canterbury was assured a pivotal position by topography. Even today, if you take the shortest way between Dover and London, you take the A 2 via Canterbury, although it lies a good deal northeast of a straight line between them. The reason: from Dover northward stretch the North Downs, a range of high chalk hills. To skirt them, the Romans (and today's engineers) had to go north to Canterbury before they could turn eastward toward London.

And finally, Canterbury can make some claim to being Mother of Literary England as the focal point and inspiration of the first great work in a language that to the average twentieth-century reader is recognizably English—Chaucer's *Canterbury Tales.*

Canterbury is a joy to visit; and though Charles Dickens preferred to live in Rochester and vacation in Broadstairs, he obviously loved it. He dwells lovingly on his description of the city in *David Copperfield;* the fanciful picture of David's mother in his youth was associated "with the sunny street of Canterbury, dozing as it were in the hot light; and with the sight of its old houses and gateways, and the stately, grey Cathedral, with the rooks sailing round the towers."

On the other hand, Jane Austen would probably have sniffed in a maidenly, mannered way something to the effect that "it's a great place to visit, but. . . ." From Southampton she regards with mock horror a possible consequence of her sister Cassandra's being too charming on a visit to Canterbury: "If that should be the case, we must remove to Canterbury, which I should not like so well as Southampton."

In any event, it *is* a great place to visit. But there is so much to see—both literary and otherwise—that unless you have unlimited time, perhaps the best thing to do is screw your courage to the sticking point, be gauche if you have to, and insist on seeing only the "must" things on your list. You'll miss a number of things on somebody else's must-list, true—but better that than failing to savor anything by trying to devour everything. (You can save the rest for that second visit recommended by Archbishop Temple.) You'll want to see more than just what's associated with literature, of course. But here the emphasis is on the literary highlights.

Start with the Cathedral. In Chaucer's day, surely, that's what religious pilgrims did, once they were established in their quarters; today's literary pilgrims may well do the same. For the Cathedral ranks as a literary monument in its own right, thanks to authors like Charles Dickens, Tennyson, Somerset Maugham, and T. S. Eliot, in addition to Chaucer. It serves also as a striking record of the passage of slow time required both for the construction of a cathedral and the creation of a literature.

When William of Sens, in 1174, began the rebuilding program that ultimately produced today's Cathedral after fire had destroyed the earlier building, a Canterburian who wanted to curl up with a good book had to settle for the likes of Wace's *Brut*—and in Anglo-Norman French at that. Thomas à Becket was a brand new saint-in-residence, having been canonized a scant three years after his death in 1170.

But by the time the nave was completed in 1421, the *Canterbury Tales* had long since been written—and in English, however "middle"—and Becket had become the town's leading industry, thanks to nearly 250 years of duly attested "miracles" that had helped people "whan that they were seeke."

And in 1503, when the Cathedral was finally finished with the tucking of the last stone into "Bell Harry," the 235-foot central tower, *Utopia's* Thomas More was getting ready to enter parliament, sonneteer Thomas Wyatt had just been born—and Shakespeare himself was a mere sixty years away. And Henry VIII, who was to put Becket's tomb and his church out of business (and cart off a reputed twenty-six cartloads of the shrine's gold and jewels) was twelve years old.

The Cathedral today still stands much as it was in the sixteenth century, save for the northwestern tower, which was the victim of a Victorian dean's misplaced zeal for symmetry. Seeing that this Norman tower didn't match its 1460 southern partner—a fact that had somehow escaped less discerning eyes for nearly 400 years—the dean, in the 1830's, had the offending tower pulled down and replaced with a more compliant Victorian version.

The most picturesque approach to the Cathedral—so much so that it has become a camera fan's cliché—is from the High Street . . . down narrow Mercery Lane, the very essence of a medieval street, whose ancient roofs frame the pinnacles of the Cathedral towers . . . through the Christchurch Gate . . . and into the Precincts.

Usually the visitor enters the Cathedral itself through the southwest porch, and proceeds along the south side of the nave, at whatever pace suits his own particular taste for—and capacity to digest—the glorious mysteries of such things as Perpendicular and Decorated, stained glass and tombs, and clerestories and triforiums.

Becket's shrine, from 1220 to 1538 (his body was moved from the crypt in 1220) was in the Trinity Chapel at the Cathedral's eastern end, which had been specially rebuilt to house and highlight it. And it must have been something to see before Henry laid hands on it. Today, however, no trace of it remains. But just behind the high altar you can gaze upon the spot, now roped off, where pilgrims knelt to pray to the "hooly blisful martir," and even imagine that among the grooves worn in the floor by their knees are those of the Wife of Bath.

To the right and left of the shrine were the "Miracle Windows," six each in the north and south aisles. Much of the original glass is gone, and some of the windows are in part reconstructions. But what remains has its own beauty and interest. There is more left to see in those on the north aisle, including a "portrait" of Becket, illustrations of his life and martyrdom, and a sampling of miracles attributed to him. Those on the south aisle, such as they are, are largely reconstructed, but the lower part of Window No. 12 is worth a pause for the modern-sounding story it tells. A William of Gloucester, it seems, was buried alive in a ditch while laying, of all things, water pipes. Happily, the intercession of St. Thomas saved him.

Looking up at these Miracle Windows, lying comfortably atop his tomb in the south aisle, is the splended life-size brass figure of Edward the Black Prince, whose untimely death in 1376, in a sense, gave rise to the War of the Roses. For had his son, Richard II, not come to the throne prematurely, there might well have been no deposing and no consequent war. But since the War of the Roses, in turn, gave rise to Shakespeare's *Richard II, Henry IV, Henry V,* and *Richard III*—and above all, Falstaff—perhaps we should bear the Black Prince no malice.

Also in the Trinity Chapel, nestling just across the aisle from the prince, is the alabaster tomb of his nephew, Henry IV—prudently close to St. Thomas's shrine, as if seeking his protection from the wrath of God for having stolen Richard's throne.

The Black Prince had wanted to be buried in the crypt below the Presbytery and Trinity Chapel, and this is where Becket first was buried and first went to work making miracles. It's possible to duck down to see the crypt before going on to the northwestern transept and The Martyrdom itself. Here, in the closing twilight of December 29, 1170, in full view of the horrified worshippers who had come in to Vespers, Thomas à Becket was hacked to death by four knights who mistakenly thought Henry II would enjoy being rid of his balky archbishop.

They had made an odd but vastly successful team, these two—Henry, gifted but mercurial, only twenty when he picked Becket for his chancellor . . . and Becket, thirty-six, who had loved rich living as a chancellor, but secretly wore a hair shirt beneath his habit and scourged himself daily when he became archbishop. It was to the crypt and Becket's tomb that Henry came in 1174 to do penance. The clash of these two powerful personalities was the very essence of drama, and George Darley, Tennyson, and T. S. Eliot wrote plays about it.

To the north of the Cathedral is King's School, reached through the Green Court, that open space which in Chaucer's day divided the monks' quarters from the service buildings—stables, brewhouses, and the like. The latter, considerably rebuilt and changed, are now part of the school whose graduates include such literary luminaries as Thomas Linacre, Christopher Marlowe, Walter Pater, Somerset Maugham, and Hugh Walpole.

Nothing is known about how Marlowe fared there, but Maugham had a thoroughly miserable time. He was a lonely, scared, shy, sickly boy who stammered. No wonder he was fair game for schoolboy barbarisms. And no wonder it took years for him to regard the school with anything but loathing. But as time passed, he mellowed. Ultimately, he gave its library the manuscripts of *Liza of Lambeth* and *Catalina,* his first and last novels, and he contributed handsomely toward a new boathouse and new science building—and even attended the dedication of the latter at age eighty-eight, though he had to come from France to do so. At his death the reconciliation was complete. His ashes lie near the Norman Staircase in the northwest corner of the Green Court.

A far more enthusiastic alumnus (who never even graduated) was the novelist Hugh Walpole. He attended the Junior School from September of 1896 to Easter of 1898, and though he was only a so-so student, he thoroughly loved it. His godfather was a canon, and Walpole enjoyed his house, garden, and library, as well as the beauty of the Cathedral and its precincts. In later life he gave King's as his school, even though he spent the bulk of his schooldays at Durham. He paid for the returfing of its Mint Yard, gave the school valuable furniture, and donated his considerable and impressive collection of manuscripts, now on display in the gate room over the Cathedral's Dark Entry. One of the boardinghouses has been renamed Walpole House.

In *David Copperfield,* King's School figures as the one conducted by Dr. Strong, "who looked almost as rusty . . . as the tall iron rails and gates" outside his house, and "almost as stiff and heavy as the great stone urns that flanked them." The school springs to life in David's description: "a grave building in a courtyard, with a learned air about it that seemed very well suited to the stray rooks and jackdaws who came down from the Cathedral towers to walk with a clerkly bearing on the grass-plot." (They still do.) Betsey Trotwood's decision to send David here proved a happy one. He rose to be head boy, and his stay here was one of the brighter periods of his life.

In *Of Human Bondage,* Somerset Maugham represents Canterbury as Tercanbury, but King's School appears under its own name, and his hero, Philip Carey, is as unhappy as Maugham himself had been there. The author's stammer has become his hero's clubfoot, but the ragging and misery the handicap occasioned are unchanged: "He had got his teeth in the pillow so that his sobbing should be inaudible. He was not crying for the pain [the boys] had caused him, nor for the humiliation he had suffered when they looked at his foot, but with rage at himself because, unable to stand the torture, he had put out his foot of his own accord. And then he felt the misery of his life. It seemed to his childish mind that this unhappiness must go on forever."

Back on the High Street, a pleasant, not too long walk in a northwesterly direction takes you to the Westgate, a massive addition to the town's defenses built in the time of Richard II, and today the largest surviving city gate in England. As you pass through, and depending on your mood, you can tingle to the recollection that Chaucer's pilgrims would have entered the city through this very gate . . . or consider gloomily that today Canterburians note with approval that a double decker bus exactly fits the archway.

Beyond the gate and a few hundred yards on the left is a row of ancient buildings with no fewer than thirteen gables among them. The one housing the hotel called The House of Agnes has been identified as the home of sweet, noble Agnes Wickfield, where David Copperfield lived while attending school. The description fits well enough: "a very old house bulging out over the road; a house with long low lattice-windows bulging out still farther, and beams with carved heads on the ends bulging out too, so that I fancied the whole house was leaning forward, trying to see who was passing on the narrow pavement below." No matter that the description generally fits other houses—or that when Dickens was showing some American friends, including Charles Eliot Norton, the sights of Canterbury, and they tried to decide which bulging house was Agnes Wickfield's, the novelist only laughed and said several "would do."

At this point, "High" Street has assumed another of its many names, having become St. Peter's Street before reaching the Westgate, and now being St. Dunstan's Street. The name comes from the church on down past the House of Agnes, past the railway crossing, on the corner where the old

London Road strikes off to the left. The church, St. Dunstan's, is notable, for it was here that the last episode in the tragic clash of wills between Becket and his king began.

The murder of his archbishop in 1170 had weighed heavily on Henry's conscience. The public outcry would not be stilled. The pressure of the Church was unrelenting. At last, in July of 1174, Henry capitulated and returned to Canterbury from Normandy to perform his penance.

He came first to St. Dunstan's Church. Alighting from his horse there, he entered the building, stripped off his royal robes, and donned a hair shirt. Then in bare feet he walked along the rough-cobbled street, through the Westgate to the Cathedral, the soles of his feet slashed to ribbons and staining the stones as he went.

Arriving at the Cathedral, Henry went directly to Becket's tomb in the crypt for a lonely, all-night watch over the body of the man his friends had butchered. Next morning, he was met by the whole community of monks, and asked their pardon. He received it, but only after they had stripped off his shirt and flogged his naked back. But at last his ordeal was over. And apparently it was worth it: on the very day Henry left Canterbury, William the Lion, King of Scotland and threatening ally of Henry's rebellious sons, was taken prisoner at Alnwick.

St. Dunstan's has another claim to fame, one of equal literary interest. It has a martyr to rival even Becket himself—Sir Thomas More, author of *Utopia*. For underneath a marble memorial stone in St. Dunstan's Roper Chapel lies all that More's family could rescue after his execution: his head. Like Becket, he had been Lord Chancellor; and like Becket, he had sorely vexed his king, another Henry, Henry VIII.

More could not subscribe to Henry's annulment of his marriage to Catherine, nor accept the validity of his marriage to Anne Boleyn. Nor could he in good conscience sign the Act of Supremacy declaring Henry head of the Church. Henry's patience with this good but stubborn man wore thin. In quick order, More was imprisoned in the Tower, brought to trial, and executed. As was the custom then, his head was exposed on the London Bridge as a gruesome warning. But his favorite daughter, Margaret Roper, somehow managed to get possession of it and spirit it off to Canterbury, where it was reverently buried in her husband's family vault. More is venerated in Canterbury, and to this day the parish of St. Dunstan's, with Holy Cross, Canterbury, holds a united commemorative service each year on the day of his martyrdom, July 6.

From St. Dunstan's, northwestward, what began as the High Street becomes the A 290, the road to Whitstable. And in the Roman Catholic part of the cemetery along this road, near the outskirts of Canterbury, is the grave of Joseph Conrad. He died August 3, 1924, at nearby Bishopsbourne, where he had lived since 1919, and was buried here following the funeral service at Canterbury's St. Thomas's Church.

His grave, with its little stone border, has an irregularly shaped tombstone, and as one gazes at the inscripton, it is hard to escape a feeling of awe at the intrepidity of its fashioner—a man who dared to take chisel in hand, knowing he couldn't spell. Boldly, letter by letter he hacked it out: JOSEPH TEADOR CONRAD KORSENIOWSKI. Teodor, maybe?

Some Canterbury leftovers: John Lyly was born here, but no one knows where, or even exactly when. Best guess is 1553 or 1554. Richard Lovelace lived here for a time in the seventeenth century. The nineteenth-century humorist Richard Barham was born in Canterbury Lane and used the city in some of his *Ingoldsby Legends*. And Marlowe fans should know that the entry of his baptism in the register of St. George's Church, destroyed by a bomb in 1942, is preserved in the Cathedral library . . . there's a thriving Marlowe Theatre (repertory) near Mercery Lane . . . and in the Dane John Gardens off Marlowe Avenue is a Marlowe memorial, a bronze statue of a muse standing on a base adorned with characters from his plays.

Yes, there's a lot to see in Canterbury.

3. ALONG THE NORTH SEA

Goodnestone—Godmersham—Bishopsbourne

A good way to take a literary jaunt around England is to establish a series of bases, or points of reference, from which to operate. Canterbury is just such a base from which to cover the rest of Eastern Kent. Within easy distance (twenty miles, forty minutes or less) are a number of towns and villages of literary interest, some worth a footnote, some worth a stop. One can take quick excursions to the likes of Goodnestone, Godmersham, and Bishopsbourne, for instance. Or take a circular day's swing through Whitstable, Birchington, Margate, Broadstairs, Ramsgate, and back to Canterbury.

Goodnestone Pronounced "Goon-stun," this little hamlet, seven miles southeast of Canterbury on a tolerable unnumbered road off the B 2046, is just west of Rowling House, where Jane Austen's brother Edward (he had changed his name to Knight) lived after marrying the daughter of Sir Brook Bridges, owner of elegant Goodnestone Park.

Jane Austen visited Rowling often, and its gentle social whirl provided her with pleasant little details for her books. In fact, often in her letters from here, Jane sounds deliciously like one of her own heroines: "Miss Fletcher and

I were very thick, but I am the thinnest of the two. She wore her purple muslin, which is pretty enough, though it does not become her complexion. There are two traits in her character which are pleasing,—namely, she admires Camilla, and drinks no cream in her tea."

Godmersham Park On the A 28, this estate, inherited by Edward Knight in 1797, is even nearer to Canterbury (to the southwest) than his Goodnestone place had been: only five miles. And Godmersham proved more fruitful of both visits and book material for his sister Jane Austen than Goodnestone. Her letters about the grand life have all the sly humor of her novels: "Yesterday was a day of dissipation all through: first came Sir Brook to dissipate us before breakfast; then there was a call from Mr. Sherer, then a regular morning visit from Lady Honeywood on her way home from Eastwell; then Sir Brook and Edward set off; then we dined (five in number) at half-past four; then we had coffee; and at six Miss Clewes, Fanny and I drove away."

And this on a quiet day: "I did not mean to eat, but Mr. Johncook [the butler] has brought in the tray, so I must. I am all alone. Edward is gone into his woods. At this present time I have five tables, eight-and-twenty chairs, and two fires all to myself."

Jane may well have used her brother's Godmersham Park as a model for Lady Catherine de Bourgh's estate in *Pride and Prejudice,* which she places in Kent. The obnoxious (but Reverend) Mr. William Collins has the rectory of "Hunsford, near Westerham, thanks to Lady Catherine de Bourgh, owner of Rosings in Kent." Elizabeth herself visits her friend at the rectory after Charlotte Lucas marries Collins.

Bishopsbourne About four and a half miles out of Canterbury, while barreling south along the A 2 on the way to Dover, the average driver is hardly likely to notice the signpost directing him off to the right, to this modest little collection of houses. But over the centuries, two of its residents left their mark on literature.

In 1595 Richard Hooker, after four years as rector of Boscombe near Salisbury, was moved to the church here. Somehow he seems to have considered it a promotion. It was here that he finished Book Five of his famous defense of the Elizabethan Church of England, *Of the Laws of Ecclesiastical Politie,* in 1597. And it was here, in 1660, that he died and was buried under a slab from his church's old altar. A memorial marking his service can be found on the south side of the chancel.

Near the church is a handsome, medium-sized Georgian house called "Oswald's." To it in 1919—after judiciously waiting several days for his wife to handle all the details of actually moving in—came Joseph Conrad. For all his career, he had struggled with poverty and obscurity. Now ironically, for his best work was done, he had begun to make money (as much as £10,000 one year), and was able to afford what for him and his long-suffering Jessie was a mansion.

It was the dower house to a large estate, with a series of gardens opening upon each other through red brick walls, and a bowling green opening upon the park, and at the back a formal Dutch garden in view of the covered porch where Conrad liked to sit in warm weather while awaiting lunch. The drawing room was a particularly fine room, with gilt chairs and Aubusson rugs. Mrs. Conrad even had a "den"—though it did have a small billiard table, at which her husband indulged in haphazard fashion in his only sport.

But the center of his life, and therefore the center of the house, was the small, unassuming, book-lined study. It was plainly furnished, for Conrad was really a man of simple tastes, but did have a special armchair facing the window, through which he loved to watch the birds hopping about his lawn, little knowing (or caring to know) one from another.

Here Conrad read, and entertained his guests, and wrote. Chief products of the study were *The Rescue,* published in 1920; *The Rover,* published in 1923; and the fragment published after his death as *Suspense.* He had begun it in June, 1920, and had finished something more than half of it when he died.

Among his earliest and most frequent visitors was his devoted younger friend, the novelist Hugh Walpole, who first came to Oswald's in January, 1920. He was used to Conrad's mercurial moods and sudden outbursts, and took them calmly. This time he found his host fulminating about one of his pet peeves: Americans (Russians were another). In selling his books in America, he snorted, he felt exactly like a merchant selling glass beads to African natives. But then, Walpole recalled, Conrad had always maintained "it was easier to have an intellectual friendship with a Chinaman than with an American."

Much of Conrad's acerbity stemmed from ill health, especially recurring battles with gout. On a visit in the fall of 1921, Walpole paints a picture that was to become increasingly typical of Conrad: "much odder than I've ever known before, bursting into sudden rages about such nothings as the butter being salt, and then suddenly being very quiet and sweet."

After a time, Conrad inevitably grew restless with any house he lived in. By the summer of 1924 he had found a new place, eight miles further down the road to Dover, and looked forward to moving there in September. But it was not to be. He died at Oswald's on August 3.

Whitstable—Birchington—Margate

Whitstable On the coast, six miles north and a little bit west of Canterbury, on the A 299, Whitstable is worth a trip even today for a taste of the oysters dredged up from the bay. In the 1880's it was one of the great oyster centers of Kent, with 80 vessels actively dredging, and a total of 300 ships, including the fishing fleet, based in its harbor.

Vicar here, since 1870, at the thirteenth-century All Saints Church, had been the Reverend Henry McDonald Maugham. For him, the parish built a new vicarage in 1871. Thirteen years later, the cheerless monotony of this household was jolted by the unwanted arrival of a suddenly orphaned nephew: William Somerset Maugham.

It was an unpromising event at best. The boy had been raised in France, and at ten was more French than English. In addition, as mentioned earlier, he was abnormally shy and had a painful stammer. It hardly helped that his new guardians were middle-aged, and childless, and on the humorless and Puritan side.

The house and grounds—still called the "Old Vicarage," though no clergyman has lived there since 1924—stand hardly changed since the day little Somerset ("Willie") Maugham arrived. And the visitor finds that they were not unattractive. The house, on an acre of beautifully landscaped grounds, is a large two-storey stone building, with twin steep roofs, looking rather like two narrow houses had been fastened together, and then two even narrower houses had been fastened on behind them. Despite the inevitable changes inside, there are still the little-used drawing room where the vicar took his Sunday naps . . . the snug dining room (now a sitting room) . . . the little study . . . and the young Willie's tiny room at the head of the stairs, with its narrow bed, bookshelves, and chair. (The ugly wood carvings of the four Evangelists apparently fell victim to some later occupant's good taste.)

Maugham casts himself as the young Philip Carey in *Of Human Bondage,* and in Philip's unhappy boyhood reflects his own. The unbending guardian-uncle-vicar became the Rev. William Carey, who rebukes Philip when his tumbling blocks disturb his Sabbath snooze, and reminds him "it's very, very wicked to play on Sunday." Whitstable itself becomes "Blackstable," but one has no difficulty in recognizing either the town or the vicarage.

The narrator in Maugham's *Moon and Sixpence* also refers to his uncle's home in "Blackstable." Maugham also used Whitstable for scenes in *Cakes and Ale;* and flashes of his aunt and uncle, the vicarage, and the town, with its Joy Lane and High Street, pubs and shops, are not hard to find. Nor were they for the townspeople of the time, who saw shadows of themselves even where none existed. Nothing is so deathless as outrage without reason, and they never forgave Maugham.

Birchington In this town on the A 28, twelve miles east of Whitstable along Kent's northern coast, and also twelve miles almost directly northeast of Canterbury, died the Victorian painter-poet, Dante Gabriel Rossetti, a most unlikely spot for a rather improbable life to end.

He came here on February 4, 1882, to recuperate, his body and strength sorely depleted by the ravages of drugs, insomnia, and illness. His home was "Westcliffe Bungalow," a commodious but undistinguished dwelling beside the sea, with a large garden, that was lent by a friend. It was ugly, though cozy, and Rossetti detested it. With near superhuman effort, he forced himself to work at two paintings, "Proserpine" and "Joan of Arc." He even managed to finish that weird supernatural poem of a Dutchman who loses his soul to the Devil in a smoking match, *Jan van Hunks,* which he had begun long before.

His mother and his sister Christina came to nurse him. But he grew steadily worse, and by February 25 the nonbeliever Rossetti was sardonically reporting: "I suppose my illness is notorious here, for today the parson called." On Easter Day, April 9, he died.

His grave can be found on the south side close to the porch of the old, grey, country flint-stone church, easily recognized by reason of the large Celtic cross that marks it. Designed by Rossetti's longtime friend (and short-time teacher) Ford Madox Brown, it has three sculptured scenes—the temptation in Eden, the Marriage of Dante and Beatrice, and the death of the painter-physician, St. Luke, all subjects readily identifiable with Rossetti and his work. The inscription reads: "Here sleeps Gabriel Charles Dante Rossetti [his name as he was christened]; honoured under the name of Dante Gabriel Rossetti among painters as a painter, and among poets as a poet. Born in London of parentage mainly Italian 12 May, 1828, died at Birchington, 2nd April 1882."

Sister Christina described the site in a sonnet, "Birchington Churchyard":

> A lowly hill which overlooks a flat,
> Half sea, half country-side;
> A flat-shored sea of low-voiced creeping tide
> Over a chalky weedy mat.

Christina and her mother also contributed a stained glass memorial window to the church, made by Rossetti's friend Frederick Shields from a drawing of the poet's and sketches of his own. Shields's first design was rejected by the vicar: "I do not think this picture is likely to inspire devotional thoughts and feelings, and fear that in some cases it might rather do the reverse." Shields tried again, and the cleric found the window the modern visitor can see, especially the second light showing Christ healing the blind, wholesomely innocuous.

Even so, Rossetti's ghost may well feel lonely and out of place in Birchington. Perhaps remembering that when one of his predecessors visited Rossetti he was turned away even though Rossetti was at death's door, a recent vicar remarked of his guest in the churchyard: "He wasn't a very nice man, actually—morally, that is."

Margate A considerable city (over 50,000) practically at the north-eastern-most tip of the Kentish coast, and four miles east of Birchington on the A 28, Margate has long enjoyed its reputation as a watering place. Thomas Gray, by now somewhat reluctantly celebrated for his *Elegy,* visited it in 1766 and captured in a phrase the merry, abandoned holiday spot it was beginning to become in the eighteenth century. He called it "Bartholomew Fair by the sea-side."

Charles Lamb first came to Margate in 1790, a visit he enjoyed so much that years later he wrote jokingly he had to pay "dreary penance" for it by vacationing in Hastings. In June of 1821 he was in Margate again with his sister Mary "to drink seawater and pick up shells." But the high spot of this visit was an extraordinarily large whale. Lamb never tired of recounting the stir caused by its capture, and its being borne off through the streets in a strong cart, past—he claimed—his very window.

Lamb also lovingly recalled the little sloop-rigged coastal vessel called a "hoy" which visitors could board for a view of the harbor. He describes it in *Last Essays of Elia* in a piece called *"The Old Margate Hoy":* "Can I forget thee, thou old Margate Hoy, with thy weather-beaten, sun-burnt captain, and his rough accommodations, ill-exchanged for the foppery and fresh-water niceness of the modern steam-packet?"

An even more gifted writer who came to Margate about this time was John Keats. He spent August and September of 1816 here, shortly after receiving his Apothecary's Certificate. It was his first glimpse of the sea, and he captured the thrill in a sonnet, "To My Brother George":

> The ocean with its vastness, its blue green,
> Its ships, its rocks, its caves, its hopes, its fears,
> Its voice mysterious.

Not a great sonnet, true. But it does breathe of the wonder and mystery Keats always found in nature. And the wonder of this "ocean with its vastness" may well have shaped a truly magnificent sonnet, "On First Looking Into Chapman's Homer," with its picture of "stout Cortez when with eagle eyes/ He star'd at the Pacific." Keats wrote that within days of returning to London from Margate.

And Margate can claim a part in the writing of *Endymion*. For although he had found it a "treeless affair," Keats was back in Margate in May of 1817. On May 10 he outlines the rigorous regimen he has set for himself: "I read and write about eight hours a day." He had begun *Endymion* about a fortnight before on the Isle of Wight, and had done something on it every day since except while en route to Margate. But the very next morning his chronic money troubles surfaced again, and he moodily declares: "So now I revoke my Promise of finishing my Poem by the Autumn which I should have done had I gone on as I have done—but I cannot write while my spirit is fevered in a contrary direction." As it turned out, he did finish *Endymion* by fall—on November 28 at Burford Bridge in Surrey.

The novelist Thackeray is usually associated with Brighton, but he stayed in Margate, too, from August 20 to September in 1840, at 1 Bridge Terrace. It was, says Thackeray, "A charming green little lodging . . . but very dear, 2 1/2 guineas a week. All our windows look to the sea, if you call this sea. A queer little sitting-room with a glass door that walks straight into the street and two neat smart bed rooms one on top of the other. We dined at the inn." Perhaps there's a bit of a sneer in that "if you call this sea." But Thackeray confessed he did enjoy the melodious ripple of the water, and "the gas lamps round the little bay look as if they were sticking flaming swords into it."

The little bay is still a charmer.

Broadstairs

This town on the A 255—with better than 20,000 year-round residents and several times that number of summer visitors—shares the northeastern tip of Kent with Margate, one flowing directly into the other. As a mecca for the Dickens devotee, Broadstairs looms large and distinct, rivaling Rochester in importance. And it is certainly as much a "must" for the general literary traveller. (Note: it's as easy to get around in, too.)

Broadstairs was by all odds Dickens's favorite holiday spot. Beginning in 1839, he visited it for stays of one to several months every year through 1851 except for the two years when he was abroad during the seasonable months, and even then he thought of Broadstairs. Italy, in 1844, had "never so fine a sunset." Switzerland, in 1846, provoked nostalgia for Broadstairs and its "good, old, tarry, salt, little pier."

The list of books he wrote at least in part while here is striking: *Pickwick Papers* (1837); *Nicholas Nickleby* (1839); *Old Curiosity Shop* (1841); *Barnaby Rudge* (1841); *American Notes* (1842); *Martin Chuzzlewit* (1843); *Dombey and Son* (1847); "The Haunted Man" (1848); *David Copperfield* (1850); and "Our English Watering Place" (1851). And *Bleak House* was planned here in 1851.

The dates, indicating when Dickens was working on each, attest at once to the regularity of Dickens's visits and his ability to work while there.

Even today it doesn't take much imagination to see Broadstairs as it was then: a little fishing village, with a couple of twisting streets feeding into the main street zigzagging along the top of the white chalk cliffs. The salt air is as fresh and inviting now as it was in June, 1840, when Dickens praised it in a sprightly spoof of Chamber of Commerce puffery: "this place is, as the guide book most justly observes, 'unsurpassed for the salubrity and purity of the refreshing breezes which are wafted on the ocean's pinions from far distant climes.' "

Stand on the cliff on a calm day when the tide is out, and squint your eyes, and you can practically see the Broadstairs he described in 1851 in "Our English Watering Place":

> Sky, sea, beach, and village lie as still before us as if they were sitting for the picture. . . . Below the cliff a brown litter of tangled sea-weeds and fallen cliff, which looks as if a family of giants had been making tea here for ages, and had observed an untidy custom of throwing their tea-leaves on the shore.

The road from Margate (the A 255) turns into Broadstairs' High Street as it approaches the cliff. At No. 12 High Street, in 1837, Dickens stayed on his first visit, working on *The Pickwick Papers* which, at age twenty-five, had just catapulted him to fame. The house is now gone, but still standing is the Royal Albion Hotel—then simply the Albion—where during his stay Dickens enjoyed a memorably "merry night" with his friend John Forster, who had come down from London to do precisely that. And it is at the Albion that the visitor should begin his tour of the town. The always useful (and friendly) Tourist Information Office is in the High Street just before it runs into Albion. And where the two streets meet, hugging the cliff with its face to the sea, is the Albion.

You can make the Albion your headquarters for your stay in Broadstairs if you like, and Dickens would have urged you to. It was perhaps, of all the hotels he stayed in, his favorite, and he declared in 1849 that it beat "all watering places into what Americans call 'sky-blue' fits." He had the highest of accolades for the hotel's keeper, in no way diminished by that worthy's special attentions to Dickens: "Mr. Ballard of the Albion Hotel—one of the best and most respectable tradesmen in England. He has a kind of reverence for me." As a modern plaque on the front of the building points out, Dickens stayed at the Albion in 1839, 1840, 1845, 1849, and 1859.

However, the Albion in Dickens's day was only a slim, four-storey building, and today's somewhat sprawling establishment is the result of gobbling up nearby houses and lots. One of these was No. 40 Albion Street (now No. 12) which is where he actually stayed in 1839, and which he describes as being "two doors from the Albion Hotel." At £ 21 a month, it was not expensive. Proudly, he emphasized that it was a house, not a lodging," with "the most beautiful view of the sea from its bay-windows that you can imagine."

The view, apparently, more than compensated for a "costively inconvenient water-closet." In turn, the w-c doesn't seem to have interfered too much with the winding up of *Nicholas Nickleby.* Nor could a cook that got "remarkably" drunk and lay down in front of the house. On September 18 Dickens exulted (in reference to the plot of the novel): "The discovery is made, Ralph [Nickleby] is dead, the loves have come all right, Tim Linkinwater has proposed, and I have now only to break up Dotheboys and the book together." At two o'clock on the afternoon of September 20, he wrote ". . . their eyes filled with tears, and they spoke low and softly of their poor dead cousin"—and the book was finished. No wonder Dickens wrote of No. 40, "We enjoy the place amazingly."

First stop after the Albion for today's visitor should be Dickens House, at the upper end of Victoria Parade and reached by slipping through a little alley to the right of the hotel. The house, a tidy, low, three-storeyed affair, now has a covered outside balcony on the middle floor, with an attractive "crinoline rail"—actually a decorative wrought iron railing. (The Victorians were wont to apply the term "crinoline" to a variety of stiffened items, such as certain kinds of wire and steel, and even to anti-torpedo netting around warships.) The core of the house was a small Tudor building that overlooked the sea. The original entrance is now the archway in the hall, and the left hand side was added toward the end of the seventeenth century. Other changes over the years included refronting in the Georgian era and the adding of the balcony in early Victorian times.

The house has a double fascination for the literary pilgrim: its owner was the original of *David Copperfield's* Betsey Trotwood, and now it harbors an excellent Dickens museum (open to the public for a modest fee) with letters, furniture, and other items "connected" with Dickens. Its owner in Dickens's day was a Miss Mary Pearson, prominent in Broadstairs society, and a favorite of the author. She waged perpetual but inconclusive war against the donkeys who seemed to prefer the grass in her sea-front yard to all others. Dickens so loved to watch her in action, shouting and flapping her apron at the invaders, that before a visit he would bribe the donkey-boys to loose their charges at the strategic moment.

He uses the incident hilariously in *David Copperfield,* of course; and a highlight of the museum is "Betsey Trotwood's Parlour," looking very like it might have an instant after she went flying out, crying aloud to her maid, "Janet! Donkeys!" The room has been most imaginatively done, and it is obvious that someone has gone to great pains to find all the objects needed to show it just as Dickens describes it, even to the two canaries. The cupboard from which Aunt Betsey produced her wondrous assortment of nostrums to restore her weeping nephew is in the left corner as you enter the room.

One is grateful that the Curator of the museum had the good taste to eschew wax figures, and let the visitor's own imagination supply the scene as Dickens's words suggest it:

> My aunt, with every sort of expression but wonder discharged from her countenance, sat on the gravel, staring at me, until I began to cry; when she got up in a great hurry, collared me, and took me into the parlor. Her first proceeding there was to unlock a tall press [i.e., cupboard], bring out several bottles, and pour some of the contents of each into my mouth. I think they must have been taken out at random, for I am sure I tasted anise-seed water, anchovy sauce and salad dressing.*

At least three of Dickens's Broadstairs holidays in the early 1840's were spent at No. 37 Albion, a few doors further down the street from the hotel than No. 40. (Since the streets have been renumbered, it's not always easy to match original house numbers with modern ones.) Like No. 40, it was a house, not a lodging, and faced the sea.

He was at No. 37 on June 1, 1840, for instance, for the first part of a two-stage vacation, contemplating with satisfaction the completion of his usual first order of business when moving into any strange quarters: The "writing table is set forth with a neatness peculiar to your estimable friend; and the furniture in all the rooms has been entirely re-arranged by the same extraordinary character," with "a good array of bottles on display in the dining parlor closet." Meanwhile, "the sea is rolling away, like nothing but the sea, in front of the house," as he sits down to work on the newly-begun *The Old Curiosity Shop.*

Other letters from other years give glimpses of him at work in this house. He is here in 1842, through August and September, toiling away on *American Notes* and managing to do a chapter a week. An occasional pause to glance outside yields a picture of his young son Charley on the beach below the house, "digging up the sand on the shore with a very small spade, and compressing it into a perfectly impossible wheelbarrow." One is happy to

---

*If you have a nagging recollection that all this belongs in Dover, not Broadstairs, you're right. Dickens moved Miss Trotwood there to avoid embarrassing Miss Pearson.

report that those same sands are still filling equally impossible wheelbarrows.

He was back at No. 37 in 1843, and a letter in September depicts him in his house vividly: "In a bay window . . . sits from nine o'clock to one, a gentleman with rather long hair and no neck-cloth who writes and grins as if he thought he were very funny indeed. His name is Boz [Dickens's pseudonym for the newspaper sketches that won him his first success]. At one, he disappears, and presently emerges from a bathing machine and may be seen—a kind of salmon-coloured porpoise—splashing about in the ocean."

The reason Dickens grinned as he wrote is that he was doing the passages in *Martin Chuzzlewit* on the "Watertoast Association of United Sympathizers," so funny that the author himself confessed, "[I] nearly killed myself at laughing at what I have done." What makes it all the more remarkable is that he was contending all the while with the noise of "donkeys and drivers out of number" at the street side of the house and a perpetually banging piano on another.

Broadstairs is to be commended for having all its literary shrines within easy walking distance. Thus it is that the pleasantest of short strolls takes you from No. 37 to where Dickens spent the second part of that two-stage 1840 vacation. You go down the hill to the bottom of Albion, turn right into Harbour Street (more lane than street), pass under an archway—and you're there.

For the archway is actually part of a small villa—called, with somewhat painful literalness, Archway House. In Dickens's day it was The Lawn House, and he loved it. It was (and is) a splendid example of Regency architecture, then separated from the sea by a cornfield. Dickens declared the house "a most brilliant success—far more comfortable than any we have had," and during the five weeks he rented it, from September on, worked away at *The Old Curiosity Shop.* (There's a shop of that name to the right on Harbour Street now, but it has no historic connection with the novel.)

The next year he rented Lawn House again for two months beginning in August. And though he managed to write enough at *Barnaby Rudge* to have each number (installment) ready as it came due, he concentrated on fun, the house usually bulging with family and friends: "I am hideously lazy—always bathing, lying in the sun, or walking about. I write a No. [Number] when the time comes, and dream about it beforehand on cliffs and sands—but as to getting in advance—!" Before deciding that Dickens has joined the Lotus Eaters, however, keep in mind his extraordinary energies, even at "idle."

No distance at all down the lane from Lawn House, standing sentinel-like at the edge of the cliff that drops to the sea, is a stern, crenellated, castle-like structure: Bleak House. Dickens knew it as Fort House, and from the mid-forties on, he rented it for a month or more almost every year until 1852 without fail. As his favorite holiday retreat, it came to be "the residence he most desired." Like Dickens House Museum, for the modern visitor it is a "must."

The Fort House Dickens knew, built in the early nineteenth century, was only about a third of today's building, the original house being the narrow, three-storey eastern wing overlooking the sea.* With a basement, ground floor, and two upper floors, it was adequate but hardly commodious, for during the last half of the decade the Dickens brood grew from five to eight.

Moreover, there was always a constant stream of guests, whom the hosts enjoyed immensely: "Here has Horne been (with a guitar) bathing at 'Dumblegap,' the flesh-coloured Horror of maiden ladies. Here has Forster been and gone, after patronizing with suavity the whole population of Broadstairs, and impressing Tom Collins with the fact that he (F) did the Ocean a favour when he bathed. Here, likewise, has Mrs. Horne been, also Wills, with a frosty nose and a dribbling pretence of shower-bath."

Yet for all the bustle in the house, Dickens was always able to combine work with his play, notably during these years with *Dombey and Son* and *David Copperfield,* as well as "Our English Watering Place." A letter of August, 1850, when he was writing as much as eight hours at a stretch at *David Copperfield* is typical: "I have been hard at work these three days, and still have Dora to kill. But with good luck I may do it tomorrow."

In 1851, in the same little Fort House study in which much of *David Copperfield* was written, Dickens plunged into preparations and planning for his next major work, *Bleak House.* It is for this study and other Dickens memorabilia—not for any conjectural influence its stern facade may have had on the novel—that today's Bleak House and its museum have their great appeal.

The study is a small room on what the English call the first floor. Dickens always liked a view when he wrote—in London he looked over the garden—so here his desk faced the semicircle of Viking Bay sparkling below. Among interesting pieces of furniture here are a desk chair, one of three claimants to being the one in Fildes's famous painting, "The Empty Chair," done the day after Dickens's death, and an oddly shaped (7½ feet high by 2 feet wide) drawing cabinet used by Dickens's best known illustrator, George

*The larger, two-storey western wing, the transformation of the original front door into a dining room window (you can still see the steps outside), and the crenellations were among major changes made in 1901—but so skillfully done one can scarcely detect new from old.

Cruikshank, with a cupboard at the side for a chamber pot. Among items on the wall are a reproduction of "The Empty Chair," a letter praising Fort House, and a rare portrait of Dickens's young actress-mistress, Ellen Ternan. Show cases house published versions of works he wrote in this room.

Adjoining the study is the novelist's high-ceilinged bedroom, with an equally spectacular view of the sea. Its dominating object is a big brass bed, which came from the one-time Bull Hotel in Rochester in 1961. The Bull was Dickens's usual stop there before he bought nearby Gads Hill Place, and the bed graced the hotel's chief bedroom. In turn, the bed was graced by the sleeping form not only of Dickens, but at least twice, of his sovereign, Victoria—not simultaneously, to be sure.

Other points of interest in the house are the billiards room, with a variety of Dickens relics, and the dining room, both on the ground floor. Outside is a summer pavilion made from the covered balcony and its decorative ironwork, removed from the house when it was enlarged in 1901.

One cannot be in Broadstairs even a few hours without sensing the town's genuine love for Dickens. The Broadstairs Branch of the Dickens Fellowship has been most active in collecting memorabilia. It stages an annual Dickens Festival in the summer, as well as a Dickens Garden Party in June on the Bleak House lawn. In turn, the visitor will find it hard not to love Broadstairs and its people.

4. RAMSGATE TO RYE: ALONG THE DOVER STRAIT

Ramsgate and Dover

Most travelers with Canterbury and Dover on their itineraries scurry directly from one to the other. But those who find themselves "diverted" (that's the Englishman's delightful word for detour) will take the Ramsgate Road (the A 255) out of Broadstairs, before heading almost due south on the A 256 to pick up Dover and the strait thereof, for Folkestone and points west where giant names like Wells, Conrad, and James beckon. The twenty miles between Ramsgate and Dover hold no such lures, but Ramsgate itself deserves some attention.

Ramsgate With Margate and Broadstairs, Ramsgate shares the northeast tip of Kent, and is, as the atlas says, "contiguous to the south with Broadstairs." Unlike Broadstairs, however, poor Ramsgate throughout the centuries seems to have been fated to be mainly the landing place people used to go elsewhere. Hengest and Horsa came ashore in neighboring Pegwell Bay in the middle of the fifth century, marking the first wave of Saxon invaders. And Saint Augustine began his more mannerly conquests for the church in 596 by landing here (a monolithic cross at Cliffs End marks the spot).

In the nineteenth century, Dickens and his friends regularly used the Ramsgate Steamer to get to and from London in the years when the novelist spent so many holidays at Broadstairs. It left every morning promptly at nine o'clock from the London Bridge Wharf, took six hours at the longest, and cost six shillings. When the weather allowed, it would pause briefly off Broadstairs to let passengers bound there transfer to a small boat. (Today a Hovercraft leaves from Pegwell Bay.)

It was from Ramsgate that Hans Christian Andersen sailed in August of 1847 to return to Denmark from his first English tour. He stayed his last night at Ramsgate's Royal Oak Hotel, but had dinner at Dickens's house in Broadstairs. To Andersen's surprise as he went to board ship next morning, there on the quay was Dickens to see him off. Andersen's account of the event is beguiling:

> He had walked from Broadstairs, to say goodbye to me, and was in a green Scotch dress and gaily coloured shirt, extremely smart English. He was the last person to shake my hand in England. . . . As the ship glided out of the harbour, I could see Dickens on the furthermost point. I thought he had left long ago. He waved his hat and finally raised one hand towards heaven. I wonder if he meant to say: "We shall meet again aloft."

Dickens's associations with Ramsgate, however, were strictly utilitarian. His preference for Broadstairs was obvious. As early as 1839 he was recording that there were "no lodgings at Ramsgate (thank Heaven!) and after spending a night at an Hotel [the Royal Oak] there, we came on here." [i.e., Broadstairs.] Jane Austen was another who snubbed Ramsgate, blithely questioning the taste of an acquaintance who proposed to live there, while noting, with mock approval, that for those who loved the ocean, Ramsgate did have the advantage of being on the water. "Ed Hussey talks of fixing at Ramsgate—Bad taste!—He is very fond of the Sea, however;—some taste in that—& some Judgement too in fixing on Ramsgate, as being by the sea." In defense of Ramsgate, however, it should be said that Coleridge was a regular summer visitor and loved its bathing.

One may make whatever one likes out of the fact that Ramsgate figures fleetingly in two of Jane Austen's novels, in neither episode to any great purpose. In *Mansfield Park,* Ramsgate is where Tom Bertram has problems with the intricacies of determining when a young lady is, in the best social terms, "out." And in *Pride and Prejudice,* Darcy's fifteen-year-old sister is taken to Ramsgate by an accomplice of the dastardly Wickham. "And thither also," Darcy tells Elizabeth, "went Mr. Wickham, undoubtedly by design." The lure, Darcy hastens to add, was not Ramsgate, but Georgiana's thirty thousand pound fortune.

Sandwich Sandwich is on the A 256, seven miles below Ramsgate and thirteen above Dover. No need to stop, but as you pass on by, you might muse on its role in the fortunes of two Thomases of note. Tom Paine, who lived for a while at 20 New Street, failed to make it as a corset maker, thus freeing himself for America and *The Rights of Man.* And Thomas à Becket came ashore here in 1170 to end his exile, avoiding the enemies waiting for him on the beach at Dover. He should have stayed in France.

Dover This is the end (or the beginning, if you like) of the A 2, the one-time Roman road that stretches all the way from London, via Canterbury. If you've come from the southwest, you enter the city on the A 20.

Beyond doubt, Dover is one of England's best known small cities, but it's not easy to determine whether this is due to Matthew Arnold's grimly darkling hymn of despair, "Dover Beach," or that glutinously sticky song of World War II that threatened "Bluebirds . . . just you wait and see." Perhaps Shakespeare deserves a bit of credit, too. For in *King Lear* the blinded Gloucester begs his son Edgar to take him to Dover and the "cliff, whose high and bending head/ Looks fearfully in the confined deep." There's even a cliff on the west side of town called "Shakespeare's Cliff" you can go see, if you're so minded.

Dover and his Aunt Betsey Trotwood are the young hero's goals in *David Copperfield.* On the sixth day of his flight, in Dover at last, searching among "some houses facing the sea," he comes to a "very neat little cottage with cheerful bow-windows: in front of it, a small square gravelled court or garden full of flowers, carefully tended, and smelling deliciously." And there, tending the flowers, is Aunt Betsey.

Dickens himself doesn't seem to have been all that fond of Dover, even though he visited it two years in a row in the 1850's. In July of 1851 he enjoyed the sea and walking in the country, but found Dover "too bandy (I mean musical, no reference to its legs) and infinitely too genteel." In 1852, he is back again, this time with Wilkie Collins, staying at 10 Camden Crescent. In *The Uncommercial Traveller,* he records his envy of the city, snugly tucked in for the night, while he has to board the packet for Calais: "I particularly detest Dover for the self-complacency with which it goes to bed."

Other literary visitors to Dover include Byron, Arnold, Henry James, and Stephen Crane. Byron spent the last two days he was ever to spend in England in Dover, waiting for a good wind to bear him off into virtual exile. While in Dover, Byron visited the grave of another controversial satirist of society, Charles Churchill, who was buried in the old churchyard of St. Mary's in 1764.

According to Boswell, it was Churchill who stung Dr. Johnson into completing and publishing his edition of Shakespeare after nine years of accepting money from subscribers for a work that never appeared. Wrote Churchill of the great man:

> He for subscribers baits his hook,
> And takes your cash; but where's the book?

Byron may have sensed something of a kindred soul. At any rate, he flung himself lengthwise on Churchill's grave as a kind of living yardstick, and, using the measurements thus obtained, left instructions for the sexton to have the grave turfed at his expense.

The connection of the other three literary visitors to Dover may be told briefly. Arnold came for several days in 1851 with his bride to begin a happy marriage. Henry James came alone in 1884 to begin *The Bostonians*. And Stephen Crane came with his brothel-wise mistress in 1899 to begin the voyage that took him to Germany's Black Forest and death.

Folkestone

Folkestone, like so many of the towns and cities along England's southern coast, runs a bit overmuch to abrupt ups and downs, topographically. You can come in to it on the A 20 from Dover seven miles to the east, or Ashford sixteen to the northwest—or on the A 259 from the southwest; but whichever way you come, to reach the cente; of town you'll have to coil round a steep hill.

There, atop a promontory with a stunning view of the sea, you'll find a big and modern carpark building, thanks to the space made available by heavy Nazi bombing in World War II. And very near the carpark, but on the edge of the overlook itself, are the Albion Villas—a row of gleaming white, attractive adjoining houses that seem to have maintained the appeal they had in Victoria's day.

Number 3 Albion Villas, marked by a plaque for the visitor's benefit, was, in the summer of 1855 when the ubiquitous Charles Dickens took it over for a holiday, a pleasant little house with the sea below and the scent of thyme sweetening the breezes from the Downs.

The rugged terrain of Folkestone had particular appeal for Dickens. Although he was writing daily at a furious pace, he still had energy aplenty to go "swarming up the face of a gigantic and precipitous cliff." Many a day, he says, he could be seen "from the British Channel, suspended in mid-air with his trousers very much torn at fifty minutes past 3 p.m."

Dickens had first come to Folkestone in 1853 for a few days on his way to Boulogne. His work-in-progress then was *A Child's History of England.* When he came back in 1855 for a holiday at No. 3, he was working on *Little Dorrit,* the book George Bernard Shaw was to call more seditious than *Das Kapital.* Today's No. 3, now called Copperfield House, isn't all that little, and an amusement park down below makes the ocean view less than idyllic; but the breezes still blow, however thymeless.

Folkestone's most loyal literary lion was H. G. Wells. In September of 1898, hoping to recuperate from a devastating kidney infection, he came to Sandgate, then actually a separate seaside village three miles west of Folkestone: "I had been driven in a comfortable carriage to Sandgate, and after a week or so in a boarding house we had installed ourselves in a little furnished house called Beach Cottage."

It had, said Wells, "a back door slap upon the sea," and he predicted "the shrimps will come in and whack about on the dining-room oil-cloth." Indeed, it was so close to the sea the waves sometimes broke over the roof. But the place proved good for his health, and it was here on October 5, that one of his happiest books had its beginnings, though it was not completed and published until 1905: "I hatched out a new project called *Kipps.*" (The egg had been laid in New Romney.) It is fitting, then, that Kipps at fourteen, since "inexorable fate had appointed him to serve his country in commerce," should be initiated into the ways and wiles of business at the "Folkestone Drapery Bazaar."

Wells was to attract a veritable "Who's Who" of contemporary writers to his three various homes in Folkestone during the years he was there. Among them were Arnold Bennett, James M. Barrie, G. B. Shaw, Joseph Conrad, Ford Madox (Hueffer) Ford, George Gissing, Henry James, G. K. Chesterton, and Rudyard Kipling.

Bennett was an early caller to Beach Cottage, and Wells enjoyed his company, confessing "his swimming and diving roused my envy." Bennett's writing, however, was another matter. Wells admitted he had a bright and busy brain, but found his work "extraordinarily unequal."

Barrie was there in October, almost before the Wellses were fairly settled in, on a delicate mission, so discreetly handled Wells nearly missed the point: did he, um, need financial help? He did not. (A similar incident had occurred in New Romney with Edmund Gosse and Henry James).

In March of 1898 the Wellses moved. For Jane had found the house for which she had been hunting almost daily. Called Arnold House, it was very near the Beach Cottage, but more comfortable and unfurnished so they could send for their stored furniture. A sturdy semidetached villa, sheltered by the sharp rise of cliff to the Leas. "It had a long narrow strip of grass," says Wells, "which ended in a hedge of tamarisk along the sea wall." The setting, he explains, found its way into his work: "Upon the beach one day the *Sea Lady* appeared, very lovely in a close fitting bathing dress and with the sunlight in her hair, and took possession of my writing desk."

In September a letter heralded the arrival nearby of a writer who for some years was to be a warm and loyal friend, despite myriad differences of background, temperament, and outlook that eventually pulled them apart. On September 11, 1898, Joseph Conrad wrote: "We are going to be nearer neighbors than I dared to hope," and announced he was moving into Pent Farm in Postling, only about six miles—or under thirty minutes by bicycle or pony cart—away.

Their first attempts to get together were almost comical. On try number one, Conrad found Wells out. On try number two, Wells was not only out—he was out calling on Conrad at the Pent. But try number three succeeded, and thereafter the Conrads and Wellses exchanged visits regularly. As Wells paints them, the Conrads en route were something to see:

> Conrad with Mrs. Conrad and his small blondhaired, bright-eyed boy, would come over to Sandgate, cracking a whip along the road, driving a little black pony carriage as though it were a droshky, and encouraging a little Kentish pony with cries and endearments in Polish, to the dismay of all beholders.

Through Conrad, Wells developed a close friendship with Ford Madox Hueffer, who in a busy lifetime turned out more than sixty books. Most notable, perhaps, were the novels of the Christopher Tietjens saga, published under the name of Ford Madox Ford: *Some Do Not* (1924), *No More Parades* (1925), *A Man Could Stand Up* (1926), and *The Last Parade* (1928). How Hueffer came to change his last name would make a novel in itself. In 1909 he had left his wife and two daughters and by 1911 had established a ménage with Violet Hunt, his former secretary (and later a novelist and biographer herself). Soon Miss Hunt was calling herself "Mrs. Hueffer," though his first wife, refusing him a divorce, stoutly claimed the same title for herself. So in

1919, apparently in a desperate effort to get shuck of ALL Mrs. Hueffers, he became Ford Madox Ford.

Anyway, at Pent Farm Conrad was collaborating with Hueffer on a novel, and early on, Wells took to his bicycle to visit Hueffer and beg him not to continue the collaboration and spoil Conrad's "wonderful Oriental style." Hueffer refused, but the friendship and the visits back and forth continued. In these early days, Hueffer thought Wells "The Dean of our Profession."

Two other nearby writers who began exchanging calls with Wells in 1899 were American—as strikingly different from each other as each was from Wells. One was Henry James, who lived in Rye, twenty-one miles down the beach in East Sussex. James was twenty-six years older than Wells and an established great man of letters. Wells was still just somebody who hoped to become one. Moreover, James had an overriding concern for social niceties, most of which Wells was still struggling to acquire. Even so, Wells could not conceal his great respect for James, and the latter in turn recognized Wells's talent, and wrote him: "You fill me with wonder and admiration."

The other American was Stephen Crane, already, at twenty-nine, acclaimed for *The Red Badge of Courage* (1895), who moved into a decrepit old mansion in Brede, five miles west of Rye. Crane was a wild, irrepressible person, but it was hard not to like him. Wells exchanged visits with him, put him and his mistress up when they were en route to Switzerland, and was the one who went off to find a doctor during a days-long Christmas party when the tubercular Crane nearly died of a hemorrhage.

Even though he had taken a three-year lease on Arnold House, Wells wanted a place of his own. And thus it was that he spent most of 1900 watching—with considerable irritation at their slowness and outmoded methods—workmen building his home. It was only 100 yards from Arnold House, up the same cliff, with an even more spectacular view of the sea. On December 8, Wells was able to write Arnold Bennett: "Got there at last! No carpets, no dining room table or chairs, little food but still—there!"

In his *Recollections,* Wells described it as a "bright and comfortable pseudo-cottage" which faced south, "with a loggia that was a sun-trap." It was (and is) a good-sized house, light and open, with a low- eaved tiled roof, a rough exterior finish, and an interior that featured open spaces and Moorish arches. Fearing that his kidney ailment might yet confine him to a wheel chair, Wells insisted that living rooms and bedrooms be on the same level. Upstairs were night and day nurseries (Jane was pregnant when they moved in), and downstairs was Wells's "pretty little study." It may have been pretty, but it was also dark. After a while Wells added to it part of what is now a large open lounge, so he could get more sunlight, plus a view of the garden and the sea.

He also had a small stone building put up at the west end of the garden, so he could work there uninterrupted when he wished.

In these various rooms, over the nine years that he was in Spade House, Wells turned out an astonishing array of books, including among others *Mankind in the Making* (published, 1903); *Food of the Gods* (1904); *Kipps* (1905); *Tono-Bungay* (1909); *Ann Veronica* (1909); and *The History of Mr. Polly* (1910).

The architect, Charles Voysey, had a thing about hearts, and wanted a large heart-shaped letter plate on the front door. But Wells protested at wearing his heart so conspicuously. So he compromised: they turned the heart upside down and made it a spade. Hence came the name of the place, Spade House, to which came all the distinguished writers mentioned above.

Conrad's wife Jessie gives us a revealing glimpse of the Wellses at home. "We spent many very happy days at Spade House," she wrote in her memoirs, adding that Wells had a passion for breaking crockery. His wife Jane handled this by providing a supply of cheap vases and the like for just such occasions. And Jane herself had a passion for tidiness. Mrs. Conrad tells of opening Wells's handkerchief drawer one day, and finding it full of neat little piles, each with its own paper label: "Handkerchiefs to lend . . . Handkerchiefs for every day use . . . Evening handkerchiefs" and so on.

Wells's stay at Spade House—and in Folkestone—came to an end in 1909, so abruptly he forgot to tell his sons in advance. He wanted to live in London for "a web of almost impalpable reasons." Not the least of these, one assumes, was the fact that his mistress was pregnant and he wanted to be closer to her.

Since Wells's day, the house has passed through a number of hands and several changes. A considerable three-floor addition was made to the west end. The original front door was moved to the right, and a bay put in its place. The name of the house was even changed to "Bay House."

But the last owner, Mrs. E. M. May, was an admirer of Wells. She restored the name Spade House. And after she established it as a vegetarian hotel, all the upstairs guest rooms were named for Wells novels: "Tono-Bungay," "Wheels of Chance," and "Kipps." (The Kipps room has a heart on the closet door!)

Since Mrs. May's death, her heirs have sought to maintain the place as a hotel for vegetarians and have been sympathetic to would-be visitors. The house is well worth seeing, but before making a trip there you'd be wise to write and ask if you'd be welcome.*

---

*Spade House, Radnor Cliff Crescent, Folkestone, Kent

Postling

A moody, tortured soul, Conrad came to hate almost every house he lived in, and after a few years would move to another as if hoping he'd find a new temperament lurking in its depths. Thus, in 1898, he moved from Essex to Kent, exclaiming ecstatically: "This opportunity is a perfect Godsend to me. It preserves what's left of my piety and belief in a benevolent Providence and also probably my sanity."

What benevolent Providence had brought him to was Postling and Pent Farm.* Postling was, and is, the tiniest of hamlets, reached today by taking the A 20 for some five miles west out of Folkestone, and then turning right on an unmarked road for a mile or so more. And Pent Farm was, and is, a pleasant, two-storey brick farmhouse, set down in gently rolling hills. You reach it by forking left by the Postling village church; it's less than half a mile down the lane on the left.

Giving Providence an assist was Ford Madox Hueffer, for it was his collaboration with Hueffer that brought Conrad to Pent Farm. Indeed, Hueffer owned the place and moved to nearby Aldington so that Conrad could move into the Pent. Conrad described it as "small and old," but ideal for his needs. Old it was: a marker on the "newer" part of the house reads 1833. Other parts date back variously over several centuries. But though it is compact, it is not exactly tiny; when Conrad was in one of his moods, any place was likely to seem cramped.

Along with the house, Conrad rented Hueffer's furniture, and an odd assortment it was. There was a writing desk that was once Christina Rossetti's (Hueffer was the grandson of that old Pre-Raphaelite chum, Ford Madox Brown), and a big table William Morris had designed, and a picture cupboard that had belonged to Brown himself. Above the front room couch were two death masks: one of Dante Gabriel Rossetti—the other of Oliver Cromwell.

Under the windows of the house was a brick path on which Conrad would often pace for hours, whipping himself up to the fury he needed for writing. For unlike Henry James, who could work with military precision from nine to eleven every morning without fail, Conrad could only do what he called the "damned stuff" by a "kind of mental convulsion" that could go on for up to a fortnight and left him absolutely limp.

Here at the Pent, and out of his anguish, came some of the best things he ever wrote: *Lord Jim* (published 1900); *Youth* (1902); *Typhoon* (1903); *Nostromo*

*Pent means "a place containing pent-up water; a reservoir."

(1904); and *Mirror of the Sea* (1906); and those two collaborations with Hueffer, *The Inheritors* (1901) and *Romance* (1903).

Isolated as it was (poor Jessie Conrad's nearest neighbor was half a mile away), Pent Farm had its share of celebrated literary guests. H. G. Wells came over often from Folkestone, and in his *Recollections* gives a report that makes the place come startlingly to life for today's visitor: "One goes downhill to the Pent, the windows of the house are low, and my first impression of Conrad was of a swarthy face peering out and up through the little window panes."

Despite their early and genuine liking for each other, however, Wells later said they never really got on together and came to think Conrad overrated. For his part, Conrad in 1918 declared, after his breakup with Wells, that he had told him their differences were fundamental: "You don't care for humanity but think they are to be improved. I love humanity but know they are not!"

Wells sometimes brought guests with him, and one of them was even more trying to the patient Jessie Conrad than Wells himself. For Jessie prided herself on her cooking, and Wells required an odd diet. But this guest was George Bernard Shaw, and to Jessie's horror he made a tea of nothing but cocoa and a dry biscuit. Conrad himself was hardly more charmed, not at all enchanted by such samples of Shavian wit as "You know, my dear fellow, your books won't *do*." No wonder Conrad confided to a friend, "G. B. S. towed by Wells came to see me reluctantly, and I nearly bit him."

Among other guests were novelists George Gissing and Stephen Crane. Crane and his vibrant mistress, Cora, frequently drove, via horses, the thirty miles from Brede and more often than not stayed the night. Crane and Conrad, aliens alike in Britain, had become the closest of friends and even bought a sailboat together. But perhaps the most welcome visitor was John Galsworthy. Many a time he would appear walking across the fields with his black cocker Chris, and always both Joseph and Jessie were delighted. Jessie said flatly he was the most easy guest to have in the house.

Galsworthy was perhaps Conrad's longest-lasting literary friend and was generous in his tribute: "He was indefatigably good to me while my own puppy's eyes were opening to literature." Galsworthy's description of The Pent is worth noting, especially by the reader who is more than five-foot-seven and ponders a visit. With accuracy that rings true today, Galsworthy described it as a "friendly dwelling where you had to mind your head in connection with the beams; and from those windows you watched ducks and cats and lambs in the meadows beyond."

But inevitably Conrad came to equate his personal problems with the place. And so by mid-July of 1907 he is once again house hunting. Pent Farm is "imperfectly watertight." It is "damnably expensive." And by September he says bitterly he is leaving it to its "green solitude:—*to its rats.*"

Today Pent Farm is a 1,000 acre section of a thriving commercial agricultural concern, its role being mainly the growing of rye and wheat. As a private place, it deserves the privacy you would accord to your own home. But if you have an abiding interest in seeing it, write and ask. The English are a gracious people.

Hythe—Aldington—Orlestone—New Romney

The direct route for the twenty-one miles between Hythe and Rye is the A 259, with only New Romney offering anything in between of much literary interest. But short sallies inland, after leaving Hythe, bring one to two more of Joseph Conrad's on-again, off-again flirtations with Kent: Aldington and Orlestone. And Hythe (Lympne, actually) and New Romney are part of Wells-country.

Lympne "Lim," or sometimes "Liminie,"—no one seems to know what happened to the "p"—is about three miles west of Hythe on the B 2067. It was to Hythe, and especially to Lympne, that Wells's Kipps came to clamber the battlements of heart's desire with Miss Helen Walshingham. Lympne was the site of a Norman Abbey, home of the archdeaconry of Canterbury. The good clerics, never reluctant to give God a helping hand, made a veritable fortress of it, so fortified, said Leland in 1536, it was "lyke a castelet embatelyd."

By Wells's time it had become a popular tourist attraction. But let Wells describe it in his own words, as he does in *Kipps:*

> Everyone who stays in Folkestone goes sooner or later to Lympne. The Castle became a farm-house, and the farm-house, itself now ripe and venerable, wears the walls of the castle as a little man wears a big man's coat . . . One climbs the Keep, up a tortuous spiral of stone, worn to the pitch of perforation, and there one is lifted to the centre of far more than a hemisphere of view. Away below one's feet, almost at the bottom of the hill, the Marsh begins and spreads and spreads in a mighty crescent that sweeps about the sea, the Marsh dotted with the church towers of forgotten medieval towns, and breaking at last into the low blue hills by Winchelsea and Hastings; east hangs France between the sea and sky; and round the north, bounding the wide perspectives of farms and houses and woods, the Downs, with their hangers and chalk-pits, sustain the passing shadows of the sailing clouds.

No wonder Kipps bursts into rhapsody when he and Helen finally reach the seclusion of the Keep, alone: "I've always been fond of scenery."

The scenery *is* spectacular: sweeping views of today's Romney Marsh, the seabed of a port in Roman days, with the real, rolling sea beyond. The castle-become-a-farm-house is still, as in Wells's day, in private hands. But it is open to the public in season, and you can go see it if you like. There are even tea and lunch available for those who crave refreshment. (And, from Hythe, a miniature railway across the marshes to New Romney, for those who crave that.)

Aldington Two miles west of Lympne (and five west of Hythe), just off the B 2067, is this tiny village where Joseph Conrad managed to stay miserable for a little over a year . . . and came close to dying. He had stormed out of Kent for Bedfordshire in mid-1907. By August, 1908, he and Jessie were back at Aldington for a holiday at Hogben House, a farmhouse with rooms to rent, and to visit Conrad's onetime collaborator, Ford Madox Hueffer (Ford), who lived at Aldington Knoll.

Even before this vacation, Conrad, as was his wont, had developed a "positive horror" of the Bedfordshire house. And so by the end of the year he was looking forward to a place in Aldington, across the road from their holiday home, even though it had disaster written all over it. Conrad himself described it as a "very small (and poky) cottage," but added, as if by way of compensation, that it was within a stone's throw of the church where Erasmus was said to have preached. Anyway, as he put it to his wife, it was only a place to "hang out" till they found something better.

Jessie describes "it" as actually two little cottages across the road from each other. They rented part of one to store their extra furniture in and crowded into four small rooms of the other with the rest of their furniture and three-year-old John. She fought gallantly to make it livable and a place where Conrad could write, after moving in, in March, 1909.

The only place suitable for writing was the big front bedroom, so she converted it to a study-sitting room. Of the cupboard-sized chamber opening off it, she made a library of sorts: at least she had bookshelves put up. The study's old oak door leaked cold air. Yet despite all this, and a complete physical breakdown that brought him close to death before it ran its course, in this room, as Jessie said, "some good work got itself written." Among other things, he finished *Under Western Eyes*.

The nearby church added its own macabre touch during Conrad's desperate illness, and Jessie vowed that never again would she live close to a church: "I would wake from my few moments sleep to hear the strange voice of my invalid repeating the burial service in hoarse gasps, and the church bell a few yards away tolling its lament for some other poor departed soul."

In fact, Jessie's days near the church were numbered. Far ahead of his usual schedule, but with more reason than usual, too, Conrad was soon waging his inevitable feud with the house in which he lived. By December 17, 1909, he was bewailing the way they were "crowded into four tiny rooms in half a cottage." By May 17, 1910, he had secured another house: "I can't stay on in this [comparatively expensive] hole. It has become odious to me after this illness."

By June he was gone to Capel House, Orlestone—five miles away.

Orlestone A pleasant village indistinguishable from dozens of its kind throughout Kent, Orlestone is just off the B 2070, five miles south of Ashford. And on the Bonnington Road running out of Orlestone to the east, is Capel House, an old, low farmhouse of red brick. Joseph Conrad lived there from June, 1910, to March, 1919, the longest he ever stayed in one dwelling in all his years in England. In this house he wrote the last of his really significant works, and when he finally had to move elsewhere he seemed, wonder of wonders, reluctant to leave.

Compared to the Aldington quarters he had just vacated, the house—two storeys, plus an attic under the high, dormer-windowed roof—and its "biggish" rooms felt truly commodious. Moreover, its isolation was complete enough to satisfy even Conrad at his most antisocial. With almost aching aloneness, it was set in the midst of one-and-a-half acres of orchard, standing off by itself in flat fields, and surrounded in turn by 750 acres of dwarf oak trees.

In announcing his securing of the house to his friend ("Dearest Jack") Galsworthy, Conrad said: "It is a very attractive place and cheap at £45. It may be folly to take it—but it's either that or a breakdown." Besides, he admitted, "the days of twenty-pounds-a-year farmhouses are over." The clincher, however, was "I require perfect silence for my work." If he couldn't get it here, it would be his own fault.

The moving-in process was the usual Conrad charade. First he arranged to be at a friend's so that Jessie was left to handle everything alone. Then he gave her a deadline of just two days in which to transport everything and install it in the new place—precisely in the position he indicated. And finally he threw everything behind schedule before his departure by repeatedly hopping out of his car to get one or another book he simply had to have with him during the forty-eight hours he would be away.

Somehow Jessie met the deadline, even to filling the lamps with oil. And the place proved congenial to its master's spirit: "I can work here," he wrote on September 2. "The soil is clay, but the house is sympathetic." Work he could, and at a pace and a persistency that for Conrad was astounding.

In August, for instance, he finished the long short story "A Smile of

Fortune," writing it in pencil at the rate of 10,000 words per month, pushing the manuscript under the door of an adjacent room for Jessie to type. By May of 1911, a little under eleven months from the day he came to Capel House, he had written 84,000 words, including four short stories, and 12,000 words on the novel *Chance,* even though for three weeks in December he wrote not one line and for seven weeks in March and April managed little more.

It was at Capel House, and through that very novel, that Conrad's financial fortunes at last turned dramatically upward, both at home and in America. Even before he finished *Chance* in March, 1912, the *New York Herald* had begun serializing it, with great popular success. *'Twixt Land and Sea: Tales* was actually an American best- seller.

Conrad couldn't maintain the writing pace of his first two years, but the rest of his Orlestone years saw some first rate work. *Victory* was finished in June, 1914, and *The Arrow of Gold,* in June, 1918, for instance. And in the autumn of 1918 he took up *The Rescue* again, the novel he had laid aside in 1899. "It struck me then [in 1918] that my time was running out," he said, "and I wanted the deck cleared before going below." The deck was cleared: he finished the book the next year in May in temporary quarters at Wye.

Although Conrad guarded his solitude ferociously when he worked, he often craved intellectual company—Jessie's talents ran more to cooking and housekeeping—and could be a lavish, if temperamental, host when he liked. Therefore, despite its remoteness, a number of distinguished visitors found their way, via the Hamstreet station, to Capel House.

As always, perhaps the most welcome was John Galsworthy, whose friendship dated back to 1892, when Galsworthy was a passenger and Conrad the first mate aboard the clipper ship *Torrens*. Galsworthy was a leader in the effort that in 1911 won Conrad a pension of £100 on the Civil List, and Conrad's younger son John was named after him.

Another frequent visitor was the poet Arthur Symons, who was a particular favorite of young John. Once, when their regular games had palled, Symons eyed the muddy waters of the moat by which they were standing, and said matter-of-factly, "Let us try walking on the water, John." "All right, Mr. Symons," said the boy. "You try first."

Not so welcome a guest was the editor and writer Frank Harris, who arrived in a Spyker 30–40 automobile with a friend one Sunday afternoon and had both the Conrads seething by the time he left. "They patronized me immensely," fumed Joseph. And Jessie reported: "Coffee was brought at once. I stayed in the room some half-hour or so, and Frank Harris, to everyone's surprise, rose and without a word to either of us coolly rang the bell for more coffee. The impertinence nearly took my breath away, and the air was tense for a few moments."

Ford Madox Hueffer (Ford) came occasionally, although the closeness with Conrad had cooled considerably since the days of their collaboration. Jessie could hardly stand him, but Joseph regarded Hueffer as "a sort of life-long habit." On one visit in 1912 Hueffer brought along the novelist Violet Hunt. Conrad referred to them sardonically as "the great F. M. H.—with the somewhat less great V. H."

In 1913 Bertrand Russell came down to Capel House to meet Conrad. The result was explosive. "We seemed to sink through layer after layer of what was superficial, till gradually both reached the central fire," Russell recalled later. "We looked into each other's eyes, half appalled and half intoxicated to find ourselves together in such a region. . . . I came away bewildered, and hardly able to find my way among ordinary affairs." The pair's respect for each other persisted, and their friendship grew. In 1921, Russell named his newborn son John Conrad.

Another friendship formed in the Capel years was with the much younger Hugh Walpole, who had already won wide popularity with such novels as *Fortitude* and *The Dark Forest*. They first met in London early in 1918, although Walpole had already written a study of Conrad's works. In June he came down to Capel House for a weekend and has left a picture of his host that glows with life: "Great and glorious day. Conrad simply superb. A child, nervous, excitable, affectionate, confidential, doesn't give you the idea anywhere of a strong man, but *real* genius that is absolutely *sui generis*. *Green Mirror* (Walpole's new book) fine—no holes to be picked—but I need more resonance. Said only thing was to be a 'glorious story-teller.' Said all 'ism's were rot.' "

Walpole was something of a literary name collector, notably of Henry James. But he was a loyal and obliging friend as well. Even in his younger days, Conrad was often a living definition of the word "irascible," and as he grew older, he was at times moody and savage, even to guests. But Walpole remained a stout ally and supporter to Conrad till his death and to Jessie thereafter.

It is likely that Conrad would have spent all his last years in Capel House if he'd been able, though he liked to play the game of house hunting even when the lease on a current place had several years to go. But their landlord suddenly died, and his son and heir announced he wanted the place for himself. And so, in March, 1919, Conrad moved from Capel House. He acted, Jessie said, like a mule.

New Romney A small town on the A 259, New Romney is almost exactly halfway between Hythe and Rye. That luckless novelist, George Gissing, stayed here in 1897 on a visit to his old school friend, Dr. Henry Hick, the town physician. Through Gissing, H. G. Wells came to know and like Hick, and in 1898 he and his wife Jane decided to include a visit to Hick during a cycling holiday along the South Coast. They wound up in New Romney all right, but hardly as planned.

For by the time they reached Seaford in Sussex, Wells had developed a severe cold, a frightening high fever, and a stabbing pain from an abscessed kidney. Only by a series of agonizing trips via local trains were they able to reach New Romney and Dr. Hick. They arrived August 9 and stayed until the beginning of September.

Wells's illness, in turn, brought two more distinguished literary men to New Romney. For during his slow recuperation, Edmund Gosse and Henry James bicycled over from James's house in Rye to probe ever so gently into Wells's possible need of help from the Royal Literary Fund. Luckily, Wells didn't need help, and hadn't the foggiest notion what they were up to.

In its own way, New Romney also made small contributions to *Kipps,* one of Wells's best received novels. For although the "egg was hatched," as he put it, in Folkestone some years later (in 1905), it was laid here. And fittingly enough, when Kipps's mother hands him over to his elderly aunt and uncle, Wells places the scene in New Romney.

5. SHOWPLACES OF KENT

Tunbridge Wells

Kent's most famous spa, Tunbridge Wells, attracted Charles and Mary Lamb in the spring of 1823 to holiday and to see two of the county's most spectacular showplaces, Knole and Penshurst. Were they making the trip today, they would surely add a third, also nearby: Sissinghurst. They didn't visit it then for the very good reason that there was nothing to see. Much of it had been scavenged for building materials, and what remained was used as the Parish Workhouse. But now a restored Sissinghurst ranks among Kent's most notable sites.

It is typical of Kent's prodigality that three such places can be found within a radius of ten miles from Tunbridge Wells. Using the latter as a base, the literary traveller can see them all in a single day—if his feet hold out and his satiation point is high. In fact, the glutton can even add a fourth stop: the Ellen Terry Museum, which is only eight miles southeast of Sissinghurst.

Even from London the circuit can still be made in a day. Or if you're lucky enough to be in Rye, Sussex—and that's very lucky indeed—you can leave after breakfast, see all three, and have dinner in London . . . but you'll have to clip along those historic halls in less than stately fashion.

Tunbridge Wells A city of about 50,000, Tunbridge Wells is a twenty-eight mile drive northwest from Rye along the A 268, A 21, and A 264 . . . or a thirty-seven mile one southeast of London via the A 21 and A 26. Somewhat déclassé (what spa isn't?), it was still thriving before World War I. In 1909, Edward VII dubbed it "Royal Tunbridge Wells" in recognition of its services to a long line of monarchs, and in 1915 men like John Galsworthy were still bringing their wives to holiday there.

The chalbeate (iron salts) spring was discovered in the time of James I, and by the Restoration the town was in full swing as a fashionable and racy resort, many coming for the powers of the water, reputed to cure almost anything that ailed you from sexual hesitancy to old age itself.

But in his *A Tour through the Whole Island of Great Britain* (1724–27), Daniel Defoe excoriates the many more who came "for Gaming, Sharping, Intriguing; as also Fops, Fools, Beaus, and the like." For whatever their reasons—and with a gamut from Colley Cibber to Dr. Johnson there had to be several—the leading authors of the eighteenth century came in throngs. John Gay came in 1723, working on *The Captives*. Garrick and Sir Joshua Reynolds came, as did Johnson. Edward Young visited often to take the waters, perhaps in hopes of shaking off the gloom of "Night Thoughts." Fanny Burney was there with Mrs. Thrale and worked a bit of the town into *Camilla* (1796). Beau Nash himself reigned over all for a time as master of ceremonies.

In the nineteenth century Tunbridge Wells was largely eclipsed by Brighton. But Thackeray came as a twelve-year-old lad the very year of Lamb's visit (1823), stayed with his parents for a long vacation in a "lovely cottage," and had a grand time scaring himself with gothic novels. So much so that he was back as a grown-up to "scribble, scribble all day" in 1842, in nearby Southborough, and in 1860 had a house on the common (now marked with a plaque) in Tunbridge Wells itself.

Alfred Tennyson came in 1840, hoping it would improve his mother's health. He didn't like it, and in the autumn of 1841 moved on to Boxley. But Tunbridge Wells need not be faulted: Tennyson had lost Hallam. He had published nothing in eight years. His "engagement" to Emily Sellwood was in limbo. And he had been turned out of the beloved Lincolnshire rectory, so filled with both sweet and bitter memories of his growing up. To remedy all this was asking a bit much, even of a chalbeate spring.

Sissinghurst Castle (and Smallhythe)

Sissinghurst Castle is one mile east of Sissinghurst village on the A 262, and two and a half miles northeast of Cranbrook, where those little-known brothers, Giles and Phineas Fletcher, were born, destined to write their lesser-known poems in a blazing competition for obscurity.

Properly speaking, Sissinghurst never was a castle, but mainly a sixteenth-century manorial pile built not as a fortress but as a country estate. And its literary interest stems not from any role it played over the centuries, but from its being restored—beginning in 1930—by poet-novelist Vita Sackville-West and her writer husband, Harold Nicolson, and from the books they wrote here.

What Vita took over was a shambles, for the history of Sissinghurst is the story of a great house nobody came to want, and amid its ruins were only a few fragments from its long-past glory. The present gatehouse and great central arch, for instance, go back to about 1530, when Sir John Baker inserted them in the center of the grand new house his family had built forty years earlier. (Oddly, Sir John's daughter Cicely married Thomas Sackville, making Vita his direct descendant.)

Sir John amassed a huge fortune one way or another (after his death he was awarded the title "Bloody Baker," perhaps unjustly). Thus about 1560 his son Richard was able to afford to build the four-storey tower, which still stands, just in time for a three-night stay by Queen Elizabeth—which may well have cost almost as much as the tower did.

From then on it was pretty much downhill for the Bakers and their home, however. During the seventeenth-century Civil War another Sir John had the bad judgment to back the wrong side and lost most of the family's wealth. And his son showed equally poor judgment by producing four daughters and no sons. Two of these girls had no children at all. And the other two had husbands with estates of their own to worry about. There was nobody left to care tuppence about Sissinghurst.

Horace Walpole, gothic novelist and charming letter writer, visited it in 1752 and found "a park in ruins and a house in ten times greater ruins." But worse things were yet to come. From 1756 to 1763, during the Seven Years War with the French, the government leased it to house as many as 3,000 war prisoners, jamming them as many as eighteen to a room. One English officer was historian Edward Gibbon, who was appalled by the stench, squalor, and misery. The prisoners responded by wrecking what was left of the place. When they left, the total value of Sissinghurst, land and all, was just £300.

Essentially, this is what Vita and Harold Nicolson took over. It had some assets for the garden spot she had in mind, such as good soil, for since 1800 it had been used primarily as a working farm. And Vita saw possibilities in the two surviving stretches of the twelfth-century moat as picturesque background, and the few "high Tudor walls of pink brick" had their appeal.

But for years the grounds had been a dumping place, and one marvels that

Vita Sackville-West's Sissinghurst, Kent

By Courtesy of The National Trust

Vita and Sir Harold could ever foresee today's beautiful gardens in the jungle they took over. But they were a formidable team. He designed the garden with classic control and symmetry. She planted it with romantic profusion and abandon. The result is stunning.

As the gardens slowly developed, the remaining buildings were gradually restored as well, the family spreading out to use each as it developed. Thus, Sissinghurst emerged not as one dwelling, but as scattered parts of a house. The parents slept in South Cottage, their sons in Priest's House. The dining room and kitchen were in Priest's House, but Vita's sitting room-study was in the tower, while Nicolson wrote in South Cottage. The library, converted from the old, dark stables, was in the North Wing. They must have forever been meeting themselves coming or going.

Vita Sackville-West died in 1962, Harold Nicolson in 1968 and today Sissinghurst belongs to the National Trust, though their younger son Nigel lives on in the South Wing. In season (roughly April through mid-October), the gardens, library, courtyard, and tower are open to the public for a small fee (or National Trust card).

Of most interest to the literary minded is the Elizabethan Tower. On the first floor (U.S. second), reached by a spiral staircase in the left hand turret, is Vita's sitting room-study, lined with her books, cluttered with her memorabilia, writing table, and couch, and looking much as she left it. Here, among other things, she wrote *Dark Island* (1934), and *Pepita* (1937), and her biography of *Saint Joan of Arc* (1936).

On the second floor, in addition to before-and-after exhibits of house and garden, is a surprisingly small printing press which was *the* Hogarth Press, on which Virginia and Leonard Woolf produced the first edition of T. S. Eliot's *The Waste Land,* as well as books by Robert Graves, Herbert Reed, Roger Fry, and others. Virginia would hand set the type, and Leonard operated the press. After treading away at it for four hours at a time he wrote "I felt as if I had taken a great deal of exercise." Until 1924 the press was installed at Hogarth, Richmond, hence the name. Then it was moved to the basement scullery of their Bloomsbury house in London. In 1930 Virginia gave it to Vita. It was the first piece of furniture to arrive at Sissinghurst after the purchase of the castle that same year.

In the turret on this floor are diaries, letters and manuscripts of both Vita and Nicolson relating the story of their discovery and restoration of the place. The top floor of the tower has some handsome photographs of other National Trust gardens. And while you're up there, you might as well clamber out on the top of the tower. The view—gardens, North Downs, valley of the Weald—is something to see.

Smallhythe Place The fifteenth-century half-timbered house called Smallhythe Place is on the east side of the Rye Road (B 2082) two miles south of Tenterden and eight miles southeast of Sissinghurst. Here Ellen Terry, one of England's most charming and accomplished actresses, lived from 1899 until her death in 1928. Today the building houses the Ellen Terry Memorial, a museum with memorabilia from her life and her long career in the theater. It's owned by the National Trust and is open in season (normally March through October).

Strictly speaking, it must be confessed, her one book hardly entitles her to be called a literary figure—especially as it was *The Story of My Life* (1908). But playwrights from Shakespeare on owe her much. She played her first Shakespearian role in *The Winter's Tale* when only eight, as the boy Mamilius, and went on to play every one of his major heroines. And she rounded out her career starring in the plays of G. B. Shaw. Which suggests one other credential: as the author of her part of the correspondence recording her celebrated (if arm's length) affair with Shaw, she can claim more avid readers than many a recognized writer.

Penshurst Place

Penshurst Place, one of the splendid country homes of England, is eight miles northwest of Tunbridge Wells just off the B 2176. Dating back to the fourteenth century, with significant additions over the years since, even into the nineteenth century, this great stone mansion has its share of magnificent hangings, fixtures and furnishings. But it is not as stately as Chatsworth in Derbyshire, say, nor is it at all as large as Knole, its neighbor up the road.

To the student of Elizabethan literature, however, Penshurst has a special appeal. For here, in 1554, was born that courtier, soldier, scholar, patron of the arts, and poet, that epitome of the Renaissance man, Sir Philip Sidney. The Renaissance man was supposed to be able to do just about anything . . . do it well . . . and do it with ease. Sidney fit this pattern.

His achievements in just literature would have been noteworthy in any man, let alone one who moved on the highest levels of Elizabeth's court, travelled on delicate diplomatic missions, served as governor of Flushing in the Netherlands—and died at thirty-two. His sonnet cycle, *Astrophel and Stella,* written during 1580–84, preceded those of Spenser and Shakespeare and ranks with both. His *Apology for Poetry* is a landmark in Elizabethan criticism. And there is nothing until the eighteenth century to rival his *Arcadia* in its importance to the development of English prose fiction.

Penshurst came into the Sidney family during the brief reign of Henry

VIII's son Edward VI, who gave it to Sir Philip's grandfather, Sir William. It passed then to his son Henry, who had grown up as Edward's favorite companion. Sir Henry made a number of structural changes and first designed the almost too mathematically formal gardens the visitor sees today. Sir Philip didn't inherit Penshurst until 1586. Since he died the very same year, his imprint on the place is slight.

Similarly, it is easy to exaggerate Penshurst's influence on him. He spent much of his youth away in Ireland and Wales, where his father was in the service of the Queen, and from age ten on, at school. Thereafter, he was largely at the court, abroad, or—occasionally in disfavor with the Queen—at Wilton House in Wiltshire, the estate of his sister, the Countess of Pembroke.

He was at Wilton, in fact, when he wrote the *Arcadia* to amuse her, and probably Wilton's gardens have as much (and as little) claim to inspiring that work as Penshurst's. As you stroll amidst the quartered geometry of Penshurst, at any rate, it's hard to see in them *Arcadia's* flowery meads where "shepherd boys pipe as tho' they would never be old," let alone "goatherd gods that love the grassy mountains" and nymphs "which haunt the springs."

Since Sir Henry's time, nonetheless, Penshurst's gardens, now restored to his Elizabethan design, and grounds have been among its greatest attractions for people of all degrees, including writers. Ben Johnson wrote a poem "To Penshurst," in which he praised the orchard fruit and garden flowers that "hang on thy walls, that every child may reach." Another seventeenth-century poet, Edmund Waller, admired the "lofty beeches," though his eye was really on Lady Dorothy Sidney, granddaughter of Sir Philip Sidney's brother. (She was the Sacharissa of Waller's love poems.)

The great seventeenth-century diarist, John Evelyn, visited it and recorded that it was "famous once for its Gardens and excellent fruit." And it was the gardens, among other things, that in 1823 made Mary Lamb say that although she was "very much pleased with Knole," she was still more [so] with Penshurst."

The public rooms of Penshurst are sumptuous, but they too, like the gardens, reflect little of Sidney himself. The elegant furnishings and furniture are chiefly seventeenth and eighteenth century, and even later. But in the sixty-foot high fourteenth-century Great Hall, with its roof of massive chestnut beams, is a poignant reminder of how magnificently he died.

In July of 1586 he had voluntarily joined a raiding party in the Netherlands and in the ensuing fight was struck in the thigh by a bullet. Somehow he managed to make it back to camp. There, as he lay on the ground awaiting aid, he was offered a cup of water, but noticed a dying soldier. "Nay," he said, pushing the cup to the soldier, "thy need is greater than mine." They died together.

No wonder all England mourned the early death of this most shining of knights. Over 200 elegies were written to honor him, including Edmund Spenser's *Astrophel*. In the great funeral procession to St. Paul's Cathedral in London, where he was buried, his helmet held a place of honor. You can see that helmet now in the Great Hall. For all its furnishing and paintings, Penshurst has no richer treasure.

Today Penshurst is owned by Viscount de L'Isle, and he opens it to the public for a fee most days of the week, from spring to fall. But it is wise to learn exactly which hours of what days before setting out.

Knole

Knole is about ten miles northwest of Tunbridge Wells at the Tunbridge end of Sevenoaks just off the A 225. It's the greatest Tudor palace of them all. And it's almost too big to talk about. It has seven courtyards, fifty-two staircases, and 365 rooms—for the days of the week, weeks of the year, and days of the year (or so they say. A person could get lost trying to verify this.) The house itself is three acres; the garden, twenty-six; and the park, 1,000.

And the thing of it is, you suspect none of this as you come into the park by the main entrance opposite St. Nicholas's church.* In the eighteenth century, Horace Walpole was similarly taken in as he viewed the deceptive west front facing the park: "A beautiful, decent simplicity," said he, "which charms one." And, as indicated above, on her visit in 1823 with her brother, Mary Lamb confessed she was "very much pleased with Knole." Charmed, yes. Pleased, yes. But one must be on guard that he's not overwhelmed, too.

Most visitors today come for the lavish rooms, furnishings, paintings, and grounds. But in truth, Knole has had important literary connections from sixteenth-century writer Thomas Sackville, who was given the place by his cousin Queen Elizabeth, to twentieth-century writer Vita Sackville-West, his direct descendant, who grew up there.

She cherished Knole for its slow, almost organic growth over the years. Thomas Bourchier, Archbishop of Canterbury, began it all in 1456 when he bought the estate and started building. Henry VIII enlarged it greatly when he snatched it away from poor Thomas Cranmer, despite the archbishop's plea that it was too small a house for His Majesty. Sackville himself, kin to Elizabeth on the Anne Boleyn side, fortunately was rich enough to afford his monarch's gift and greatly remodelled it between 1603 and 1608. Later Sackvilles added their touches, too.

The unmatched collection of furniture and paintings grew over the

---

*John Donne preached here annually from 1616 to 1631.

centuries similarly, especially seventeenth- and eighteenth-century pieces; some are so precious they have to be protected from sunlight and are examined close-up only with flashlights. And, while some of the Sackvilles were collecting material things, others were collecting writers as well.

Thomas Sackville set the precedent for this interest in literature, writing with Thomas Norton that earliest of tragedies, *Gorboduc* (1561), and the *Induction* to the *Mirror for Magistrates*. *Gorboduc's* chief value may be to convince the doubtful that Elizabethan drama certainly did improve a lot in the thirty years between it and Shakespeare, but the *Induction* has its moments.

Sir Thomas's grandson, Richard (third Earl of Dorset), was one of the seventeenth century's most accomplished gamblers and wastrels; he even managed to put Knole in hock. But he befriended a number of writers, among them Ben Jonson, Michael Drayton, and John Fletcher, and from time to time had them as houseguests. No great chore, 'tis true. He had 111 servants, and goodness knows, rooms aplenty.

Charles Sackville, the sixth Earl, a lover of Nell Gwynn, was an even greater patron of writers of the latter part of the century. Among those he supported with his friendship and entertained at Knole were not only Dryden, Pope, Wycherly, and Matthew Prior, but also Thomas Shadwell, the much abused "hero" of Dryden's "MacFlecknoe" who "never deviates into sense." Dryden dedicated both his *Essay on Satire* and *Essay of Dramatic Poesy* to the Earl, and in the latter casts him as Eugenius. This master of Knole, who could turn out deft and witty verse himself when so moved, was a notable host. Says Prior: "A freedom reigned at his table which made every one of his guests think himself at home."

Vita Sackville-West's father was the third Lord Sackville, and it is sad to think that had she been a male she would have inherited the Knole she loved so much—sad, that is, until one realizes that had she done so, there would have been no Sissinghurst. (Her father was succeeded by his younger brother.)

She has left her personal monument to Knole, however. Her *Knole and the Sackvilles* (1922) is a classic. So, in its own strange way, is *Orlando: A Biography* (1928) by her good friend Virginia Woolf, which presents the great house and its past through the eyes of its artist-hero. Vita's son Nigel tells of her reception of the novel: "She loved it. Naturally, she was flattered, but more than that, the novel identified her with Knole forever. Virginia, by her genius, had provided Vita with a unique consolation for having been born a girl, for her exclusion from her inheritance, for her father's death earlier that year. The book, for her, was not simply a brilliant masque or pageant. It was 'a memorial mass.' "

Virginia gave the manuscript of *Orlando* to Vita, who gave it to Knole, where you can see it if you wish. For in 1946 Vita's Uncle Charles, fourth Lord Sackville, gave Knole to the National Trust and, in season (March through November normally, but you'd better check) it is open to the public for a small fee or a National Trust membership.

SUSSEX

God gives all men all earth to love,
But since man's heart is small,
Ordains for each one spot shall prove
Beloved over all.
Each to his choice, and I rejoice
The lot has fallen to me
In a fair ground—in a fair ground—
Yea, Sussex by the sea!

"Sussex," by Rudyard Kipling

Kipling was only one of a number of eminent writers who lived and wrote in Sussex, from Henry James and Thackeray to Aubrey Beardsley and Stephen Crane. But it's surprising how many of them are Victorians. True, there is a Shelley before them, and a Virginia Woolf after. But in the main it is as if a whole wave of English writers suddenly discovered Sussex together in the latter part of the nineteenth century.

This is strange, for Sussex is among the loveliest of English shires. The Downs, rising to the heights of 800 feet, with the tree-strewn Weald below and the English Channel beyond, provide breathtaking vistas. The villages are ancient and charming. The beaches are alluring. Often enough it takes the stranger but one visit to some place in Sussex to make it "beloved over all."

And it's not as if Sussex hasn't been there all the time. Way back in 477, an Anglo-Saxon visitor named Ella grounded his boat here, jumped ashore, and proceeded to knock the natives about until they accepted him as king. And almost six hundred years later another visitor, a Norman, did the same thing—with more lasting results. Never mind that the Battle of Hastings didn't take place in Hastings. It *was* in Sussex, and it was 1066.

Modern Sussex is an area of nearly 1,500 square miles bounded on the north by Surrey, the northeast by Kent, the south by the English Channel, and the west by Hampshire. And, actually, there are two counties—East and West Sussex—each with its own government. Each county warrants its own section . . . and attention.

EAST SUSSEX

East Sussex

1. The Reaches of Rye
2. Brighton and its Neighbors

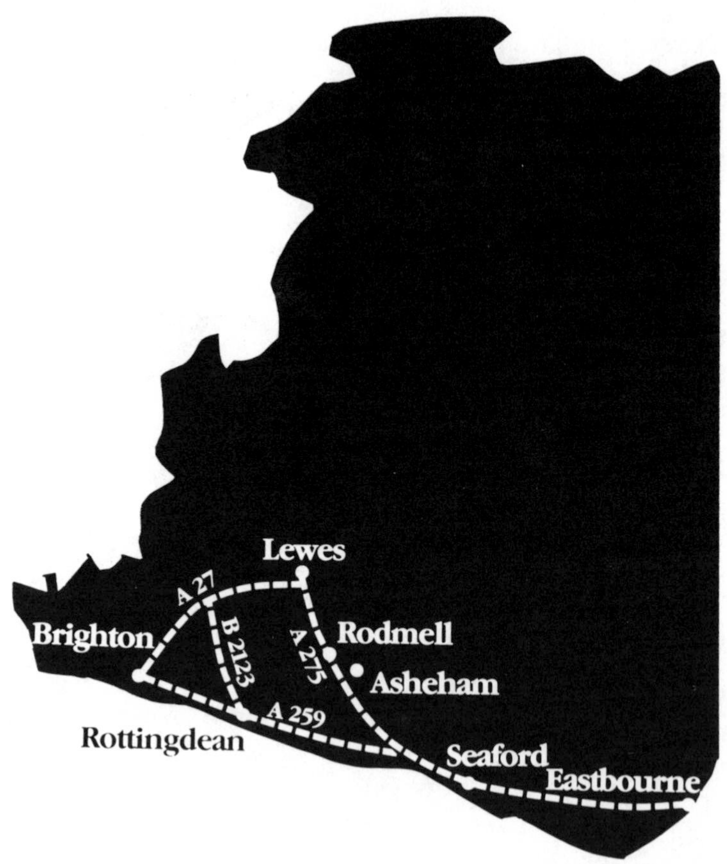

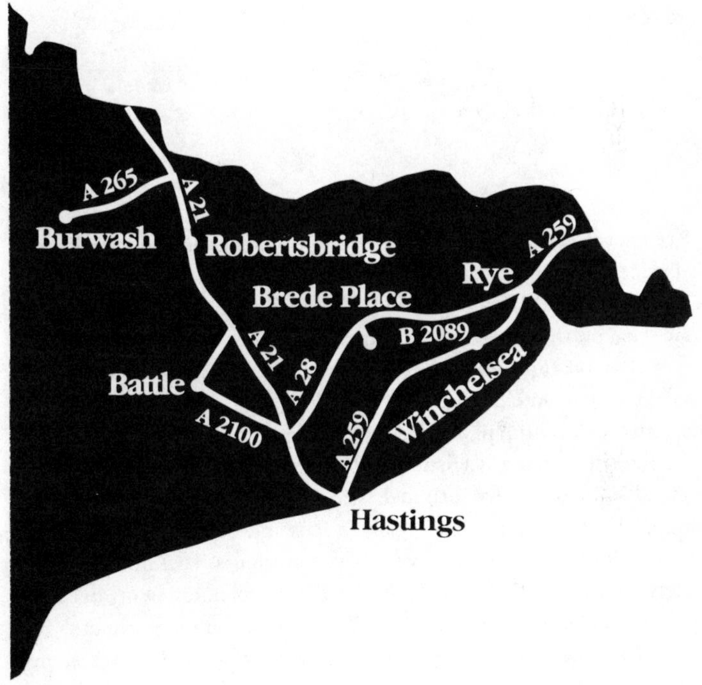

English Channel

The literary highlights of East Sussex are best discussed and explored in terms of the two major cities along its southern coast: Rye and Brighton. They mark the county's farthest stretches, east and west. And they can serve as the two anchor points for exploration afield. Very special anchor points they are, too.

1. THE REACHES OF RYE

Rye

If Rye hadn't existed for Henry James to discover, someone would have had to invent it for him. But it was there and had been since 1229 and before, when he came to nearby Point Hill in the summer of 1896. All he had to do, as he sat there on the terrace of his borrowed house working on *The Spoils of Poynton,* was to look up, and see Rye perched there a mile across the valley—red-roofed houses, old church tower, and all.

Once, in the dim, dim past, Rye had been an island. Even before William the Conqueror arrived it was a fishing village. King Henry II (Becket's loving nemesis) added it to the five original "Cinque Ports." The French found it irresistible, visiting it again and again to loot and burn. Queen Elizabeth visited and dubbed it "Royal Rye." The notorious Hawkhurst gang of smugglers came in the 1750's and took over its best hotel, following belatedly on the heels of George I, who stayed briefly and took over its best house. This was the very house James was to acquire almost two hundred years later. Today it alone would place Rye high on the must itinerary of the literary traveller.

When you come to Rye, you enter either on the A 259 (from Hastings, twelve miles to the west; or from New Romney, twelve miles to the east), or on the A 268 from Tunbridge Wells, twenty-eight miles to the northwest. In any event, you'll want to head at once for one of the several good hotels and get settled before venturing out again so that you can give Rye your undivided attention once you start. It deserves it.

The oldest and most picturesque hotel, as it turns out, is also the best: the three-star Mermaid. It is a handsome, half-timbered building that dates back to 1420, erected to replace a 1300 A.D. building burned in a French raid of 1377. The street (now Mermaid) was then called Middle Street and was the main entrance from the sea through the Strand Gate. Hard as it is to believe now, as one looks at the bare trickle of water that is "Rye Port," the anchorage below the Mermaid then had twenty feet of water, with as many as 2,000 boats at a time at anchor.

The Mermaid has its own interest for the visitor: not only its quota of Tudor linen-fold paneling and Caen-stone fireplaces, but also its secret staircases and priest holes, which must have proved an extra bonus for the Hawkhurst smugglers when they took over the place. Queen Elizabeth had made it her headquarters, too, when she came to Rye. Most distinguished visitors to Rye who were not privately housed stayed here.

In the early twentieth century the prominent of the community and its environs belonged to the Mermaid Club and met regularly in a large half-timbered room. Henry James was a member and sponsored Stephen Crane (the American writer was living in nearby Brede), as well as—reluctantly to be sure—Crane's mistress Cora for admission to the club's woman's corner.

The Mermaid makes an excellent starting point for a foot tour of Rye. The streets are steep, however, and the famed cobble stones protrude as much as two inches. Good walking shoes will in no way diminish the city's charm.

First stop should be Henry James's house, a few hundred yards up Mermaid Street, then right on West Street to where it curves toward St. Mary's Church. And there it is: Lamb House, James's home from 1897 until his death in 1916. It's a handsomely simple, modest-sized mansion, with (James's words) a "nice old red-bricked front" and a "high old Georgian doorway" with a canopy.

The building dates back to 1722–23 when a newcomer to Rye, James Lamb, rebuilt an existing building. He went on to become mayor, and through the centuries his house was considered the town's most elegant. Noting that it had a "King's Room"—the principal bedroom—James boasted that George I, forced ashore in 1726 by a storm, commandeered Lamb House as the house "then most consonant with his grandeur." James was understating things: George II also stayed there under similar circumstances in 1736.

James got to Lamb House in three stages. In the summer of 1896 he had borrowed a small house on Point Hill, Playden (one mile north of Rye). When he had to give it up he rented the Old Vicarage of Rye's St. Mary's for two months (about which, more anon). And here, just down the street, he discovered and fell in love with Lamb House. But when he asked about a

Henry James's Lamb House, Rye, East Sussex

By Courtesy of The National Trust

lease, the answer was a flat "no!" In 1897, however, the owner's sudden death and his son's preference for gold mining in the Klondike left the house available. With some apprehension, for £70 a year, James signed for this "smallish, charming cheap old house . . . for 21 years." Two years later, when the would-be gold miner died, with even more trepidation James bought Lamb House for £2,000.

It was more than ample for his needs. On the ground floor was a little parlor of old oak, a squarish dining room, a kitchen and breakfast room, and a small white-paneled room that came to be known as the "Telephone Room." James had one of the instruments before there was anyone else much to call in Rye.

Above were three bedrooms, a dressing room, and the "Green Room" (green paneling) which James used as a second study. The main study, separate from the house, was one of its major attractions: "most delightful little old architectural garden-house, perched alongside of [the main house] on its high brick garden wall." Called the "Garden Room" (or Garden House) it was at right angles to—and to the right of—the front door. A large bow window furnished a view down steep West Street.

Commodious and safe from distraction, it was ideal for writing. James jokingly dubbed it the Temple of the Muse. Winters he wrote in the Green Room; summers he wrote here. His friend, novelist E. F. Benson, describes the incredibly disciplined daily routine of "the Master" at work in this room, dictating—as was his wont in later years—his novels to his secretary in what he called "Remingtonese":

> [His voice] boomed out through the open window between the tassels of wisteria, now louder, now softer, as he paced up and down the length of the room, and the metallic click of the typewriter made response. From breakfast until the stroke of the gong for lunch he was thus invisible though not inaudible. . . .

Although he was already fifty-five when he moved into Lamb House, James wrote some of his best things there. In the five years 1898–1903 alone he wrote *The Awkward Age, The Sacred Font, The Ambassadors, The Wings of the Dove,* and *The Golden Bowl*—some say the latter three were his greatest—as well as such short stories as "The Turn of the Screw," "The Soft Side," and "The Better Sort."

Lamb House figures peripherally in *The Golden Bowl.* For when George I was there in 1726 he attended a christening and presented the baby with a golden bowl. James saw this bowl in 1902 in a bank vault and it worked its way into the symbolism of the novel, along with the "silver cord, the golden bowl" of Ecclesiastes and Blake's "silver rod, golden bowl." The bowl, real gold and flawless, serves as a contrast to the gilded, cracked-crystal bowl Maggie gets.

Even without these rich associations with James's own work, Lamb House would be a literary shrine simply for the writers who visited there. Among the more or less illustrious were Stephen Crane, Joseph Conrad, George Gissing, H. G. Wells, G. K. Chesterton, Rudyard Kipling, Max Beerbohm, Hugh Walpole, Rupert Brooke, Ford Madox Hueffer (Ford), Logan Pearsall Smith, Violet Hunt, Edith Wharton, and Virginia Woolf.

Crane came often in the months he was at Brede, dressed in riding breeches and cowboy shirt and charging up to the high-canopied door on a huge horse—once to the consternation of Mrs. Humphrey Ward, who was presiding over the tea urn. James was apparently always glad to see the younger American, but his view of Crane's work was mixed. (Among James's less than beguiling traits was a tendency to temper his praise of fellow writers. At a Beacon Hill reception in Boston he assessed Crane as "a Cockney—oh, I admit of the greatest genius, but a Cockney still.")

Joseph Conrad came to Lamb House now and then, too. His wife recalled with relish a tea party in the oak parlor when James inadvertently passed the first cup of tea to Ford Madox Hueffer's wife instead of to Jessie Conrad. In the carriage going home, for they had come together, Mrs. Hueffer asked angrily: "Did he give me the tea first because he thinks I'm older than you?" Jessie's answer was innocence itself: "You could hardly expect me to make a scene, could you?" Jessie couldn't stand Mrs. Hueffer. And besides, the Hueffers had tricked the Conrads into not dressing up for the tea, and then had shown up resplendent themselves.

Conrad and James were a strange couple, anyway. Aliens both, but at bottom sharing little more than a fluency in French. Conrad made James uneasy; James found Conrad "curious" and "interesting." But each had vast respect for the other's art. James had the highest praise for Conrad's *The Nigger of the Narcissus* and *Lord Jim,* and Conrad addressed James as "très cher maitre."

James and H. G. Wells visited back and forth while Wells lived at Folkestone. On one such visit to Lamb House in June, 1901, Wells brought along his house guest, George Gissing, a pathetic, skin-and-bones figure whose powerful proletarian novels, notably *New Grub Street*, had been greeted with impressive indifference. It must have been a remarkable evening, even for Lamb House, for the three novelists spent the whole night talking—especially James—with reminiscences of Turgenev in Paris. James thought that "poor Gissing" was "peculiarly marked out to be a writer," and that his "style [is] ugly but really describes the lower-middle-class circles."

Another time Wells arrived to find himself smack in the middle of a contretemps between Henry James and his equally famous philosopher-brother William. The incident had its irony, for these two elegant (though admittedly American) gentlemen appealed to the humbly-born Wells to adjudicate what a well-born gentleman does and doesn't do.

William, it seemed, excited at the news that the distinguished writer, G. K. Chesterton, whom he longed to meet, was staying at the Mermaid just over Lamb House's high garden wall, clambered up a ladder to have a peep. Henry caught him at it and was furious. Well's decision was Solomonic: he ended the quarrel by carting William off with him to Sandgate. Best of all, whom should they run into on the way but Chesterton!

Wells thought James a "strange, unnatural human being, a sensitive man lost in an immensely abundant brain." His description of James and his home recalls the meticulous discipline of the latter's way of writing: "His life was unbelievably correct and his home at Rye one of the most perfect pieces of suitably furnished Georgian architecture imaginable."

A less than enraptured guest was Edith Wharton, who in 1903 had herself chauffeured to Rye for an overnight stay. She and James were old friends, but later to intimates she sniffed at his "anxious frugality," which included serving the same "dreary pudding or pie" two meals in a row. Henry, she said, had a terror of being thought rich, worldly, or luxurious. (One should remember, however, Edith's own enormous wealth.)

Perhaps, the most frequent and welcome guest at Lamb House in James's later years was Hugh Walpole, on the threshold of a career as one of the most prolific and popular novelists of his time. As some people are social climbers, Walpole was a literary climber, but in so unabashed a way as to be forgiven. Just twenty-five, he first met James at his London Club—for dinner alone—through the simple expedient of writing a shamelessly flattering fan letter.

In September Walpole's adulation was rewarded with his first visit to Lamb House, and he confided to his diary that he was thrilled "to hear all about Thackeray, Stevenson, Dickens, Carlyle and the rest intimately from first hand." At the end of each year, Walpole would list in this diary his leading fifteen friends (later he had a second list of thirty) in order of merit. This first year, James made number four.

Walpole came thereafter whenever he could. In a letter to Walpole in 1912, when he was seventy-three and Walpole, twenty-eight, James picturesquely describes the close, almost father and son relationship that developed: "the old grizzled and blear-eyed house dog looks up . . . and grunts and wags his tail at the damaged but still delectable Prodigal Son."

Lamb House's literary ties did not end with the death of Henry James. He left the house to his nephew and namesake, who preferred to lease it. Among early tenants were the Benson brothers, writers both. Arthur Christopher

(A.C.) Benson, Master of Cambridge's Magdalene College, wrote fifty books. Never heard of him? He wrote the words to "Land of Hope and Glory." Edward Frederick Benson (E. F.) was the author of such popular novels as *Dodo*. Before he died in 1925, A.C. had written three novels, a two-volume reminiscence, and a Greek anthology in Lamb House. And E. F. wrote all his later works here, including *David of King's Mezzanine,* and the "Lucia" series, and served as mayor of Rye before dying in 1940.

Rye and Lamb House itself are featured in one of E. F. Benson's most successful novels, *Miss Mapp,* published in 1922. He tells how the plan for it grew as he looked upon the ladies of Rye shopping in the High Street:

> I outlined an elderly atrocious spinster and established her in Lamb House. She should be the centre of social life abhorred and dominant, and she should sit like a great spider behind the curtains of the Garden Room, spying on her friends, and I knew that her name must be Elizabeth Mapp.

A few months after Benson's death, while the house was still empty, a German bomb demolished the Garden Room and badly damaged the main structure. The house stood empty for ten years. Then in 1950 it was given to the National Trust, which has done a remarkable job of restoring the house and recovering some of James's far-flung possessions.

Lamb House is now open to the public (small fee or N. T. card) Wednesday and Saturday afternoons in season. On view, all on the ground floor, are the hall, the "Telephone Room," and especially the Morning Room, which is rich in James furniture and relics. The garden is also on view. The rest of the house is let to tenants. One of these, James Haynes-Dixon, wrote his autobiographical novel, *Home Made Trousers,* here. His wife was Rumer Godden, who brought novel writing back to the Green Room.

Leaving Lamb House, the foot tour takes you along West Street. A few steps bring you to the Old Vicarage of St. Mary's on your left. This is where James came for two months in July of 1896 when his loan of Point Hill ran out. He found it a letdown, "Shabby, fusty", but the rent was reasonable, and it did have more rooms, more tumblers, and more saucepans. Today it houses some rather elegant flats.

Another few steps, on the right, is the Norman fifteenth-century St. Mary's Parish Church with its unusual old clock. James mentioned it specially when he talked of moving into Lamb House: its chimes "will sound sweet in my goodly old red-walled garden." They still do.

The church is at the top of Lion Street, down which, a hundred yards or two on the left, is the "Ancient" Vicarage (as distinct from the "Old" one). In this Tudor house, partly fronted in 1701, was born Jacobean playwright John Fletcher, son of the vicar of Rye (who as Bishop of London was to have the dubious pleasure of attending Mary Queen of Scots at her execution). Today the Fletcher House is a charming tea shop, and you'll enjoy it—if you can get in. There's a plaque on the wall; so you can't miss it.

One last stop on a stroll about Rye is the Ypres Tower, pronounced by the natives, James hooted, "Wipers." (And so some of them do to this day.) Even so, it was part of the ancient flavor of the town that so captivated him. It was built about 1250 by order of Henry III, largely destroyed by the French in the fourteenth century, bought by a John de Iprys in 1430, and finally re-purchased by the town corporation. Now it houses a public museum. Through its arch you can catch a glimpse of all that's left of the Rye River, the empty stream that depends on a rising tide to float even the tiniest of fishing boats.

The stream, the tower, and the town itself belong in the past. But therein lies the irresistible charm Rye had for Henry James—a charm undiminished by time.

Winchelsea

Winchelsea, two and a half miles south of Rye on the A 259, is one of those once-bustling ports the sea deserted—and one gets the feeling the people deserted it, too. You reach it through the old, narrow, stone-arched Strand Gate, up the steep, twisting hill road to the tiny, well-nigh empty town with its handful of wooden houses, gleaming white in the sun. In its own right Winchelsea's claim to literary fame is muted. Here, in a pleasant cottage in the early years of the twentieth century lived the prolific novelist Ford Madox Hueffer (Ford), already mentioned in connection with both Postling and Aldington in Kent.

Because of him, on the roads leading into Winchelsea at that time two more imposing writers might have been seen hurrying along—one going to meet him, the other scurrying to get out of his way. The first would be Joseph Conrad, for whom Hueffer, as Conrad put it, was a sort of lifelong habit, but a better fellow than the world believed. Conrad would often take his carriage the twenty three miles down from Pent Farm for an "afternoon rush" to "let the air flow through me" after what he described as a convulsion of writing.

The man trying to avoid Hueffer would be Henry James. James also loved a refreshing jaunt to Winchelsea, often to show it off to his Lamb House guests. "Rye," he said, "dares to be cheerful; Winchelsea has the courage of its desolation." But for James, a little of Hueffer was grace abounding.

Once, seeing Hueffer coming toward him along the Winchelsea road, James made his secretary jump a dike to avoid meeting him. Another time he pulled her behind a tree until his would-be worshipper was past. One can almost hear the relief in an invitation James sent to H. G. Wells, suggesting that for the moment Hueffer is in check: "Conrad haunts Winchelsea, and Winchelsea (in discretion) haunts Rye. So foot it up."

Conrad himself thought of settling in Winchelsea and to test it borrowed Hueffer's cottage for a fortnight in 1906. James was happy to come over to them for tea and was voluble in his concern for the pregnant Jessie Conrad. Winchelsea was not for Conrad, however; he decided to stay at Pent Farm.

James in his knickers, astride his bicycle but impeccably groomed, must have been quite a sight. But nothing as compared to an earlier visitor to Winchelsea, the poet-painter Dante Gabriel Rossetti. Already becoming a strange, alien, exotic, even slightly sinister legend, Rossetti nonetheless enjoyed his five day stay in the fall of 1866. He found it a "most delightful old place for quietness and old-world character." The old church so struck him that he got a picture of it. And he wrote a gleeful account of a solemn civic procession he witnessed, consisting in total of seven persons, including the mayor in splendid robes of scarlet lined with sable and three other officials in blue robes, one of whom was the parish barber and another, the carpenter. Said Rossetti: "It was viewed in the street by a mob of one female child and ourselves," i.e., Rossetti and his friend Frederick Sandys.

The church is indeed worth seeing. It is in the center of town—or more correctly, it represents such center as the town can now muster. Rossetti's summary will still serve: "The outside is fine—partly a ruin—and quite embedded in ivy, and the inside contains some fine tombs with effigies."

The church was built in 1190 by Edward I and dedicated to England's latest and "chic-est" thing in the way of saints, the new martyr Thomas à Becket. Only the chancel is left of that church, five waves of French marauders having done much of Winchelsea in. But the tombs with the effigies Rossetti mentioned remain, and they are splendid: twelfth-century tombs of the local leading family, the Alards, with a nearly life-size recumbent figure of an armed man with a crouching lion at his feet on each.

Rossetti's friend, the eminent painter Sir John Everett Millais, was so taken with the Alard figures he painted them in his "Safe from the Battle's Din." What's more, he urged Thackeray to go see them. The novelist's visit found expression in his *Denis Duval*.

If you're on the A 259 anyway, going either way between Hastings and Rye, and have a few moments to spare, you might well spend them on Winchelsea and its grand old church.

Brede Place

Brede is a tiny village eight miles north of Hastings on the A 28, and six miles west of Rye via the B 2089. Just out of Brede to the east in a massive, almost forbidding fourteenth-century manor hiding itself in brooding isolation, American novelist Stephen Crane lived out the ten penultimate months of his colorful, hectic, and finally tragic life.

Called simply Brede Place, the house was built in the 1370's in the reign of Edward III and added to in early Tudor times when the original plaster and timber exterior gave way to the gray stone and brick of today. When Cora "Crane" first saw it in 1898 it was badly run down and neglected, the weeds high against the walls and ivy almost obliterating the leaded windows. But this seemed to make it all the more romantic to Cora, and she communicated her enthusiasm to Stephen, then in Oxted, Surrey. Cora could be beguiling.

She had met him in 1896 when he came to the sporting house she ran in Jacksonville, Florida, a place with the improbable name of Hotel de Dream. She was a plump but vivacious thirty-one; he was already famous as the twenty-five-year-old author of *The Red Badge of Courage*. Now she was living with Crane as his wife and called herself Mrs. Crane, though there is no record of their marriage. However, there is also no doubt that she was devoted to him.

When Cora first saw Brede Place in 1898, it and its 100 acre game park were owned by Clara Jerome Frewen, sister of Winston Churchill's mother. The Frewens had lived in it briefly in 1885, but since then only the farm bailiff used a couple of its numerous rooms, leaving the rest to its resident ghost and the bats.

There was no denying its romance. It had a "Gallows Room" over a private dungeon, with a spot of blood that neither soap nor time could erase. And overhead in the room was an oak beam from which the lord of the manor was said to have hanged his wives. He was one Sir Goddard of sixteenth-century vintage. His was the ghost that came with the lease (both for £40 a year rent), along with the sound of little children crying. Sir Goddard's diet, it seems, included a small child for dinner each night. No matter that the real Sir Goddard was a kindly old gentleman who had attended Henry VIII.

The basement was a network of subterranean passages in which the household priest hid from Cromwell's vigilantes, and which later served the local smugglers well (the passages connected to the Brede river a mile away) while the house stood empty a hundred years and more.

Stephen and Cora moved in, in February, 1899, and speedily discovered there were drawbacks aplenty to more than balance the undoubted assets of atmosphere, spacious grounds, and privacy. The stone floors were perilously drafty for a man with Crane's tubercular lungs. None of the doors or locks would stay shut. The only illumination was by lamp or candle, there was only one indoor toilet, and the only heat came from fireplaces, with most of it going up the chimney. Moreover, bats flew in through the bedroom windows.

One of the upstairs bedrooms had a door that opened on to a thirty-foot plunge straight downward into the private chapel below. Cora chose for her bedrom the vast ballroom, her huge four-poster looking like a toy bed on the orchestra dais where it stood. And, because of the ghost, no servants would stay in the house overnight. The cook, whom Cora found superb at her craft, at times had to be bribed with a bottle of brandy before she would prepare dinner.

But Cora struggled valiantly to make it liveable. She turned the long, baronial, oak-paneled hall into their main living room, decorating it with Crane's swords and Mexican blankets. And she managed to furnish a dozen other rooms with odds and ends, including a bed or two that had seen previous life as chicken coops. All the other rooms she closed off.

She chose the room over the entrance porch as Crane's study—though he worked any place in the house where the fancy struck—and painted it his favorite red. It was a cheerful room, and through its single window Crane could catch a glimpse of the spire of Brede's lovely little Norman church. Here he worked on *Active Service,* the novel he hoped would win him literary immortality. He was fated never to finish it.

As respite from his desk, Crane gloried—as perhaps only a determinedly classless American could—in his role as the "Baron of Brede," riding one of his two huge, white carriage horses (Horsa and Hengist) about the countryside, dressed in riding breeches and a cowboy shirt. Most of all, he loved playing the lavish host he really couldn't afford to be.

Particularly devoted to him were the Joseph Conrads, who came with their baby son Borys in June of 1899 for a two week visit. Crane had met Conrad in 1897, after writing him that he thought *The Nigger of the Narcissus* "a crackerjack." Their friendship ripened rapidly, and Conrad came to admit about Crane's work, "I am envious of you—horribly." He once wanted to share a house with Crane—and Crane wanted to write a play with Conrad. In her memoirs Jessie said "In both our hearts Stephen had a little shrine" till the day he died.

It was Jessie who reported the ritual that attended the brandy bribing of the cook. An hour or two before dinner, she would appear and dramatically announce that she was departing forever, then and there. Cora would panic and appeal to Stephen. Stephen would ring the bell for the butler. The butler would ceremoniously hand over a bottle of brandy to the cook. And the cook would then prepare the dinner, complete in every detail.

Henry James came over on his bicycle from Rye a number of times and entertained Stephen and Cora at Lamb House. James and Crane's first meeting, at a London studio party, had been most unlikely for so formal a man as James: Crane rescued the older man from an outrageous young woman who was pouring champagne into his silk hat.

Different as these two displaced Americans were, they had genuine affection for each other. Crane admitted James had ridiculous traits and could make a "holy show" of himself, but added: "it seems impossible to dislike him. He is so kind to everybody." In June of 1900, a month after Crane left Brede Place a dying man, James wrote Cora: "I constantly think of him and, as it were, pray for him."

Crane's career as a hospitable master of Brede Place reached its undoubted climax in a Christmas party that, in a twinkling, turned from glorious to ghastly. Sixty people were invited for the holiday week, though there were only three or four furnished bedrooms. No matter! Two of the cold, cavernous, unused rooms were opened and converted into dormitories, one for the men, one for the women. They could bring their own bedding and blankets.

Worse, the house's one toilet facility, dating from the seventeenth century at that, was accessible only through the Girls' Dormitory. Consequently—according to H. G. Wells, who was lucky enough to arrive early and so get one of the precious bedrooms—"the wintry countryside next morning was dotted with wandering, melancholy, preoccupied men guests."

Even so, Wells termed the party "an extraordinary lark." It reached its hilarious peak three days after Christmas with a play acted by the guests and put on in the Brede Hill Schoolhouse. The play depicted the plight of the Brede Place ghost: the time is 1950 and tourists coming there ignore him because they no longer believe in ghosts. Chief writer was Crane, but he wangled brief contributions from nine "collaborators," among them no less than Henry James, George Gissing, Joseph Conrad, Rider Haggard, and H. G. Wells.

Next night, following a gala ball, disaster struck. Most of the guests had retired. Crane was alone with one or two stragglers, softly strumming his guitar. Suddenly he collapsed over the strings.

Awakened by Cora, who announced Stephen had hemorrhaged badly, Wells rode off on his bicycle to fetch a doctor from Rye. It was only a matter of time, however. Cora, fighting to stave off the inevitable, took Crane to the Black Forest in Germany in May. But even as she closed the door on Brede Place for the last time, she must have known it was futile. Crane died on June 5.

The mansion is reached by a very long and tortuous lane, at the end of which a sign firmly announces that it is a private home and is *not* open to the public. Alas, however, it is no longer open to anyone. In 1979, almost within minutes, fire destroyed what had survived the ravages of six hundred years. The great stone shell, with five huge chimneys starkly standing, and ponderous beams that defied the flames give some notion of its massive grandeur. But Brede Place is gone, a victim to the very isolation its owners cherished.

Hastings and St. Leonards

For every schoolboy who ever studied English history, Hastings (on the A 259) has enjoyed a rather spurious fame. The best-known battle and date in that history never took place—at least, not there. William the Conqueror's fateful victory over Harold no more happened at Hastings (though it *was* in 1066) than the first major engagement of the American Revolution took place at Bunker Hill. The English affair was at Battle; the American, at Breed Hill.

Today's Hastings, "downtown" anyway, has a bustling air about it that is also on the spurious side. The plentiful hotels and guest houses along its wide, shingled (gravel) seafront have a seedy air, and the "old town," which has most of literary interest, looks neglected rather than quaint. Here narrow streets twist about and reach upward to clutch at the rocky prongs of West and East Hills. Atop West Hill are the scanty ruins of a castle where Thomas à Becket served as Dean.

On display at the Royal Victoria Hotel (actually in adjoining St. Leonards), on the landing between the lower and upper ground floors, is its guest register dating from 1855. The inquisitive visitor can inspect it and find that Tennyson, Gladstone, and the Queen herself were among those who enjoyed their stay there.

Earlier in the century, however, Charles Lamb found Hastings rather less enchanting. He came in June of 1823 and in his essay "The Old Margate Hoy" calls it "doing dreary penance" for having enjoyed Margate so much. "There is no sense of home at Hastings," he wrote. "It is a place of fugitive resort, an heterogeneous assemblange of sea-mews and stock-brokers, Amphitrites of the town, and misses that coquet with the Ocean."

He is scathing on the tourists who come only because it is the fashion and spoil the nature of the place. He is more gentle on the simple folk who wander about the shingles, tire of picking up cockleshells, and soon long to "exchange their sea-side rambles for a Sunday walk on the greensward of their accustomed Twickenham meadows!"

Lamb and his sister Mary found their quarters cramped and their landlord very ugly; but they delighted in the turbot and smuggled Hollands (gin), and the view from the cliffs, especially when the sea was shipless: "the salt sea is never so grand as when it is left to itself. One cock-boat spoils it."

It was on this vacation—according to De Quincey, who got it from Coleridge—that Lamb tried sea bathing to cure his stammer, with unexpected results. The plan was for him to stand in his bathing machine at water's edge, a stout servant on either side, ready to dunk him in the cold sea on command. He began bravely: "Hear me, men! Take notice of this—I am to be dipped . . . "

But it came out "di-di-di-di . . . " and when he finally finished the word, the eager attendants took it as the command and promptly dunked him. He came up spluttering, tried to explain what he meant, came again to "di-di-di-di . . . " and was dunked one more. His third attempt reached the same icy end. Only then did the gasping Lamb manage to conclude his sentence: "I say, I am to be dipped but once!"

Leigh Hunt, Byron, Thomas Hood, Thomas Campbell, and Keats were others who came to Hastings in the early part of the century. Hunt started his major poem, *The Story of Rimini,* while here in 1812. Byron stayed with his half sister Augusta near All Saints Church—an ironic neighborhood for a couple accused of incest. Hood spent his honeymoon here in 1825, and Campbell lived here for nearly a year in 1831–32.

Keats visited Hastings twice, in 1815 and 1817. It was on his second visit that he met Isabella Jones, the "lively lady from Hastings," given more credit than probably she deserves for inspiring the *Eve of St. Agnes*. While here in 1817, Keats was working on *Endymion,* and the coastline is reflected in Book II:

> Wide sea, that one continuous murmur breeds
> Along the pebbled shore of memory!
> Many old rotton-timber'd boats there be
> Upon thy vaporous bosom . . . .

One of the leading Victorian discoverers and boosters of Keats's poetry was the poet-painter Dante Gabriel Rossetti, and for him Hastings had especially anguished memories. He first came in 1852, a darkly handsome, charismatic youngster of twenty four with great promise in both arts. His lover-model, Elizabeth Siddal, had come down from London for her health, and he followed her. It was the first of a number of such flights to Hastings, and as Elizabeth's health grew worse, the visits became more cruel.

Their stay in May and June of 1854 was typical. Elizabeth ("Guggums" or

"Gug") took a room with a Mrs. Elphic at No. 5 High Street. Rossetti was at 12 East Parade (now part of the Cutter Hotel). But after three days Rossetti moved into Mrs. Elphic's, too—only because, he hastened to assure his pious mother, it was so much cheaper. In those days of his youth he was far from the libertine he was later supposed to have become, and there is something almost pathetically ingenuous in his attempts to reassure "My Dearest Mother": "No one thinks it at all odd my going into Gug's room to sit there; and Barbara Smith [a friend] said to the landlady how inadvisable it would be for her to sit with me in a room without fire."

Despite the brave front, however, these were desperate days. Elizabeth was a near-invalid, making the marriage Gabriel couldn't bring himself to face even less likely. His own career had reached the agonizing point where he couldn't tackle either painting or poetry wholly for being torn between the two. And for city-bred Rossetti, Hastings soon became intolerable.

In June he wrote a friend: "There are dense fogs of heat here now, through which sea and sky loom as one wall, with the webbed craft creeping on it like flies, or standing there as if they would drop off dead. I wander over the baked cliffs, seeking rest and finding none." But the image and the mood are strikingly retained in a poem Rossetti wrote five years later, "Even So":

> But the sea stands spread
> As one wall with the flat skies,
> Where the lean black craft like flies
> Seem well-nigh stagnated,
> Soon to drop off dead.

The doomed affair dragged on until mid-April of 1860, when Rossetti inexplicably decided on the marriage. They came down from London and, after several postponements, were wed on May 23 at the church of St. Clement in Hastings. It was a dreary ceremony, with only the clergyman and two strangers as witnesses. As Rossetti mournfully wrote his mother, it had been—like all the important things he meant to do in his life—deferred almost beyond possibility.

St. Clement is a handsome old church standing near the south end of High Street. If you look closely, you can see two cannonballs in the steeple wall, one on either side of the window. One was lobbed up there by the French during one of their raids. The other was put there by a vicar of St. Clements who thought a single cannonball "looked a bit untidy."

Inside the church are melancholy reminders of Rossetti. On the wall immediately to the left as you come in the side door, in a simple wooden frame, is the message: "Dedicated to the Memory of Dante Gabriel Rossetti, whose glory it is to have done so much to strengthen the love of beauty in art, in literature and in life." Below this is a copy of his glorious painting, "The Annunciation," for which sister Christina and brother William Michael posed; and below that is his sonnet of the same name: "This is the blessed Mary, etc." The large sanctuary lamp in the chancel is also in his memory, given by his aged mother.

At the other end of High Street is another church associated with a Victorian poet, the Roman Catholic St. Mary Star-of-the-Sea. Coventry Patmore lived from 1875 to 1891 in Mansion House, between High Street and the Old London Road, to be close to his daughter's convent. Here he wrote such things as "The Unknown Eros" and "Amelia," as well as his religious meditations. He became the chief contributor when St. Mary's was proposed, and in 1883 it was dedicated to his second wife.

Other literary names associated with Hastings included Thomas Carlyle, who stayed at 117 Marina in 1864, and Lewis Carroll, who followed Lamb in trying to cure a stammer . . . Henry James and John Addington Symonds, who followed Rossetti in getting married at St. Clement . . . and Rider Haggard, who bought North Lodge on Maze Hill to spend his winters.

Hastings figures, too, in H. G. Well's *Kipps* as the site of "Cavendish Academy," the "Academy for Young Gentlemen" that occupied a battered private house. Kipp's colleagues turned out to be a motley lot, many of whom "had parents in 'India' and other unverifiable places." But the school satisfed Kipp's mother's desire for a middle class academy that not only had mortar boards and gave every evidence of a higher social tone, but also was remarkably cheap.

One last note on Hastings: if you go there, drop in the White Rock Pavilion on the Promenade and see the Hastings Embroidery. In twenty-seven panels this unique piece of needlework depicts 900 years of English history, including Thomas à Becket's murder, the Battle of Agincourt and Henry V, Richard III's sad little princes in the Tower, Chaucer's Canterbury Pilgrims, and so on all the way down to the WW II Battle of Britain and D-Day. As lagniappe, in the center is a scale model of the battle that never took place in Hastings: Harold and William and their cohorts having at each other in one-inch minatures.

Battle and Robertsbridge

Battle: The origin of the name is simplicity itself: it is called "Battle" because it (and not Hastings) is where *the* battle actually took place—the battle on October 14, 1066, that changed William of Normandy's name from William the Bastard to William the Conqueror and made him King of

England. Today it is a considerable town of over 5,000 people, seven miles northwest of Hastings at the junction of the A 2100 and the A 269, and indubitably one of the favorite tourist centers of Southern England. Tennyson called it "O Garden, blossoming out of English blood." More recently, the Federation of Sussex Amenity Societies staged a contest to find the worst environmental black spot in the county: Battle placed second. This seems to have stung the town, however. One rejoices to announce that the next year (1979) it won the regional competition for "Best Kept Village," in 1980 was runner up for "Best Kept" in the whole of East and West Sussex, and in 1982 reached the top.

When William the Norman and Harold the Saxon pitched battle for England's destiny that October day, however, there was no town, no abbey, not even a name. Just a grassy, tree-dotted hill on top of which Harold had dug in, blocking William's march north from Hastings and his Pevensey landing place.* It was a ripsnorting fight: it took all day and involved either 6,500 or 8,000 men on either side (one notice on the site gives the first figure, another, the second). As darkness began to fall, after losing both brothers during the day, Harold himself fell. Henceforth England would be Norman.

To keep a pledge he had made to God for Victory, William immediately began building a memorial abbey. The plans were elaborate, the church alone to be over 300 feet long with its high altar on the precise spot where Harold fell. The first abbot was appointed in 1076, and the abbey flourished until Henry VIII tore most of it down during the sixteenth-century Dissolution, though it never reached the magnitude of William's dream.

What remains for today's visitor is a ruined potpourri of the centuries. Although much still awaits the archeologist's careful excavation, there is enough to see to suggest the scope of the original establishment. From the Early English period (around 1200), there is a lovely shell—walls and gable—of what was either a refectory or a dormitory, and beneath it, a vaulted crypt that housed facilities like the monks' day room, parlor, and calefactory (a heated apartment used as a sitting room). From Chaucer's time (about 1340) is a splendid gateway with triple archway and octagonal towers. And from Henry VIII's time are two watch turrets, survivors of a mansion a Sir Anthony Browne made of the Great Hall when Henry gave him what was left of the abbey.

There are also some "gothic" looking buildings dating from Victorian

---

*The hill is now called Senlac Hill, and hence some call it the "Battle of Senlac." But that's no more accurate than calling it the Battle of Hastings: the hill had no name in William's day.

times and later, and these are principally used for a girls school and are normally closed to the public. The Victorians took a keen interest in the Abbey, reflecting their overall interest in things medieval. Two such were Tennyson and Bulwer-Lytton, who came to survey it while preparing his works on Harold. Bulwer-Lytton dedicated his novel, *Harold, the Last of the Saxon Kings* (1848), to Tennyson's uncle: Tennyson reciprocated by dedicating his play, *Harold* (1875–76) to Bulwer-Lytton's son.

The Abbey and its grounds are just a few steps from the center of town and have their own extensive parking facilities. Ruins and grounds are open to the public for a nominal fee (not National Trust) most days of the week all year round, but it's best to check days and hours in advance. One hour should do nicely for the whole tour.

Robertsbridge This is a pass-through village five miles north of Battle and ten miles northwest of Hastings. It's on the A 21, and therefore you go through it if you're travelling between London and Hastings. It was here that Dante Gabriel Rossetti came in the spring of 1870 to try to restore his health and to await the publication and public reception of his first book of poems—a period filled with apprehension and misgivings. He had ample reason for both. The critics, he feared, were waiting to pounce on him as the evil leader of a "fleshy school" of poetry. And among the poems he would publish were those he had tenderly (and remorsefully) buried in the coffin with his wife in 1862—only to have the grave opened in the dead of night seven years later and the manuscripts retrieved.

He left London in March for Scalands, the Robertsbridge cottage of Mme. Barbara Bodichon, the Barbara Smith who had harbored his ailing wife before they were married. For this least pastoral-minded of city dwellers, it was an unfortunate choice. "Barbara [his absent hostess]," he confided to a friend, "does not indulge in bell-pulls, hardly in servants to summon thereby . . . what she does affect is any amount of thorough draft, a library bearing the stern stamp of 'Bodichon' (her husband), and a kettle-holder with the uncompromising initials B.B."

It was lonely, too, even though William Morris, friend of Pre-Raphaelite days and fellow poet, came down several times, and his wife Janey—whom Rossetti passionately loved—even stayed on a while after her husband returned home. Rossetti's brush wth country life took some strange turns. Once he saw a "poor dear little mole" lying dead and was so touched he tried to get a pair to take home to his own garden. He did get one which he kept in a glass box—until it bit him.

Nor was Robertsbridge conducive to writing. He had hoped to do a new narrative poem, "God's Grael," and finish "The Stream's Secret." Some work did get done on the latter, but only nineteen lines were ever written of "God's Grael." Mainly, Rossetti fussed endlessly with details about his upcoming book and wrote a few sonnets. By mid-May he was happy to be back in London. The book was out, and he thought he was safely past the abuse he feared. He was wrong: it came the following year.

Burwash

Twelve miles northwest of Hastings (in a straight line only a bird can negotiate) and five miles from Battle (via roads that go north then west—the A 21 and the A 265) lies Burwash, as pleasant a little one-street town as you'll come across . . . and with one of the best literary shrines in all of England, Bateman's, where Rudyard Kipling lived and wrote for thirty-four years.

He bought the place in June of 1902 for £9,300, a truly handsome sum for the time and nearly five times what Henry James had recently paid for his house in Rye. But he could afford it. Money was coming in, in great amounts, and he had become almost a cult throughout the British Empire. He and Caroline (Carrie) had been looking for a house for several years, for their home in Rottingdean had become too full of painful memories since the death of their six-year-old daughter, Josephine. And the "trippers" (tourists) from nearby Brighton had become so thick Carrie often had trouble reaching her own front gate.

Bateman's had been a grand old house, built at the peak of the region's prosperity as an iron-making center. The master of a local forge had owned it. But then the industry moved elsewhere. The house was first neglected and then finally abandoned. It had long been empty when it was bought, along with 100 acres, and restored in the 1890's by an artist-architect. Driving down what Kipling called its "rabbit-hole of a lane" they fell in love with it first in 1900, but before the Kiplings could act someone else snatched it up. When it became available again in 1902, they were the snatchers.

It was (and is) a big, imposing house, square and sturdy, built of local dressed stone in the customary E shape, though the north wing of the E has disappeared with time. A stack of six tall brick chimneys spring from its roof like a battery of so many cannon. The house stands at the foot of a lane that drops steeply from the village, and therein lies a tale. Once the purchase contract was safely signed and pocketed, the seller dared ask Kipling how he proposed to handle the four-mile climb up the hill to the railroad station, saying he had worn out two teams of horses doing it. "By motorcar," said Kipling. Said the seller: "Oh, those things haven't come to stay."

Kipling's own description of the place could serve today: "A grey stone lichened house—A.D. 1634 over the door [still visible]—beamed, panelled, with old oak staircase, and all untouched and unfaked . . . a good and peaceable place standing in terraced lawns . . . a walled garden of old red brick . . . two fat-headed oast houses." (Oast houses are kilns used to dry hops).

Among Bateman's attractions was its comparative nearness to several fellow writers who were Kipling's friends and with whom he could now exchange visits. Henry James's Lamb House in Rye was only eighteen miles away; Conrad and his Pent Farm in Postling were twenty-five; H. G. Wells and Spade House in Folkestone were thirty. To facilitate such trips (and cover the steep four miles into Burwash) Kipling indulged in a £1,000 car, a Lanchester. And, indicative of how small was the market for any car then, let alone so luxurious a car, Mr. Lanchester delivered the car to Bateman's door in person.

Owning a car in those early days was an adventurous thing, even if you had a driver, which Kipling did. One of his first expeditions was to visit James, and "Amelia," as he had dubbed the car, made the trip in great shape, the natives of Rye flocking 'round to see their first automobile. Lunch, too, went off in lively fashion, the host perhaps telling the author of *The Jungle Book* that he was even then writing "The Beast in the Jungle." But when the time came to go, Amelia balked; despite all efforts, the car wouldn't move. The Kiplings wound up going home by train.

James enjoyed visiting Burwash (even though he mockingly insisted the villagers pronounced it "Burridge." Truth is, oldtimers still say something that sounds suspiciously like "Burrish.") And James liked "the great little Rudyard" and had served as best man when Kipling married Carrie. But, as always, James had his reservations: "I can't swallow his loud, brazen patriotic verse. . . . Two or three times a century—yes; but not every month."

H. G. Wells was another Kipling friend and guest whose private praise of his host could be moderate. But in his *The New Machiavelli* (1911), Wells has his hero accurately reflect Kipling's national standing before the turn of the century: the prevailing force among undergraduates was "Kiplingism." And, although critics later tore him to shreds, in the middle nineties "this spectacled and moustached little figure" became "almost a national symbol. He got hold of us wonderfully."

Two other visitors to Bateman's were Stephen Leacock, the humorist and McGill University professor, and H. Rider Haggard. Haggard was among the early friends Kipling made in London in 1889, and they remained close until Haggard died in 1925. Kipling allowed the lesser known man to work at his own long writing table and made suggestions that Haggard often used.

Kipling chose for his study an ample first (U.S. second) floor room to the right of the seventeenth-century oak staircase that rises up to it from the ground floor. Here, at his incredibly cluttered table—ten feet long, and with blocks under his chair legs to raise the diminutive writer to the table height—Kipling did all the writing of his last thirty-four years. Among the best known of these are *Traffics and Discoveries* (1904), *Puck of Pook's Hill* (1906), *Rewards and Fairies* (1910), and "If" and "The Glory of the Garden."

He was a meticulous craftsman, writing and crumpling and discarding page after page in a suitably huge wastebasket, only to write and crumple and discard again. Except toward the end when he turned to the typewriter, he wrote on large, pale blue, specially made pads with a thin silver pen. A hard sofa stood at right angles to a small fireplace. Here Kipling could mull things over between spurts of writing.

Two of his books were directly inspired by Bateman's grounds. From the western windows of the upper floor you can see a long spur running from Dudwell Brook to Burwash Common. The Kipling children knew it as Pook's Hill and pitched their "theatre" at the foot of a grassy slope by the brook to present such things as *Midsummer Night's Dream.* Son John would be Puck, daughter Elsie, Titania, and Kipling himself, Bottom in a realistic cardboard donkey's head—once to the consternation of a village policeman who was passing and must have been startled to see this apparition crowning a tweed-clad figure.

This idyllic setting was, of course, that of *Puck of Pook's Hill,* as well as of *Rewards and Fairies,* where Dan (who is really John) and Una (who is really Elsie) find Puck and through him meet characters from history—including not only Queen Elizabeth but even George Washington.

Kipling died in 1936; and when his wife died three years later, she left Bateman's to the National Trust. It is open to the public most days of the week from spring to fall (modest fee or N. T. card) and rivals Carlyle's house in Cheyne Row, London, and G. B. Shaw's at Ayot St. Lawrence, Hertfordshire, in providing a nearly unique glimpse of an author's home, for much of it is precisely as Kipling left it.

On the ground floor the hall and drawing room are full of Kipling's furniture and furnishings, showing a wide range of cultures, countries, and centuries. On the floor above, the study lacks only Kipling himself to be complete. There, in the large square room, are the book-lined walls, the Indian rugs, the master's personal trinkets—as well as his littered work table with its "working tools," the great pewter inkpot, and, handy to all, the yawning wastebasket.

Next to the study is a good-sized room, once the guest room, which now exhibits an array of Kipling memorabilia, including eight plaques by his father to illustrate Rudyard's works.

The garden, too, largely the work of the Kiplings, is a delight to see.

And, at the bottom of the garden is the old water mill which appears in *Puck of Pook's Hill, Rewards and Fairies,* and *Below the Mill* and for which Kipling wrote:

> See you our little mill that clacks
> So busy by the brook?
> She has ground her corn and paid her tax
> Ever since Domesday Book.

Dating from 1196, the mill came to house one of the area's first electrical outlets when Kipling removed the waterwheel and installed a turbine. The wheel has now been put back, the mill restored, and may well be England's oldest working mill of its kind, grinding the corn (i.e., wheat) you can buy at the Gift Shop.

Much to see? Yes indeed! But then, there's a Tea Room to refresh you when you're through.

2. BRIGHTON AND ITS NEIGHBORS

Brighton

Brighton lies on the English Channel where the South Downs slope into the sea. It is fifty miles due south of London's Victoria Station, from whence it can be reached by fast (about an hour) and frequent trains. It can also be reached by excellent roads, the A 217 and A 21. In season, both railway and highway are packed with tourists heading for Brighton. Yet the overly fastidious find it easy to stay away from this "London by the Sea," population 165,000. There is something raucous about its bustle. The sun and sea are too insistent in their glitter. And the Royal Pavilion too blatantly reminds you that a Regent can be as vulgar as a commoner, though much more expensive.

Writers from Dr. Samuel Johnson on have hurled brickbats at the town. Said Dr. J. in 1765, the place was "so truly desolate that if one had a mind to hang oneself for desperation at being obliged to live there, it would be difficult to find a tree on which to fasten a rope." Faced with the prospect of having to visit it, Jane Austen agreed with her sister Cassandra: "I dread the idea of going to Brighton as much as you do." Charles Lamb was bored with it, and D. H. Lawrence was overwhelmed by it.

Yet, Brighton *is* a place to see, at least once, if only so that one can be properly condescending about it. And to balance the amusement pier, toy railroad, dolls museum, aquarium, waxworks, and the like along the seafront, there are the long, well-tended terraces, reminders of the best part of the Regency, with their cream-colored facades, bow windows, and decorative ironwork. This is the Brighton that Virginia Woolf used to like to visit from her country place in nearby Asheham—admittedly, for just six hours.

Besides, located as it is at the junction of the A 27 and the A 23, Brighton makes an excellent base of operations for seeing the eastern portion of East Sussex and has numerous literary ties of its own. Even Jane Austen, for all her dread, uses Brighton in *Pride and Prejudice.* Jane Bennet worries about Brighton and its whole campful of soldiers, but her sister Lydia thrills to think of them and happily joins the wife of the regiment's colonel to get there, from which she elopes with the unscrupulous Wickham.

Daniel Defoe, who wrote that delightful travel book, *Tour through the Whole Island of Great Britain* (1724–47), was in Brighton during a great storm in 1703 and was moved to write a long article about storms. "Brighthelmston," he wrote [it didn't officially become Brighton until 1810], "being an old built and poor, tho' populous town, was torn to pieces, and made the very picture of desolation." Brighton then was little more than the large fishing village it had been in the days of William the Conqueror, when the annual rent was 4,000 herring. What made Brighton prosperous were a doctor and a prince.

The doctor was Dr. Richard Russell of nearby Lewes, who in 1753 heralded the curative powers of sea bathing, fresh sea air, and tossing off a saltwater cocktail each day. Brighton, he suggested, would be just the spot for all three. Among those who began to throng to Brighton were Henry Thrale and his wife Hester, intimate friend of Sam Johnson (and later, as Mrs. Piozzi, his biographer). By 1779 they had their own house near the bottom of West Street.

The Thrales often had Johnson, as well as the novelist Fanny Burney, come to Brighton to stay with them. On one occasion, in 1765, Johnson so impressed a fellow bather with his swimming that the man exclaimed, "Why, sir, you must have been a stout-hearted gentleman forty years ago." Johnson could hardly have been flattered: he was then only fifty-four. On this visit he was working on his *Lives of the Poets*. On Sundays he worshipped at St. Nicholas Church at the west end of Church Street, and a tablet can be seen on the chancel end of the north wall indicating where the Thrale pew used to be. As for Fanny Burney, her diary gives a vivid account of the Brighton social whirl, especially after the success of her best-selling *Evelina* (1778) made her a celebrity.

The prince who made Brighton—"invented" is the better word—was

George August Frederick of the House of Hanover, Prince Regent and ultimately George IV, who first came in 1783. The Royal Pavilion he built off Castle Square, now Brighton's major tourist attraction, is a fantasy of Oriental opulence that borders on the obscene. The cost of building and maintaining it so staggered even Byron, hardly a paragon of frugality himself, that he wrote in *Don Juan* (1819–24):

> Shut up—no, *not* the King, but the pavilion,
> Or else 'twill cost us all another million.

If you care for such things as "bamboo" furniture that's actually cast iron and a forty-five foot high domed ceiling made to resemble an Eastern sky, you can see the Pavilion for yourself—for a fee—all but five days of the year.

Byron, then a Cambridge student, came to the Pavilion in 1808 for a lavish celebration of the Prince's birthday, accompanied by a strange duo: a boxing champ named "Gentleman Jack," and a pretty girl whose masquerading boy's jacket and trousers fooled no one once she opened her mouth to address Byron in a loud and shrill cockney voice as "Bruvver!"

Charles Lamb and his sister Mary paid a visit in the summer of 1817, which he recalled in his essay, "Old Margate Hoy," where he said he had been "dull at Worthing one summer, duller at Brighton another, and dullest at Eastbourn a third." Even so, Mary told Dorothy Wordsworth that she and Charles had liked walking on the Down, which they thought almost as good as the Westmoreland mountains.

A much more enthusiastic and frequent Brighton visitor was Charles Dickens, who seemed to favor it particularly as a place for his wife Kate to recuperate from bearing a child—and she bore him many. Usually he stayed at the Bedford Hotel (destroyed by fire in 1964) or at the Old Ship on King's Road, still a good hotel (three-star) and rich in literary associations. He first came in 1837 while he was working on *Oliver Twist* and, like Defoe, was met by a great storm: "It blew a perfect hurricane," and the air "darkened with a shower of black hats (second hand) blown off the heads of unwary passengers."

In 1841 he was back with Kate and again at the Old Ship to celebrate the arrival of their fourth child, "a jolly boy" named Walter Landor. As always, Dickens worked while vacationing, this time on *Barnaby Rudge*. In 1847 the occasion was the birth of child number seven—Sydney Smith Haldimand Dickens—and the father was in the throes ("convulsions," he called them) of *Dombey and Son*.* And, by coincidence, he was in Brighton again—at the

---

*Yes, Joseph Conrad also called writing "convulsions"—but he *meant* it!

Bedford—when he finished *Dombey* the following March.

Brighton and *Dombey* are especially connected, of course. Mr. Dombey first entrusts his son, frail and pathetic little Paul, and his sister to that great manager of children, the "marvellous ill-favored, ill-conditioned old lady" Mrs. Pipchin, whose boarding house was on a steep Brighton bystreet where the houses were "more than usually brittle and thin," and the gardens inexplicably produced nothing but marigolds, regardless of what was planted. And Paul next goes to Dr. Blimber's school, "a mighty fine house, fronting the sea," with "sad-coloured curtains," modelled perhaps on Chichester House on Chichester Terrace. And Mr. Dombey, Captain Cuttle, and others stay at the Bedford Hotel.

Dickens himself is back at the Bedford in December of the same year (1848), finishing "The Haunted Man" after "crying my eyes out over it . . . these last three days." Two months later he was back again with Kate, to recuperate from the birth of child number eight, Henry Fielding Dickens. Initially they took lodgings, but their landlord and his daughter suddenly went raving mad, and Dickens fled to the Bedford. Here he spent the time mulling over titles for his next novel. First came the evolution of the hero's name: "Mr. Thomas Mag" . . . to "David Mag of Copperfield House" . . . to "David Copperfield." Then the title itself: *The Copperfield Disclosures, The Copperfield Records,* and several more led at last to a twenty-four-word title that was cut to *The Personal History of David Copperfield.*

He was deep into the book when he next came to Brighton in March, 1850: "Such weather here!" he wrote. "So bright and beautiful! and here I sit, glowering over Copperfield all day." *Copperfield* was safely behind him on his visit in 1853, also in March; but he was still glowering over a book, this time *Bleak House.*

Perhaps even more associated with Brighton than Dickens was his onetime friend and fellow novelist, William Makepeace Thackeray. He was there frequently, especially during the 1840's, staying at the Old Ship or, more often, at the Albion House, still an elegant hotel (four-star) on the seafront near the Old Steine.* Like Dickens, Thackeray usually came to combine work with vacationing. In 1843 he was doing pieces under the pseudonyms of Fitzboodle and Michael Angelo Titmarsh when he stayed at the Albion in May "to be alone, and avoid good dinners and do some magazine work." In the summer of 1844 he was again at the Albion working on *Barry Lyndon* and going "early to bed, where the bugs played deuce with me."

In February, 1846, he was torn between the pro's and con's Brighton

*It's now known as the Royal Albion.

offered a writer: "A little fresh air down here does one a power of good: only as the deuce will have it there are dinner-givers here too: whose hospitalities undo the service of the fresh air." In progress was *Book of Snobs* for *Punch* magazine. But a stay in October the next year spurred him on as he worked away on what was to be his greatest book, *Vanity Fair:* "just back from Brighton, where I found kind friends, fresh air, and a little renovation of health & spirits."

Brighton appears in *Vanity Fair,* and if you stay at the Old Ship, you'll feel the novel truly coming to life. For this is the hotel where George Osborne and Amelia Sedley honeymoon and run into the equally newlywed Becky Sharp and Rawdon Crawley. And Thackeray's picture of the hotel and its view still glows with vitality:

> . . . that beautiful prospect of bow windows on the one side and blue sea on the other . . . the ocean—smiling with countless dimples, speckled with white sand, with a hundred bathing machines kissing the skirt of his blue garment . . . Brighton, a clean Naples with genteel lazzaroni . . . Brighton, that always looks brisk, gay and gaudy, like a harlequin's jacket . . . which used to be seven hours distant at the time of our story [1815]; which is now [1847–48] only a hundred minutes off.

Two figures of the later part of the Victorian period had rather improbable connections with Brighton in view of the sensational images they struck in the public mind: Aubrey Beardsley and Oscar Wilde. Beardsley, whose fantastic drawings helped give the *Yellow Book* of the 1890's a reputation for decadence it hardly lived up to, was born in Brighton at 12 Buckingham Road in 1872. By age nine he was playing piano duets at the Royal Pavilion.

Wilde, whose "Salomé" Beardsley illustrated, made several visits to Brighton, usually staying at the Albion. On one stay in 1894 he was driving along the Hove seafront to the west when his horse bolted and didn't stop until he crashed, carriage and all, into the railings of Regency Square. The Brighton paper hailed Wilde's coolness and courage. More discerning viewers said he was merely bored. The Albion for lunch, by the way, was a favorite of Evelyn Waugh's when he was a schoolboy at nearby Shoreham.

After *Vanity Fair*, Thackeray used Brighton as a setting again in a later novel, and Henry James recalled this on a visit in 1906. James, too, was taken with the "shining silvery shimmery sea"—the water can be implausibly so here—and said: "It's like the old Brighton that you may read about (Miss Honeyman's [kindly Brighton lodge keeper]) in the early chapters of the 'Newcomes.' " And James himself used Brighton as a setting in "Sir Edmund Orme."

D. H. Lawrence was equally ecstatic about Brighton and its sea when he came in 1909, but his reaction was to move on. He had bicycled down from Croydon and lay for an hour "on the sharp, shelving shingle of the beach." Apparently, that was enough: "Brighton is splendid—big, stately, magnificent, with a sea like pale green jewels—is lapis lazuli green?—and all wavering, shimmering, intermingling with purple-lovely-inexpressible. But Brighton is stately, and I am not. So I pushed my way through the wind, and here I am at Rottingdean."

Twice more Lawrence came to Brighton, at Christmas in 1910 and in May, 1915. The latter visit was particularly bitter. He was ill, bankrupt, hounded and reviled for his antiwar views, and totally ignored by the publishers. "How pleasant it would be," he wrote despairingly from Brighton, "to walk over the edge of the cliff" into another, brighter sort of world.

In contrast, Arnold Bennett's career was at its peak during these years, though compared to Lawrence, his was but talent compared to genius. Bennett reveled in Brighton and used it both for *Clayhanger*—where the real Royal York hotel figures as the "Royal Sussex" with its eagle-eyed inspector of rooms—and for its sequel, *Hilda Lessways.*

So there is Brighton—called everything from boring to brassy, but always brightly shimmering in the sun, and with far more literary associations than its latter-day, rather amusement-park image might suggest. And there are those who love it dearly still. Laurence Olivier and his wife, Joan Plowright, have made it their home since 1961. And when he was created a Life Peer in 1970, he chose the title Baron Olivier of Brighton. But perhaps the Oliviers can be excused: it was while playing together in *The Entertainer* at the Brighton Hippodrome that Olivier and Joan fell in love.

Rottingdean

Rottingdean sits at the edge of the sea (the English Channel) and on the A 259, four miles east of Brighton. It can be reached by train, bus, or car. D. H. Lawrence got there by bicycle—against the wind at that. And little old ladies think nothing of walking there from Brighton along the cliffs. Whatever the mode of transportation you prefer, let it take you to Rottingdean sometime. It's utterly charming. Miss Pankey, that "mild little blue-eyed morsel of a child" in Dickens's *Dombey and Son* would have felt her weekly distress at leaving Rottingdean for Brighton even without Mrs. Pipchin waiting at the other end.

For all its pungency, Rottingdean owes the name to deplorably prosaic circumstances: "dean" was an Anglo-Saxon word for valley, and in early times one Rota ruled it—hence "valley of Rota's people." Before it became the lovely, quiet retreat of today, Rottingdean had the regular quota of Sussex smugglers, and many of the best houses had secret tunnels that ran to the "gap," where boats came under cover of darkness.

Not the least of the town's present charms are the ease and pleasure with which the literary traveller can explore it. If the weather's fine, start in the lounge of the old White Horse hotel in the High Street . . . get some sandwiches and wine . . . find a table on the sun-drenched terrace overlooking the sea . . . and do your homework in sheer bliss. Then head up the hill toward the village green. Everything to see—mainly connected with Rudyard Kipling—is on this street, and it can be done in an hour or so.

First, on the left, is Plough Inn where Kipling liked to drop in for a drink and a chat with the villagers. Then, just beyond, on the right, is the town library, formerly the vicarage, and dating from the early 1800's, with interesting, but hardly overwhelming, Kipling memorabilia.

Next, a very short way up the street (the name abruptly becomes "On the Green"), on the right, is the lovely little Church of St. Margaret's; the tower goes back to 1200 and has walls four feet thick. (The planners of California's Forest Lawn Cemetery were so taken with it that they wanted to cart it off but had to settle for an exact replica, called "Church of the Recessional" after Kipling's poem.) A sixteenth-century patron of St. Margaret's was Sir Thomas Sackville, contributor to *A Mirror for Magistrates* and coauthor of *Gorboduc,* an early English tragedy. The church has the closest ties to Kipling: here he was married, here his aunt and uncle's ashes are buried, and here he worshiped for five years.

The aunt and uncle were Sir Edward and Lady Georgiana Burne-Jones. A noted painter, Burne-Jones had been an intimate friend of Rossetti, Swinburne, and Morris and was an important illustrator of books—including the eighty-seven illustrations for the much-acclaimed edition of Chaucer by the Kelmscott Press (1897). The Burne-Jones home was Kipling's only refuge during his miserable boardinghouse days, from age six to eleven with strangers in Southsea, and again during his schooldays at Westward Ho!. With a number of other families interrelated by blood or marriage, the Burne-Joneses had their summer home in a conclave centered about Rottingdean's village green. Here the young Kipling was always welcome.

No wonder, then, he chose Rottingdean and St. Margaret's for his wedding in 1892. Somewhat to his own surprise, however, the novelist Henry James found himself a major figure in the ceremony: "I today . . . 'gave way' Caroline Balestier to Rudyard Kipling—a queer office for *me* to perform." It was also, he said, an "odd little marriage."

James was back at St. Margaret's in 1898 for a more melancholy occasion, the funeral of Burne-Jones, whom he loved and called "one of the greatest of boons to our most vulgar of ages." The visitor to St. Margaret's can view Burne-Jones's work as well as his grave. In the chancel and tower are seven of his stained glass windows. His and Lady Georgiana's ashes, with those of their grandaughter Angela, are buried outside the church in a little corner formed by the south wall of the nave and west wall of the aisle. Angela Thirkell succeeded Trollope as a chronicler of Barsetshire. Perhaps best known for *Love Among the Ruins* (1948), she also left a picture of the Rottingdean conclave in her autobiographical *Three Houses*.

From the church it's only a step across the street to North End House, the Burne-Jones home. It's a big, white, rambling structure, looking like three houses jammed together, marked with a plaque. In 1897 his aunt offered it to Kipling while he sought a place of his own. The Kiplings moved in on June 2, a day British enough for even so professional an Englishman as he: it was Derby Day of the Queen's Diamond Jubilee Year.

At North End House, Kipling began to put together the animal stories with which he had amused his children while living in Vermont, and which—as the *Just So Stories* (1902)—are among his most popular works. He also tried to do a Jubilee poem, but it didn't jell, and he put it aside. Several days later, as he sat with an American guest, Miss Sally Norton, cleaning out his desk, he threw it into his wastebasket.

It caught Miss Norton's eye, and she asked if she might see what it was. When Kipling consented she fished it out and found it was a short poem entitled "After." After reading it, she said it was too good to throw away; it must be printed. Kipling demurred, but agreed to abide by whatever his Aunt Georgie decided. She said "Yes." So Kipling cut it to five stanzas and, at Miss Norton's suggestion, made a refrain of the first stanza's last lines:

> Lord God of Hosts, be with us yet,
> Lest we forget—lest we forget!

The poem was, of course, "Recessional."

By September, the Kiplings found a place of their own, "The Elms," just across the Green from North End House. It's a large house, with a great chimney and dormer windows sprouting from the roof; on the high wall that surrounds it is a commemorative plaque. The Kiplings regarded it as a stopgap until they found something permanent and rented it for three guineas a week. But they were there for five years, and in this house Kipling wrote *Stalky and Co.* (1899), *Kim* (1901), and completed the *Just So Stories*.

And to this house came various literary figures. An early guest was W. E. Henley, author of "Invictus," so crippled he could go abroad only in a Bath chair. James Barrie came down that first year, too, and he and Rudyard would go for great walks across the Downs. And Henry James came over from Rye now and then. The Kiplings were both fond of him. Carrie called him that "nice man, much beloved," and Rudyard much admired his writing. For his part, though James remained devoted to the Kiplings, his regard for Rudyard's work lessened with time. In 1890 he used phrases such as "infant prodigy" and "star of the hour." By 1893 he was saying privately of Kipling, "I doubt if he has anything more to give."

In 1902, as noted in the Bateman's section, three things moved the Kiplings to abandon The Elms for Burwash at the other end of East Sussex. First, those "trippers" (gaping tourists) from Brighton had become intolerable. Second, their six-year-old daughter Josephine had died during a trip to the United States, and The Elms seemed haunted by memories of her. And, third, the house in Burwash they had loved and lost in 1900 again became available. On June 10, 1902, they bought it.

Rottingdean's literary associations do largely center on Kipling. But before we leave it, a note on two other, if lesser, writers of the first quarter of the twentieth century. Both also lived there for a time; both, oddly enough, in Steyning Road. One was dramatist, novelist, and poet Maurice Baring, best known for *Cat's Cradle* (1925), *Tinker's Leave* (1927), and *In the End is My Beginning* (1931). The other was that poet of the sea and fairy land, Alfred Noyes, whose works include *Drake* (1908) and *The Torchbearers* (1922–30).

Lewes—Asheham—Rodmell—Seaford—Eastbourne

To the east of Brighton lie several places with some literary links, not worth a special pilgrimage, perhaps, but (in both senses of the word) of passing interest. Three of these—Lewes, Asheham, and Rodmell—are within eight miles of Brighton and have connection with Virginia Woolf. A fourth, Seaford, marked a black period in the life of George Meredith. And the fifth, Eastbourne, is associated with some interesting noms de plume.

Lewes A fair-sized town (15,000) on the A 27 and the Ouse River, Lewes is eight miles northeast of Brighton. There are a number of reminders of its ancient past, including parts of the old town wall, a Norman castle, and a half-timbered Tudor house in the High Street, open to the public, where Anne of Cleves lived after Henry VIII sent her packing.

In the seventeenth century John Evelyn, famous diarist, grew up in the Lewes area at his grandmother's, first at Cliffe and then in the Southover district. When it came time for him to leave his "too indulgent" grandmother for Eton, he simply refused to go and attended the Southover free school instead. Southover Grange, his grandmother's home, is now owned by the city council and its grounds are public gardens.

Another Lewes literary landmark readily seen is the Bull House in the High Street (No. 92) by the West Gate: it's now a restaurant. Here, from 1768 to 1774, lived Thomas Paine, fiery writer for the American Revolution. He came to Lewes in 1768 as a minor tax official and began agitating for better working conditions and higher pay. By 1774 he had managed to lose his wife and job and go broke; his response was to go to America, write *The Rights of Man,* and coin the name "the United States of America." Bull House has some Paine relics and some rooms on display.

Twentieth-century writers with Lewes connections are John Galsworthy and Virginia Woolf. Galsworthy came in 1909, first to visit the jail, then to interview its prisoners, in order to further his efforts at prison reform and to get background for his play, *Justice,* produced in 1910. And for Virginia Woolf, Lewes was her nearest shopping center for the last thirty years of her life (1912–1941) when she lived at Asheham and then at Rodmell. Moreover, she actually bought and planned to live in the Round House, a converted windmill in Lewes, just before she moved to Rodmell.

Asheham (Asham) In this hamlet, seven miles northeast of Brighton on the B 2109, was (and is) Asheham House, the retreat of Virginia and Leonard Woolf whenever they could get away from London, from their marriage in 1912 until 1919. It's a solid, charming, commodious two-storey structure, with a one-storey wing at either end. Arched lights over the windows, according to David Garnett (one of the younger members of the Bloomsbury group), gave the facade a curiously dream-like character. The house came equipped with live-in ghost, which may have suggested Virginia's *A Haunted House* (1943).

Garnett declared: "for a full understanding of Virginia . . . Asheham would greatly help." This is surely true; there is so much of what she relished in and about the place. The house looked across the valley of the Ouse, a view she loved and a river that had a fascination for her that was to prove fatal. And from her bedroom window, she had an enchanting glimpse of the ever-changing Downs which she loved to climb. This was but one of the diversions Asheham House offered both Woolfs from the strain of writing and the turmoil of London. There was gardening "until we both rained sweat." And moles to kill, rabbits to repel, wood to cut. And always servants to cope with—including a burgeoning eighteen-year-old virgin whose dropsey one night turned into a nine-pound baby.

Virginia and Leonard also did much writing here, working in separate rooms, he on things like an article on labor, or a review of French literature, or a history of the Woman's Cooperative Movement; she, at first, mainly literary reviews and criticism. But both worked on novels, too—for him *The Wise Virgins* (1914), and for her *The Voyage Out* (1914) and *Night and Day* (1919).

Often there were overnight guests, especially from that talented collection of politicians, musicians, artists, philosophers, mathematicians, and writers loosely (too loosely) known as the Bloomsbury group. Among the writers were: Lytton Strachey, a frequent caller; E. M. Forster; Katherine Mansfield and John Middleton Murry; and Christopher Isherwood. The Woolfs entertained informally—invitations always included an admonition not to bring dinner clothes. (During the war years, to be sure, they were admonished to bring their rations of butter and tea.) Mornings they were left to their own devices; evenings there was talk—and such talk it must have been.

In January, 1919, however, the owner of Asheham House announced that beginning in September he would need it for his farm bailiff. September 1 they made the move to Rodmell. Asheham House still stands, divided now into flats. But you can see it from the outside. And, as any visitor will attest, good manners work wonders with the English. If you write, "Occupant" in advance, you might even be invited in for a look.

Rodmell This village to which Virginia and Leonard Woolf moved in 1919 is on the A 275 only half a mile from Asheham and, like it, about seven miles northeast of Brighton. Here Virginia was to live out her life, work on the books that placed her among England's great novelists, and die her tragic death.

On their walks in the area, they had often noticed a house that stood off a lane between Rodmell church and the village street, and peering over a wall, had admired its orchard and garden. The afternoon of July 1, 1919, they bought it at auction for £700. It was an old house—the deeds ran back to 1707—and was, Virginia admitted, "very humble and unromantic." To this day, despite the additions the Woolfs made, it remains a modest, basically clapboard house, easy to overlook. But the Sussex Downs and River Ouse Valley made a charming setting. "I like the morning sun in one's window," Virginia reported, but "what I like best is the water meadow onto which the garden opens. You see every down all the way round you."

When they moved in September, two farm wagons sufficed to carry all they owned. Trouble began immediately. The kitchen flooded and had to be disemboweled. The red brick sitting room floor oozed moisture, the whole house was damp at times, and the dining room carpet turned to mould.

There was no running water, and they had to use the loft for an earth closet. Worst of all, there was no central heating; on cold days wind whistled through the wooden walls from all directions.

Small as the house was, it was frugally furnished, mainly with castoffs and hand-me-downs. But there were books everywhere, even spilling so thickly up the stairs there was room to place only one foot at a time. Only over the years, as Virginia's books began to sell, could they improve their somewhat Spartan living conditions, each improvement an event. Virginia was almost breathless in reporting the first such in 1921: "My great excitement is that we're making a beautiful garden room out of a toolhouse with large windows and a view of the downs."

In 1927, the year *To the Lighthouse* came out, they added to one end of the house: a sitting room and an honest-to-goodness bathroom upstairs, a bedroom for Virginia downstairs. And in 1928 Virginia produced a best-seller with *Orlando,* making them comfortable financially for the first time. They bought some new furniture and built a tiny pavilion in the garden—one fair-sized room on the ground floor, plus a small upper room under the slanting roof, reached by outside stairs. It was in this pavilion that Virginia Woolf did most of her writing from 1928 on.

At Monk's House, as the place was called, the routine was well established. Mornings were for writing, he in the house, she in the pavilion. Afternoons they walked together or, while he gardened, she would walk alone, mulling over scenes and phrases for the next day's work. Virginia liked to bicycle and to indulge in simple, childlike pleasures. Once she confessed to Hugh Walpole, the novelist: "I feel like driving off to Rodmell on a hot Friday evening and having cold ham, or sitting on my terrace and smoking a cigar with an owl or two." And she loved to bowl with Leonard. She competed firecely; he usually won.

And always, it seemed, there were guests, including the same Bloomsbury coterie so often at Asheham House: Roger Fry, the painter; Maynard Keynes, the economist; and such writers as Lytton Strachey and E. M. Forster. Strachey, whose *Eminent Victorians* has become a classic, was among Virginia's dearest friends. Indeed, he had once proposed to her; but realizing his sexual tastes might make marriage with any woman, even Virginia, awkward, he was soon suggesting Leonard Woolf marry her. Leonard obliged.

Forster, already a success with *A Room with a View* (1908) and *Howards End* (1910) liked to visit, though he and Virginia were never completely at ease with each other. Once, when they were both writing in the garden room, she wryly noted in the letter she was writing: "I have to exercise great discretion in not sneezing or knocking things over."

Two poets who came to Monk's house were Stephen Spender and T. S.

Eliot. Eliot, whose *Waste Land* the Woolfs had introduced on their Hogarth Press, came often, though it took three years for him to unbend enough to call them by their first names. And on one walk he froze with embarrassment when Leonard dropped behind him and Virginia to relieve himself. Vita Sackville-West was another writer who came often for a while, especially when she was in love with Virginia and carried on an "affair" whose dimensions are still debated. Virginia wrote *Orlando* for Vita—Vita in actuality being the hero, Orlando, who halfway through the book turns into a female.

Orlando is but one—and in Virginia's eyes hardly the best—of the books she wrote at Monk's House: *Jacob's Room,* published in 1922: *Mrs. Dalloway* (1922); *To the Lighthouse* (1927); *The Waves* (1931); *The Years* (1937); and *Between the Acts* (1941), as well as other works. But the last novel came hard, and even as she showed her latest revision to Leonard in February of 1941, she realized she was in trouble.

They had spent the war winters of 1939–40 and 1940–41 in Monk's House after their London place was bombed, and brutal winters they had been. Even in Rodmell air raid warnings sounded and German airplanes flew low and ominously over the house. Barbed wire and pill boxes sprang up on the Monk's House grounds. Virginia feared another summer would not come to a free Rodmell and kept a supply of poison on hand against the fully expected Nazi invasion. Leonard was a Jew. And, terrifyingly reminiscent of the insanity that had struck her down in that other, earlier World War, she began to hear voices.

On March 28, 1941, she wrote two letters, one to her sister Vanessa, one to Leonard. To Leonard she wrote:

> Dearest,
> I feel certain I am going mad again. I feel I can't go through another of those horrible times. And I shan't recover this time. I begin to hear voices, and I can't concentrate. So I'm doing what seems the best thing to do. You have given me the greatest possible happiness. . . . "

And then she took her walking stick and, about noon, crossed the water meadows to the river. There she paused to leave her stick on the bank and put a large stone in her pocket. Her body wasn't found for three weeks.

In their garden the Woolfs had two tall elm trees which they called Virginia and Leonard. Her ashes were buried at the foot of her tree, which unfortunately has since blown down. But you can still see the other, as well as the busts of each—with accompanying plaques—placed at either end of one of the low flint walls that divide the garden into sections.

Monk's House was acquired by the National Trust in 1980, and following a painstaking campaign spearheaded by devotees of Virginia Woolf's works, now has several rooms open to the public two days a week (in season) with a gratifying number of the novelist's furnishings and possessions. To get to Monk's House when approaching Rodmell from Lewes, you turn left at the Holly Public House, and Monk's House is the last one on the right. There never were, by the way, any monks at Monk's House.

Seaford A considerable town (about 18,000 people) on the A 259 and the Channel coast, Seaford is ten miles southeast of Rodmell. In the summer of 1856, it was a nondescript fishing village when George Meredith came there to reach a pivotal point in a personal domestic tragedy that was to find expression in *Modern Love* (1862), that series of monodramatic poems that so shocked the Victorians.

Meredith found Seaford an "ill-conditioned sort of place with a straggling row of villas facing a muddy beach." But no place, perhaps, at that juncture would have appealed. His marriage to Mary Ellen Nicolls, widowed daughter of poet-novelist Thomas Love Peacock was nearing collapse. They were apart more and more and when together spent most of the time quarreling violently, despite a three-year-old son, Arthur, they both adored.

At first, Seaford offered Meredith some compensations: the towering South Downs, grand for walking, and cheap lodgings with good food at the home of the local carpenter. But by December his despair is clear: "I remain here as I can work better than elsewhere, though, engaged as I am, the DULNESS is something frightful, and hangs on my shoulders like Sinbad's Old Man of the Sea." Mary Ellen, one should add, was regaling herself elsewhere.

The truth was, she had fallen in love with Henry Wallis, a promising young artist—and Meredith not only knew Wallis, he knew about their affair as well. Mary Ellen had posed for Wallis's "Fireside Reverie," for which Meredith had written a four-line epigraph; and Meredith himself was said to have been the model for Wallis's most popular work, "The Death of Chatterton."

The rest can quickly be told: The summer of 1857 Mary Ellen was openly visiting the holiday spots of northwest England with Wallis, and then eloped with him to Capri, though Meredith begged her not to. All too soon, Wallis abandoned her, leaving her to bear alone their child the following April. She registered the father's name as "George Meredith, author." But the pathetic saga that reached its turning point in Seaford was over. Meredith would not let his wife return to him, nor ever again let her see Arthur.

Eastbourne On the Channel coast nine miles west of Seaford, Eastbourne now surpasses Brighton in the number of elegant seaside hotels. This was not so in Charles Lamb's day, however; while he found Worthing dull and Brighton duller, he found Eastbourne dullest. Subsequently, some twenty to thirty years apart, two characters walked its streets little noticed by the passersby, though their pen names today are known to millions. Who in Eastbourne in the late Victorian period would have guessed that Mr. Charles Lutwidge Dodgson, the shy mathematics teacher who lodged in Lushington Road with the Dyers, was really Lewis Carroll, author of *Alice in Wonderland?* And who would have thought just before World War I that Eric Blair, the sad-looking schoolboy from St. Cyprian's, would grow up to be George Orwell and write books like *Animal Farm* and *Nineteen Eighty-Four?*

Lewis Carroll obviously loved Eastbourne. As Dodgson, the college don—he kept his two identities scrupulously separated—he came here for his summer holidays from Oxford every year from July of 1877 until his death in 1898. He always stayed with a Mr. Dyer, a postal worker, and his wife. For most of this time the Dyers occupied a small, semidetached house at 7 Lushington Road, and here Carroll had a "nice little first floor sitting room with a balcony, and bedroom adjoining." Today a plaque marks the spot.

His life at Eastbourne was pleasantly uneventful: enjoying the sea, going for very long walks, attending church, writing. *Alice* and *Through the Looking Glass* were well behind him, but during these later years he wrote *Rhyme? and Reason?* (1883), *A Tangled Tale* (1885), and *Sylvie and Bruno* (1889 and 1893), as well as the solid mathematical works (e.g., *Euclid and His Modern Rivals*) which were the only books of his that he would publicly acknowledge.

Perhaps because of his shyness, Carroll had a great fondness for young girls, whom he would love with devotion until they neared womanhood. Then, almost invariably, the attachment would become strained and broken. It was for one such love, Alice Liddell, a daughter of an Oxford dean, that Carroll had written *Alice in Wonderland.* In Eastbourne, during his very first stay there in 1877, he met one of the several successors to Alice. She was twelve-year-old Agnes Hull, the pretty daughter of an Eastbourne barrister. Carroll adored her and wrote her loving notes and letters. But in 1881 she warned him that she was nearing sixteen, and their relationship must change.

Eric Blair, the boy who was to become George Orwell, came to St. Cyprian's school in 1911 when he was only eight years old. Run by a Mr. and Mrs. Vaughan Wilkes, it was located in a sheltered bowl below the great chalky cliff called Beachy Head and consisted chiefly of two large, late Victorian houses and the football-cricket playing field. In their place today is a typically middle class suburban street, from which the Downs rise steeply to the cliff.

The school was then only twelve years old, but had already achieved a reputation for preparing boys (cramming would be more accurate) for acceptance by Eton and other great English public schools. From the start, Blair was an outsider and a loner. He was sensitive and mature beyond his years. But worse, he was a poor boy at special rates among the sons of upper-upper middle class families, a sprinkling of South American millionaires, and even a genuine aristocrat or two. His unhappiness here won for the school a distinctive place, however negative, in his later writings.

In his essay, "Such Such Were the Joys," so bitter that it could not be published in England during his life for fear of libel, Orwell attacks the beatings, the cramming, the baseless suspicions, the poor food, and the utter mindlessness that were the everyday fare of St. Cyprian's. He was even more appalled at the snobbery the masters encouraged in their charges. In the autobiographical parts of *The Road to Wigan Pier* (1937), Orwell includes portraits of "Sambo" and "Flip" which are based on the school's headmaster and wife.

St. Cyprian's even wins, anonymously, a niche in *Nineteen Eighty-Four.* When critics charged that the torture scenes in that grim and prophetic novel reminded them of the behavior of school bullies, Orwell retorted that for those who grew up amid the safe conventions of democratic England "the only English parallel for the nightmare of totalitarianism was the experience of a misfit boy in an English boarding school."

The only bright spot for young Eric Blair was the friendship of another gifted boy who was destined to be a writer, Cyril Connolly. He was just Eric's age and arrived in 1914, Blair's third year at the school. In his *Enemies of Promise* (1938), Connolly has left his own assessment of the place and its products (he calls it St. Wulfric's)—less bitter, but hardly more flattering: "Muscle-bound with character, the alumni of St. Wulfric's would pass on to the best public schools, cleaning up all houses with a doubtful tone, reporting their best friends for homosexuality and seeing them expelled."

Connolly was, like Blair, bright, precocious, and unusually mature for his age; he became Eric's first close friend. The adult Orwell recalled their staying up all one night, when about eleven, snatching H. G. Well's collection of short stories, *The Country of the Blind,* from each other's hands—and getting caned in the bargain. They served as critics for each other's early attempts at writing. Of a Connolly poem written at thirteen, for instance, Eric gravely commented: "*Dashed* good . . . scansion excellent . . . The whole thing is neat, elegant and polished."

And an effort by Eric that same year became his first published work—its only distinction, to be sure, as a sample stanza indicates. The year was 1914, and World War I had just begun:

> Oh! Give me the strength of the lion,
> The wisdom of Reynard the Fox
> And then I'll hurl troops at the Germans,
> And give them the hardest of knocks.

It must be conceded that however dubious its merits, St. Cyprian's did enable both boys to win scholarships to other schools. After five years there, Blair won awards to both Wellington and Eton and attended both. Connolly won a scholarship to Eton, too. Connolly went on to become a distinguished journalist and essayist, and author of *The Rock Pool* (1935). Eric Blair went on to serve with the Indian Imperial Police in Burma. It was not until 1933, with the publication of his first book, *Down and Out in Paris and London,* that he became George Orwell: George, because it was so characteristically English a name . . . Orwell from a river in Suffolk.

WEST SUSSEX

A Tale of Two Roads

West Sussex

1. Along the Channel–The A 259

2. The A 272–And a Few Asides

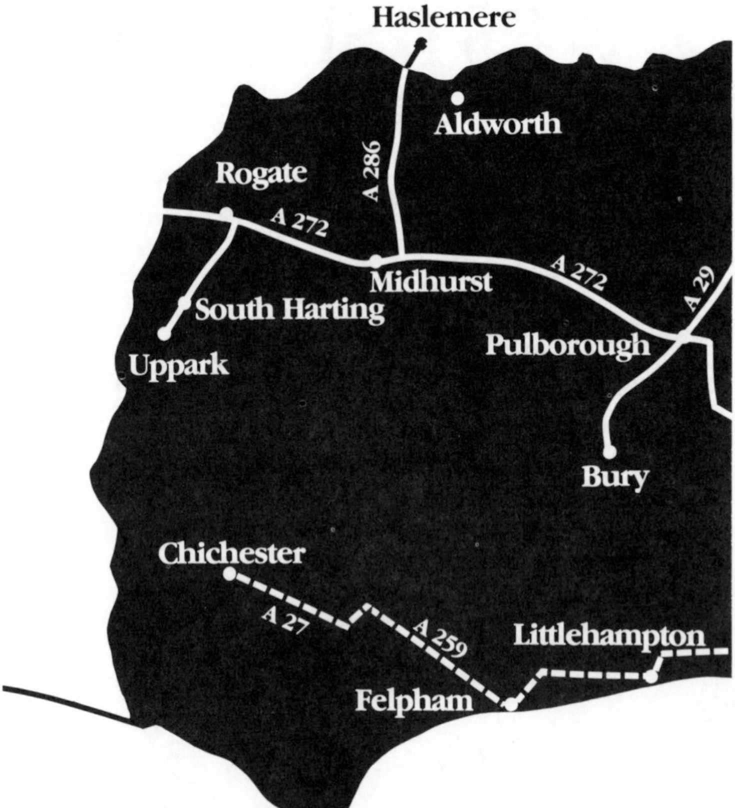

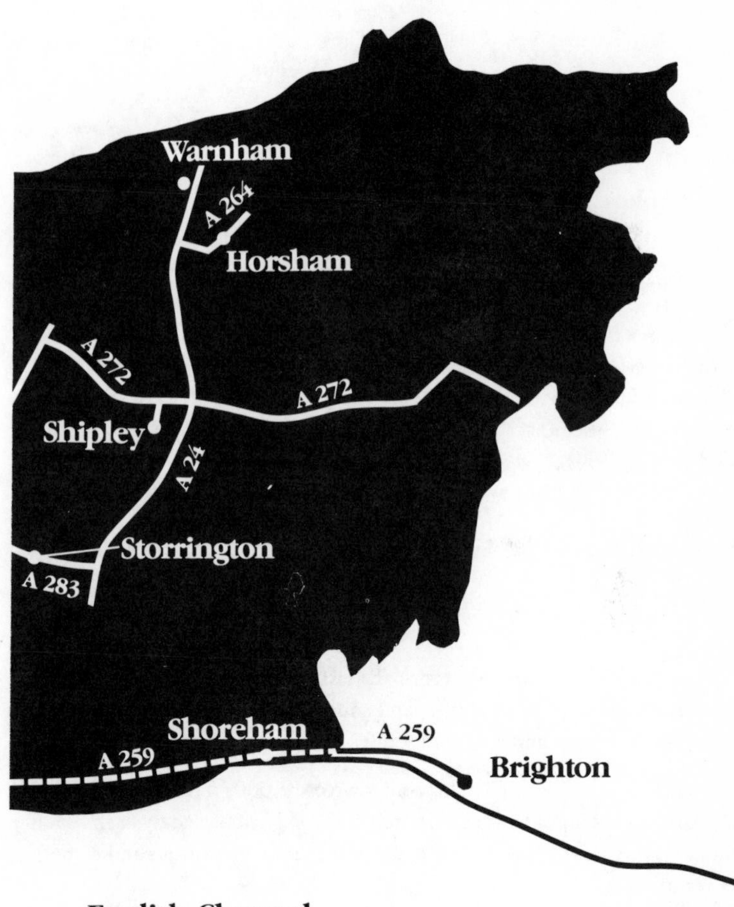
Warnham
A 264
Horsham
A 272
A 272
Shipley
A 24
Storrington
A 283
Shoreham
A 259
A 259
Brighton
English Channel

I know no country to compare with West Sussex except the Cotswolds. It has its own colour, a pleasant colour of sunlit sandstone and ironstone and a warm flavour of open country because of the parks and commons and pine woods about it.

H. G. Wells, *Experiment in Autobiography*

Roads in England go east and west with the greatest reluctance. But in West Sussex two such highways provide the most convenient means of seeing both its beauty and its considerable literary heritage: the A 259 along the Channel Coast from Shoreham to Chichester (from Waugh to Keats). . . and the A 272 at the county's waist from Shipley (and Hilaire Belloc) to Midhurst (and H. G. Wells).

1. ALONG THE CHANNEL—THE A 259

Shoreham to Felpham

The A 259 is not the shortest or the fastest way to negotiate the distance between West Sussex's southeast and southwest corners, but its occasional glimpses of the sea and its literary offerings make it worth the taking.

Shoreham-by-Sea This thriving town of 10,000 on the sea (and on the A 259), is just six miles west of Brighton at the eastern boundary of the county. Chief literary ties are two novelists who planned to be painters and wound up as writers anyway.

One was George Moore, novelist, dramatist, and short story writer, who in the later 1800's often stayed with Shoreham's leading family, the Bridgers. Squire Bridger's manor, Buckingham, with its gables, ornamental porches, and seventy-acre park appears as "Woodview" in Moore's best-known novel, *Esther Waters* (1894), and in *A Mere Accident* (1887), which was planned there.

The house is now gone, but the grounds remain as a public park.

The other was Evelyn Waugh, who attended Lancing College, a school just north of Shoreham, from 1917 to 1921. Its Victorian Gothic Chapel has England's largest rose window and was about the only thing that aroused much enthusiasm in him. He came as a fourteen-year-old and managed to be as miserable as schoolboys were supposed to be. The food, he said, would have "provoked mutiny in a mid-Victorian poor house."

He planned to be a painter, but he did write at Lancing: a novel, which he quit writing after it turned into "a bloody sweat," a play that was well received, and a poem that won the Scarlyn prize. He describes his schooldays in his autobiography, *A Little Learning* (1964).

Littlehampton Further down the A 259, twenty miles from Brighton, are Littlehampton and the Beach Hotel, a favorite holiday haunt of John Galsworthy, and still an inviting hotel (three stars). A rambling, three-storey building with gables and rustic balconies, it dates back to about 1900, but it was new when Galsworthy with his bride, Ada, went there for the first week of their long-delayed marriage. He had just finished *The Man of Property,* the first of what was to be *The Forsyte Saga*, and had already begun what ultimately became the second, *The Country House* (1907). Ada had been his model for Irene.

Ada loved the Beach Hotel, and they came often in succeeding years. Galsworthy was here the Christmas of 1917, working on *Saint's Progress* (1919), when a telegram came from the Prime Minister, Lloyd George: "Please wire by return whether you accept offer of knighthood." Feeling a writer should be free of all titles and rewards, Galsworthy's answer was "No thanks," but somehow his name was included in the year's honors list anyway, and it cost him a good deal of joshing from friends before he could set the record straight.

Felpham An appealing little place on the A 259 just east of Bognor Regis, Felpham is where William Blake—engraver, poet, and artist—saw more than heaven in a grain of sand. He saw Milton in his garden and heard Satan roaring on the open sea.

Blake came to Felpham in 1800 at the invitation of William Hayley, a would-be patron of the arts, versifier, and friend of poet William Cowper. Felpham was then a tiny marine village set in fields that ran to the edge of the wide sandy beach. Hayley's unique Marine Turret house, where Blake stayed at first, was less than a ten minute walk from the ocean, and the poet was enchanted. With Hayley's encouragement, he decided to move his engraving shop to Felpham.

From the landlord of the Fox Inn, where he stayed for a while, Blake rented for £20 a year a sturdy thatched cottage about a quarter of a mile from the sea. And in mid-September, with his youngest sister Catherine and sixteen heavy boxes, plus portfolios of prints, printing press, plates, and much too much printing paper, he moved in, after a trip that required seven different chaises, seven drivers, and seven shiftings of all that gear. To start a new life at this tiny outpost, at forty-three, was bold indeed. But Blake wrote ecstatically to his friend John Flaxman:

> Away to sweet Felpham, for Heaven is there
> The ladder of Angels descends through the air.
> On the turret its spiral does softly descend,
> Thro the village then winds, at my cot it does end.

For all the three years he spent in Felpham—the only time he lived outside of London—Blake continued to be delighted with his home: "Our cottage is more beautiful than I thought, & also more convenient, for tho' small it is well-proportioned." It was (and is) a lovely place, with "thatched roof of rusted gold," and not all that small. It had two storeys, six rooms. and its front door faced across the small garden toward cornfields, meadows, and the sea.

Odd as he was (in London many thought him crazy), Blake seems to have gotten along well with the people of Felpham. "The Villagers of Felpham are not meer [sic] Rustics," he wrote a friend, "they are polite & modest. Meat is cheaper than in London, but the sweet air & the voices of winds, trees & birds, & the odours of the happy ground, makes it a dwelling for immortals. Work will go on here with God speed."

And despite the demands of engraving the works of others, Blake's own writing did go on apace. In this house he did some of his most significant work. He completed the *Four Zoas,* wrote most of *Milton*, and conceived *Jerusalem.* The physical presence in Felpham of some of the principals in *Milton* was intensely real to Blake: "I beheld Milton with astonishment. . . descending down into my Cottage Garden, clothed in Black, severe & silent." And there was Ololon, "trembling in the porch" on the seaward side of the house. Out past the shore, "loud Satan thunder'd, loud & dark upon mild Felpham shore." At the end of the poem, when Milton has achieved wholeness, "Jesus wept & walked forth from Felpham's Vale clothed in clouds of blood."

In August of 1803, however, a bizarre event ended Blake's stay in Felpham. Some soldiers were stationed there, and Blake got into an altercation with one, a Pvt. John Scofield, in his garden. He wound up marching Scofield by the elbow to the nearby Fox Inn, "raging and cursing." Scofield retaliated by getting a warrant against Blake for assault and sedition (i.e., damning the king).

It was a serious and potentially dangerous charge, particularly for one who supported the French revolutionists as vehemently as Blake did. Fortunately, these sympathies were not known to the jury, in Chichester, who tried Blake in January of the next year, and he was acquitted. Blake's revenge was typical: he gave Scofield the dubious immortality of a footnote. Scofield appears in both *Milton* and *Jerusalem* as a villain. But Blake's days in Felpham were over.

Both Blake's house and the Fox Inn are still standing. You reach them by going through the village—if you're coming from Littlehampton on the A 259—turning left at Vicarage Lane, and continuing on until it runs into what is now called Blake's road. There, on the left, is The Fox. It's still a pub, and lunch on its outside court, if the weather is pleasant, is a delight.

Blake's cottage is only some fifty yards down Blake's Road, to the right and across the street, and recognizable by its handsome thatched roof. It is now a private dwelling and is shut in by high walls. But you can see the upper half of it. Hayley's Turret House around the corner on Limmer Lane was pulled down a few years ago and replaced by a block of flats. The builders were able to retain the old wall and gateway, however, and Hayley himself is buried in little St. Mary's Church.

Chichester

At Bognor Regis the A 259 turns its back on the sea and climbs seven miles northwest to Chichester, where it is absorbed by the A 27 and seen no more. Most who know Chichester know it for its Festival Theatre. It's a fine theater, and its first director was Sir (now Lord) Laurence Olivier.

But the city's real charm is, as it was for Blake and Keats, its authentic and apparent antiquity. You feel it the moment you glimpse its Cathedral tower, tall and slenderly elegant as a junior-size Salisbury, even as you approach the city. You feel it in the Cathedral itself and its clustering outbuildings, dating variously from Norman times through the Middle Ages. You feel it in the remnants of the town walls; in St. Mary's Hospital, a thirteenth-century almshouse; and in the sixteenth-century Market Cross, on the spot where people came to sell their cattle.

Keats felt it, too, and with happiest results. But before we get to him, a few words about some lesser poets—to apply the word generously. William Collins was born here in 1721, and it must be admitted he wrote a few graceful lyrics. He died in Chichester, too, in 1759, and in the southwest tower of the Cathedral is a white marble *bas relief* memorial, with a verse that says in part:

For this the ashes of a bard require
Who touched the tenderest notes of pity's lyre,
Who joined pure faith to strong poetic powers. . . .

"Strong poetic powers" may be a bit much—but not in comparison with the gifts of another Chichester son, William Hayley, the friend and over-zealous patron of Blake. Hayley was an astoundingly prolific producer of bad poetry, which was reputed to be found on every girl's sofa. But Sam Johnson and Robert Southey were nearer the mark. Johnson tried to read Hayley's best-seller, *Triumphs of Temper,* and couldn't get past the first two pages. And Southey said, "Everything about that man is good except his poetry." Hayley was offered the poet laureateship in 1790 but had the good sense to refuse.

During his three years at Felpham at the beginning of the next century, Blake came often to Chichester and liked it: "Chichester is a very handsom [sic] City, Seven miles from us; and we can get most Conveniences There." Moreover, the townsfolk were "Handsomer than the people about London." It was in Chichester's bleak, gray Guildhall just within the old city walls, however, that Blake's trial for sedition was held.

John Keats came to Chichester early in 1819 and was captivated, its atmosphere complementing and reenforcing the powerful pull of the medieval and romantic he was already feeling. The result was immediate. "I took down some of the thin paper," he announced to his brother and sister, and "wrote on it a little poem call'd 'St. Agnes Eve.'" Chichester's medieval air breathes through such early passages as:

He follow'd through a lowly arched way,
Brushing the cobwebs with his lofty plume,
And as she mutter'd "Well—a—well—a—day!"
He found him in a little moonlight room,
Pale, lattic'd, chill, and silent as a tomb.

But "little poem" indeed: "The Eve of St. Agnes" signalled the arrival of one of England's greatest poets.

Keats's unfinished "Eve of St. Mark" was inspired by Chichester, too, and bears easily recognizable traces of his stay, especially the "rain-cleansed streets" crowded well with "pious companies" heeding the Cathedral's Sabbath bell and passing through its "arched porch, and entry low." The porch, the entry and even the "clamorous daws" still work their magic to this day.

2. THE A 272—AND A FEW ASIDES

Shipley—Horsham—Warnham—Storrington

The two towns that mark the entrance and exit of the A 272 in its passage through West Sussex are impressive in their literary insignificance. Hayward's Heath on the east is where England's most famous nine-year old novelist, Daisy Ashford (her *The Young Visitors* was a sensation in 1919), went to school. And Trotten, on the west, is where the father of playwright Thomas Otway (his *Venice Preserv'd* was big in 1682) was curate. But on the forty miles of the A 272 that twist and climb between the two, and the byways that beckon off it, are some of the most interesting literary spots and most beautiful vistas to be seen.

Shipley A couple of pubs and a few houses—that's Shipley, six miles south of Horsham and just off the A 272, fifteen miles from its eastern entrance into the county. Here is King's Land, home of Hilaire Belloc from 1906 until his death in 1953, where he wrote novels, essays, verse, histories, and biographies beyond counting. The Jebb branch of his descendants still own it.

It is a good-sized red brick building framed in friendly trees and can be seen from the road. Inside it is a labyrinth of rooms and periods, the furnishings intact since Belloc bought it. Among its curiosities are its own little chapel, dating from the fifteenth century; its own tiny bakery; a hall built especially to house an old staircase Belloc had been given; a couch that had belonged to Joseph Priestley; and a Tudor table that belonged to Oxford University. The walls of Belloc's study are lined with books, most of which he wrote himself. Because the house he had meant to buy before he bought King's Land burned down from a faulty fuse, he never installed electricity.

The house, of course, is not open to the public, but the mill on the grounds (Belloc ground his own whole meal flour to make his own bread) is and can be seen for a slight fee weekends in season, along with some Belloc relics.

Horsham Horsham is an agreeable old market town on the A 264, is six miles north of Shipley, and came close to having a literary celebrity on two occasions. It missed being Shelley's birthplace by two miles (his grandfather did live in Horsham) . . . and missed being Tennyson's home by five miles and a few mishaps.

Shelley was born at nearby Warnham. As for Tennyson, he and Emily came to Warninglid, five miles southeast, in 1851, after the wonderful year that witnessed his marriage, his appointment as poet laureate, and the publication of *In Memoriam*. They were delighted with their old, secluded house and its exquisite view of the South Downs.

But Tennyson's luck had run out. The fireplaces smoked, the doors banged, and the windows were drafty. Wind blew down part of the bedroom wall, and rain poured in. To cap it all, the poet learned that a notorious cutthroat gang had once lived in the house, and a baby was buried somewhere on the grounds. Since Emily was pregnant, that was enough for Tennyson; he moved her to the nearby inn. Alas for Warninglid: *Maud*, and *Idylls of the King*, and all the rest were written elsewhere.

Warnham Really Shelley's birthplace, Warnham is just south of the county's northern boundary and two miles north of Horsham. On the outskirts of town, down a long, lovely lane, is Field Place. Here Shelley was born, did his first writing, and in his teens came to be an exile in his own home.

Ancestral seat of the Shelleys, long the local squires, Field Place is a roomy, gracious, two-storey country house of stone with a grey Horsham slate roof lined with chimneys. In an upstairs bedroom, Percy Bysshe Shelley was born on August 4, 1792. In its pastoral setting, with its own little brook and lake amid its own park, Shelley's father hoped to raise him to be the landowner, hunter, and horseman his destiny obviously called for.

But as early as age ten, when he first left Field Place to go to school, the rebel in Shelley began to show. It burst forth fully in 1811 at Oxford when he was eighteen. He wrote an essay with the deliberately inflammatory title, *The Necessity of Atheism*, and was expelled. He returned to Field Place as a virtual outcast, even with his mother. "I sometimes exchange a word with my mother on the subject of the weather," he wrote a friend, "upon which she is irresistibly eloquent; otherwise all is deep silence!"

He compounded matters in August of the same year by running off to Edinburgh to get married. His father responded by barring him from his home until he recanted and was accepted once more by Oxford. Shelley refused. In 1814, while his father was away, his mother invited Shelley for a visit so secret that when he was outside the house he wore a friend's military uniform and posed as "Captain Jones." After a few days, however, he left. He was never to see Field Place again.

The house and grounds are still handsomely maintained. But it remains a private dwelling, and is not open to the public.

Storrington You reach Storrington by driving south on the A 24 where it crosses the A 272 just before Shipley, and then going south another five miles, then west for two miles on the A 283. It's a friendly little place, Storrington, and the people are happy to direct you to the modest little brick

Our Lady of England Church at the edge of town. It's the only church of that name in the country, and at the priory attached to it lived, from 1889 to early 1890, a gifted young poet born out of his time: Francis Thompson.

Thompson's stay at the priory, still run by Norbertine monks, no doubt saved his life. He had been sent there for recuperation by a compassionate editor who had found him on the streets of London starving and wracked by drugs. Under the monks' loving care he gradually grew strong enough to write, and it was at the Storrington Priory that he began his greatest poem, "The Hound of Heaven." Two other of his well-known poems written here were "Daisy" and "Ode to the Setting Sun."

He loved to walk on the Downs outside town, and "Daisy" was the result of meeting a little local girl of that name on one such walk. The poem reflects the beauty of this part of the country:

> The hills look over on the South
>   And southward dreams the sea;
> And with the sea-breeze hand in hand
>   Came innocence and she

"Ode to the Setting Sun," the first evidence of Thompson's true poetic powers, was inspired directly by an impressive crucifix in the cloister, near life-size. He describes how the sinking sun's "straight long beam lies steady on the Cross," until at last the "Cross stands gaunt and long."

Hilaire Belloc was a frequent worshipper at the church, driving down from Shipley. He was especially fond of three small paintings in the hall depicting "The Annunciation," "The Visitation," and "The Birth of Our Lord," and wrote a poem called "Courtesy":

> On monks I did in Storrington fall,
> They took me straight into their Hall,
> I saw three pictures on the wall
> And Courtesy was in them all.

Belloc goes on to describe each picture in turn, the last being particularly charming:

> The third it was our Little Lord
> Who all the Kings in arms adored;
> He was so small you could not see
> His large intent of Courtesy.

But you can enjoy the pictures for yourself. They're still there in the hall—and the good monks still make visitors welcome.

Bury and Midhurst

Pulborough is a typical Sussex town at the junction of the A 283 and the A 29, four miles northwest of Storrington. One day in 1926 John Galsworthy was lunching in Pulborough with his favorite nephew and niece, Rudo and Vi Sauter. After lunch he dropped in on the local housing agent to talk about buying a house for the young people. What he had in mind was something in the £3,000 range—a cozy little place where the Sauters could live comfortably, but with an extra room or two where the Galsworthys could stay when they liked.

Did the agent have anything to recommend?

Well, yes. There was that place down in Bury.

So they went and took a look, and Galsworthy bought it on the spot, to Rudo's horror: it cost £69,000 and had twenty-two rooms! The thought of trying to run such a big house staggered the youngsters. No trouble, said the uncle: he and Aunt Ada would buy the house, and Rudo and Vi could stay with them. And so it was. Here Galsworthy lived until his death in 1933, and here he wrote the sequel to *The Forsyte Saga, A Modern Comedy*. His ashes are sprinkled amid the neighboring hills.

Bury Bury is a five mile drive south from Pulborough along the A 29; the village is just off the highway. Bury House itself is a Soames-sized mansion, modern in Galsworthy's day, but built in Tudor style of grey, hand-hewn stone. It is an E-shaped structure, with a gable atop each arm, and faces a pool and what was a spacious garden. In Ada Galsworthy's day there were 10,000 blossoms that required five gardeners. Hugh Walpole, a welcome guest, has left a feeling description: "A really lovely house, pearl-gray stones fronting lawns that run straight to the open fields . . . very like a special edition of one of John's own books."

Galsworthy apparently had not intended to do much writing at Bury House. He told Walpole soon after he moved in that when the Forsyte book then in progress—*Swan Song* (1928)—was done, he'd probably never write another line. But he went on writing every morning as if on a rigid schedule, in the billiards room, on the terrace, or, sometime, in his little study at the top of the house, balancing a pad on his knee. There was a steady flow of books: *On Forsyte 'Change* (1930), *Maid in Waiting* (1931), *Flowering Wilderness* (1932), and, published after his death, *Over the River* (1933).

Writers who were guests at Bury House included James M. Barrie, fellow dramatists John Drinkwater and Harley Granville-Barker, Arnold Bennett, and, as mentioned, Hugh Walpole. Once Walpole was there in 1928 when Bennett came driving up in his Rolls Royce and began going on about how much money he was making. Wrote Walpole scathingly in his diary: "a guttersnipe cocking snooks from the street." With equal bluntness Walpole reported his host as a terrible loser at croquet on the terrace: "He has no sense of fun about games. They are battles for Galsworthian justice." But to wife Ada, Galsworthy could do no wrong: "John is God. And John deserves to be God, too."

Since the mid-forties, Bury House has been a county home for the aged. You can see it from the road.

Midhurst On the A 272 where it makes its final run to the county line, seven miles to the west, is Midhurst. It's the kind of town you stumble upon by chance and want to tell your friends about—but not too many, lest they spoil it. It has changed very little in the hundred years since H. G. Wells discovered, with delight, its "shops and schools were grouped in rational, comprehensible relations; it had a beginning, a middle, and an end."

Wells came to Midhurst in 1881 to learn to be a chemist in a Mr. Cowap's "bright little shop, with its drawers full of squills and senna pods," and he loved it. But he had to leave after a month when the apprenticeship proved to be more than his mother could afford. He was then somewhat briefly at the recently reopened Midhurst Grammar School and—despite his own scanty education—later returned to the school as an usher (assistant teacher) as well as student. For a while Wells's mother was a housekeeper at the Angel Inn on North Street, and during his second stay at the school he shared a bedroom with a fellow usher over a little sweetshop next to the hotel.

These youthful days figure prominently in Wells's noteworthy novel, *Tono-Bungay* (1909). The hero, George, comes to his Uncle Ponderevo's chemist shop in Wimblehurst (obviously Midhurst); and his uncle, like the real Mr. Cowap, invents a wondrous elixer. And, like Wells, George goes to the grammar school, newly reopened. But Uncle Ponderevo hardly shares Wells's love for the town: "Sac-remental wine!" he snorted, "this isn't the world—it's Cold Mutton Fat! That's what Wimblehurst is! Cold Mutton Fat!—dead and stiff!" The grammar school appears also in *Love and Mr. Lewisham* (1900), with Mr. Lewisham pinning to his wall just such a "scheme" as Wells himself devised to give every moment in the day its appointed task.

The Midhurst of Wells, actual and in fiction, is easy to see, for it's either on or near North Street. The fifteenth-century Angel Inn is midway down the street; the sweetshop (still in business) is next to it; and the school is a few hundred yards farther up and across the street, identified by the "Schola Grammaticalis" over the door. On the southern end of town, past Church Hill where Mr. Cowap's chemist's shop was, is South Pond, near which was the comfortable old house of the headmaster, where Wells first boarded.

Those impressive ruins at the northeast edge of the town, across the Rother River? They're what remains of the great Cowdray mansion, built in the early sixteenth century on land held by the Earls of Arundel, whose antiquity is attested by a charming little rhyme:

Since William rose and Harold fell,
There have been earls of Arundel.

Somehow the mansion survived Cromwell and the Civil War in the seventeenth century, even though its occupants then, named Montague, were notably Catholic. But a fire in 1793 burned it beyond restoration.

Actually, since they're on the east bank of the Rother, the ruins are in Eastbourne parish. And they have no discoverable literary importance. Still, if you've a mind to, a conducted tour is available. Apply to the custodian at the Round Tower.

Aldworth—South Harting—Uppark

Three of the more notable "asides" from the A 272 lie inside a seven mile radius of Midhurst—the homes of three of England's most successful writers. Within this small area lived Alfred, Lord Tennyson, and Anthony Trollope as adults, and H. G. Wells as a boy. Two remain in private hands, but the third belongs to the National Trust and is open to the public in season.

Aldworth Scattered about England are a number of houses of literary importance that have been rescued from ruin and restored to graciousness by the loving efforts of their modern owners. Aldworth is one such. It is six miles due north of Midhurst on a small road off the A 286.

The beauty of Aldworth's setting earned its own poem:

You came, and looked, and loved the view
Long known and loved by me,
Green Sussex fading into view
With one grey glimpse of sea.

Prologue "To General Hamley"

The poet is Tennyson. . .the "you" is General Hamley. . .the view is a spectacular look at the famed Sussex Weald and Downs, stretching to the English Channel forty miles away. Sir Edward Bruce Hamley had served with distinction in the Crimean War, and when he visited Aldworth in autumn of 1883, Tennyson's poem about that war, "The Charge of the Heavy Brigade" (yes, indeed, there's one for the heavyweights, too), provided a warm link between the two. In consequence, when Tennyson reprinted the piece in 1885 he wrote the above prologue to honor his guest.

Harried by the ever-growing number of tourists that in summer swarmed about his house on the Isle of Wight, Tennyson had in 1867 bought thirty-six acres atop 900-foot-high Blackdown at the northernmost edge of West Sussex. (Today the very next house to it is called Surrey End, for the adjoining county.) It is a lovely spot with rich wooded slopes interlaced with narrow smugglers' trails and small sparkling streams that still supply the house with purest water. Here Tennyson built his summer retreat, laying the foundation stone, appropriately enough, on Shakespeare's birthday, April 23, 1868.

In July, 1869, they moved in. Since there was no road over the hill, semi-invalid Emily was pushed in a basket chair, younger son Lionel rode sidesaddle on a donkey, and the rest walked. They called the place Aldworth after the Berkshire village where Emily had lived.

Aldworth is a large, attractive house, even imposing in its own way, but in no sense massive. It looks as if the winds and rains have beaten upon it for years, as no doubt they have. Built of local sandstone and with a green slate roof, it is gothic in style, but with untypically large windows, and with a colonnaded porch so Tennyson could walk in bad weather. It also had a brand-new luxury—hot running water. Tennyson was so delighted he took three baths a day, racing down the stairs to dump pitchers of bath water on the new lawn—or sending it cascading out the window to the consternation of Emily sitting below.

All this grandeur provoked among the natives a less than ecstatic reaction to their new neighbor and his show-off "Gothic" mansion. The resident earl rode over one day to see it . . . was intercepted by a sign that said "No Tresspasers" . . . ejaculated "the bloody blighter can't even spell" . . . and went home. Thereafter Tennyson was left alone in the privacy he had sought.

He needed all the privacy he could get, for he had much to do. The crowning feature of Aldworth was its library upstairs—a large oblong room with tall windows providing him with a splendid view as he wrote. Although he was nearing sixty when the house was built, the writing went on apace: the later *Idylls of the King (The Holy Grail, Pelleas and Ettarre, Gareth and Lynette,* and *The Last Tournament)* . . . a number of plays like *Queen Mary* . . . and many shorter poems. And isolated as it was, Aldworth often had guests—among them Turgenev, George Eliot, and Henry James.

When Tennyson at last accepted a title in 1884, he included both his homes in the name he selected for himself, becoming Baron Tennyson of Aldworth and Farringford. And it was at Aldworth that he died in 1892 in an upstairs room, his Shakespeare in his hand and a full moon streaming in upon his face.

His son Hallam kept Aldworth until 1921, selling it at last to His Highness Sir Sayaji Rao Gaekwar, a maharaja of India. Since then it has had a variety of owners, including one who installed a rather good-looking bust of Tennyson that's still there in the garden. Originally it showed the poet's naked chest, but this was later changed to a more discreet—and Tennysonian—cape. During World War II the house was taken over by the Admiralty, the insides painted an "institution buff," and used, among other things, as a convalescent home.

Today Aldworth is once more an elegant private home, rehabilitated after long years by its present owners. It's still isolated, set well back from the road so a decent view in passing is hard to come by. But after all, that's what Tennyson built it for, isn't it—privacy.

South Harting Five Miles west of Midhurst, along the A 272, is Rogate; and at Rogate a little road—so little it has no number—runs off from the highway south, passing after three miles what there is of South Harting. And, just before you get to South Harting is the house that Anthony Trollope, easily the most prolific of Victorian novelists, leased in 1880. It was an act of commendable optimism. Trollope was sixty-five at the time—and the lease was for seventeen years.

Called North End House, later changed to The Grange, its current name, the place was made by joining two farmhouses together, but the present facade of white-painted brick conceals where the two were joined. A plaque on the house indicates someone named Crostlethwaite built it in 1800, but part of it had to be redone after a fire in 1840. It's a good-sized house, as it was in Trollope's day, with a long line of windows and doors that open on the lawn.

At the Grange, Trollope continued his steady pace of writing with *Kept in the Dark, The Fixed Period, Mr. Scarborough's Family, An Old Man's Love*, and *The Landleaguers*—an incredible performance for a man his age who had already written forty-two novels and countless short stories and articles. But, alas, the optimism of the lease signing was not to be justified. After only eighteen months, he died.

The Grange today is a handsome private home, but you can see it from the road.

Uppark Uppark is two miles southwest of South Harting and five miles southeast of Petersfield; and you come upon it suddenly—very suddenly—as you bounce and twist along the B 2146. Uppark now belongs to the National Trust and is open to the public in season. It has the stuff of at least half-a-dozen movies, including an "Upstairs-Downstairs" in which H. G. Wells and his mother would appear in real life roles—downstairs.

H. G. Wells's Uppark, West Sussex

By Courtesy of The National Trust

The first movie would star the builder of Uppark, a Lord Grey who, among other things, ran off with his eighteen-year-old sister-in-law, was sent to the Tower after an ill-planned plot against Charles II, fought (badly) for Monmouth's doomed rebellion, and was taken prisoner by James II. Even so, he managed to build Uppark. The date is uncertain, either 1685 or 1690. The setting was superb, high on the Downs, with a view as far as the coast beyond Chichester. Typically Queen Anne, the house is a two-storeyed, hip roofed, red brick, nearly square building with, as a 1694 passerby reported, "nine windows in ye front [on each floor] and seven in ye sides." Added in 1810–1813 were the north portico and the long connecting passage by which today's visitor enters.

Since Lord Grey, the house has had a number of other film-worthy inhabitants and guests. In 1746 a Matthew Fetherstonhaugh (FEATH-er-stone-haw) was living in blissful, bucolic obscurity when he was told that a distant kinsman had left him an enormous fortune on two conditions: he buy a baronetcy and a country seat. In no time at all he was Sir Matthew Fetherstonhaugh, Bart., of Uppark.

Sir Matthew's son Harry, himself no run-of-the-mill libertine and wastrel, was responsible for two of Uppark's more notable guests, Emma Hart and the Prince Regent. Emma, you see, who came in 1780 as an ignorant, fifteen-year-old unwed mother, was Sir Harry's mistress. She was to become the Lady Emma Hamilton who caught Lord Nelson's fancy. As for the Prince Regent, he came so often he had his own room and occasioned parties so lavish and bacchanalian guests had to be carried from the banqueting hall back to the main house in wheelbarrows.

When H. G. Wells's mother arrived as housekeeper in 1880, the owner of Uppark (Wells spelled it "Up Park," and some maps still give it that way) was Miss Frances Fetherstonhaugh. Only her name wasn't really Fetherstonhaugh, and she was just the uneducated daughter of the park keeper when her sister, the head dairy maid, married the aging Sir Harry and took Frances to live with her. Upon her sister's death, Frances Bullock inherited the place and changed her name.

Wells was thirteen years old when his mother took the housekeeping position—one a bit beyond her capabilitites—and twenty-six when she left. During these years, he was away from his mother most of the time as a grammar school and college student, teacher, and journalist. But he spent his vacations there, and one four-month convalescence at Uppark was particularly influential on his life. In between prowling the beech woods and the bracken dells, he filled in the great gaps, especially literary, in his education. He devoured books, from Spenser to Stevenson to Hawthorne, to "learn the elements of this writing business." And as he observed, he imitated—then burned the manuscripts. It was a priceless prelude to his writing career.

Uppark educated Wells in other ways. "My glimpses of life below stairs at Up Park," he said, "helped me to meet fresh social occasions with a certain ease." And he was unconsciously absorbing material for the novels he would write. This is particularly true of the semiautobiographical *Tono-Bungay* (1909), in which Uppark appears as Bladesover House, the "complete, authentic microcosm," with its 117 windows "looking on nothing but its own wide and handsome territories."

Uppark's Miss Frances Fetherstonhaugh, née Bullock, and her equally aged companion in their black velvet dresses become *Tono-Bungay*'s Lady Drew and cousin Miss Somerville, who lived "like dried up kernels in the great shell of Bladesover House," spending "whole days in the corner parlour just over the housekeeper's room, between reading and slumber and caressing their two pet dogs."

One of the novel's most hilarious episodes actually happened, "Coo-ees" and all, to Wells himself when he ran away from his draper's apprenticeship in Portsmouth one Sunday morning and fled back to Uppark. He had left without breakfast and walked the seventeen miles to come upon his unsuspecting mother and the whole Uppark staff on their way up the hill from church in South Harting. George Ponderevo in the novel tells what happened:

> Presently, down the hill, the servants appeared, straggling by twos and threes, first some of the garden people and the butler's wife with them, then the two laundry maids, odd inseparable old creatures, then the first footman talking to the butler's little girl, and at last, walking grave and breathless beside old Ann and Miss Fison, the black figure of my mother.
>
> My boyish mind suggested the adoption of a playful form of appearance. "Coo-ee, Mother!" said I, coming out against the sky, "Coo-ee!"

Wells reports that his mother was not amused. Nor was George's.

Uppark and other houses on the grounds are still lived in by descendants of Miss Frances's heirs, though the main house and much of the estate were given to the National Trust in 1954. From late spring to early fall, twelve of its rooms are open to the public for a fee (or N. T. card) and offer a lavish display of furniture, furnishings, and paintings, mainly of the eighteenth century. Of special interest to the literary minded are the ground floor saloon and the housekeeper's room in the basement.

The saloon is quickly identified as the one described in *Tono-Bungay*, and the visitor recognizes the immense chimneypiece (one of two) adorned with a "wolf and Romulus and Remus, with Homer and Virgil for supporters." And there is a big portrait of George III, though it is not "twice life-size" and Wells makes him the pre-king Prince of Wales. And there is a massive glass chandelier—one, though, not three.

The Housekeeper's room below, where Mrs. Wells wielded her limited scepter, is of appeal, too, giving, as it does along with the kitchen and butler's pantry, a fascinating look at the lower domain of the Upstairs-Downstairs kingdom. Tono-Bungay's George, like Wells himself, recalled sitting here of a winter's evening, warming his toes and sipping elder wine, and hearing the two old ladies bumping about over his head. And envying them not at all.

THE ISLE OF WIGHT

The Isle of Wight

1. The Right Little Isle: East
2. The Right Little Isle: West

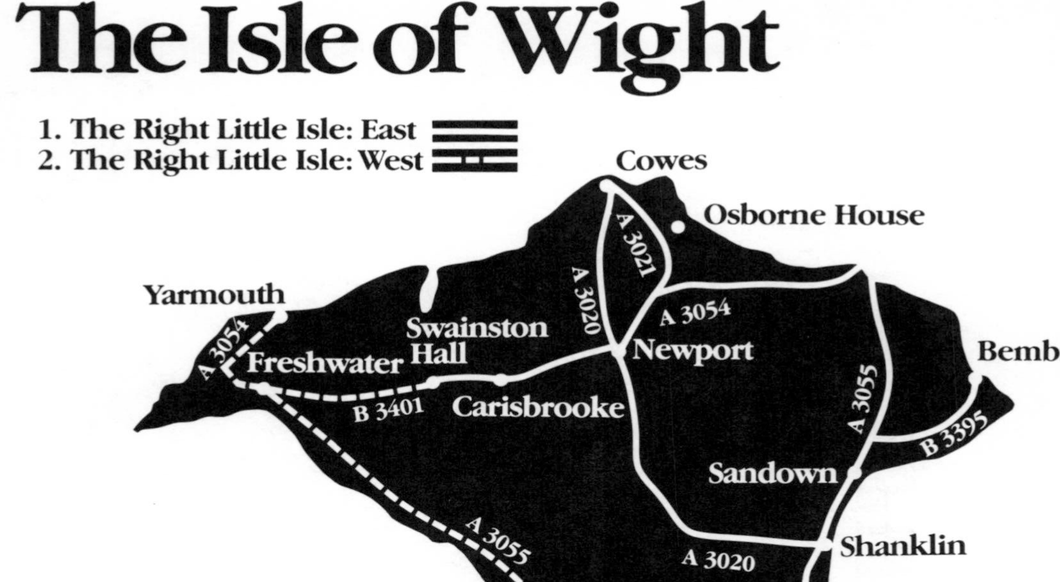

A little kingdom of serenity in this most troubled world.

Old Guide Book

If England has everything that's lovely and literate in miniature, the Isle of Wight has everything that England has—in miniature miniature. Even its literary pretensions are low key. Only twenty-three miles long from east to west and thirteen from north to south, it is shaped like a rough diamond. Its 94,000 acres—rolling now up to 787 feet, now down to the sea—are sheer heaven.

The island is separated from the mainland by the narrow waters of the Solent and is reached by ferry from Lymington, Southampton, or Portsmouth—the latter two within an hour of London by fast train. If it suits your itinerary, it's most fun to arrive by one ferry and leave by another. None takes over forty-five minutes.

With distances so short, the island is quickly and easily covered, even by bicycle, if your legs are stout. Places of literary interest divide conveniently into two halves—east and west—and are mainly on or near the coast, which is also where the chief highways are. The following tour arbitrarily begins in the east; you can just as easily reverse everything and begin in the west. If you plan right, you can even wind up sleeping in Tennyson's house. It is truly a tight, as well as right, little isle.

1. THE RIGHT LITTLE ISLE: EAST

Osborne House

This was Queen Victoria's favorite summer getaway for more than fifty of the last years of her life, and if Tennyson took the place seriously—and he surely did—so, perhaps, should we. Well, not too seriously. It's a grandiose, Italianate affair in the Palladian manner, with two 100-foot campanili, an upper floor loggia, and pseudo-Renaissance terraces. Basically, the Mediterranean Villa style was Albert's idea and, as someone has said, suggests he wished the Solent were really the Bay of Naples.

But it was Victoria's own house, as the grossly (in several ways) overstuffed interior attests. She built it in 1846–48 out of her personal savings, selected the 2,000 acre site, and had her husband's and children's well-being in mind in model housewifely fashion as she approved each detail . . . down to a Swiss chalet in which her youngsters could prepare practically for the days to come: the little princes learning carpentry, and the princesses, housekeeping and cooking.

Only twelve miles from Osborne House lived Alfred Tennyson; as the years passed he came there a number of times and grew to be a real friend to the lonely Queen. Her first invitation was in April, 1862. After her beloved Albert's death the previous December, she had found her greatest consolation in Tennyson's *In Memoriam.* Was there anything she could do for him?, she asked. There was: Would she shake his children's hands? Next year, the invitation was for the whole family. One such visit, in 1883, was particularly memorable. She gave the poet the rare privilege of not only sitting (not standing!) with her for the whole hour—but in the Prince Consort's own room. When the visit was over, she thanked him warmly and described their meeting in her journal at great length. Not long after came the offer of a barony, making him Alfred, Lord Tennyson.

After Victoria's death in 1901—it was at Osborne House—Edward VII lost no time in giving the place to the government. Much of it is now a state-run convalescent hospital. But Victoria's private quarters and the state rooms have been kept precisely as they were in her day and are open to the public in season, for a small fee. It's on the A 3021, just four miles northwest of Fishbourne Slipway, Ryde, where the Portsmouth ferry docks.

To see the Queen's sitting room, with its jumble of chintz upholstery and confusion of bric-a-brac—along with a life-sized marble statue of her favorite dog—is to see (if not salute) the Victorian Age as it was. And the Horn Room has to be seen to be believed, if then. Everything in it is made of antlers or other former attachments of a deer. The chair legs, for instance, are hooves. Real hooves.

Cowes—Newport—Carisbrooke

Cowes The island's northernmost point, Cowes is just two miles northwest of Osborne House. It stands at the head of the A 3020 and serves as the terminal of the Southampton ferry. Charles and Mary Lamb stayed here with a Captain Burney in 1803, and Lamb quickly proved he was no sailor.

On a jaunt to Newport by boat, he innocently cast loose the mast, sprit, sails, and all to go crashing into the sea. Lamb thereupon decided he didn't like his abode on the island: "Nothing in this house goes right till after supper; then a gentle circumambience of the weed [tobacco] serves to shut out Isle of Wight impertinent scenery."

Newport With 23,000 people one of the island's major cities, Newport is five miles south of Cowes, and on the Isle of Wight one could almost say "all roads lead to Newport." The A 3020 from the north and south, the A 3054 from the east and west, the B 3401 from the west, and the B 3323 from the southwest all take one to Newport.

Keats had lodgings here during a vacation in 1817, where he found somebody had scratched on a window pane: "O Isle spoilt by the Milatory." Keats wasn't enamoured of the place, either. He complained he could not get wholesome food and thought so much about poetry he "became not over capable in my upper stories." Even so, it was here that he began *Endymion*. And he was here again in the summer of 1819. He wrote Fanny Brawne, his sweetheart, "I do not pass a day without sprawling some blank verse or tagging some rhymes." He was working on, among other things, *Otho the Great*.

Carisbrooke Carisbrooke is only two miles southwest of Newport on the B 3401. Keats went there in 1817 because its central location made it a good headquarters for the walks he planned to take to all parts of the island. Also, he wanted to see Carisbrooke Castle, which had housed Charles I, first as an honored guest and then as a prisoner, before he was hauled off to London, trial, and death.

Keats was entranced with the castle: "I have not seen many specimens of Ruins—I don't think however I shall ever see one to surpass Carisbrooke Castle. The trench is o'ergrown with the smoothest turf, and the Walls with ivy—Keep within side is one Bower of Ivy—a Colony of Jackdaws have been there many years. I dare say I have seen many a descendant of some old cawer who peeped through the Bars at Charles the first, when he was there in Confinement."

He stayed at a Mrs. Cooke's, now Canterbury House, on the Castle Road; he could see the castle from his window. His first move was to arrange his books and swap the picture of a French ambassador in his room for a print of Shakespeare in the hall. Then he got down to working on *Endymion* and writing a sonnet, "On the Sea." But within a week he grew restless, complained of the food, and departed for Margate in Kent. Mrs. Cooke apparently didn't mind: she gave him the Shakespeare print to take with him.

Bembridge—Sandown—Shanklin

Bembridge It's nine miles east of Newport in a straight line—but you can't get to Bembridge in a straight line from anywhere. You have to get to the A 3055 somehow and then take the B 3395 east. However, if you have a passion for John Ruskin, it's worth going there. The Bembridge School has the greatest single collection of Ruskin's work in the world, including over 300 Ruskin drawings in water color and pen and pencil. You can locate the school by its tower, visible for miles, and it's safest to get in touch with the curator in advance.

Sandown On the A 3055, seven miles southeast of Newport, Sandown rates less than stellar billing in a book of this sort. Its collection of bars, bingo halls, hotels, and "B and B's" comes this side of a literary Valhalla. But it is blessed with a natural coastal beauty that has attracted visitors from David Garrick to Charles Darwin and Lewis Carroll. And for an extra fillip—brace yourself—Hall Caine wrote his first novel here.

Shanklin The A 3055 is the Isle of Wight's longest highway, girdling all but its upper extremities. And in its passage along the coast from eastern anchor to west, the next stop after Sandown is Shanklin. It's a pleasant little cliff-top town and drew the attention of both Keats and Longfellow.

Keats came to Shanklin first in 1817, but found it too expensive. He returned at the beginning of July, 1819, and initially was delighted with it. In a letter to Fanny Brawne, he wrote: "I am now at a very pleasant Cottage window, looking into a beautiful hilly country, with a glimpse of the sea: the morning is very fine." But cares and anxieties were closing in upon him from all sides. His finances were desperate. The threat of death from tuberculosis was a lengthening shadow. Marriage to Fanny, reason told him, was out of the question. "I have two luxuries to brood over in my walks," he wrote her, "your Loveliness and the hour of my death."

The specters that haunt his great sonnet, "When I Have Fears," seemed all too real in Shanklin. To defeat them he wrote at a furious pace. By July 12 alone, he had finished Act I of *Otho the Great*, the potboiler he hoped would solve his money problems, and the first 400 lines of *Lamia*. It was a heroic effort. The climate turned oppressive. His lodgings began to seem like a coffin. Said Keats, "I begin to dislike the very door posts here."

You can't blame him. Mrs. Eglantine's Cottage, No. 76 High Street, where he had an upstairs room, was a thin little two-storey bulding, but all that Keats could afford. And today—though the front part has been changed, and the former back door made the front—it still has a melancholy air about it. Though it boasts the names of both "The Eglantine" and "Keats

Hotel," it is only a "B&B" at best. One can stand before it, gazing at the commemorative plaque that bears his name, and ache for John Keats . . . age twenty-four and already fatally stricken.

Just down the High Street from the Eglantine is the Crab Inn, a two-storey stone and brick thatched building where Longfellow stayed in 1868. His verse, placed on a brick pillar from which trickles a spring, commemorates his visit:

O, traveller, stay thy weary feet;
Drink of this fountain pure and sweet;
It flows for rich and poor the same.
Then go thy way, remembering still
The wayside well beneath the hill,
The cup of water in His name.

Bonchurch

Further down the A 3055 and three miles south of Shanklin is Bonchurch, another charming little village perched above the sea. An impressive number of writers have enjoyed its beauties, among them Keats, Macaulay, Tennyson, Thackeray, Dickens, Swinburne, Hardy, and Anna Sewell, who wrote *Black Beauty*.

Tennyson came to Bonchurch a number of times, but the visit of 1850 was surely the one he would never forget. He got the scare of his life. He had gone up to his room to get the butcher-ledger-like book in which he had written the only copy of the "Elegies" on which he had been working for sixteen years, so that he could read a couple of poems to a local artist. But the book wasn't there. Alarmed, Tennyson wrote his friend, the poet Coventry Patmore. Had he borrowed it by any chance? If not, would he see if Tennyson had left it in the London lodgings he'd recently vacated? But hurry, please. Patmore dashed to the flat, brushed aside the startled landlady, and began a wild search. And there, at last, at the back of the cupboard where Tennyson kept his tea things, it was. The "Elegies," renamed *In Memoriam*, established Tennyson's reputation.

It was while in Bonchurch in 1853 that Tennyson heard of Farringford, near the western edge of the island. The following year he paid a return visit to Bonchurch, walking over the downs from Farringford, now his home, and returning along the seashore—an incredibly arduous thirty miles of ups and downs. But then, Tennyson did like to walk.

Charles Dickens, who usually summered in Kent, in 1849 rented one of Bonchurch's better houses, Winterbourne (now a two-star hotel with a great view of the sea). Dickens called it "a delightful and beautiful house," but he was even more enraptured with a small waterfall which he had a carpenter convert into a perpetual shower bath. Although he soon claimed the climate was ennervating, he did manage to do some work on *David Copperfield* here, perhaps thanks to those shower baths.

Playmate for Dickens's children was a twelve-year-old boy named Algernon, with a shock of flaming red hair. He and his parents, Admiral Charles and Lady Jane Swinburne, lived almost next door in East Dene (now a guest house). Young Swinburne came back to Bonchurch on school holidays every year until the family moved away in 1861, and he never lost his love for the cliffs and the "wonderful waters." The sea, particularly, provided recurring images for his poems.

On the slope of St. Boniface Down—the island's highest point and source of the "Bon" in the town's name—is the so-called "New" church. And, in its churchyard, in graves marked with grey stone near the gardenlike path, lie the Swinburne family, the poet among them. To this site came novelist Thomas Hardy, to pay homage. His poem, "A Singer Asleep," is a tribute to Swinburne and this spot where he is "pillowed eternally":

> In this fair niche above the unslumbering sea,
> That sentrys up and down all night, all day.

It is possible, however, that Bonchurch is no happier with having Swinburne's grave than Birchington is with Rossetti's. As late as the middle of this century, at least, a local guide book sniffed: "Algernon Charles Swinburne was endowed with the gift of song, but his use of it will always be questioned. . . . He had no stability of character and judgment, and was not fit to go about the world alone."

St. Lawrence

The last point on the A 3055's southeastern leg of its circumnavigation of the island, just before it turns upward and northwest, is St. Lawrence, today a well-to-do village with nearly subtropical vegetation. Its literary interest is indeed subdued, even for the Isle of Wight.

Here, at Lisle Combe, lived poet Alfred Noyes, from 1929 until his death in 1958. Most of his best poetry, mainly about the sea or fairyland, had already been done, but some of *The Torchbearers* (1922–30) was written here. One of Noyes's visitors was the novelist Hugh Walpole, who came in 1939. The visit, however, turned sour: when he began to praise James Joyce's *Ulysses*, Walpole was practically ordered out of the house.

2. THE RIGHT LITTLE ISLE: WEST

Had Queen Victoria ever considered sharing any of her power with another—something her eldest son Edward would be the first to describe as sheer fantasy—she might have kept the eastern half of the Isle of Wight for herself and given the western half to Tennyson. His is the dominating literary figure there. And ever since 1853, his Farringford has made Freshwater a mecca for tourists, lettered and unlettered alike.

Freshwater

Fourteen miles of the A 3055 stretch between St. Catherine's Point, at the island's most southern tip, and Freshwater near its most western. And what miles! Up and down you go, each rise providing a vista of the sea more breathtaking than the last, each dip plunging you back to the sea itself. And for a climax, as you reach Freshwater, there are the sheer chalk cliffs, abrupt and majestic as Dover's own. No wonder Tennyson was caught and held when he came this way, in 1853, from Bonchurch.

Farringford, the house that caught his eye, was a modest-sized late Georgian structure of yellow-tinged brick, standing on a rise and surrounded by farmland. To the north there was a fine view of the English coast, now hidden by trees. To the south was—and is—an enchanting look at Freshwater Bay and the rounded swell of St. Catherine's Down. Southward, between house and bay a mile away, rose High Down with its precipitous chalk face 500 feet above the sea.

The Tennysons moved in, in November, 1853, happy to be rid of the gapers who pestered them in Twickenham. For the next two and a half years they rented the place, but by April, 1856, profits from *Maud* and *In Memoriam* allowed them to buy it. While her husband toiled at *Idylls of the King*, Emily tore into the task of redoing Farringford—redecorating throughout, getting their stored furniture from London, and buying more where needed. While all this was going on, who should drop in, amid all the debris and confusion, but the Prince Consort. To make things worse, he was so charmed, he said, that he must bring the Queen herself over one day. Emily lived in terror until they had Farringford back in shape, but the Queen never came.

Emily's favorite room was the ground floor drawing room, with the splendid view of the bay and down that had caused Tennyson to take the house in the first place. Here she played the piano and entertained a parade of

Tennyson's Farringford, Isle of Wight

Robert M. Cooper

notable guests. The poet's favorite room was a small study in the attic, aptly dubbed the "fumitory." Here he wrote—though it was dark and harmful to his weak eyes—and here he took overnight guests to talk and smoke the night away after Emily had gone to bed. In 1858, however, Tennyson built a small summer house overlooking the fields and thereafter did much of his writing there. Later he added an upstairs study in the west wing.

The first important work written at Farringford was *Maud,* that rather murky monodrama of the Crimean War, done in late 1854 and early 1855. Farringford itself appears as where the orphaned hero is "living alone in an empty house/ Here half-hid in gleaming wood," within sound of "the scream of a madden'd beach dragg'd down by the wave." *Maud* was published in July, 1855, and greeted with widespread disapproval. One critic said one of the vowels ought to be dropped from its title—it didn't matter much which. But a spin-off from the Crimean War, written during a pause from *Maud*, a ballad inspired by a news item in the *Times*, was one of the most popular poems he ever wrote: "The Charge of the Light Brigade."

Tennyson was always a regular as well as a rapid writer, and the works flowed forth steadily, both here and in his summer home in Sussex, almost until the day he died. Beginning with "Merlin and Vivian" in 1856 came a succession of poems that wound up at various times as parts of *The Idylls of the King,* as well as countless shorter poems from "Enoch Arden" (1864) to "Death of Oenone" (1892), and a stream of plays.

But Farringford was a place of fun as well as of work, and he always found time to romp with his sons, take long walks (up to thirty miles) on the downs or along the beach, and to entertain guests. The two boys often accompanied their father on his walks, and he sometimes rowed them and the maids around the Needles, three prongs of chalk rising out of the sea to a height of 100 feet. Another favorite sport with them was flying kites from Farringford's roof.

At first the Tennysons had no carriage. Visitors had to walk the three miles from the Yarmouth ferry, leaving luggage for the gardener to fetch in a donkey cart. But, from the Prince Consort down, they came anyway. In time entertaining reached such proportions that the Tennysons had to have a housekeeper, butler, lady's maid, cook, kitchen maid, two footmen, housemaids, coachmen, grooms and gardeners.

The *Rubaiyat's* Edward Fitzgerald, Arthur Clough of "Thyrsis" fame, and Coventry Patmore were early guests, Patmore bringing the manuscript of his *The Betrothal.* Lewis Carroll came uninvited and caught Tennyson cutting the grass. Actress Ellen Terry came as a bewildered child bride. Queen Emma of the Sandwich Islands came and required a throne in the garden made of great ilex. Thomas Woolner, the sculptor, came with a story that grew into

"Enoch Arden." Arthur Sullivan came with music to put to a Tennyson song cycle ("The Window"). And Jenny Lind came to sing.

Swinburne came as a second year student at Oxford, listened to the poet read *Maud*, and patiently heard his advice to study Virgil intensely. As a result, Tennyson thought the young man very modest and intelligent and "particularly admired him" for not pressing any of his own verses upon the laureate.

Edward Lear, artist and writer of limericks and nonsense verse, was a frequent and welcome guest. He adored Emily and once raved about her as the distillation of angel-woman-philosopher-minor prophet-doctor-school mistress in one. In turn, the Tennysons were very fond of Lear, especially enjoying his singing and playing at Emily's piano, often doing Tennyson's poems set to his own music.

Today you can sit in the very drawing room where Emily entertained all these notables and relish the very view they relished. For Farringford is now a hotel, and it is a good one (three stars). This room, now a lounge, is only one of the many reminders of Tennyson the hotel provides. The dining room was his children's playroom. His upstairs library, where he wrote so much, is now the television room and lounge and houses his cap, cloak and scarf, clay pipes, spirit flask, and microscope. It was in this room that in 1890 Tennyson recorded some of his poems for Thomas Edison. At one end of the room is an arched door leading to turret stairs that wound down into the garden. It was Tennyson's secret escape hatch when he heard visitors coming up the regular stairs.

The hotel has four bedrooms in what used to be Tennyson's attic, where the fumitory was. In the hall outside fixed against the wall beneath a narrow window, there is still a ladder with four or five steps. Tennyson used it to climb out on the roof to a platform he had built between the "V" of the roof slants so that he could study the stars—and fly his kite.

While staying at the hotel, the ambitious can duplicate one of Tennyson's favorite walks—a mild word for an awesome undertaking—and climb High (now "Tennyson") Down. Atop it is the Tennyson Monument, a large Iona cross of granite, visible for miles.

Tennyson died in 1892, and is, of course, buried in Westminster Abbey. But Freshwater's All Saints Church has seven memorials to the Tennysons. Emily is buried in the churchyard by the east wall. And there is a stone honoring the poet. It says his happiest days were spent at Farringford and adds:

> Speak, living voice, with thee death is not death;
> Thy life outlives the life of dust and breath.

One of Tennyson's favorite neighbors, Julia Margaret Cameron, an outstanding woman photographer, was far more attentive to the poet's needs than he cared for. Once she badgered him so much to have a vaccination that he finally gave in—and was sick for six months. As it happened, she was also the great aunt of Virginia Woolf, and Virginia knew Freshwater, having stayed there as a girl with another aunt.

In 1923, largely for her own amusement Virginia wrote a play called *Freshwater*. It's a hilarious spoof about Tennyson, Mrs. Cameron, and the painter George Frederick Watts and his bride, Ellen Terry. When they came to Farringford in 1864, Watts was forty-seven; his bride was sixteen. Virginia and her friends finally got around to staging the play in 1935 in her sister Vanessa's London studio. Vanessa and Virginia's husband Leonard played Mr. and Mrs. Cameron.

Swainston Hall

Six miles east along the Newport Road (the B 3399–3401) from Freshwater, just before you reach the village of Calbourne, lies what's left of Swainston Hall (pr. "Swanston"). Here, in 1853, lived Sir John Simeon, a hearty fox-hunting squire, who quickly became one of Tennyson's closest friends. Many a night found them at Farringford or Swainston, talking and smoking for hours. When Sir John died, Tennyson wrote a poem in his honor, "Swainston," calling him "Prince of Courtesy," and saying: "Three dead men have I loved, and thou art last of three."

Sir John is credited with urging Tennyson to write *Maud,* and his mansion figures in the poem as the heroine's: "on the landward side, by a red rock, glimmers the hall," with its mighty cedars "sighing for Lebanon." And the grounds inspired what may well qualify as the most banal lines Tennyson ever wrote:

> Come into the garden, Maud,
> For the black bat, night, has flown.

The eighteenth-century hall itself burned in a WW II air raid, but a thirteenth-century oratory remains and can be seen from the road.

Yarmouth

Yarmouth is barely two miles northeast of Freshwater via the A 3054, and its ferry to Lymington provides a pleasant half-hour trip back to the mainland. Contrary to England's pub hours, while the boat is in passage the bar is open, even as early as 6 A. M. and as late as 11 P. M.

Tennyson used this ferry regularly to go between his two homes, Farringford and Aldworth. On one such trip, in the fall of 1889, on the Lymington-to-Yarmouth leg, into his head sprang the lines:

> Sunset and evening star
> And one clear call for me!

Indeed they, and all the rest of the poem, "came in a moment," he said. Traditionally, "Crossing the Bar" comes at the close of any Tennyson section of an anthology. It seems appropriate to end with it here, as we quit the little Kingdom of Serenity that he loved so well.

HAMPSHIRE

Hampshire

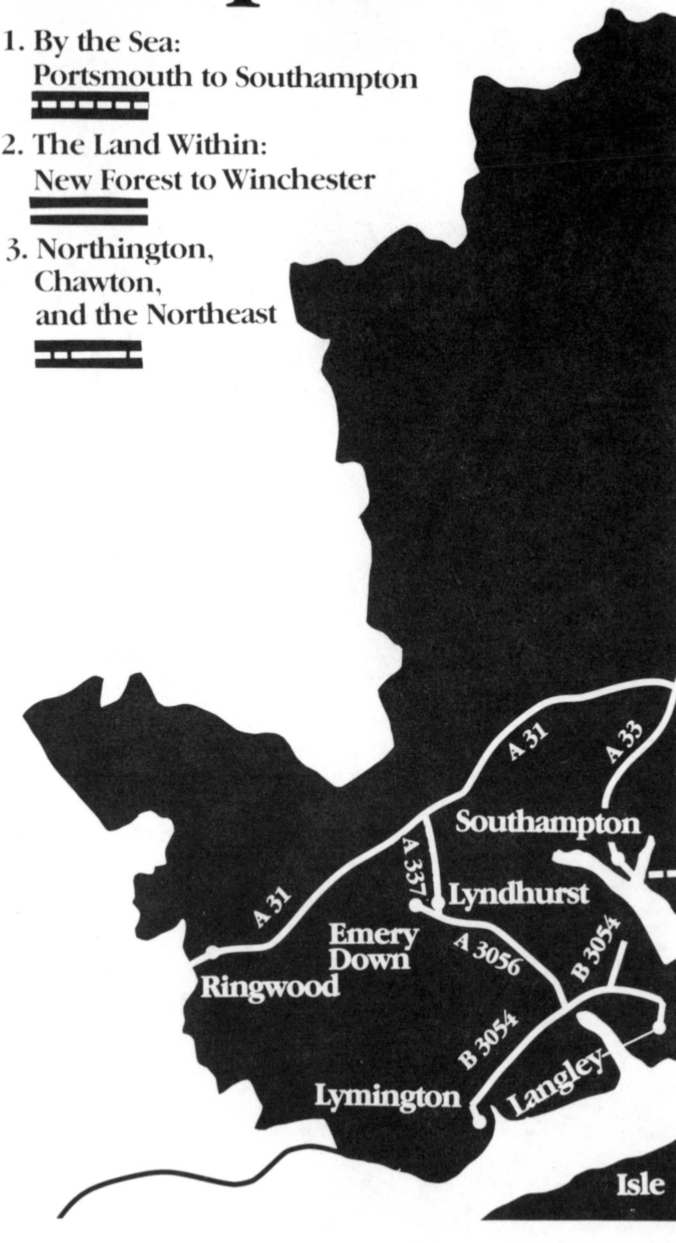
1. By the Sea:
Portsmouth to Southampton
2. The Land Within:
New Forest to Winchester
3. Northington,
Chawton,
and the Northeast
A 31
A 33
Southampton
A 337
Lyndhurst
A 31
Emery
Down
A 3056
B 3054
Ringwood
B 3054
Langley
Lymington
Isle

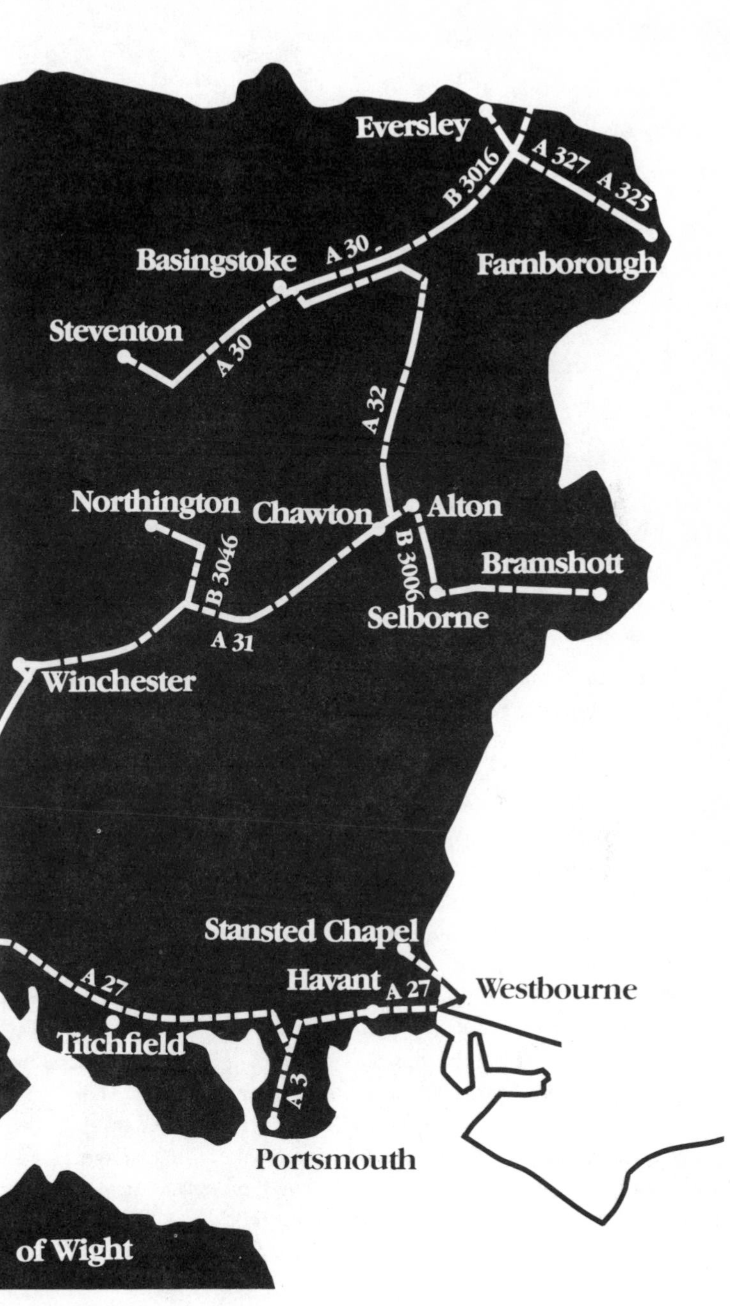
Eversley
A 327
A 325
B 3016
A 30
Basingstoke
Farnborough
Steventon
A 30
A 32
Northington
Chawton
Alton
B 3046
B 3006
Bramshott
Selborne
A 31
Winchester
Stansted Chapel
Havant
A 27
Westbourne
A 27
Titchfield
A 3
Portsmouth
of Wight

> "How beautiful the season is now—How fine the air. A temperate sharpness about it. Really, without joking, chaste weather—Dian skies—I never lik'd stubble fields so much as now—Aye better than the chilly green of the Spring. Somehow a stubble plain looks warm—in the same way that some pictures look warm—This struck me so much in my Sunday's walk that I composed upon it."
>
> John Keats

What Keats composed was his immortal "Ode to Autumn"—a Hampshire autumn. For Hampshire rivals the two Sussexes for natural beauty. If the beauty contest Paris had to judge had been among these three counties rather than three godesses, he would have been even more sorely tried than he was.

Wedged between Surrey and West Sussex on the east and Wiltshire and Dorset on the west and resting atop the English Channel, Hampshire is 1,500 square miles of loveliness and anomaly. Its New Forest is 900 years old. Its genuine one-and-only Round Table was built more than 700 years after Arthur's death—if there was an Arthur. Its abbreviation is "Hants.," but nobody who lives there will tell you why. Cricket was born there, and so was Charles Dickens. Americans can understand Charles Dickens.

A tidy way to explore Hampshire's places of interest—and there are a number—is to organize your investigation in two parts. First, make a trek by the sea from Portsmouth (overflowing with writers-to-be, most of them unhappy) to Lymington (Tennyson) and then make a circular sweep of the land within, with Winchester as the hub. You'll meet Jane Austen coming, going, and in between—but there are others, too.

I. BY THE SEA, BY THE SEA: PORTSMOUTH TO SOUTHAMPTON

Standsted Chapel—Bedhampton

The year 1819 was John Keats's *annus mirabilis,* the wonder year that —though he was only twenty-four—saw most of his great poems written. He began the year with visits to Standsted and Bedhampton. Both left their mark on his work.

Standsted Chapel On the grounds of Standsted House, just inside the Hampshire boundary with West Sussex and about four miles northeast of Havant, this chapel had as curious an origin as any connected with the Anglican Church. It was built from a fifteenth-century hunting lodge core by a Lewis Way for the purpose of converting Jews to Christianity—a project on which he had already spent £100,000. Its style was Gothic à la Regency. To its dedication on January 25, 1819, came, among others, John Keats.

Keats had recently been in Chichester, whose cathedral and atmosphere had reinforced his love for the medieval that, even at that moment, was finding expression in "Eve of St. Agnes." Standsted supplied additional material and inspiration. The chapel had stained glass triple-arched windows in the nave, with family scutcheons, rosy shields, and diamond panes. And the house, open to the public for the occasion, offered great tapestry rooms, a wainscoted saloon, and an oak room with fine paneling. Under Keats's "magic hand of chance," the various details merge:

> A casement high and triple-arch'd there was,
> All garlanded with carven imag'ries
> Of fruits, and flowers, and bunches of knot grass,
> And diamonded with panes of quaint device,
> Innumerable of stains and splendid dyes,
> As are the tiger-moth's deep-damask'd wings;
> And in the midst, 'mong thousand heraldries,
> And twilight saints, and dim emblazonings,
> A shielded scutcheon blush'd with blood of queens and kings.
>
> Stanza XXIV, "The Eve of St. Agnes"

The chapel, still occasionally used for services, is not normally open to the public. It can be seen lying far back from the road—but even the road (unnumbered) is hard to get to from Westbourne, the nearest village.

Bedhampton On the A 27, Bedhampton is a village adjoining Havant on the eastern edge of Hampshire. Keats came here twice. His first visit was in January, 1819, when he and his friend Charles Brown walked the thirteen miles from Chichester to stay with Mrs. John Snooks, sister of another friend. The Snooks lived in the Old Mill House, and normally Keats would have loved the story that went with it. For in the eighteenth century, it seems, the mill had always enjoyed phenomenal prosperity, even when the milling business was abominable. And, if among the sacks of grain that entered the mill and the sacks of flour that left, a sack or two of tobacco or other contraband should find their way, who was there to notice?

Keats's visit, however, was plagued by a "sore throat"—actually a preliminary of the tuberculosis soon to destroy him—and he left the mill only once, to ride over to Standsted Chapel. This unwilling retirement, though, bore the richest of fruit. While staying at the mill Keats finished "The Eve of St. Agnes," an event now commemorated by a plaque on the house erected by the Keats-Shelley Association.

In September of 1820, Keats by chance was at the mill again. He was en route to Italy, feeling that another winter in England would kill him. When contrary winds forced his ship to put into Portsmouth, just seven miles from Bedhampton, Keats seized the opportunity of visiting the Snooks. It was to be his last night in England.

Portsmouth

Portsmouth is the sort of city that seems interminable—and is. It's a big (well over 200,000 people) sprawling place that offers more pleasure in the getting there than the arrival. It is splendidly accessible via the good A 3 highway from London (and one-hour trains). . . the equally good A 27 from east and west along the Channel coast. . . and by Hovercraft and ferry from the Isle of Wight. Four of the nineteenth-century's top novelists spent some of their earlier days in Portsmouth—and three of them managed to be fairly miserable about it.

The city is actually four towns in one. In the southwest is Portsmouth proper, where the military is concentrated. The northwest is Portsea, with England's largest naval station and 500 acres of royal dockyard where you can visit Nelson's flagship "Victory." The northeast is Landport, where the dockyard people and artisans live. And the southeast is Southsea, the better residential quarter and watering place. Portsmouth can claim a number of literary associations, real and fictional. Unfortunately, however, Portsmouth suffered horibly from the WWII blitz—ninety percent of its buildings were destroyed or hit—and therefore few actual landmarks remain for you to see. In one that does remain, Charles Dickens was born.

By 1800 the threat of invasion by Napoleon had made the British navy a booming business. Portsmouth was particularly affected, new districts popping up outside the city walls to house the swelling dockyard population. One such was Landport, in the northeast adjacent to Portsea. To No. 1 Mile End Terrace—it was the end of a mile from Portsmouth's main gate—in the summer of 1809 came John Dickens with his new bride. He was a naval pay clerk and had just been transferred from the London office. His pay was only £110 a year—and for No. 1 Mile End Terrace he was paying £35 rent. He was already deep into his lifelong role of Mr. Micawber.

What Mr. Dickens got for his money was the southernmost of four attached red brick houses, each two storeys, with a neat paneled door between narrow white pilasters, two windows to the right on each floor, and a dim attic with one low rectangle window in its sloping roof. On the ground floor were a lounge and a dining room, and upstairs, two small bedrooms. A tiny attic room housed the maid; the kitchen and storage were in the semibasement.

In one of the upstairs bedrooms, on February 7, 1812, just before dawn, was born Charles John Huffman Dickens. His mother had been out all night dancing and barely made it home. Charles was her first son. He was to have few memories of the place, however. Following a pattern that was to plague all Charles's early years, his father began a series of financial slides downward, each marked by a dwelling lesser than the last. Five months after Charles was born the family was at No. 16 Hawke St., in a meaner section of Portsea, with no front yard, a cramped little sitting room, and a bay window that actually hung over the paving stones. By the end of 1814 they were back in London.

Next time Charles Dickens saw Portsmouth it was 1838 . . . he was twenty-six and the celebrated author of the *Pickwick Papers* and *Oliver Twist* . . . and was doing research for *Nicholas Nickleby*. He was back in 1859 on a reading tour. But, strangely enough, it wasn't until 1866, on another reading tour, that he took the trouble to seek out Mile End Terrace. And then he couldn't ascertain which of the four houses was his.

Research has since established precisely which house it was, and in which bedroom he was born. Providentially the house was bought by the Portsmouth Corporation in 1903 and now houses excellent Dickens memorabilia. In 1968 it was thoroughly renovated and imaginatively transformed into the kind of place it must have been when the novelist was born there—the Regency-furnished home of a young couple struggling for middle-class status, with a few finer pieces reflecting wedding gifts from Mrs. Dickens's more affluent relatives.

The bed canopy and hangings, the wallpapers and carpets were specially made for the restoration of this house. The couch in one bedroom is the very couch on which Dickens died at Gads Hill. On the wall of the other bedroom, appropriately enough, is a quotation from Carlyle, to whom Dickens was devoted: "Man of genius! Hast thou any notion what a man of genius is? Genius is the inspired gift of God." And the dresser in the kitchen basement was indubitably the Dickens's: it had been firmly built into the wall when the house was constructed and couldn't be removed.

The whole house, except the attic, is open to the public year round for a modest fee. The street is now called Old Commercial Road, and the house is 393. The area is well posted with directional signs; so it's easy to find.

Dickens had Nicholas Nickleby come to Portsmouth as a member of Mr. Vincent Crummles's tatterdemalion acting company. The Theatre Royal in the High Street was demolished in Dickens's lifetime, and you'll search in vain for Mr. Crummles's lodgings in St. Thomas's Street, with the ship mast in the back yard. But a number of houses from Nicholas's day survive on the Common Hard, where he and Smike had two small rooms—"pernicious snug"—over a tobacconist's shop.

George Meredith was born in Portsmouth in 1828, sixteen years after Dickens, at 73 High Street. The house, standing just where the street begins to curve toward the Point, was then a spacious old red brick, red-tiled building, though at a later date a stucco front was put on over the brick. Meredith's grandfather, Melchizedek Meredith, had been a prominent and prosperous naval outfitter (tailor), and George's father purported to carry on the business, which was on the ground floor. The family lived upstairs: from their parlor window, young Meredith could see the Isle of Wight.

His earliest days must have been happy ones. But his mother, whom he adored, died when he was five, and his father carried on an affair with the housekeeper whom George despised. Moreover, George was a lonely boy, holding aloof from the neighboring children. Their school was the lowly, nearby Frost's; he went to St. Paul's. They retaliated by calling him "Gentleman Georgy." And to top it all, the family fortunes that had been slipping steadily downward since his mother's death, crashed utterly in 1838 when he was ten. Mr. Meredith was hailed up to London and bankruptcy, and George was consigned to relatives in the Hampshire countryside. His adult view of his father is understandable: "a muddler and a fool."

In later life Meredith deliberately obscured his Portsmouth origins. Told in the 1901 census that he must indicate where he was born, he said, "Well, say Petersfield"—twenty miles away. And as for his income: "Don't call me Author. Put in 'private means'." Nevertheless, Meredith made considerable use of his Portsmouth background, especially in *Evan Harrington* (1860). In this novel the grand-mannered tailor, "the great Mel," is obviously his own grandfather Melchizedek, and Lymport is Portsmouth itself.

Meredith and Dickens may have been somewhat unhappy in Portsmouth. But Rudyard Kipling and H. G. Wells were downright wretched. And if in later life, after they became friends, Kipling and Wells ever argued about which of the two was the more miserable there, Kipling might well have won, if only because he came younger and stayed longer. He was not quite six when his father and mother brought him and his three-year-old sister to a house in Campbell Road, Southsea, where a retired naval couple provided lodgings for children of Englishmen living in India.

Without preparing the children in any way, without even a goodbye, the Kiplings slipped off secretly, leaving Rudyard feeling abandoned. He was there for the next five-and-a-quarter years, and his unhappiness was acute. He called it the "House of Desolation," and his misery is reflected in the haunting short story, "Baa Baa, Black Sheep," in which Kipling himself is the black sheep, the despised, beaten, tortured boy, Punch.

Herbert George Wells was fourteen when, in 1881, he conveyed his small portmanteau "with sinking heart" to Mr. Edwin Hyde's Southsea Drapery Emporium in Kings Road—the kind of sweatshop for which Portsmouth was then infamous. Indentured as an apprentice for four years, he stuck it out for nearly two, each day more wretched than the one before. It was little better than slavery, and crushingly boring slavery at that, with "freedom" at the end represented by a detested career as a draper.

At sixteen young Wells could stand it no longer. One Sunday morning, before breakfast, he simply disappeared, walking the seventeen miles to Uppark to enact that scene so hilariously presented in *Tono-Bungay* (1909), popping out at his mother and shouting "Cooee, Mother."

Portsmouth and the Drapery's major contribution to Wells's writing, however, was *Kipps* (1905), the jolly, uncomplicated novel that perhaps was his best. Kipps was drawn from a fellow apprentice, a boy, says Wells in his autobiography, with "an amusing simplicity of mind, a carelessness of manner, a way of saying "Oo-er," and a feather at the back of his head."

In *Kipps*, Wells gives a devastating account of the boy's thirteen-hour days:

> His round began at half-past six in the morning, when he would descend, unwashed and shirtless, in old clothes and a scarf, and dust boxes and yawn, and take down wrappers and clean the windows until eight. Then in half an hour he

> would complete his toilet, and take an austere breakfast of bread and margarine and what only an Imperial Englishman would admit to be coffee, after which refreshment he ascended to the shop for the labours of the day.

Finally, at nine at night, Kipps (Wells) had a supper of bread and cheese and watered beer. And then "the rest of the day was entirely at his disposal." Wells had little reason to love Portsmouth.

One morning in July, 1882, a young doctor put a brass plate on the railing of No. 1 Bush Villas, Elm Grove, Southsea, announcing his first practice. After midnight that night, he crept out to polish it himself so that the neighbors wouldn't know he was too poor to afford a maid. It was a narrow but fine red brick house. But the upstairs windows facing the street were always kept curtained to keep the neighbors from discovering that only two rooms in the whole three-storey structure were furnished: a consulting room on the ground floor, and one bedroom upstairs with odds and ends bought at auction, including a bed but no mattress. The name on the brass plate? Doyle—Conan Doyle (without the "Arthur" then).

Doyle did have a bebuttoned page boy to open the door for his customers: his ten-year-old brother Innes. By eating bread, potted meat, and bacon cooked over a gas ring in the back room, the pair of them could get by on a shilling a day, which was a good thing. For the customers came slowly. And when they came, Innes was wont to let his enthusiasm run away with him. Typical was the time he opened the door to find a woman whose flourishing figure promised business, and soon. Up the stairs went Innes's piping voice: "Arthur! Hooray! It's another baby!"

It was in this house that Sherlock Holmes was born, making his first appearance in *A Study in Scarlet*, along with Dr. Watson, modeled after a Portsmouth doctor-friend of Doyle's with that name. It was a short novel—only 200 pages—and Doyle began it in March and finished it in April of 1886. By May it had already been rejected in a way that must have doubled the sting: So interesting, said the editor, he'd kept it an unusually long time because he wanted to finish it. But a "shilling dreadful" all the same—and both too long and too short for his magazine. Several more rejections came, but at last it was published in 1887, and one of the best known characters in all of literature was launched—ironically because an editor's wife liked the book.

In time, Doyle managed to afford a study at the top of the house, with light blue wallpaper and a bear's skull on his desk. Writing began to take over. By the time he left, in 1890, to go to Vienna to study the eye, Dr. Doyle of No. 1 Bush Villas had also written *Micah Clarke* (1889), *The Sign of Four*

(1890) and *The White Company* (1891) and was no longer polishing his own brass plate.

Titchfield

"Others abide our question," Matthew Arnold wrote of Shakespeare. "Thou art free. We ask and ask—" and nothing happens. There are a number of puzzling questions about Shakespeare still to be resolved. Titchfield—an undemanding little town on the B 3334, midway between Portsmouth and Southampton—may have the key to one such question, asked repeatedly and answered all too variously: When Shakespeare wrote in Sonnet 18,

> Shall I compare thee to a summer's day?
> Thou art more lovely and more temperate,

who was the young man he was asking? Did he once live in what is now the ruined splendor of Titchfield Abbey? It's as tenable a theory as any other.

That the onetime Abbey, then a great manor house, was owned by one of Shakespeare's dearest friends and benefactors is indisputable. He was Henry Wriothesley, third Earl of Southampton. To him Shakespeare lovingly dedicated *Venus and Adonis* (1593) and *The Rape of Lucrece* (1594). Only twenty then, Southampton was, like the young man in the sonnets, greatly gifted, extraordinarily handsome, and reluctant to marry. Even, say some, give his initials a twist and you get "W. H.," initials of the mysterious "only begetter" so teasingly mentioned in the sonnets' dedication. Southampton, master of Titchfield, might indeed be the poet's beloved.

But if Southampton was in fact the third leg of the Shakespeare—Dark Lady—Young Man triangle, there's more than a little irony here. For the grandfather of the man Shakespeare thought so far above him socially was a parvenu and a Tudor carpetbagger. As assistant to Thomas Cromwell in carrying out Henry VIII's dissolution of the monasteries, Thomas Wriothesley furnishes a masterful sixteenth-century case history of how such Algerian traits as ability and ambition—plus a bit of ruthlessness, cunning, and greed—spell success. In 1538 he was Master Wriothesley . . . in 1540, Sir Thomas . . . in 1544, Baron Titchfield . . . and in 1547, Earl of Southampton, thanks to the titles passed 'round by the council appointed to govern for the boy king, Edward VI. Wriothesley was one of the council.

Helping Henry wreck the monasteries had other rewards, too: Wriothesley got one of them for his own—the Premonstratensian abbey at Titchfield, dating from 1232. He quickly transformed it into a great mansion, pulling down and selling for building materials what he didn't want. He kept the monks' frater (refectory) as his great hall, and built his gatehouse into the nave opposite, much of which he retained as domestic apartments. By 1543 one passerby reported:

> Mr. Wriothesley hath builded a right stately house embateled and having a goodely gate and a conducte [conduit] casteled in the midle of the court of it, yn the very same place where the late monasterie of Premonstrateneses stoode, caullyd Tichfelde.

Wriothesley called it Place House.

The converted nave and Tudor Gatehouse are the chief parts of the ruins that remain today, open to visitors regularly for a slight fee (not National Trust). They're pleasant ruins, especially for the nonbuff: easily negotiated, quickly seen, and guaranteeing a good photo or two. Besides, you can feel that you're treading where Shakespeare trod. For in his dedications, Shakespeare speaks of his indebtedness to the earl for recent favors, which certainly would include his hospitality; and plays like *Twelfth Night* suggest that Shakespeare was no stranger to great country homes. Very likely, then, Shakespeare was at Titchfield at least a time or two in the 1590's; so some of the sonnets were probably written there, and perhaps one or more of his earliest plays, such as *Love's Labor's Lost.*

It's tempting to go further, and wonder if maybe Place House had even a showing or two of the comedies suitable for staging at a manor and flattering to a courtly audience. But that would be to "ask and ask" indeed.

Southampton

In the magic of Shakespeare's theater, the trip from London to Southampton is accomplished in one short breath of Chorus:

> The King is set from London, and the scene
> Is now transported, gentles, to Southampton
>
> *Henry V*, Prologue Act II

We, in our mundane modern world, must negotiate the seventy-seven miles by train (fast and regular) or by car (arriving via the A 33). There are also M-ways from the east and west. But the most fitting way to approach Southampton, perhaps, is by water—via hydrofoil, say—from the Isle of Wight.

For Southampton has been best known for centuries as one of England's finest ports, thanks in part to the fact that its harbor enjoys a double tide, first by way of the Solent, followed two hours later by one from Spithead.

Southampton saw Richard the Lion-Hearted go forth to the Crusades in the Holy Land and Henry V depart for victory at Agincourt. From its docks sailed the Mayflower to settle a new world and the Titanic to meet disaster.

In the eighteenth century the city attracted such visitors as Pope, Gray, and Voltaire. And born there were two of the century's most popular writers of songs: Isaac Watts and Charles Dibdin. Dibdin was an actor, dramatist, and novelist, as well as a writer of show tunes. Several of the latter figured in a production of Shakespeare, fantastic even in a century noted for its high-handed "improvements" of the playwright. In Kilkenny, Ireland, in 1793, was staged "the tragedy of Hamlet, originally written and composed by the celebrated Dan Hayes of Limerick, and inserted in Shakespeare's works."

The program goes on to announce that the characters would be dressed in Roman costumes, and "the parts of the King and Queen, by the direction of the Rev. Mr. O'Callaghan, will be omitted, as being too immoral for any stage." Best of all, Ophelia would sing several of Mr. Dibdin's latest hits from his London revue, *The Oddities,* including "The Lass of Richmond Hill" and "We'll All be Happy Together."

In the nineteenth century Jane Austen came, in 1805, to live in Southampton for the next four years, first in lodgings, then in "a commodious old-fashioned house in a corner of Castle Square." John Keats stopped briefly in 1817 to comment dryly: "I know nothing of this place but that it is long—tolerably broad—has by streets—two or three churches—a very respectable old Gate with two lions to guard it—the men and women do not materially differ from those I have been in the Habit of Seeing." He goes on, "the Southampton water when I saw it just now was no better than a low-water Water which did no more than answer my expectations—it will have mended its Manners by 3."

William Makepeace Thackeray's view of Southampton was hardly that lighthearted. He came there as a six-year-old schoolboy and was wretched: "What a dreadful place that private school was," he said later, "cold, chilblains, bad dinners, not enough victuals, and caning awful!"

Southampton is another of those English towns that accommodate the visitor with literary interests in the kindest sort of way. Everything to be seen is nicely laid out along High Street (which for its northern half adopts the alias of Above Bar Street). A pleasant and leisurely stroll covers it all. If you have a car to dispose of first, there's even a car park near the Tourist Information Centre where High Street switches names, and that's a convenient place to start the walk.

From this spot to the bottom of High Street pretty much covers the highlights of the ill-starred end of Richard, Earl of Cambridge, Lord Scroop of Masham, and Sir Thomas Grey of Northumberland, that Shakespeare presents so swiftly and dramatically in *Henry V.* First stop is the Northern Bar Gate, built by the Normans—Keats's "very respectable old Gate" with the two lions on guard. One can't miss it: it's just south of where Hanover Buildings runs into High Street, and it's so big the arch has a passageway sixty feet deep. Before this gate, the trio were summarily executed for treason after being found guilty of plotting with France against the King, and their heads suspended from the wall above.

A few blocks further down the street (south) immediately past Bernard Street and on the left is the Red Lion Inn, a late medieval timber building and Southampton's oldest pub. Inside is a handsome half-timbered bar known as the Henry V Court Room, where the three traitors were supposed to have been tried and convicted. If, indeed, they did get a trial, it was news to Shakespeare. He simply has Henry turn to the three—smile on face, no doubt—and ask whom he has lately appointed royal commissioners. Why, here we are, they say. Great, says the King, and here are your commissions. What he hands them, instead, is their death sentence. Not the highest kind of justice, to be sure—but you can't beat it for dramatic punch.

Continue to the end of High Street, to the left near Town Quay, and you come to the final scene of the piece, the chapel of God's House. Under its floor the bodies of the luckless three were buried. Originally, three black marble flags marked their graves, but these disappeared somewhere along the way. In 1766 the 1st Earl of Delaware placed a tablet on the south wall that says:

> Richard, earl of Cambridge, Lord Scrope of Masham, Sir Thomas conspired to murder Henry V in this town as he was preparing to sail with his army against Charles VI of France, for which conspiracy they were buried near this place in the year MCCCCXV

Since the sixteenth century, the chapel has been used as a French Protestant church.

Continuing west along Town quay, you come to Mayflower Park and a bit beyond it, West Gate. This is Pilgrim country. Through the West Gate the Pilgrim Fathers filed to board the Mayflower and the Speedwell, an event duly celebrated in the park by a fifty-foot monument of Portland stone. Since the Speedwell was dismissed at Plymouth as unseaworthy, leaving only the Mayflower to make the trip to the New World, one is all the more amazed at the numbers claiming descent from these dauntless few—and awed by their ancestors' virility. John Alden, by the way, was a Southampton man.

Back at the Bar Gate, one goes north through the shopping precinct and up Above Bar Street to reach Isaac Watts's domain. Challenged to name the five leading writers of the eighteenth century, few would dream of including Watts. But if by "leading" one means having effect on future generations, Watts may single-handedly surpass any quintet of the century you might come up with.

What did Pope or Swift or Dr. Johnson ever write that has such powerful impact on people today as Watts's "O God, our help in ages past" or "Jesus shall reign"? Johnson was perhaps righter than he knew when he said in his *Life* of Watts "he has provided instruction for all ages." Few of our modern intelligentsia have even heard of it, perhaps, but Watts's *Divine and Moral Songs, for the Use of Children* has sold over seven million copies since he wrote it in 1720, even if it does invite the parodist with such gems as:

How doth the little busy bee
Improve each shining hour,
And gather honey all the day,
From every opening flower.

Lewis Carroll, in *Alice in Wonderland*, answers gloriously with

How doth the little crocodile
Improve his shining tail?

Similarly Watts's

'Tis the voice of the sluggard
  I heard him complain . . .

becomes Carroll's

'Tis the voice of the lobster
  I heard him declare
You have baked me too brown
  I must sugar my hair.

From the Bar Gate, a walk east along Hanover Buildings, then north of Vincents Walk takes you to a Marks and Spencer department store. On this site, on 17 July 1674, Isaac Watts was born. Unless, of course, he was born at 41 French Street—if he wasn't born somewhere else "without the bar." Southampton's own designated biographer of Watts puts it succinctly: "There is some doubt about the place of Watts' birth." However, a plaque at the rear of the store does provide what is accepted fact:

ON THIS SITE STOOD
THE ABOVE BAR CONGREGATIONAL CHURCH
FOUNDED IN 1662 AND
DESTROYED BY ENEMY ACTION IN 1940

AMONG THOSE WHO WORSHIPPED THERE WAS
ISAAC WATTS

AUTHOR AND HYMN WRITER

It was also in this church that a number of Watts's hymns were heard for the first time.

Further up Above Bar Street is the imposing new Civic Centre, further testimony to the Blitz—and to Watts. For its clock, from eight o'clock on each morning, sounds the tune of "O God, our help" every four hours. (The local radio station regularly uses the first four notes of the same hymn.)

At the top of Above Bar, on the left, is Watts Park with a statue of Watts in white marble—usually complete with live sea gull on his head. On the grey pedestal are bas reliefs, details of his birth and death, and lines from "From all that dwell below the skies."

Aficionados of Watts's hymns may want to make a short side trip to Bitterne, a suburb just to the east where the A 3024 comes in from Portsmouth. The Church of the Ascension in Bitterne Park has four windows commemorating Watts that are well worth seeing. Celebrated in refreshingly different pictures and texts are seven of his best-known hymns. "O God, our help in ages past," for instance, shows a tree with a serpent and at the top the Holy City. Depicted, too, are the various ages of man: Father Time at the bottom with a baby; and on a road leading to the City a youth, a soldier, and an old man. For "Jesus shall reign" and "When I survey" there are figures of ordinary people through the ages against a background of the Southampton Civic Centre and Bar Gate; the Christ crucified, with the world and the sun; and at the top Christ in glory.

2. THE LAND WITHIN: NEW FOREST TO WINCHESTER

New Forest

New Forest takes up much of Southwest Hampshire and is 900 years old, which isn't exactly new even to the English. It has no monumental literary ties, but there are a few links with literature you might as well know about as you pass. William Rufus generally gets blamed for its name and its existence, being charged with creating a whole new hunting ground for himself in the eleventh century by demolishing entire villages and planting trees. Vainly, natives insist the destruction-of-villages business is exaggerated. And besides, it was Rufus's father, William the Conqueror, who started it. But no one listens.

Anyway, the Forest's chief inhabitants are wild horses. At least they think they're wild, which may be just as good; and when they take a notion they may wander into the nearest town. Among the officers who keep things decorous are the regarders: they go about "regarding" trespassers against the law. They have a lot of ground to cover. Stretching between Southampton Waters and the Avon River and vaguely girded on the north by the A 31, New Forest is about as big as all of the Isle of Wight.

Daniel Defoe thought the Forest a shocking waste of land and wanted it chopped up into small holdings. But Tennyson, visiting it at the end of a trip to Portugal, thought it finer than anything he'd seen abroad and later returned with his whole family in tow. After he bought Aldworth in Sussex, of course, he passed through the Forest regularly on his annual trips between his two homes, catching the Isle of Wight ferry at Lymington.

Lymington—Langley—Lyndhurst—Emery Down—Ringwood

Lymington Lymington is a little town at the southern edge of the Forest on the A 337 and the Solent. Tennyson had just left Lymington on the ferry for Yarmouth, noted earlier, when "Crossing the Bar" flashed entire into his head. Few of us are likely to be struck by the same divine lightning, but the trip to the Isle of Wight is worth it anyway.

Who of literary note lived in Lymington? Well, William Allingham, whose "Up the Airy Mountain" marks the modest pinnacle of his poetry, was a customs officer here from 1863 to 1870. Frederick Marryat, whose sealife novels had a vogue in the first half of the nineteenth century, lived for awhile on Brockenhurst Road. And though "Abide with Me" was written elsewhere, at least its author, Henry Francis Lyte, was curate here from 1820 to 1824.

Langley This hamlet at the Southeastern edge of New Forest is where T. E. Lawrence lived between the ages of five and seven (1894–96) in a red brick villa called Langley Lodge. Favorite pastimes were watching the fleet at Spithead pass by and collecting and identifying fossils he found along the beach, foreshadowing the interest in archeology that, as an adult, first took him to the Middle East.

Lyndhurst Nine miles due north of Lymington, Lyndhurst is a little town where seven roads meet—and in the summer every single one of them seems jammed with tourists. Most of them will be heading elsewhere, but some, who are Lewis Carroll fans, may be heading for the churchyard. For here is the grave of Mrs. Reginald Hargreaves, the Alice Liddell for whom *Alice in Wonderland* was written.

Lyndhurst is in the very heart of the Forest, and Tennyson chose it when he escorted an American actress, Mary Anderson, on a trip in 1888 to gather atmosphere for a production she planned of his play, *The Foresters*. The poet was as frolicsome as a boy and played at ducks and drakes on the ponds as he showed her choice scenic spots like the "Queen's Bower." He was seventy-nine at the time. Tennyson never had much luck with his plays, however, and this one was no exception. Before she could get it under way, Miss Anderson decided to retire from the stage.

Emery Down Conan Doyle dearly loved the New Forest, and always associated it with his own favorite among his books—not a Sherlock Holmes adventure, but a historical romance, *The White Company* (1891). It was written in Doyle's little top-floor study in Southsea, but it owed its existence to Emery Down.

Emery Down is the tiniest of villages just off the A 35, a mile west of Lyndhurst. Doyle stayed at a cottage on the Down the Easter of 1889, coming with friends for a brief holiday to take walks by day and play whist at night. But he was soon back alone, with a cart full of books on the Middle Ages. By the time he returned to Southsea in autumn, he had steeped himself in the period, and the shape of the novel was clear in his mind. It gives a glimpse of life in 1366 that is ringingly true and, among other things, presents a vivid picture of how the monks lived at nearby Beaulieu ("Bewly") Abbey, now picturesque ruins well worth seeing. (Old car buffs, by the way, come from all over the World to visit the National Motor Museum in Beaulieu's Palace House.)

Ringwood Ringwood, at the western edge of the New Forest, may not claim the best known writer in Hampshire. Indeed, its most successful writer was not only determinedly anonymous, but his best-selling work is as little known today as his name. Yet in him Ringwood has an all-time literary champion. His name was Harold Begbie, and the best-seller was *The Mirrors of Downing Street*. His championship? He was the greatest writer of poetry-by-the-foot England ever produced. Writing for a London newspaper, Begbie once received a check for 136 inches of poetry at 2s 6d an inch!

Winchester

> . . . an exceedingly pleasant Town,
> enriched with a beautiful Cathedrall

and surrounded by fresh-looking country.

John Keats, 1819

John Keats's words are so true—still. Although nearby Salisbury is almost the same size (in the neighborhood of 35,000), Winchester seems much more town than city. And far more than one expects, Winchester has not only the stamp of history stretching back to Alfred the Great (871–901) and before, but also the clean, orderly lines of the post-Restoration and eighteenth century. Its national role has been significant ever since there was a nation unified enough to call England.

Sixty-five miles southwest of London, Winchester often vied with the latter to be capitol of the kingdom. Indeed, Sir Thomas Malory, author of *Le Morte D'arthur* says it was the site of King Arthur's court. When Alfred made Wessex the center of a united kingdom, he made Winchester its capitol, as did successors like Canute. (Both are buried there.) The last of the Anglo-Saxon kings, Edward the Confessor, was crowned in its Cathedral. Playing it safe, the first of the Normans, William the Conqueror, displayed his crown in Winchester every Easter—but also at Westminster at Whitsuntide and Gloucester at Christmas.

Rudyard Kipling said that he never passed through Winchester without feeling that, other than Stratford, it was the holiest place in England because of Jane Austen and Izaak Walton. Both are buried in the Cathedral. But Winchester has literary importance well beyond this. In addition to being Malory's Camelot, it was (in part at least) Trollope's "Barchester," and Hardy's "Wintoncester," where Tess was hanged. And, most of all, perhaps, it was here that Keats wrote the last of his great odes.

He had come to Winchester from the Isle of Wight with good friend Charles Armitage Brown in August, 1819. Strapped for cash, they found "tolerably good and cheap lodgings." Here Keats resumed the furious pace of writing that had produced 1,500 lines in two months, including "Pot of Basil" (i.e., "Isabella"), "St. Agnes Eve," half of "Lamia," four acts of *Otho the Great,* and parts of "Hyperion."

After a day's hard work, Keats liked to stroll about the lovely town before dinner; and one afternoon the beauty of the surrounding country captured him utterly. The "Dian skies" and their clouds, the soft twilight, the warm "stubble plain," he wrote to his brother George, "struck me so much in my Sunday's walk that I composed upon it." What he composed was the "Ode to Autumn," in which the details of his letter grow even richer:

Where are the songs of spring?
Ay, where are they?

Think not of them, thou has thy music, too—
While barred-clouds bloom the soft-dying day,
  And touch the stubble-plains with rosy hue. . .

Title and theme of the poem are all too tragically symbolic of the poet himself. The ode marked not only the autumn of his most productive year ever, but the autumn of his very career, though he was only twenty-four. Seventeen months later he was dead.

When pressed to admit that Winchester was the Barchester of his Barsetshire series of novels, Anthony Trollope liked to say that "Here and there may be detected a touch of Salisbury, sometimes perhaps of Winchester—but no more than that." Besides, he'd growl, he hardly knew the town. Truth was he'd attended Winchester College for three years, 1827–1830, arriving as an admittedly big and awkward, "ill-dressed and dirty" twelve-year-old. His prefect was his older brother Tom, who thrashed him daily out of fraternal concern for his moral well-being.

What touches here and there of Winchester he uses in his novels each reader must decide for himself. But there is no doubt that, in a way, the town is responsible for there being a Barchester or a series at all. For a newspaper attack on the Winchester charity known as St. Cross suggested the plot of *The Warden* (1855), whose success—Trollope's first—led to all the others.

Coming into Winchester from the south on the A 31-A 33, which join near Otterbourne, you cross the pretty little River Itchen and hit The Broadway, guarded by a heroic statue of Alfred the Grat, erected in 1901, on the millennium of his death. On down the street (now High Street) on the left is the Tourist Centre with excellent information sheets and a city map, free. And a little further down still, on the left, is the Cathedral. Here's where to shuck your car, if you have one, and begin your foot tour of the town. A mile or so, round trip, covers everything: it's an easy, pleasant walk. Start with the Cathedral itself.

From the outside Winchester Cathedral is hardly a heart stopper, even though it's 900 years old and the longest Cathedral in England. It has an embarrassed air about it, as perhaps it should. There's a sense of something unfinished, as if the builders had quit for lunch one day and never came back. Suddenly you realize what it is: there's no tower.

Start your tour of the inside at the west entrance, of course, and head down the south aisle of the nave. Almost immediately on the right is the Wykeham Chantry. Wykeham's the bishop who founded illustrious Winchester College as well as New College, Oxford. But the main reason for pausing at his tomb is one of those touches of humor this cathedral offers. At the feet of Wykeham sit three frocked figures, alert to serve him still—his secretaries.

Next, in the south transept, in the Sylkestede Chapel, is the grave of Izaak Walton, whose *Compleat Angler* (1653) made him beloved of fishermen. The tablet on the floor says in part:

> Alas, he's gone before, gone to return no more.
> Our panting breasts aspire after their aged Sire.

This forerunner of the Hallmark school of poetry is hardly made easier to read by the seventeenth-century fashion of making the "S's" look like "fs." On the wall behind the grave a memorial window shows Walton, in a pilgrim-like hat, reading, his fishing rod beside him; the rest of the window appropriately illustrates biblical references to fish.

Outside this chapel, on the right, stairs lead up to the Cathedral library, England's oldest, a twelfth-century addition. Its treasures include the Winchester Bible, dating from about 1150; *Eikon Basilike;* the scaffold speech of Sir Walter Raleigh; and the first Bible printed in America—a translation into Indian. Raleigh was found guilty of conspiracy in 1603 after an outrageously rigged trial in Winchester, but wasn't executed until 1618. His final moments reflected the gallantry for which his name has become a symbol. He ended his speech with: "So I take leave of you all, making my peace with God. I have a long journey to take, and must bid the company farewell." Then he demanded to see the executioner's axe and felt its blade. "This is a sharp medicine," he said with a smile, "but it is a sure cure for all diseases."

The choir, in the center of the Cathedral, holds two things of interest—England's most amusing misericords . . . and the tomb of her least lovable monarch, William Rufus. The son of William the Conqueror, Rufus was beloved, so far as history discloses, by no one. One old chronicler tersely said, "He was loathsome to his people." To this day there are those who insist that the hunting accident that killed him in the New Forest was actually no accident at all. When he was brought to Winchester Cathedral for burial, the bishop saw to it he got a good deal less than the standard deluxe funeral: no mourners, no prayers, no tolling of the bell. Gossip has it that Rufus struck back, and the tower collapsed upon his dishonored grave. Could be, and at least it does explain why Winchester now has its stump of a tower. But if so, Rufus took seven years to get around to it.

As for the misericords in the choir stalls—they're delicious. So, for that matter, is the word itself. It comes from miseri (pity) plus cordis (of the heart), reflecting the compassion some long-ago superior had for his monks who had to stand through long services. The little wooden half-seats provided just the support needed while allowing the monks technically to remain standing. The vergers—a knowledgeable, friendly breed at

Winchester, omnipresent in their black robes—are happy to show off the misericords, whose carvings, like caricatures in wood, further prove this Cathedral's sense of humor. Especial fun are the saucy fellow whose tongue clacks at you and the blissful cat with a mouse in its mouth.

Between the choir and the west entrance, half way up the north aisle, Jane Austen is buried. The stone in the floor merely applauds "the benevolence of her heart, the sweetness of her temper, and the extraordinary endowments of her mind." It makes no mention of her as a writer, and Cathedral legend says a young Victorian verger, puzzled by the many visitors to her grave, asked "Is there anything particular about the lady?" In 1872 a brass plate was placed on the adjoining wall to correct this omission, and in 1900 a memorial window was erected, depicting St. Augustine, David with his harp, the sons of Korah, and St. John with a book and the first sentence of his gospel: "In the beginning was the word."

The houses where Jane Austen and Izaak Walton died are both almost literally in the shadow of the Cathedral and within several hundred yards of each other. Walton's comes first, reached by leaving the Cathedral through a door in the south aisle and going straight across the close to Dome Alley at its southern edge. Here, in 1663, Cathedral officials built a row of four attached houses, two-storey red brick buildings, each with twin gables. In the most western one, No. 7, lived Dr. Hawkins, a prebendary, son-in-law to Walton. Here Walton came to live in late life, and here he died in 1683. The house is still in use and not open to the public.

The same is true of Jane Austen's last quarters, No. 8, at the beginning of College Street, the second street south of Dome Alley. It's a neat, compact, three-storey affair, marked by a gray slate oval plaque. One can still see the bow window of Jane's "neat little drawing room," where she spent most of her time on a sofa, vainly hoping for the cure from Addison's disease that had brought her to Winchester. But it was not to be. She left her Chawton home the end of May, 1817. July 18 the same year she died, her last words a weary, "I want nothing but death." She was forty-one.

While in Winchester, Jane wrote nothing of any worth, having suspended *Sanditon,* the novel then in progress. She did manage a tolerable jingle or two, one of them just three days before her death, giving a comic version of why Winchester's patron saint, St. Swithin, sent forty days of continuous rain. It begins:

> When Winchester races first took their beginning
> It is said the good people forgot their old Saint
> Not applying at all for the leave of St. Swithin
> And that William of Wykeham's approval was faint.

Jane was not particularly good at doggerel.

Jane Austen's house is next door to Winchester College, whence the street gets its name. Bishop Wykeham founded it in 1382, and it claims to be the oldest public school in England. Eton, for instance, didn't get started for another sixty years. Among writers who attended Winchester, in addition to Trollope, were Nicholas Udall, Sir Henry Wotton, Sir Thomas Browne, Thomas Otway, Edward Young, Sydney Smith, and Matthew Arnold. And it was in this school's library that, in 1934, was found a manuscript of Malory's *Morte D'arthur* contemporary with William Caxton, who first printed that work. A valuable find it was, for the manuscript contained much that was not in Caxton's text.

The route back to the High Street takes you past the City Museum on the Square. It advertises a display of "personal belongings" of Jane Austen, but don't expect much. In a tiny room above the office is a small case on the wall; in the case are a manuscript of one of her jingles, two little beaded purses, an ivory spool case, and a photo of the College Street house. That's the display.

To reach what remains of Winchester Castle, next to last stop on this tour, you climb the hill of High Street to the West Gate, and there go left one hundred yards or so down a lane. At the end of the lane is the Great Hall, and on the left, just before you get to it, are some excavations still in progress. Already uncovered are parts of the Roman city wall and the bases of William the Conqueror's Norman Keep. The Hall itself dates from the thirteenth century.

Inside the Great Hall, on the western wall, is a tabletop. Obviously it is round. Undeniably it is huge enough to have seated a king and his twenty-four knights. Indisputably the king, who is shown on his throne at the head of the table rising out of a red and white Tudor rose, is called Arthur; and the names of his knights have a familiar ring, though the spelling looks odd: Gallahalt, Launcelot, Gaweyn, Kay, Mordrede. If only there weren't modern technology, surely this would be *the* Round Table of Camelot. But, alas, science says the wood in the oak tabletop can't be older than the fourteenth century. And Arthur, if there ever was one, was about the sixth.

Still, it is imposing. It has been repainted a number of times, once as part of a public relations job Henry VIII mounted for the benefit of visiting Emperor Charles V in 1522 to impress him with the ancient royal roots of the Tudors. Actually, Henry was simply carrying on the family face-lifting inaugurated by his father, Henry VII, who—as the first of the Tudors and with suspect rights to the throne—was all too aware of his nouveau status among the monarchs of Europe. That's why the seventh Henry named his first son, who had fortuitously been born right here in Winchester Castle, Arthur, and had him christened in Winchester's Cathedral. Whether or not

Charles V was duly impressed with all this is not known. Reports do say, however, that the entertainment provided was "sumptuous."

Last stop in Winchester is St. Cross's Hospital, the charity which gave rise to Trollope's *The Warden*. But it is a mile and a quarter from the castle, and the foot weary may want to switch to a car. The easiest way to reach it from the High Street is to turn right on to Southgate just below the castle and continue on for a little over a mile as it becomes Saint Cross Road and the A 333. At this point, on the left, in the loveliest of spots by still, lily-padded waters, is St. Cross Hospital. Bishop Henry de Blois built it in 1137, he said, for "thirteen poor impotent men so reduced in strength as rarely or never able to raise themselves without the assistance of another." For centuries it has sheltered poor pensioners and distributed Wayfarer's Dole of bread and ale to needy travellers.

St. Cross's caught Trollope's attention because one dull day in the early 1850's, hard pressed for news, the *London Times* launched an attack on it. Since de Blois's day, thundered the paper, his charitable trust had grown enormous. But while the warden of the place received a fine house and £800 a year for doing nothing, the twelve old bedesmen got a niggardly 1 shilling, 4 pence a day.

Not long after, as he paused on a little bridge in Salisbury, this news item sprang into Anthony Trollope's head as the plot for a novel. St. Cross's becomes the fictional Hiram's Hospital, and the warden, the gentle Mr. Harding, is so distressed by the attacks he resigns.

There are still pensioners of St. Cross to be seen, easily recognizable in their black gowns and silver cross of Jerusalem. And the public is still made welcome, but check open hours in advance. If you like, you can even receive the Wayfarer's Dole at the gatehouse to the south. But as always, you've got to ask for it.

3. NORTHINGTON, CHAWTON, AND THE NORTHEAST

> Look on my works, ye Mighty,
> and despair!
>
> "Ozymandias," by P. B. Shelley

Northington: The Grange

It was eight miles northeast of Winchester and fifty-seven miles from London, the last few from the railroad station reachable only through narrow country lanes—ladies and infants in a carriage, gentlemen and maids in an omnibus, luggage in a wagon. Yet in the mid-nineteenth century "The Grange" was one of the most glittering social centers in all England. Prime ministers, cabinet members, lords and ladies thronged with artists, bishops, and writers, keeping the staff of thirty (plus their own servants) busy as they pursued, in Thomas Carlyle's words, their "strenuously-idle life."

Set in an enormous, lake-studded park, the great mansion sits atop a rise overlooking a tributary of the Itchen River. It is seven-tenths of a mile from the gatehouse to the approach to the main building. The approach itself is another one third of a mile. At its end, framed by trees, is the house, with soaring Greek pillars and splendid pediments. Carlyle's wife Jane described it in her usual tart-tongued manner:

> The place is like, not *one*, but a conglomeration of Greek temples set down in a magnificent wooded Park five miles in length. The inside is magnificent to death—the ceilings all painted in fresco—some dozen public rooms on the ground floor all hung with magnificent paintings—and fitted up like rooms in an Arabian nights' entertainment—but the finest part of it is the entrance hall and staircases—which present a view of columns, frescos and carved wood and Turkey carpet—that one might guess at a quarter mile long! In the hall which indeed resembles a church, Lord A. reads prayers every morning to a numerous congregation consisting of men and women servants ranged on opposite sides, and his own wife and daughters kneeling beside him.

Lord A. is Lord Ashburton. Originally, the place had been the grange for the monks of Winchester, but had been in secular hands for three centuries when the Ashburtons acquired it. Inigo Jones in the seventeenth century and Sir John Soane in the nineteenth were among famous architects involved in its design. In the eighteenth century, George IV had lived in the great house when he was Prince of Wales. The Ashburtons, Lord and Lady alike, were fitting successors.

William Bingham Baring, 2d Lord Ashburton, was a member of one of Britain's most powerful financial families. His father had served Wellington as Chancellor of the Exchequer, transacted the sale of Louisiana to the United States, and helped settle the boundary between Canada and Maine. With a yearly income of £ 40,000, he was also one of England's wealthiest men. In his wife, Lady Harriet, he had a redoubtable partner.

Birth, marriage, appearance, and personality combined to make her the social leader of her day. Daughter of the Earl of Sandwich, she was a big, buxom, handsome woman, and gay, witty, and intelligent. Carlyle, who grumped about almost everyone who touched his life called her "the greatest lady of rank I ever saw." Years younger than Carlyle, she treated him with a somewhat demanding filial devotion, summoning him to dinners and visits rather imperiously—and, loudly bemoaning the time lost from his work, the great man obeyed.

Had she been nearer his age, or he not so unlikely a candidate for such a thing, one might have suspected an affair. Jane Carlyle did not like the closeness of their attachment in any case. No doubt she resented Lady Harriet's power over her husband, and perhaps even was a bit jealous that he was so constantly made the center of attention. In addition, neither of the Carlyles was enamoured of the way of life at the Grange. But still they came, year after year, sometimes for as long as five weeks, until Lady Harriet's death in 1857—and even after.

"It is the ruling Principle of the Host and Hostess," Jane once wrote her Cousin Jeannie from the Grange, "to keep the house always full." These "idle, restless" people made her nervous. "A whole household of brilliant people," she said, "shining all day and every day, makes me almost of George Sand's opinion, that good honest stupidity is the best thing to associate with." Brilliant they were. Among writers alone at one time or another, there were T. B. Macaulay, J. S. Mill, Arthur Clough, Tennyson, and Thackeray, in addition to Carlyle.

Often Carlyle lamented the "incurably dietetic hours"—the breakfasts at 9:30 A.M., the dinners at 8:00 P.M.—that made writing impossible. But he was allowed privacy to read. While at the Grange, for instance, he did some of his research for *Latter-Day Pamphlets* (1850) and *Frederick the Great* (1858–65). And he retreated into himself: "Lonely I, solitary almost as dead," he wrote, while the Grange burst to the seams with people. But he would have said that at home in Cheyne Row. For Carlyle was a man who took his loneliness with him.

Yet he often enjoyed fellow guests who were writers. Of Macaulay, who in 1851 had recently begun to publish his *History of England,* he wrote, "He and I did very well together. . . . A man of truly wonderful historical memory." And though Macaulay spoke "with a kind of gowstering [blustering] emphasis," Carlyle concluded that he was "on the whole a man of really peaceable kindly temper, and superior sincerity in his Whig way." Thackeray, an old acquaintance, was there the same Christmas, and Carlyle wrote contentedly of their spending eight days together, he on his reading for *Frederick*, and Thackeray writing away at *Henry Esmond* (1852).

Another Christmas found Carlyle at the Grange with Alfred Tennyson, a longtime friend and smoking companion. They rejoiced in escaping to the huge conservatory for glorious talk and comradely clouds of smoke, though Tennyson missed his "little fumitory" at Farringford. Said he, with a touch of disdain: "Here they smoke among the oranges, lemons, and camellias." Only once did they differ. When Tennyson reached for *Maud*, his new poem, to read aloud to the assembled guests, Carlyle headed for his walk. He couldn't stand to hear anyone read aloud, not even the poet laureate.

The Grange continued as a show place until fairly recently. People now living in the gatehouse still remember dances in the handsome building, like a small Greek temple, back of the main house. But a few years ago overwhelming death duties forced the owner, also a Baring, to place it in permanent trusteeship with the Department of the Environment.

You reach the Grange by turning north off the A 31 at New Alresford on to the B 3046 and going about four miles (past Swarraton) to a white picket fence on the left that says "The Grange," with a little lane running through the fields. Unless things have changed very recently, there is nothing to bar your way, but be prepared for a shock.

At the end of the lane, the huge stone pillars still stand staunch against the wind, but they protect an empty shell. The ceilings drip down their last shreds of frescoed gold, the windows sag vacantly, the inner walls are down to crumbling brick. And as a final, profane indignity, a small tree is growing out of the roof. It's like looking for an elegant, distinguished gentleman—and coming upon his skull.

It helps not at all that outside, all around, the sheep graze on in oblivous content.

Chawton

On July 26, 1809, Jane Austen wrote to her brother Francis with more glee than felicity:

> Our Chawton Home, how much we find
>   Already in it to our mind:
> And how convinced, that when complete
>   It will all other houses beat. . . .

Through the generosity of another brother, Edward, Chawton Cottage was to be her home—with her mother and sister—for the rest of her life. In its ground floor dining parlour, she would work away, surreptitiously, on all six of her novels.

It was well situated, at the junction where the Winchester (now the A 31) and Gosport (the A 32) roads came together. Alton, just a mile to the north, was near enough to walk to for shopping, and Winchester was an easy sixteen miles to the southwest by carriage. It was a commodious, comfortable house, too. A nearly square, two-storey red brick building, it had been built in the days of William III as a posting inn. Now it belonged to Jane's brother as part

Jane Austen's Chawton, Hampshire

By Courtesy of Jane Austen Memorial Trust

of the inheritance from his adoptive parents. When he offered it to his mother and sister, then living in Southampton, they eagerly accepted.

Jane chose the dining room for her writing largely because the door to the adjoining vestibule creaked, enabling her to hide her manuscript if she heard anyone coming. She was most secretive about writing novels; none bore her name in her lifetime. She had begun writing them as far back as 1796–97, when she was twenty-one, with something called *First Impressions*. It was refused by the publisher almost as soon as it was offered to him. Immediately Jane turned to *Sense and Sensibility*, only to lay it aside. Next came a draft of *Northanger Abbey*, which in 1803 actually found a purchaser, but he merely tucked it away in his desk and forgot it.

Chawton seems to have sparked a new interest in writing, however. She got right to work redoing *Sense and Sensibility* and published it at her own expense in 1811. She at once began *Mansfield Park*, but when *Sense and Sensibility* proved an unexpected success, she put the new novel aside to rework *First Impressions*. By January, 1813, she was reading proofs of what was now called *Pride and Prejudice*, and saying "I must confess that I think [Elizabeth Bennet] as delightful a creature as ever appeared in print, and how I shall be able to tolerate those who do not like *her* at least, I do not know."

In quick succession—Jane was a rapid writer, but a meticulous reviser—came the completed *Mansfield Park* (1814), the first wholly done at Chawton; *Emma* (1815); *Persuasion*; and *Northanger Abbey*. The latter Jane had bought back from the diffident publisher in 1816, without ever troubling him with the knowledge that she was the author of the highly successful *Sense and Sensibility* and *Pride and Prejudice*. *Persuasion* and *Northanger Abbey* were published posthumously in 1818.

In 1948 Chawton Cottage was bought and restored as a memorial to Jane Austen. It is now open to the public, year round, for a small fee, but check which days and hours in advance. It's well worth a visit. The various rooms, furnishings, and Austen relics on display give a good sense of the novelist and her times. And the creaking door that preserved her anonymity still creaks.

Northeast Hampshire

One reason the English love history so much may be that there is so much of it to love. This goes for literary history as much as any other kind and for Hampshire as much as any other county. Sometimes the town or village itself flashes by your train, bus, or car. Sometimes it's only a signpost beckoning down some country lane. But there they are, in abundance—Alton, Selborne, Bramshott, Steventon, Basingstoke, Farnborough—each with its contribution, large or small, to our literary heritage.

Alton On the A 31, seventeen miles northeast of Winchester, is Alton. It's one of those little towns where you feel you're being deliberately taken through a back alley first so the Town Centre can be sprung on you. Jane Austen walked here from Chawton for her shopping and used its long High Street, abustle with little shops, and its red brick bow-windowed houses in part for the "large and populous village, amounting almost to a town" she called Highbury in *Emma*, though she placed it in Surrey.

In *Vanity Fair*, by Thackeray, Alton was one of the stops Jos Sedley made on his bibulous journey from Southampton and added its bit toward the besotted condition in which he arrived in London: "at Alton he stepped out of the carriage . . . and imbibed some of the ale for which the place is famous." Alton also appears in several of the novels of Compton Mackenzie, as "Galton."

In real life, Alton sheltered Edmund Spenser in 1590 when he returned to England to publish the first three books of *The Faerie Queene*. A plaque at 1 Amery Street marks the spot, and gossip-biographer John Aubrey records the event: "Mr. Spenser lived sometime in these parts, in this delicate sweete aire, where he enjoyed his Muse, and writt good part of his verses." Among the verses were some for his *Complaints*.

John Henry (later Cardinal) Newman, as a fifteen-year-old boy came to live in Alton in 1816, the year that marked three pivotal points in his life—one financial, one intellectual, and one spiritual.

It was a financial crisis that brought the Newmans to Alton in the first place. When his London bank suddenly collapsd, the elder Newman desperately accepted a position as manager of an Alton brewery. It was the first stop on a downward slide that was never reversed.

It was in 1816 that young Newman's intellectual development took a decisive turn, too. He matriculated at Oxford, where he was to meet Pusey, Keble, and others, and with them eventually to launch the Oxford Movement.

And in the very days when the family was moving to Alton, Newman was undergoing his religious conversion, the spiritual experience that so shook and shaped him. Even thirty-five years later he thanks God: "Thy wonderful Grace turned me right round when I was more like a devil than a wicked boy, at the age of fifteen."

Little wonder that when, as an adult, he returned on a visit, memories made it almost too painful to bear. Newman's is now No. 59 High Street and called Swarthmore.

Selborne Four miles south of Alton, on the B 3006, is the village beloved of Gilbert White: Selborne. Here he was born in 1720; here he died and was buried in 1793; and here, in between, he served as curate. And here was his great "outdoor laboratory" that furnished the stuff for his *Natural History and Antiquities of Selborne* (1789), a book which turned close observation of nature into literature a hundred years before Thoreau and *Walden*. Selborne has many reminders of his presence: the zigzag path he made up steep Hanger Hill . . . the great old yew by the church, twenty-six feet round . . . his favorite inn . . . the home where he died facing the church where he served. His home, The Wakes, is now the Oates Memorial Library and Gilbert White Museum. The church, on a beautiful site chosen by the wife of Edward the Confessor, has a white memorial window and a triptych over the altar. White's grave is outside near the vestry door, but you can easily miss it. For it is more than modestly small and bears only his initials and his dates.

Bramshott If noticed at all, Bramshott is to most people a spot off the A 3 above Liphook, but they'd probably recognize the few lines of poetry that were born there. One day in the late 1860's a poet on a walk stumbled upon a series of wooded pools outside Bramshott called Waggoner's Wells. One was a wishing well with ivy-leafed toadflax growing in the crevices of the grey stone. The poet captured the scene in one of his loveliest lyrics:

Flower in the crannied wall,
I pluck you out of the crannies,
I hold you here, root and all, in my hand,
Little flower—but *if* I could understand
What you are, root and all, and all in all
I should know what God and man is.

The poet, of course, was Tennyson.

Steventon On January 3, 1801, Jane Austen wrote to her sister from Steventon, a hamlet on an unmarked road five miles south of Basingstoke: "We have lived long enough in this neighborhood: the Basingstoke balls are certainly on the decline, there is something interesting in the bustle of going away, and the prospect of spending future summers by the sea or in Wales is very delightful." Her father, the vicar, had retired, and they were moving to Bath.

It must have been a wrench to leave, however. She had been born in the vicarage in 1775 and had spent all the twenty-five years of her life there. Hers was a happy childhood—playing in the garden, learning French, playing the pianoforte, and, like Catherine Morland in *Northanger Abbey*, "rolling down the green slope at the back of the house."

She began to write at twelve. The first versions of *Sense and Sensibility, Pride and Prejudice*, and *Northanger Abbey* were all written here, and the world would come to know them well. But all too little known is a piece she wrote before any of these, *The History of England by a partial, prejudiced, & ignorant Historian*. She was fifteen at the time. After warning "N. B. There will be very few dates in this History," she goes on to give thumbnail sketches of eleven of England's rulers—from Henry IV through Charles I.

A few samples suggest the flavor. "Henry the 4th ascended the throne of England much to his own satisfaction in the year 1399." Of Henry V: "This Prince after he succeeded to the throne grew quite reformed & Amiable. . . . During his reign, Lord Cobham was burnt alive, but I forgot what for."* Edward V "lived so little a while that no body had time to draw his picture—so there is none." And finally, Elizabeth I: "It was the peculiar Misfortune of this woman to have bad Ministers—Since wicked as she herself was, she could not have committed such extensive mischeif [sic] had not these vile & abandoned men connived at & encouraged her in her Crimes."

The vicarage is gone now, and all that remains to remind us of Jane is, out in a field near the church, the iron pump that once stood in the wash house—or at least a convincing stand-in for that pump.

Basingstoke This junction in Northern Hampshire where the A 30, A 339, A 33, and M 3 all come together now, is where Jane Austen found the balls beginning to pall. It need not detain us, though there may be those who will rejoice to know that in the eighteenth century all three Wartons, those less than celebrated poets—Thomas the Elder and sons Thomas and Joseph—lived there, and that on July 11, 1912, Hugh Walpole, while on a brief stay, finished "Fortitude."

Eversley If you're planning to go on to Farnborough from Basingstoke, but you're in no hurry, and it's a pleasant day, and you enjoy meandering down backroads, *and* you're a Charles Kingsley fan, take a detour to Eversley. Kingsley was curate then rector there from 1842 till his death in 1875. In between sermons he wrote such novels as *Yeast* (1848), *Alton Locke* (1850), *Hypatia* (1853), *Westward Ho!* (1855), and *The Water Babies* (1863), as well as his review of Froude's *History of England,* famous now for impugning the integrity of John Henry Cardinal Newman. Out of the ensuing controversy

---

*Jane's Lord Cobham was the Sir John Oldcastle who, by the magic of Shakespeare's metamorphosis, became the Falstaff of *Henry IV.I*. And the real life "what for" that Jane forgot was a series of Lollard conspiracies that threatened no less than Oldcastle's one-time benefactor, the king himself.

came Newman's magnificent spiritual autobiography, *Apologia pro Vita sua* (1864).

There is a plaque honoring Kingsley inside the church, and he is buried in the churchyard beneath a marble cross inscribed "Amavimus, Amamus, Amabimus" (We have loved, we do love, we shall love.)

You get to Eversley by going northeast on the A 30 to Hartfordbridge and the B 3016. Then almost immediately turn left (north) onto a little unnumbered road. You'll see the church about the time signs begin to announce the junction with the A 327. To continue on to Farnborough, take the A 327 and the A 325 southeast. The whole Eversley detour is perhaps twenty-five miles.

Farnborough This thriving, bustling city on the A 325 just before it crosses into Surrey needs but three quick notes at best. An important military center, it had a John Hume Ross in its RAF photography school in 1922, until the press discovered he was T. E. Lawrence and hounded him out. Rudyard Kipling was often here in 1911–1913 when his son was attending nearby Wellington College. And if you've always had a hankering to see the mausoleum of Napoleon III, you can—it's in St. Michael's church.

With that, it's time for Surrey.

SURREY

Surrey

1. Southward Ho:
London to Farnham (the A 30)
2. Southward Ho:
London to Haslemere (the A 3)
3. Southward Ho:
London to Dorking (the A 24)

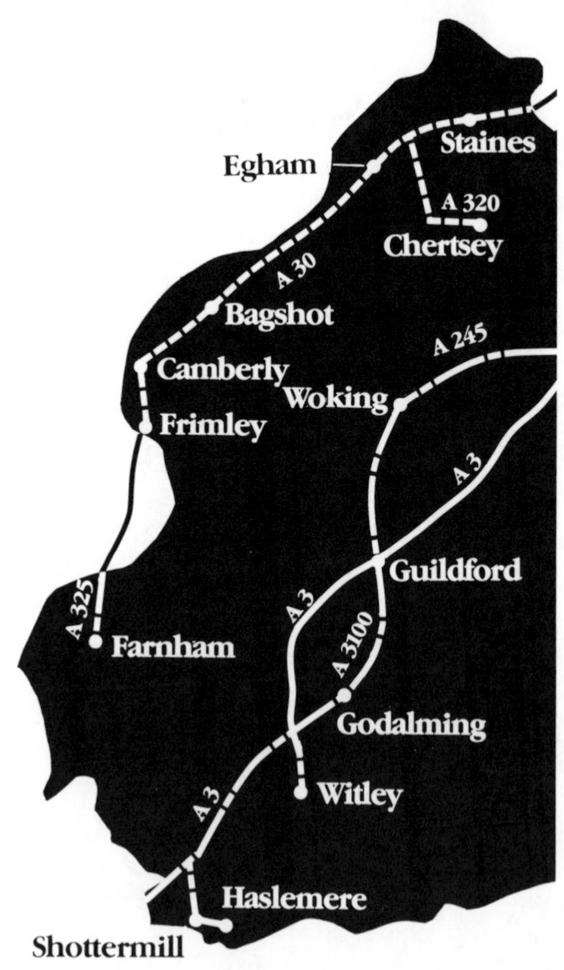

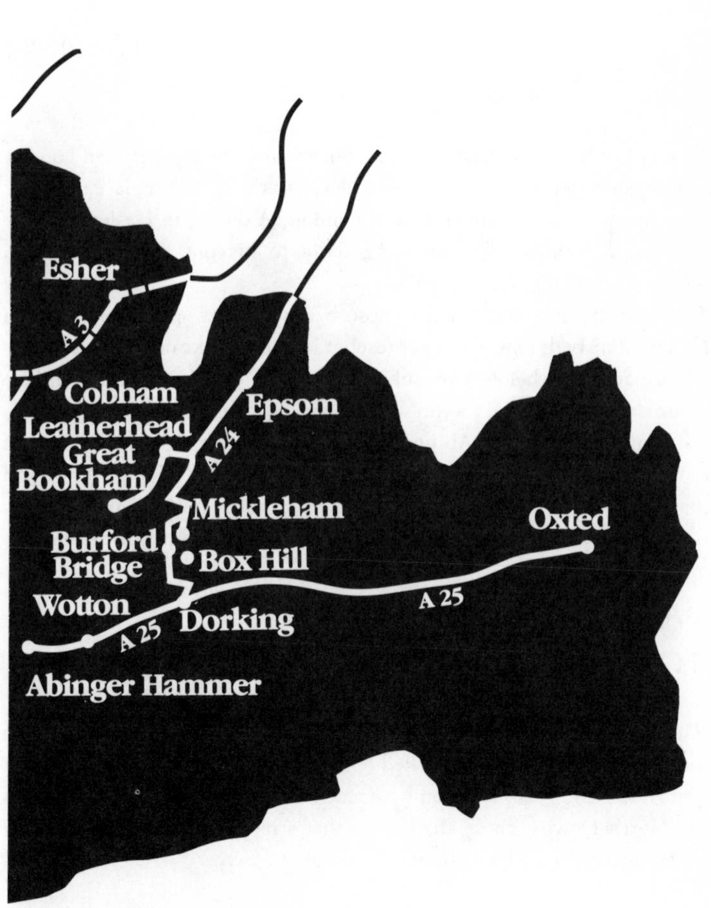
Esher
A 3
Cobham
Epsom
Leatherhead
Great
Bookham
A 24
Mickleham
Oxted
Burford
Bridge
Box Hill
A 25
Wotton
Dorking
A 25
Abinger Hammer

It was a sweet view,—sweet to the eye and the mind. English verdure, English culture, English comfort, seen under a sun bright without being oppressive.

Emma, by Jane Austen

One of England's smallest counties, Surrey fills the gap between London and Hampshire-Sussex to the south and Kent to the east. No place in Surrey is more than an hour's train ride from London. A doctor in Haslemere, say, would think nothing of commuting daily to his practice at a London hospital. And therein lies the rub.

Increasingly, Surrey has had to absorb the capital's spillover. Too often called London's bedroom, its upper reaches look more like one vast, unsupervised carpark. Yet below this suburban sprawl the sweet views of Jane Austen's days remain, the picturesque villages with their enticing names—Godalming, Shottermill, Abinger Hammer, Polesden Lacey—beloved of writers as various as Jonathan Swift and Lewis Carroll, George Eliot and Richard Brinsley Sheridan. Just as surely as all roads lead to London, they lead out as well, if you're so minded. Three such lead south to the heart of Surrey.

1. SOUTHWARD HO: LONDON TO FARNHAM (THE A 30)

The A 30, as it takes you southwest out of London and past Heathrow Airport and Staines, is a jam-packed bore of a road. By the time you leave it for the A 325 and Farnham, you have reached the farm-studded beginnings of the North Downs, those chalk hills that stretch ninety-five spectacular miles to the Dover Cliffs in Kent.

Staines—Egham—Chertsey

Staines On the A 30 eighteen miles southwest of London, Staines is in the main a bustling suburb, but it—and its own satellite, Laleham—share a pleasant bit of the Thames. It was in Laleham, which somehow still manages to keep a touch of the village about it, that Matthew Arnold was born in 1822. He lived here for six years, until his father, the then unheralded Dr. Thomas Arnold, accepted the headmastership of a rundown school called Rugby.

Matthew Arnold came back to live, in later life, at nearby Cobham, and, though he died in Liverpool in 1888, he is buried in the Laleham churchyard. His boyhood home is gone, but there is a brass tablet in his honor in the church.

Egham Two miles further down the A 30 from Staines, Egham might lay claim to being the largest little memorial center in the land. Clustered here are the memorial to President Kennedy, the Royal Air Force memorial, and Runnymede, where King John signed the Magna Carta in 1212. Runnymede is among the sights in "Cooper's Hill" (1642), a heavily moralizing poem by Sir John Denham celebrating the famous views to be seen from this local hill. Among them are St. Paul's Cathedral, "that sacred pile, so vast, so high" . . . Windsor Castle, with its "crown of such majestic towers" . . . the Thames, "though deep, yet clear, though gentle, yet not dull" . . . and Runnymede, "Here was that charter sealed wherein the crown/ All marks of arbitrary power lays down." These samples of his verse suggest why Denham is rarely dubbed the Milton of Egham.

Chertsey Not actually on the A 30 but just off it on the A 320, Chertsey is two miles southeast of Egham. Here the poet Abraham Cowley came to live in 1660 after the Restoration. He died in 1667 and was given a splendid funeral in Westminster Abbey. For in his day he was a much celebrated writer, and even a century later Samuel Johnson, in his life of Cowley, described him as a leader of the metaphysical school of poetry. Once, apparently, there was a plaque on the house in Guildford Street where Cowley lived; but not only has the house gone, so has the plaque. It was, according to Nathanial Hawthorne who visited it in 1856, "an ancient house, gabled, and with the second story projecting over the first."

Farnham

The way from Chertsey to Farnham, forty miles southwest of London, goes through Bagshot and Camberly on the A30 and Frimley on the A 325. Daniel Defoe said Bagshot was "horrid and frightful to look upon, not only good for little, but good for nothing"—a distinction it has since lost. Bret Harte, the American writer, died in Camberly in 1902 and was buried in Frimley in St. Peter's churchyard.

Farnham is a thoroughly pleasant town on the Wey River. Although it has a castle that is partly Norman and the ruins of Waverley Abbey, founded in 1128, it is mainly eighteenth century and has some fine Georgian buildings. Farnham was a favorite destination of Lewis Carroll on walks he loved to take when staying with his sisters in Guildford, ten miles to the east. To one such walk, in 1874, we owe that "agony" in eight fits, "The Hunting of the Snark." Into his head suddenly popped the last line of the poem: "For the Snark *was* a Boojum, you see." Four days later came the other three lines of the last stanza, and in the next several months, all the rest.

There is much of literary interest to see in Farnham, beginning with the southern part of the town and Swift, Scott, and Barrie. Jonathan Swift came to Farnham in 1689 as the twenty-two-year-old secretary to Sir William Temple, retired diplomat and an essayist of some skill. Temple's home was Moor Park, an imposing three-storey mansion overlooking a vast sweep of lawn and gardens. Here Swift lived, off and on, for the next ten years; and here he wrote some of the verse that prompted his kinsman, John Dryden, to say, "Cousin Swift, you will never be a poet." More to the point, here he wrote his first two important satires, *The Battle of the Books* and *A Tale of a Tub*, both finally published in 1704.

The most distinguished visitor to Moor Park in Swift's time was King William III. Temple had helped arrange William's marriage to Mary. Among guests of literary note, in addition to that obliging Cousin Dryden, were the essayists Joseph Addison and Richard Steele. One nineteenth-century visitor was Charles Darwin, then working on his *Origin of Species* (1859). He wrote his wife: "It is as pleasant and rural a scene as I ever saw, and I don't care a penny how any of the beasts have been formed."

Today the place is Moor Park College, a school for Christian Adult Education. Although the main building was considerably altered after Swift's day, the front overlooking the lawns looks pretty much as it did then, white, gleaming, and handsome. School officials make visitors welcome, but courtesy suggests: write first. Entering town on the A 325 from the north, one gets to Moor Park by taking South Street at the center and—soon after the name changes to Waverley Lane—turning left on Old Compton Lane and Moor Park Lane.

About a mile further down Waverley Lane, on the right, are the ruins of the abbey that gave the street its name. Dating from the twelfth century, it was the first Cistercian house in England, and its chronicles, the *Annales Waverlienses*, are believed to have suggested to Sir Walter Scott the title of the first novel in his famous Waverley series. The ruins are no great shakes as ruins go, which is just as well. For they sit far off in the middle of farm fields that are barred to the public.

Near the onetime lodge that guards these ruins is Stella's Cottage. Here lived one of the two mystery women in Swift's life, and perhaps his wife—if he ever had one, which is doubtful. "Stella" was Esther Johnson, daughter of a companion to Temple's sister, and Swift met her early in his Moor Park days. She became devoted to him, and he felt for her all he could feel for any woman. He supervised her education and wrote her graceful little poems and earnest prayers. And, most important for literature, he addressed to her the intimate, charming letters recording his daily life, published in 1766, after his death, as *Journal to Stella*.

If the two ever did marry secretly, as some have suggested, no evidence of it has ever been found. There is no denying the depth of their relationship—yet the one souvenir of her found among his relics bore the laconic label: "Only a woman's hair."

Three quarters of a mile almost due west of the Waverley ruins, on Tilford Road, is the elegant, many-gabled, white stucco house called, in the early 1900's, Black Lake Home. In the pine woods behind it lurked Peter Pan, Wendy, the pirates, and all the rest. For this was the summer home of James M. Barrie, where in 1904 he wrote his most famous play, based on stories he had told the five young Davies boys. He had met them in London and practically adopted them, though both their parents were then still living. In the summer of 1901, Mrs. Davies and her sons came to Farnham to stay in a rented cottage nearby, and the boys were with "Uncle Jim" constantly.

For them he turned the Surrey pinewoods into tropical forests and Black Lake across the road into a South Seas lagoon, taking innumerable photographs as they romped and played. He put the pictures in a book called *The Boy Castaways of Black Lake Island* and had two copies privately printed. One copy went to the boys; the other became a major source of *Peter Pan*. Now called Lob's Wood Manor, the house is still a private residence, and so it is closed to the public. But you can have a look at it from the road, if you like.

The rest of the things to see in Farnham can be reached on foot, once you have tucked your car away in a carpark near the center of town. If a break for a rest, a pint, or a lunch is in order, the William Cobbett pub in Bridge Square will do nicely. It's only two blocks south of the main street, Borough, and is named for one of England's most vigorous, earthy, pugnacious—and now largely forgotten—writers. Cobbett was born in this pub, then run by his father and called The Jolly Farmer, in 1763. He died in 1835 and is buried in Farnham's St. Andrew's churchyard, which has a *bas-relief* in his honor.

Cobbett was self-educated and made a career out of controversy. Twice when things got too hot for him in England, he fled to America. And twice he fled America for home when things got too hot for him there. In between he wrote reams of stuff on dozens of subjects—politics, economics, history, manners, gardening, and even grammar. His best-known book, *Rural Rides* (1830), is a kind of travel book, with a liberal sprinkling—often peppery—of political and agricultural comment, plus autobiography. Not at all your lovable curmudgeon—his pseudonym was Peter Porcupine—but a true original.

Farnham's main street is called Borough for one block, in the very center of town. To the east it's called East Street, and to the west, predictably enough, West Street. At 10 West Street a stone plaque marks the birthplace of Augustus Toplady, born in 1740, one of whose works is a good deal better known than he is. He wrote "Rock of Ages."

Last stop in Farnham is the castle, up steep (what else?) Castle Street, which runs north from Borough. Some of the castle is Norman, and the red brick tower is fifteenth century. But it's all rather unassuming and domestic, though the view of the city below is dramatic. It remained over the centuries the residence of the Bishops of Winchester until 1927 and, as the Bishop's Palace, had a literary link or two. Izaak Walton was steward to one of the bishops and wrote part of his lives of Hooker and Herbert here. And in fiction it appears in *Vanity Fair* during Jos Sedley's Southampton-London trek: "At Farnham he stopped to view the Bishop's Castle and to partake of a light dinner of stewed eels, veal cutlets and French beans, a bottle of claret." Since he had begun the day with a copious and not altogether dry breakfast at Southampton and made numerous and liquid stops along the way, it was no wonder that "when he drove into [London] he was as full of wine, beer, meal, pickles, cherry brandy and tobacco, as the steward's cabin of a steam packet."

2. SOUTHWARD HO: LONDON TO HASLEMERE (THE A 3)

The A 3 is the main highway between London and Portsmouth, seventy miles to the south. It's a good road, with frequent enough stretches of "dual carriageway" so that you're never held up too long by slower moving traffic. Even better, it takes you through some scenic country and charming places, once it shakes free of the lengthening shadow of London, and past spots where Meredith, Arnold, H. G. Wells, and Aldous Huxley, as well as George Eliot and Lewis Carroll, felt at home.

Esher

Esher (EE-sher) today is one of the wealthier London commuter havens, fifteen miles southwest of the capital and on the A 3. But when George

Meredith came there in 1859 with his six-year-old son, shortly after his wife ran off with Henry Wallis, it was a cozy little village surrounded by woods and gorse and heather.*

At first the pair lodged at a pleasant old house that had been a coaching inn. But soon Meredith moved into Copsham Cottage on the Commons, a simple little four-windowed house then two miles from town. Here he stayed five years.

The house saw Meredith come of age as a writer, although he was thirty-one and had already published *The Ordeal of Richard Feverel* (1859) when he moved in. In this tiny cottage he wrote his then-shocking *Modern Love* (1862), the sonnet sequence based on his own unhappy marriage; *Evan Harrington* (1860), in which he gave away many of the details of his own family history which he spent the rest of his life trying to hide; *Emilia in England* (1864); and most of *Rhoda Fleming* (1865). Rose Jocelyn, in *Evan Harrington,* is modeled on Janet Duff Gordon, a seventeen-year-old living in Esher. Meredith accidentally had come upon Janet and recognized her as the girl he had fallen in love with when she was an eight-year-old.

It was at Copsham Cottage, too, that Swinburne began writing one of the poems that so outraged the Victorians. It was during a wild visit in 1862. Meredith tells the story:

> He greeted me with a triumphant shout of a stanza new to my ears. It was Fitzgerald's "Omar Khayyám", and we lay on a heathery knoll beside my cottage reading a stanza alternately, indifferent to the dinner-bell, until a prolonged summons reminded us of appetite. After dinner we took to the paper-covered treasure again. Suddenly Swinburne ran upstairs, and I had my anticipations. He returned with feather pen, blue folio-sheet, and a dwarf bottle of red ink. In an hour he had finished 13 stanzas of "Laus Veneris."

If Swinburne hoped to shock the proper people of his day with lines like

> Behold, my Venus, my soul's body, lies
> With my love laid upon her garment-wise . . . .

he succeeded. For his day, the poem was a sizzler. Victorian gentlemen might lie upon their loves like a garment, but they didn't talk about it. Not in poetry, at least.

Meredith's stay in Esher ended in 1864 when he married again. The

---

*The details of this scandalous and pathetic story were given in the Seaford section on page 106.

Cottage was obviously too small, and the couple moved to Flint Cottage in Mickleham.

Cobham—Woking

Cobham This Cobham is nineteen miles south of London, four miles below Esher on the A 3.* And though a fair number of its ten thousand townsfolk take the train in to work each day, it manages to keep a bit of its own identity. Matthew Arnold chose Cobham as his final home, coming in 1873 and staying till his death in 1888.

As readers of his poetry know, nature had a soothing effect on Arnold, and he found much to soothe him in Surrey. Soon after coming to Cobham he wrote, "the country is beautiful—more beautiful even than the Chilterns, because it has heath and pines, while the trees of other kinds . . . are really magnificent." The house he chose was Pains Hill Cottage, roomy and comfortable enough for his needs, but in no way impressive, and he only rented it. Yet, he said, "we are planting and improving about our cottage as if it were our own, and we had a hundred years to live there."

Poetry for Arnold was largely over when he got to Cobham, but at Pains Hill Cottage he wrote a number of his telling prose works, including *God and the Bible* (1875), *Last Essays on Church and Religion* (1877), *Mixed Essays* (1879), and *Discourses in America* (1885), which included the famous "Literature and Science." The cottage is no more, but there is a "Matthew Arnold Close" to mark the site.

Woking Woking is big—80,000 people—and looks it. So does its cemetery, England's largest. Not actually on the A 3, but three miles west of it on the A 324, Woking is six miles west of Cobham. H. G. Wells came to Woking in 1895, a twenty-nine-year-old determined to prove that his recent decision to chuck teaching for a career as a writer was a sound one, and that the success of his just-published *The Time Machine* was no fluke.

In his autobiography, Wells describes his lodgings as "a small resolute semi-detached villa with a minute greenhouse in the Maybury Road." It faced a railway line where trains shunted and bumped in the night. Nearby, however, was a pretty, rarely used canal in a pine woods grove. During his year and a half here, Wells wrote *The Wheels of Chance* (1896), *The Invisible Man* (1897), and *The War of the Worlds* (1898). He got his exercise by learning to ride a bicycle, as reflected in *Wheels of Chance:* the fall in Chapter I rings all too true, and Wells himself rode wherever he has Mr. Hoopdriver ride in the novel.

---

*Not to be confused with the other Cobham, of Dickens fame, in Kent.

Guildford

Although it has 60,000 people, Guildford—seven miles due south of Woking and on the A 3—retains a certain charm and more narrow streets than it needs to. Malory said it was Astolat, the home of Elaine in Arthurian legend. It has castle ruins that date back to the eleventh and twelfth centuries, and England's newest cathedral, dedicated in 1961. It was, with Oxford and Eastbourne, one of the three cities that shared Lewis Carroll in later life.

When he first arrived in Guildford in August of 1868, "Lewis Carroll" was already famous as the author of *Alice's Adventures in Wonderland* (1865). But chances are no one that day recognized the writer in the earnest thirty-six-year-old clergyman-teacher down from Oxford to find a house for his six sisters. Carroll had already acquired the knack of keeping his true identity as Charles L. Dodgson a secret.

He decided upon The Chestnuts, a practically new but Georgian-looking three-storey red brick house, "close to Guildford," he said, "with a splendid view." For atmosphere, it had the castle ruins almost in its front yard.

Carroll spent all his Christmas holidays thereafter in this house, and he grew fond of the town. One year he joined in elaborate amateur theatricals put on by Guildford friends, playing the part of a doctor. In the audience, he noted were "Mr. and Mrs. A. Trollope"—the novelist and his wife. He also liked to preach in St. Mary's church, only a few steps from the house. This took more courage than it sounds, for he stammered badly and confessed he was a nervous wreck before each sermon. It didn't make the choirboys happy either: Carroll took twice the usual time to get through a service. His own funeral was in this very church, for he died in Guildford in 1898 while on his usual holiday.

The Chestnuts is on Castle Hill, a block south of the High Street, nowadays the heart of the city. It can be nicely seen from the street, for it sits close to the sidewalk. The awninglike trellis over the front steps has gone since Carroll's day, and the right and left wings are changed; but otherwise the house looks much as it did when he selected it. There is a plaque on the left gatepost announcing that he lived and died there; and it's charmingly decorated with figures of Alice, Humpty Dumpty, the Cheshire Cat, the White Rabbit, and the Red King. Carroll's grave is in the cemetery at the top of the hill, marked by a monument with three steps surmounted by a marble cross.

Sixty yards from The Chestnuts, on Quarry Street just past St. Mary's church, is the Guildford Museum, open on weekdays. It runs the usual town museum gamut from Bronze Age spears to an 1880's bicycle, but one tiny alcove does house a few interesting Carroll relics; and in the Muniment Room there is an extensive collection of Lewis Carroll documents that can be examined by appointment.

Godalming—Witley

Below Guildford, in the southwest corner of the county, the rolling lift of the Downs and the almost manicured vales of the Weald offer matchless countryside. And in between, the towns are small, warm, and unspoiled: Godalming, Witley, Shottermill, Haslemere. This is Surrey at its best. Here Aldous Huxley spent the happiest of boyhoods. Alfred Tennyson built his summer home just over the border in Sussex. And George Eliot was so entranced by a four-month visit she came back to spend the last years of her life.

Godalming (GOD-al-ming) On the A 3100, four miles southwest of Guildford, Godalming still has its quota of narrow streets and half-timbered houses and takes care that you see them, even if all you had in mind was to pass through the town as expeditiously as possible. In its environs Aldous Huxley was born and grew up. His birthplace (1894), called Laleham, is an agreeable, middle-sized, late-Victorian house with an abundance of gardens. The talented, spirited Huxleys stayed here until 1901, when they moved to Prior's Field, two miles away. The new house was also moderate in size, but in it Mrs. Huxley, Matthew Arnold's niece, opened a school with three teachers and seven pupils—six girls and Aldous. It prospered, nevertheless.

Witley Four miles southwest of Godalming on the A 283, Witley is where, in 1876, George Eliot (Mary Ann Evans) and George Henry Lewes dared to buy a country home and live openly as man and wife. It was a bold thing to do in that Victorian era, for Lewes already had a wife, however unfaithful to him she might be, and for twenty-two years George Eliot had been paying the penalty. Even her own brothers and sisters had repudiated her.

Mr. and Mrs. Lewes, as they called themselves, had succumbed to Surrey's spell seven years earlier, while staying in Shottermill near Haslemere. The minute they saw the Witley house they wanted it. Called simply The Heights (now Roslyn Court), it was a commodious vine-covered brick house, much begabled, the red-tiled roofs sprinkled with chimneys. After costly alterations and improvements, they moved in, in May 1877, only to run into such settling-in woes as furniture arriving late, water pipes malfunctioning, and troublesome mattings.

Once shaken down, however, The Heights pleased them greatly. George

Eliot worked on such things as *Impressions of Theophrastus Such* (1879)—her major novels were behind her—played her piano, and acted as hostess to the considerable number of guests who came despite convention. One of these, surprisingly enough, was that very embodiment of Victorian propriety, Henry James.

The visit was sheer disaster. Lewes was more ill than he himself realized and had to struggle not to show it. Outside, as James glumly recounted later in *The Middle Years,* it was a "dreadful, drenching afternoon." Inside was equally bleak. James sat for a while, looking at his "bland, benign, commiserating hostess beside the fire in a chill desert of a room." Then, seeing no signs of preparation for tea, he left. But not without one final turn of the screw: as James paused in the doorway, Lewes thrust into James's hands the two volumes of James's latest novel, *The Europeans,* apparently unread.

After Lewes's death, George Eliot married John Cross in May, 1880. At forty he was twenty years her junior. They bought a house in London, but planned to keep The Heights as a summer place. On December 22 of that year, George Eliot died in the new London house.

Shottermill—Haslemere

Shottermill Six miles southwest of Witley, Shottermill is just outside of Haslemere on the B 2131. Here on May 2, 1870, George Eliot and George Henry Lewes rented a "queer little cottage" from Mrs. Alexander Gilchrist, widow of the Blake biographer. It doesn't really look all that queer: called Brookbank, it is a good-sized two-storey house with a dormer above of stone and brick and red tile. The novelist was then in the midst of one of her greatest works, *Middlemarch,* and found the Surrey countryside highly conducive to her writing.

For diversion, there were glorious walks and visits from and to Alfred Tennyson, who braved the aura of scandal hovering over the Eliot-Lewes liaison. Aldworth, Tennyson's summer home, was only a couple of miles away on Blackdown, and he often walked over to read aloud poems of his like *Maud*, the "Northern Farmer," and "Tears, Idle Tears." Mrs. Tennyson received them at Aldworth and once came over with her husband. It was a doughty thing for Emily Tennyson to do, proper as she was. Well, maybe not all that doughty. When her journal was published in 1897 an entry, reading "we called on Lewes and George Eliot," was discreetly canceled.

Brookbank is on the Liphook road just before it enters Haslemere. It looks much as it did and is still one building; though it is now two homes with two names, the original Brookbank and Middlemarch. Across the street is Cherrimans, a brick and stone two-storey house with a strikingly long, high, sloping red tile roof. This is where Lewes and George Eliot moved for their last month in Shottermill when they had to vacate Brookbank. The houses are still private residences, but they are right on the road and are quite visible. The lane next to this road, by the way, is now called Eliot Drive.

Haslemere (HAY-slemere) A gentle little town on the A 286, Haslemere is at the very bottom of the southwest corner of Surrey where it runs into West Sussex and Hampshire. It was the post office address for Tennyson's summer home, Aldworth, but the house itself is actually in West Sussex and is described in that section. (See pages 124-126). However, the approach to the house is by way of Haslemere, and Tennyson must often have alighted at its railway station. So must Gerard Manley Hopkins, who came frequently to visit his parents at Court's Hill Lodge. St. Bartholomew's Church in Derby Road has a stained glass window for each poet.

3. SOUTHWARD HO: LONDON TO DORKING (THE A 24)

As the A 3, heading south out of London, crosses the Thames and reaches Clapham Common in Lambeth, it seems suddenly to make up its mind and strikes out resolutely southwest for Portsmouth. In helpful fashion, the A 24 begins here to accommodate those going more directly south. But, like the A 3, the A 24 takes a while to win one over. About halfway to the Sussex line, however, beyond Leatherhead, it, too, begins to offer the North Downs and then the Weald, whose beauties drew sightseers like Meredith, Arnold, Hawthorne, and Jane Austen's Emma. Places of literary interest include Epsom, Leatherhead, Mickleham, Burford Bridge, Box Hill, Dorking, and Wotton.

Epsom—Leatherhead—Great Bookham

Epsom Fifteen miles south of London, Epsom is still too much that city's handmaiden to have much charm of its own. It is the Epsom of the Derby, however, and the famous salts, which both John Aubrey and Samuel Pepys in the seventeenth century found beneficial. Pepys is, if anything, too plain spoken in his endorsement: "We got to Epsum [sic] by eight o'clock, to the well; where much company, and there we 'light, and I drank the water; they did not, but go about and walk a little among the women, but I did drink four pints, and have had some very good stools by it."

In the next century the dramatist Thomas Shadwell featured the spa in

Epsom Wells (1773). Some say it's his best play. But that's not saying much. Dryden's devastating accolade for his fellow playwright wasn't much amiss:

> The rest to some faint meaning make pretense,
> But Shadwell never deviates into sense.

Leatherhead On the A 24 and the River Mole, just before the first upward thrusts of the North Downs, Leatherhead's literary claims are tenuous at best. The Running Horse Inn may be the tavern of the alewife in Skelton's *Tunning of Elynor Rumming* (sixteenth century), which, even if true, hardly makes it a mecca. Some claim that Leatherhead is the prototype of "Highbury" in Jane Austen's *Emma* (1815), but nothing you can see there today supports this. And Sir Anthony Hope Hawkins was buried in its cemetery in 1933, but far more people know *The Prisoner of Zenda* (1894) than the name of its author.

Great Bookham For all its grandiloquent name, Great Bookham is a bit of a village two miles southwest of Leatherhead on the A 246. Fanny Burney lived here after her marriage to General D'Arblay in 1793 and wrote *Camilla* (1796), a novel which netted her the not inconsiderable sum of £2,000. Among the village's fans was twenty-one-year-old Jane Austen, who in later years stayed at the Great Bookham vicarage with her cousin and used nearby Box Hill in a novel of her own, *Emma* (1816).

Just outside Great Bookham, to the south, is Polesden Lacey, once the estate of dramatist Richard Brinsley Sheridan. He bought it in 1796 after his second marriage to a girl a year older than his own son. Exuberantly, he proceeded to play the country squire as if it were a role in one of his own plays—but without the laughs of *The School for Scandal.* Rains ruined the harvest, scarlet fever wracked the family, and the debts piled ever higher. He wound up mortgaging the place, and after his death in 1816 it was sold at auction.

Today nothing remains of Sheridan's house, for in the 1820's it was replaced by a Regency villa. Subsequent owners added their own touches; and early in this century the Ronald Grevilles, its final private owners, also remodeled much of the interior and furnished it as a glittering, luxurious tribute to Edwardian taste and a brewer's fortune. It is now owned by The National Trust and is open to the public during the season. (Fee or N. T. Card.)

Mickleham

Four miles south of Leatherhead, the A 24 takes a jog to avoid running into the village of Mickleham. But there is a road that continues straight ahead right through town—the Old London Road. In the parish church at its upper end, the novelist Fanny Burney married, in 1794, General Alexandre D'Arblay, a French refugee who had served Lafayette. She had come to Mickleham to visit her sister. D'Arblay, along with Talleyrand, Mme De Staël, and others had fled the French Revolution and established a kind of colony there in Juniper Hall. The Hall is still in use, not far down the road from the church, but it's considerably altered and is in no way impressive.

It was in this church, too, in 1864, that George Meredith married his second wife. She was a Mickleham girl, and in 1867 the couple came back to live, as it turned out, for the rest of their lives. The house, called Flint Cottage, is on the zigzag Box Hill Road only fifty yards or so from where it leaves the Old London Road to start climbing the hill. It's a small two-storey brick house, only three windows wide, but the setting is superb among fir trees on the green slope of the hill with vistas of the ridges of Leith, Ranmore, and Norbury.

Here, beginning with *The Adventures of Harry Richmond,* Meredith wrote and rewrote the novels that, with painful slowness, finally won him recognition from the begrudging public and critics alike. The birth of first a son, then a daughter, finally made writing in the cramped quarters of Flint Cottage impossible; so in 1877 Meredith built a two-room Swiss chalet on the slope above: "the prettiest to be found, the view is without a match in Surrey." Here, among others, he wrote *The Egoist* (1879) and *Diana of the Crossways* (1885), the book which at last brought him success. He was fifty-seven.

Flint Cottage saw a number of distinguished writer-guests, especially as Meredith's stature grew. Among them were R. L. Stevenson, George Gissing, Thomas Hardy, Henry James, J. M. Barrie, Robert Bridges, G. K. Chesterton, H. G. Wells, James R. Lowell, Edith Wharton, Alphonse Daudet, and Arthur Conan Doyle.

Stevenson came a number of times and was genuinely fond of Meredith, although he once confided to Henry James, "He is not an easy man to be with—there is so much of him, and the veracity and high athletic intellectual humbug are so intermixed." Stevenson was the model for Woodseer in Meredith's *The Amazing Marriage* (1895).

Although both his tongue and pen could be cutting, Henry James was an innately kind man, and he spent long hours on regular visits to Flint Cottage. He deprecated Meredith's style with the "general mystery of his perversity," but he admired his wit and hearty self-laughter, as well as the courage with which, from 1879 on, he faced the increasing pain and incapacity of a progressive spinal ailment. It was Henry James who took both Alphonse Daudet and Edith Wharton to Mickleham to meet Meredith.

Meredith's Chalet, Mickleham, Surrey

By Courtesy of The National Trust

The Daudet visit came in 1895, and Meredith was so pleased and flattered—he had long admired the French novelist—that he served a bottle of rare wine he had been saving for ten years. It was a moving occasion, for the foreigner was as badly crippled as his host and later described it to James as "two novelists dragging a wing, like two wounded seagulls, maimed birds of tempest, punished for having affronted the gods."

In 1909 James brought Edith Wharton, the American novelist, to Flint Cottage. She was delighted to find the old man—Meredith was eighty then—enthroned in his Bath chair and reading her latest book, though he had no notion James was bringing her with him.

Conan Doyle made a call in 1892 with J. M. Barrie and the young Arthur Quiller-Couch. He was welcomed by Meredith at the gate and barraged by war stories, leaving him not at all sure he liked their host. Even so, he was back in 1894 and took credit for persuading Meredith to finish his long-abandoned *The Amazing Marriage,* after having the first two chapters read to him.

By 1896 Meredith's writing career was largely over, and, though guests came to the end, he was almost wholly confined to Flint Cottage. He died there of a chill in May of 1909, typically enough, after enjoying a bottle of beer and a cigar. The cottage is now owned by The National Trust, but it is rented for revenue and so is not open to the public. It is much as Meredith left it and is viewable from the road. So is the charming chalet, still intact on its hillside perch.

Burford Bridge

A stone's throw from Flint Cottage, at the junction where the Old London Road rejoins the A 24, is the elegant (four-star) Burford Bridge Hotel. Long, long ago, however, it was called the Fox and Hounds and was smaller and not so elegant; though Lord Nelson had spent his last night in England there with his Emma. In one of its rooms, the night of November 21, 1817, a twenty-two-year-old Londoner sat writing to a friend: "At present I am just arrived at Dorking to change the Scene—change the Air, and give me a spur to wind up my Poem, of which there are wanting 500 lines."

A week later, in the same room, he was writing the last of those 500 lines:

> She gave her fair hands to him, and behold,
> Before three swiftest kisses he had told,
> They vanish'd far away!—Peona went
> Home through the gloomy wood in wonderment.

He had finally finished the poem begun so long ago in April, in London, with

> A thing of beauty is a joy forever

and worked on since on the Isle of Wight, in Margate, and Oxford. The poem was, of course, *Endymion,* and the poet, John Keats.

Since then, the hotel has drawn more than its share of literary people, with this association with Keats as much an attraction as the inn's location at the very foot of Box Hill. It was both that drew Meredith there in 1861, some years before he even met Marie Vulliamy, the Mickleham girl he married. "I marched me to the Vale of Mickleham," he wrote in a letter. "The walk has made me a new man. I am now bathed anew in the Pierian Fount. I cannot prose. I took Keats with me to read the last lines of *Endymion* in the spot of composition."

It was Meredith himself, in turn, who in later years was to draw a number of writers to the hotel. One such was Robert Louis Stevenson who, as an unknown of twenty-eight and author of a few essays, came for the specific purpose of meeting Meredith. He was armed with a letter of introduction and an admiration the intensity of which at first alarmed the novelist. But this passed, and they became good friends.

In 1895 Meredith was the magnet that attracted to the Burford Bridge Hotel one of England's most glittering literary functions, the annual country dinner of the Omar Khayyám Club, whose members included many of the country's leading editors and writers. Meredith wasn't up to attending the dinner but did come in for an hour or so afterwards. He was greeted by a standing ovation and responded by making what he said was the first speech of his life. There followed tributes by both Thomas Hardy and George Gissing.

Box Hill

Box Hill looms above the Burford Bridge Hotel and is reached by the same steep and serpentine road that runs past Meredith's Cottage. One of the highest points in southern England, it is a bold, rolling sort of hill, bulging up from the valley of the Mole River. From its top it offers spectacular views of that valley with the town of Dorking and its thin, graceful church spire set amidst the neat and tidy farmlands.

Even in the days of Jane Austen and John Keats, Box Hill was well known, and its appeal has held up over the years. Jane Austen makes it one of the attractions for Mrs. Elton's "exploring party" in *Emma*, and Keats paused one night from the winding up of *Endymion* to explore it, too. "I like this place very much," he wrote while there in 1817. "There is Hill & Dale and a little River—I went up Box hill this Evening after the Moon—you a' seen the Moon—came down and wrote some lines." In his vigorous days, Meredith was "every morning on the top of Box Hill." It charmed Matthew Arnold, too. "Here we are at this pretty place under Box Hill," he wrote from Burford Lodge in 1886, "which looks really precipitous as it raises straight from the river at the back of the garden."

If the view from Box Hill hasn't suffered since Arnold's day, the hill itself has. On a Sunday afternoon, particularly, there is but one word for it—trashy. It is crawling with people, alive with arrogant, aggressive motorcycles roaring and snarling their way up and down its car-crammed roads. Alas, a thing of beauty isn't necessarily a thing of beauty forever.

Dorking—Wotton—Wescott—Abinger Hammer—Oxted

At Dorking the A 24 crosses the A 25, one of the few, and so, necessarily principal east-west highways of southern England. Along the A 25 on both sides of Dorking are points of interest.

Dorking Dorking is one of the pleasanter towns on the A 25 and gave its name to that five-toed fowl, a favorite of English tables, celebrated by Edward Lear:

> There he heard a Lady talking
> To some milk-white Hens of Dorking—

Benjamin Disraeli, the novel-writing prime minister, wrote most of *Coningsby* (1844) here at Deepdene, the estate of a friend. Matthew Arnold enjoyed the town and especially its church on his visit to Burford Bridge in 1886. George Gissing lived at 7 Clifton Terrace in 1895. And George Meredith's ashes were buried beside his wife in the Dorking Cemetery in 1909.

In fiction, *Pickwick Papers'* Sam Weller plants himself on top of the Arundel Coach to go to Dorking to pay his respects to his dad. Mrs. Weller's "Marquis of Granby," the pub that was "quite a model of a road-side public house . . . just large enough to be convenient, and small enough to be snug," may well have been patterned after Dorking's King's Head in North Street. At least, when asked if it was, Dickens didn't deny it.

Wotten (WOO-ton) Two miles southwest of Dorking on the A 25, Wotton was the family home of the Evelyns; and John Evelyn, the famous diarist and author of *Sylva,* was born at Wotton House in 1620. In his later years he returned to live there and is buried in the little church nearby.

In 1856 Nathaniel Hawthorne made a pilgrimage to Wotton House and describes it as it was then: "The house is of brick, partly ancient, and consists of a front and two projecting wings, with a porch and entrance in the center. It has a desolate, meagre aspect, and needs something to give it life and stir and jollity." Hawthorne was particularly fascinated with three books in the Evelyn library: the manuscript of Evelyn's diary; the prayer book Charles I carried to the scaffold and stained with his royal blood; and a collection of his letters written during his imprisonment, including a pathetic one apologizing for being unable to pay a piddling beer bill.

Wescott At the Rookery in Westcott, just east of Wotton, was born in 1766 Thomas Robert Malthus, whose celebrated *On the Principle of Population* (1798) gloomily declared that people multiplied far faster than their ability to produce food, and man's only hopes for checking this were war, famine, and pestilence—and, he added with a delicate denial of sex, "moral restraint." (Incidentally, Malthus became curate of Albury, only six miles west of Wescott, the very year his book came out.)

Abinger Hammer This tiniest of towns, on the other side of Wotton was E. M. Forster's home from 1902 to 1945. It was where he wrote *The Celestial Omnibus* (1914) and *The Eternal Moment* (1928), as well as the essays he collected as *Abinger Harvest* (1936).

Oxted Oxted, fourteen miles east of Dorking on the A 25, received "Mr. and Mrs. Stephen Crane" from America in June, 1896. They set up housekeeping in Ravensbrook Villa, a plain brick house next to the town laundry. When asked, they would explain that they had met in Athens, feeling it quite unnecessary to mention that first meeting in Jacksonville, Florida at "Mrs. Crane's" bawdy house—or that they had never gotten around to marrying.

Crane was already famous as the author of *The Red Badge of Courage* (1895). At Oxted he wrote *The Third Violet* (1897) and a number of other pieces, including his best known short story, "The Open Boat." The Cranes left Oxted for Brede Place in Sussex in January, 1899. Ravenswood has since been turned into flats, and small villas have been built in what was the garden. But there is a reminder of the American writer: one of these villas is called "Cranes."

SOUTHERN WILTSHIRE

Where the West Begins

Southern Wiltshire

1. Marlborough–Calne–Devizes
2. In and Around Salisbury

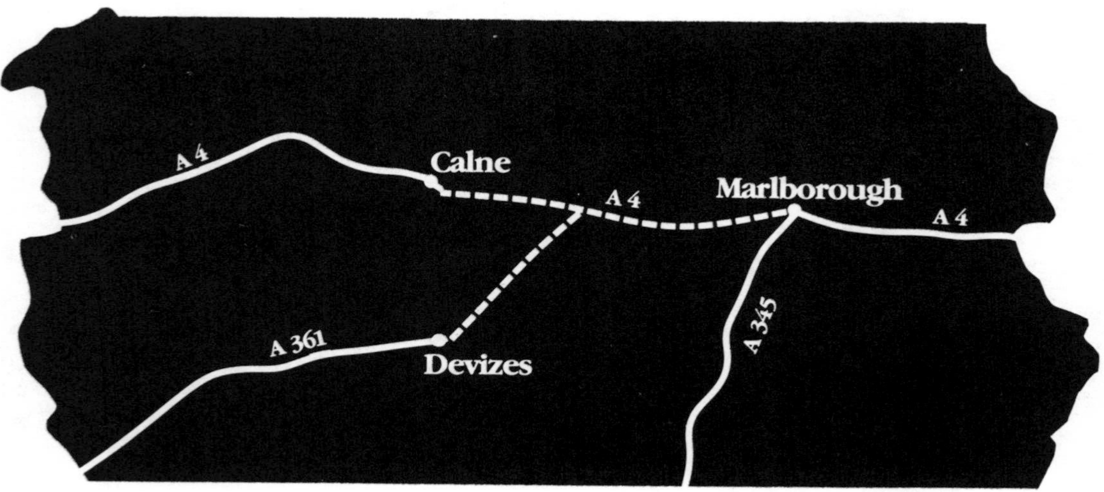

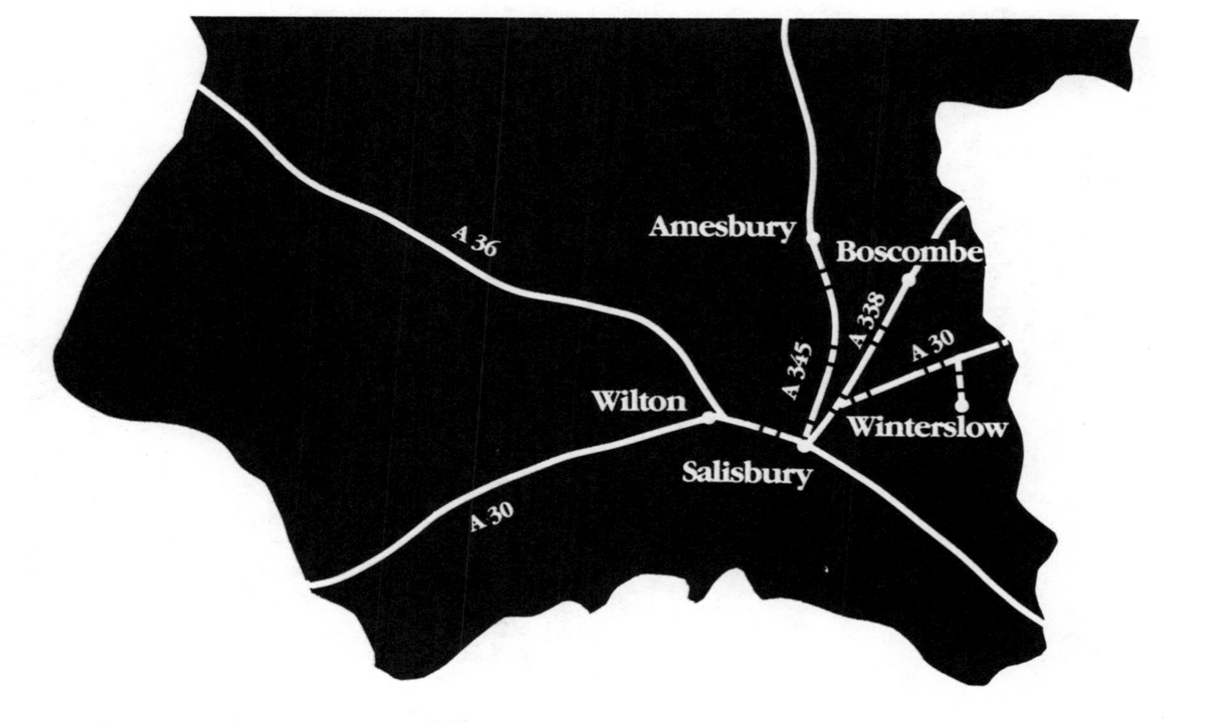
Amesbury
Boscombe
A 36
A 338
A 345
A 30
Wilton
Winterslow
Salisbury
A 30

Meantime you gain the height, from whose fair brow
The bursting prospect spreads immense around;
And snatch'd o'er hill and dale, and wood and lawn,
And verdant field, and darkening heath between,
And villages embosom'd soft in trees,
And spiry towns by surging columns mark'd
Of household smoak, your eye excursive roams.

James Thomson, *The Seasons,* "Spring"

Thomson was in Wiltshire when much of the "Spring" section of *The Seasons* (1726–30) was written, and his poem reflects its appeal. The county is still largely agricultural, and over half of it is taken up by the bursting prospects of the Marlborough Downs and the verdant fields of the Salisbury plain. Salisbury is the dominating city. In Wiltshire, England begins to thin out and, unlike Surrey or Kent, the literary traveller no longer has a bewilderment of sites to select from. Rather, there are several clusters, each with a few points of interest. In Wilton House and Longleat, Wiltshire has two of the grand country homes of England. But though it has associations with some writers of note—Tennyson, Coleridge, Addison, and Sidney among them—it has nothing in literature to match the architectural glory of its Salisbury Cathedral or the ageless spell of Stonehenge.

Marlborough—Calne—Devizes

By the same authority that says a line from Bristol to Margate delimits the beginning of Southern England, the A 4 marks the start of Southern Wiltshire. Roughly paralleling the old Roman Road and the route Chaucer's Wife of Bath might have taken to get to the Tabard Inn, the A 4 is Bath's

"London Road." Along it, or just south of it, Marlborough, Calne, Bronham, and Devizes in Wiltshire are worth a mention, however brief.

Marlborough (MAHL-bruh) Seventy-five miles west of London on the A 4, Marlborough is an agreeably open little town with a broad High Street and some fine old houses. In the eighteenth century the most elegant belonged to the Countess of Hertford. It was while here, enjoying her hospitality, that Thomson worked at the "Spring" section of *The Seasons*, and he dedicated it to her. Dr. Sam Johnson said that Thomson "took more delight in carousing with Lord Hertford and his friends than assisting her ladyship's poetical operations, and therefore never received another summons." But he apparently got this from Richard Savage, whose veracity was at best ephemeral. In fact, Thomson corresponded with—and visited—the Countess for many years.

Her mansion later became one of England's most famous country inns and was celebrated in *The Castle Inn* (1898), a novel by one Stanley Weyman. In 1853 the building became the nucleus of Marlborough College, which grew to be a leading boys' school. Among its alumni were William Morris, Anthony Hope (Hawkins), Siegfried Sassoon, Louis MacNeice, and both of Alfred Tennyson's sons. On one visit to Hallam, the elder of the two, Tennyson agreed to meet with the sixth form and bowled them over with his sonorous reading of *Guinevere*.

Lytton Strachey had a house, The Lacket, in Marlborough early in this century, and Virginia and Leonard Woolf were among the members of the Bloomsbury Group who came to visit him.

Calne Calne is a dozen miles west of Marlborough on the A 4. Coleridge lodged here from 1814 to 1816 with his friend John Morgan; Charles Lamb also came to Calne in 1816 to see Morgan. Lamb's verdict on the town, in a letter to Wordsworth, remains unchallenged: "Calne is famous for nothing particular that I know of."

Devizes Fourteen miles southwest of the A 361, Devizes has a comfortable sixteenth-century coaching inn, The Bear (two-star), on the Market Square. Here, in the eighteenth century, a pair of lady novelists stayed at different times. Fanny Burney came with Mrs. Thrale, friend and biographer of Dr. Johnson, in 1780. And nineteen years later Jane Austen and her party put up at the same place. Jane gave it high marks: "We had comforable rooms and a good dinner, to which we sat down about five; among other things we had asparagus and a lobster, which made me wish for you, and some cheese—cakes, on which the children made so delightful a supper as to endear the town of Devizes to them for a long time."

In and Around Salisbury

Salisbury, where four roads—the A 30, 36, 338, and 354—all come together, somehow manages to seem larger than it is: it has about 40,000 people. Its name most readily calls to mind its Cathedral and Trollope's Barchester novels. But it does have a number of other literary associations.

John Foxe, the author of the *Book of Martyrs* (1563), was a canon here, though hardly a popular one: he objected to the wearing of the surplice and refused to contribute to the repairing of the cathedral. Philip Massinger, the Jacobean playwright, was born in Salisbury in 1583 and was baptized at St. Thomas's. George Herbert, hymn writer and author of such poems as "The Pulley" and "The Collar," was rector of St. Andrews, 1630–32. The Cathedral has a window commemorating him and his hymn, "The God of Love my Shepherd is." In the next century Henry Fielding married a Salisbury girl and was practicing law at the Wiltshire sessions of court when he wrote his first novel, *Joseph Andrews* (1742). In *Richard III,* Shakespeare prepares for poor Buckingham's execution with the grim setting: "Salisbury. An open place." And Thomas Hardy's "Melchester" in *The Mayor of Casterbridge* (1886) and other Wessex novels is really Salisbury.

But it is the Cathedral that gives Salisbury its true distinction. Unique in an age when cathedral building was a leisurely, two- or three-century business, (Canterbury's took over three), Salisbury's was finished in just thirty-eight years (1220–1258). Oddly enough, the incredibly beautiful spire, 404 feet high, was an afterthought, added a hundred years later.

Pepys came to see the Cathedral in 1668 and was much impressed: "the Minster most admirable; as big, I think, and handsomer than Westminster." During his Wiltshire holiday in 1809, Lamb, too, was struck by its beauty, but hardly impressed by the story that a party of eight people had recently dined at the top of its spire. Henry James spoke for all visitors, ancient and modern, when he proclaimed it simply "a blonde beauty among churches."

And it was in Salisbury, by the Cathedral precincts, that Anthony Trollope, in 1851, gave birth to what was to grow into perhaps the most popular series of novels ever written. For the plot of *The Warden* "surfaced ready-made," he recounted, "as I leaned upon the parapet of the little bridge that spans the stream by Salisbury Close." As was noted earlier, the actual event that sparked this plot occurred at Hiram's Hospital for aging pensioners in Winchester, but with novelist's license Trollope was describing Salisbury when he wrote: "The London road crosses the river by a pretty one-arched bridge, and looking from this bridge, the stranger will see the windows of the old men's rooms." Out of *The Warden,* of course, came the whole Barchester series.

In the novel Trollope denies that Barchester is, in fact, Salisbury: "The

Rev. Septimus Harding was . . . a beneficed clergyman residing in the cathedral town of ______; let us call it Barchester. Were we to name Wells or Salisbury, Exeter, Hereford, or Gloucester, it might be presumed something personal was intended. . . . Let us presume that Barchester is a quiet town in the West of England, more remarkable for the beauty of its cathedral and the antiquity of its monuments, than for any commercial prosperity."

When asked point blank about the model for Barchester, Trollope insisted, with more vehemence than truth (he went to school in Winchester): "I have never lived in any cathedral city,—except London, never knew anything of any Close, and at that time had enjoyed no peculiar intimacy with any clergyman." Ah well, Barchester's cathedral has two towers. Salisbury's, however awe-inspiring, has but one.

Amesbury—Boscombe—Winterslow

Within ten miles or less of Salisbury are Amesbury, Boscombe, Winterslow, and Wilton. The first three have but modest claims for inclusion here. Wilton, however, has some of the great names of the Elizabethan era.

Amesbury Eight miles north of Salisbury, there's a Woodhenge Circle to match the Stonehenge one. It's in Amesbury, where Joseph Addison went to school before he entered Charterhouse. He was born two miles to the north, in 1672, in his father's vicarage at Milston. It is to the "holy house at Almesbury [sic]" that Tennyson's penitent Queen Guinevere retires to die. And at Amesbury Abbey, then the seat of the Duke of Queensbury, John Gay wrote *The Beggar's Opera* (1728).

Boscombe Six miles northeast of Salisbury on the A 338, Boscombe had Richard Hooker as its rector from 1591 to 1595. He built the north transept of the church and plugged away at the first four books of *Ecclesiastical Politie* (1594).

Winterslow Winterslow is seven miles northeast of Salisbury, and you can reach it via an unnumbered road off the A 30—if you're dead set on going there. However, William Hazlitt liked it and lived there from 1808 to 1812. For a time he was at what is now the Pheasant Inn (two-star), where he wrote some of the essays collected after his death as *Winterslow* (1839). Charles and Mary Lamb came to Winterslow a number of times to see Hazlitt.

Wilton

Three miles west of Salisbury on the A 30 is Wilton House, one of England's most magnificent country homes. The story of its origins has a familiar ring: Henry VIII rewards a favorite with one of the abbeys seized

Sidney's Wilton House, Wiltshire

By Courtesy of The Earl Of Pembroke

during the dissolution. Favorite pulls down abbey, builds great house, and promotes self to Earl. In this instance, the favorite was William Herbert, brother-in-law to Henry (by way of marrying a sister of Catherine Parr), and the abbey was Wilton. And the title, attained when the guardians of Edward VI promoted each other, was Earl of Pembroke.

His son Henry, second Earl, took as his third wife Mary Sidney—and thereby came most of the literary interest of Wilton House. For Mary was both a great patron of literature herself and the gifted sister of Sir Philip Sidney. Edmund Spenser, in "Colin Clouts Come Home Againe" (1595) honors her as "Urania," and his praise is lavish:

> . . . but in the highest place
> Urania, sister unto Astrophell,
> In whose brave mynd, as in a golden cofer,
> All heavenly gifts and riches locked are.

"Astrophell," of course, is Sidney himself, subject of Spenser's elegy by that name.

It was for this same Mary, Countess of Pembroke, that Sidney wrote his prose romance, the *Arcadia,* in 1580, while staying at Wilton House, chiefly to amuse his sister. The seventeenth-century chronicler said of the Countess, "She was the greatest patronesse of wit and learning of any lady of her time." Among writers often at Wilton House in her day were Philip Massinger, Nicholas Breton, Ben Johnson, and, of course, Spenser. The poet Samuel Daniel was her son's tutor. And apparently Shakespeare was there, too, for the production of his own *As You Like it* before no less than King James. From late October to mid-December, 1603 the Court was at Wilton, and there is record of a request from Lady Pembroke asking her son to bring James I to see the play and noting "we have the man Shakespeare with us." As added fillip, tradition says that Shakespeare was given to playing the role of old Adam himself.

Shakespeare's connection with the Pembrokes remained close. In recognition of their support Shakespeare's fellow actors, Heminges and Condell, in 1623, dedicated their First Folio of Shakespeare's plays "to the most noble and incomparable paire of brethren," William, third Earl of Pembroke, and his brother Philip. And there are many who stoutly maintain that this earl, and not the Earl of Southampton or anyone else, was the mysterious boy friend of Shakespeare's sonnets. The dedication is to "Mr. W. H. the only begetter of these ensuing sonnets." The initials, at least, fit William Herbert.

Wilton House is still the family home of the Earls of Pembroke, but it is open to the public for a fee during the warmer months. A number of its

Apartments and State Rooms are on display, including the almost overwhelming "Double Cube" room—sixty by thirty by thirty feet of gilded opulence. Of special literary interest are the decorations below the dado rail on all four sides of the room, with scenes from the *Arcadia* done by Emanuel de Critz in the seventeenth century.

For a final stop in Wiltshire, Wilton House provides a more than a lavish last memory.

DORSET

Dorset

1. Bournemouth and Beyond

2. Dorchester and the Land of Lawrence and Hardy

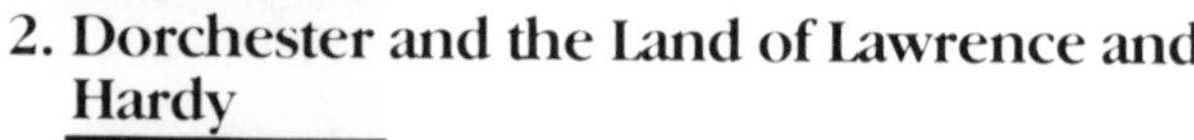

3. Lyme Regis and Racedown

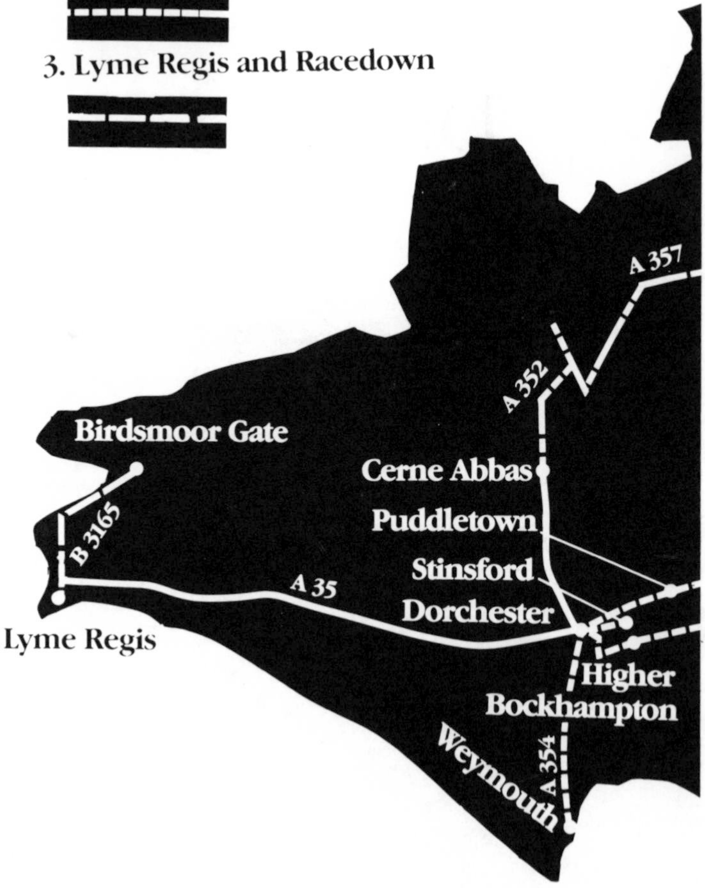

A 357
A 352
Birdsmoor Gate
Cerne Abbas
Puddletown
Stinsford
Dorchester
B 3165
A 35
Lyme Regis
Higher Bockhampton
Weymouth
A 354

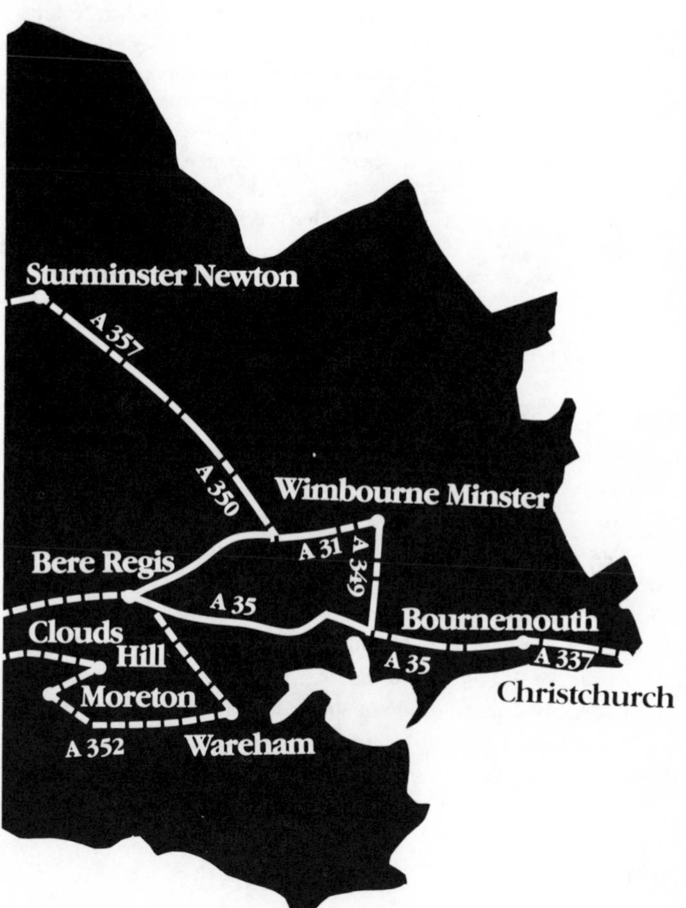
Sturminster Newton
A 357
A 350
Wimbourne Minster
A 31
A 349
Bere Regis
A 35
Bournemouth
Clouds
Hill
A 35
A 337
Christchurch
Moreton
A 352
Wareham

The hills are open, the sun blazes down upon fields so large as to give an unenclosed character to the landscape, the lanes are white, the hedges low and plashed, the atmosphere colourless. Here, in the valley, the world seems constructed upon a smaller and more delicate scale; the fields are mere paddocks, so reduced that from this height their hedgerows appear a network of dark threads overspreading the paler green of the grass.

Thomas Hardy, *Tess of the d'Urbervilles*

"Wessex," Hardy called it—the land of *Tess* and *The Return of the Native* and *The Mayor of Casterbridge* and the others. It embraces some of Cornwall, Devon, Somerset, Wiltshire, Berkshire, and Hampshire. But, in the main, Wessex is really Dorset. For this is Hardy Country, and his heart quite literally belongs to Dorset. His ashes are buried in Westminster, but his heart is entombed in the family churchyard at Stinsford.

Bounded by Somerset, Wiltshire, and Hampshire, Dorset remains largely what Hardy paints—a mixture of chalk hills and fertile valleys. But its southern edge has one of England's loveliest stretches of shore and two of its best known resorts: Bournemouth in the southeast corner, beloved by Henry James and Robert Louis Stevenson, and Lyme Regis in the southwest corner, immortalized by Jane Austen's *Persuasion.* An utterly beguiling county, Dorset—and largely unspoiled to this day.

1. BOURNEMOUTH AND BEYOND

Bournemouth

Thirty miles due south of Salisbury, Bournemouth is the showpiece of the Dorset coast. In *Tess of the D'Urbervilles,* it figures as "Sandbourne," where

Angel Clare goes to seek Tess upon his return from Brazil, and Hardy does the town full justice:

> This fashionable watering place, with its eastern and western stations, its groves of pines, its promenades, and its covered gardens, was, to Angel Clare, like a fairy place suddenly created by the stroke of a wand, and allowed to get a little dusty. . . . It was a city of detached mansions; a Mediterranean lounging-place on the English Channel.

Hardy wasn't far wrong about that magic wand, either, for that's just about what one Captain Lewis Tregonwell wielded as he set about creating Bournemouth in the 1830's and '40's. He had stumbled upon the site while trying to track down a real life Gulliver—a giant of a man and a notorious smuggler named Isaac Gulliver. Charmed by the place, Tregonwell returned with his bride, built a house, and went into the land development business, Gulliver by then had conveniently retired to open a wine shop. The result was Bournemouth.

What Tregonwell and his cohorts built was no less than an exclusive winter playground and year 'round health resort, the haven of the well-to-do lame, halt, and dying. But with its warm and gentle air and the improbably symmetrical arc of its beach—one great, graceful, beautiful sweep from Sandbanks to Hengistbury Head—what a place to die! The news of Bournemouth's "salubrious air" reached Queen Victoria herself, and she recommended it to her prime minister, Benjamin Disraeli. He, in turn, brought his whole cabinet down, and the Royal Bath Hotel on Bath Road (five-star!) still points out the room in which they held an official meeting to consider, among other things offering titles to Alfred Tennyson and Thomas Carlyle. (Both refused.)

Bournemouth prospered as a refuge for the ailing. In Westover Gardens you can see the "Invalid's Walk," specially built to accommodate bath chairs. John Keble, a leader of the Oxford Movement, came with his sick wife for the winter of 1865 but died himself the following year. He stayed in Exeter Lane in what is now part of the White Hermitage Hotel and worshipped regularly at St. Peter's. The church now has a window in his honor, in a chapel named after him. Years later William Gladstone, four times prime minister, came often to Bournemouth in his retirement and attended services in the Keble Chapel. Aware of the old man's deafness, an obliging sacristan provided him a seat in the choir. A brass plate now marks the oak stall where Gladstone made his last communion in 1898.

St. Peter's is also where Shelley, or at least his heart, is buried. (Dorset seems to run to buried hearts.) The story of how the heart got to Bournemouth is a romantic one. Practically driven from England in 1818, Shelley had gone to Italy. There, in 1822, he drowned in a boating accident that rumor hinted was no accident. By Italian law, his body was burned on the beach where it had washed ashore, with his friend Edward Trelawney and fellow poets Leigh Hunt and Byron standing by.

When the flames subsided, strangely enough, Shelley's heart had not burned; and while a guard wasn't looking, Trelawney snatched it from the ashes, though he burned his hand. Hunt dutifully conveyed the heart to Mary Shelley, the poet's widow (and author of *Frankenstein*) who took it with her when she returned to England to live with their son, Percy Florence. There she kept the heart, wrapped in a page of Shelley's elegy to Keats, *Adonais,* until her own death in 1851.

Percy Florence Shelley was then living in Bournemouth, and he acquired a family vault on the steep, grassy slope of St. Peter's churchyard. There Mary was buried along with her father and mother, William and Mary Wollstonecraft Godwin, whose bodies were brought from London, and, at last, Percy Florence himself. It was in his coffin, in 1889, that Shelley's heart finally found sanctuary.

Bournemouth has added interest for Shelley scholars, for in 1978 a unique collection of books, paintings, and memorabilia associated with the poet was given to the Bournemouth Museums. Valued at about £10,000, the collection came from the Shelley Museum in Lerici, Italy, which Margaret Brown established in 1972 at Casa Magni in Lerici, Shelley's last home. When that house was sold, Miss Brown moved the collection to Bournemouth's Boscombe Manor, Shelley Park, long the home of Shelley's son. (Open Monday–Saturday, June through September—Thursday–Saturday other months—for an absurdly low fee.)

Amid the aging convalescents, Victorian Bournemouth also harbored a group of youngsters at Saugeen, "A Preparatory School for Boys for the Public Schools and Navy." To it in 1876, at age nine, came Master John Galsworthy to prepare for Harrow and to sing in the St. Swithun's choir. John was happy here, and stayed for three years. The school is gone now, however; the building was demolished in 1935 and replaced by houses.

It was another schoolboy, Lloyd Osbourne, who drew Robert Louis Stevenson to Bournemouth. He was the writer's stepson, and Stevenson first came to visit him at a little school run by a local clergyman, in 1881. It was for Lloyd that Stevenson wrote his first popular success, *Treasure Island* (1883), heeding Lloyd's request for action after action, and "no women!" But perhaps Stevenson would have come to Bournemouth anyway, for with his history of tuberculosis, he was made for it.

In 1884 the Stevensons took lodgings there, first at Wensleydale in West Cliff Gardens, and then at Bonallie Towers in Branksome Park. In February, 1885, they bought a secluded villa on the cliffs of Westbourne. It was a tall, trim,yellow brick house with a blue slate roof, with the deep slash of Alum Chine at the back dropping sharply to the sea. Stevenson named the place "Skerryvore," after the famous lighthouse his engineering family had built. His wife made a "seductive little labyrinth" of paths, stairs, arbors, and seats where he wrote, with board on knee, such novels as *The Strange Case of Dr. Jekyll and Mr. Hyde* (1886) and *Kidnapped* (1886).

Stevenson was not overly fond of Bournemouth, however, "that nest of British invalidism and British Philistinism," as he called it, and made very few friends while there. One was his barber, who often stayed to meals. Another was none other than Sir Percy Shelley, who gave the Stevensons a portrait of his father to hang in their dining room. And a third was himself an outsider—Henry James.

James's sister was one of the Bournemouth invalids in the 1880's; and on one visit to see her in the spring of 1885, James stopped by to see the master of Skerryvore. He was at first mistaken for a tradesman, but the two writers speedily became fast friends. For the next ten weeks, James came night after night—so often that the large blue armchair he commandeered became known in the family as "Henry James's chair." James would sit, Stevenson would pace and chainsmoke, and both would talk, talk, talk. The Stevensons were genuinely fond of their guest, and Mrs. Stevenson said after he left: "the evenings seem very empty, though the room is always full of people." When Stevenson died in 1894, James wrote: "the loss of charm, of suspense, of 'fun' is unutterable."

James came back to Bournemouth several times, often staying at the Royal Bath Hotel. It was there, in 1897, for instance, that he finished *What Maisie Knew.* But Stevenson left the town in 1887, when hemorrhaging warned him that staying anywhere in England, even Bournemouth, might be fatal.

Skerryvore was the victim of a German land mine in 1943; the hit so weakened the structure that it had to be torn down. But the outlines of the house can still be seen on the site, now a public garden, along with a model of Skerryvore lighthouse. The street outside is now called Robert Louis Stevenson Avenue.

Two consumptives for whom Bournemouth proved a pivotal point were Aubrey Beardsley, of *Yellow Book* fame, and D. H. Lawrence. It was at No. 2 Exeter Road that Beardsley was converted to Catholicism, shortly before his death in 1898. And in 1912 D. H. Lawrence was transformed from a teacher to a writer when his doctor gave stern orders that he was never again to enter the classroom. Lawrence's response was the jubilant repetition of the line: "For him no more the sitting class shall wait."

While in Bournemouth Lawrence stayed at Compton House, a boarding house in St. Peter's Road, and was very popular with the other guests, though he spent much of his time writing at a furious pace. He was reworking *The Trespasser* (1912) and managed up to 3,000 words a day. A modern office block, also called Compton House, now stands on the site.

Another who came to Bournemouth was George Russell, the Irish poet known as "A.E." He spent his last years here and died in 1935 at Stagsden Nursing Home, 14 West Cliff Road, where there is still a similar facility called Portal House Convalescent Home.

It is possible to tour Bournemouth on foot, but one needs to be more than merely young at heart. For Bournemouth, like most South England coastal towns, aspires to the perpendicular. A combination of foot and car does nicely, and a good place to start is the Royal Bath Hotel on Bath Road. Adjacent is a carpark, and it's an easy stroll down Westover Road to the Tourist Information Centre to get a map and your bearings.

Handy to the Centre, at the foot of St. Peter's Road, is St. Peter's Church, with the Keble Chapel and the graves of the Shelleys. You can't miss St. Peter's: the graceful spire soars 202 feet in the air.

Then go back to the Royal Bath, if you like, for a closer look at the hotel where Disraeli had his cabinet meeting and Henry James finished *What Maisie Knew.* Next, up Bath Road, is the Russell-Coates Museum and Art Gallery, an incredible melange outside (from Edwardian to Pompeian to Arab) and in (from gems to junk). There's nothing all that literary, but a quick look inside will tell you much about the last years of the nineteenth century, including furnished morning and dining rooms, Henry Irving memorabilia—and a room jammed to overflowing with assorted furniture and furnishings, looking for all the world like a Victorian Goodwill Industries repair shop.

After catching your breath, aesthetically and actually, you can go back down past the Royal Bath to the Rothsay Museum, catty-cornered across the street, to pay homage to the machine responsible for more bad books than anything since the invention of the printing press: the typewriter. The Rothsay has the world's largest collection of typewriters, including one of wood . . . an electric one over seventy-five years old . . . one that cost $1,000,000 (the story's too long to tell here) . . . and the machine on which Edgar Wallace produced novels as if they were loaves of bread.

Also worth seeing are the site of Stevenson's house—and garden (but the prudent will use a car to get there . . . "there" being where West Cliff Road runs into Alum Chine Road) and, of course, the Shelley collection at the Bournemouth Museum.

Christchurch and Mudeford

Christchurch, just east of Bournemouth on the A 337, has been a magnet for tourists ever since the Romans looked in in A.D. 43. For the last 800 years, a big attraction (in all senses) has been the Priory Church that gave the town its name, boasting a "Miraculous Beam" and, for the last hundred years, a monument to Shelley.

Originally, the town was called Twinham, and the priory house of worship was called Christe's Church. But in time church name became town name. As for the miraculous beam, legend has it that while the church was abuilding in the eleventh century, a mysterious carpenter joined the crew, though he would accept neither food nor money. One afternoon a beam, meant to straddle the nave, was cut too short and tossed aside. Yet next morning workers found it firmly fixed in its destined place. The strange carpenter was never seen again. But when they named the church, he was remembered: they called it Christe's Church.

It's a huge building, 311 feet long, which is why Shelley's monument is there. For the poet's son, Sir Percy Shelley, had intended the sculpture for his own St. Peter's Church in Bournemouth, but it proved too large. So the Priory got it, and there it sits under the tower. It's an impressive thing, a white marble panel depicting the drowned poet lying across the knees of his grieving wife. The atheist Shelley might well have been bemused at being thus memorialized by a Pietà. The dedication honors both Shelley and Mary, and is followed by these appropriate lines from Shelley's own elegy to Keats, *Adonais:*

> He has outsoared the shadow of our night;
> Envy and calumny and hate and pain,
> And that unrest which men miscall delight,
> Can touch him not and torture not again;
> From the contagion of the world's slow stain
> He is secure, and now can never mourn
> A heart grown cold, a head grown gray in vain;
> Nor, when the spirit's self has ceased to burn,
> With sparkless ashes load an unlamented urn.

One of the rectors of the Priory Church, by the way, was the Elizabethan dramatist John Marston. He deserted the theater for the church, took religious orders in 1607, and served at Christchurch from 1616 to 1631.

Attached to Christchurch is the fishing village of Mudeford (MUDdy-ford), worth a line or two. Here fishermen in colorful caps still catch salmon much as they did in the thirteenth century when the canons of the Priory demanded as their right the first fish of the season. And here, in the late eighteenth and early nineteenth centuries, lived William Stuart Rose, an eccentric who loved tents so much he built his house like one. He fancied himself a poet and patron of the arts and entertained a host of writers, painters, and musicians, including Coleridge, Southey, and Sir Walter Scott. It was while visiting Rose that Scott wrote *Marmion* (1808), and the work is dedicated to him.

Wimborne Minster

Wimborne Minster, ten miles northwest of Bournemouth on the A 31, is a well-knit little town of 5,000-plus, with a decent hotel, the King's Head (three-star), and a dominant church—the "minster." The church, St. Cuthburga's, is a thoroughly satisfactory, cope-able gem of a minster, a grand old affair with two towers, the red sandstone central one dating back to the Normans. Among those buried within the church are Isaac Gulliver, John and Margaret Beaufort, and the two daughters of Daniel Defoe.

Gulliver was that notorious early nineteenth century smuggler in pursuit of whom Captain Lewis Tregonwell discovered the spot he later developed into Bournemouth. Gulliver, himself, wound up as one of Wimborne's most esteemed citizens, and lived in a house in West Borough that still bears his name. Indeed, his tombstone, in the floor of the crossing between the north and south doors of the church, is dedicated to the memory of "Isaac Gulliver Esquire."

As for the Beauforts, they were the grandparents of Henry VII, hailed as the Savior of England in Shakespeare's *Richard III,* and John Beaufort was the grandson of John of Gaunt, he of the dreadful deathbed puns of *Richard II.* You'll find the alabaster tomb with their curiously complacent effigies in the presbytery at the top of the stairs. As for the Defoe girls, they're in St. George's Chapel, but you won't find them: their memorial stone has disappeared.

Among the minster's many other attractions are a seventeenth-century chained library and the "jack-o'-clock," or quarter jack, celebrated by Thomas Hardy. The library, reached via the old vestry by ascending a challengingly steep spiral staircase, was founded in 1686. It contains 240 old books, mainly classical and theological, including three Breeches Bibles, a Polyglot Bible, and by way of diversion, perhaps, the works of Machiavelli. There's also a copy of Sir Walter Raleigh's *History of the World* (1614). Somehow in the early years of the library this book got damaged, but was speedily repaired, supposedly by the young Matthew Prior—whom some blamed for damaging it in the first place.

Prior had been born in Wimborne in 1664, the son of a carpenter, and had attended the town's grammar school before going to Westminster. His verse is hardly renowned today, and even he said he was "only a poet by accident," but he had few rivals for epigrammatic rhyme, spiced by wry humor, such as this, at age forty, to an alluring nymph of five:

> For as our different ages move
> 'Tis so ordained, (would Fate but mend it!)
> That I shall be past making love
> When she begins to comprehend it.

The minster is twice celebrated in poetry by Thomas Hardy, who lived in Wimborne from 1881 to 1883 in a house called Llanherne on The Avenue (now No. 16 Avenue Road). It's still called Lanherne (without the extra "l") and still lived in by members of the family that bought it in 1886, but needless to say, it has changed much over the years. In "Copying Architecture in an Old Minster," Hardy heralds the "jack-o'-clock" on the exterior of the west tower, a perky carved figure of a British grenadier that still strikes a pair of bells every quarter hour. (Installed in 1612 and carved by a Blandford craftsman for ten shillings, the figure originally was a monk, until the Napoleonic wars suggested something more belligerent.) In the poem, the jack also calls the minster ghosts from their tombs.

Hardy again treats of the minster's dead in "The Leveled Churchyard," but this time comically. A renovation project has moved the churchyard tombstones about, and Hardy depicts the fear of the departed that their identities might be mixed up, come Judgment Day:

> Here's not a modest maiden elf
> But dreads the final Trumpet,
> Lest half of her should rise herself,
> And half some sturdy strumpet.

Wimborne Minster is also the setting of a Hardy novel, *Two on a Tower* (1882), which he wrote while at Llanherne. In the novel, the town is called Warborne, "where they draw up young gam'sters brains like rhubarb under a ninepenny pan."

Sturminster Newton

Fifteen miles northwest of Wimborne Minster, on the A 357, is a small, winsome potpourri of cob and thatch, medieval, Georgian, and Victorian houses called Sturminster Newton. And among the Victorian houses is a small, dark grey semidetached dwelling, remarkable only for its location atop an escarpment that slopes down to the lovely, water-lily strewn Stour River. It's easy to miss the small slate plaque to the right of the bay window in front, reading:

Thomas Hardy
Novelist and Poet
Lived Here 1876–78

But those two years, he was to say sadly in later life, were "our happiest time."

Here he came with Emma, his first wife, to swim, row, and explore the countryside—and in the small side room off the lounge, on the ground floor, to write *The Return of the Native* (1878)*. Modest though the house was, with only three rooms on each floor, all small, Hardy hated to leave it. But Emma yearned for the social life and acclaim of London, and so they left. One day, as an old man of eighty-two, on a sudden whim, he returned to the house with a friend. Pausing, he stared at the giant monkey tree near the bay window, marvelling at its growth; it had been only shoulder high when he'd planted it. But his thoughts were elsewhere. "She had long golden hair," he said.

The tree remained until 1960, when its branches so blocked the light from the window it was cut down. Even so, the very memory of the tree refutes those who insist that the Hardy plaque is on the wrong house—that he actually lived in its partner to the left. For natives still remember Hardy's monkey tree, and where it was: on the right!

In Hardy's day, the house was owned by Robert Young, one of the two Dorset dialect poets connected with Sturminster Newton. Hardy was friendly with both. For the other, and more famous of the two, was William Barnes, who, in Dorchester, had helped Hardy with his Greek when the latter was an architectural student. The place, no longer called Riverside Villa as it was in Hardy's day (it's now South House), still stands much as it was then, a quarter-mile from the town centre at the end of Rickett's Lane. But it remains a private dwelling, and the passerby should scrupulously respect it as such.

Cerne Abbas

Cerne Abbas is only eleven miles southwest of Sturminster Newton on the A 352 . . . offers a beguiling collection of little thatched or slate-roofed

*Sturminster Newton appears in *Tess of the d'Urbervilles* as "Stourcastle."

houses huddled about a medieval church . . . and down past the church, appropriately at the end of Abbey Street, has the ruins of the Benedictine Abbey (established in 987) that gave "abbas" to the town name. And if that weren't enough, it has the largest, most naked, and most indubitably male giant you're ever likely to see.

What's more, the town itself and the surrounding villages abound in Hardy material. Six miles to the northwest is Melbury Osmund, the original of "Great Hintock" in the first edition of *The Woodlanders* (1887). Later, Hardy moved his fictional Hintocks to where the real High Story was—but High Story is even closer to Cerne Abbas—three miles north. Moreover, a mile south of Melbury Osmund is Evershot, the "Evershead" of *Tess of the d'Urbervilles*. It is in a barn in Evershead that Tess recognizes in the "ranter" who was preaching the very Alec d'Urberville who has seduced her. Alec then pursues her across the desolate upland, and at the spot called "Cross-in-Hand" on the hill atop nearby Batcombe makes her swear on a rude pillar (still extant) never again to tempt him with her charms or ways. After she swears, he abruptly leaves her, to go on to keep a preaching engagement in Cerne Abbas itself—for Cerne Abbas is Hardy's "Abbot's-Cernel."

Cerne Abbas's abbey provided the monk whose refound eucharist vessel occasioned the miracle that led to the erection of the same Cross-in-Hand—at least so Hardy says in his poem, "The Lost Pyx." (Tess, however, is told by a shepherd that the pillar never was a cross, but an ill omen put up by the relatives of a malefactor who'd been tortured and hanged there.) The abbey's ruined gatehouse figures in Hardy's short story, "The First Countess of Wessex." And, in harking back to Naploeon's expected invasion of the Wessex coast, Hardy refers to the town's celebrated giant, describing "Boney's" rumored eating of "rashers o'baby flesh" as "for all the world like the Cernel giant in old ancient times."

What *IS* the giant of Cerne Abbas, and how did he get there? Well, it's easier to answer the first than the second. The giant is the outline of a naked male, 180 feet high, carved out of the turf and into the chalk of Giant Hill. Who made him and why? Some say Celts of the Iron Age, centuries before Christ, to honor their fertility god. Some say Roman invaders of the second century A.D. to honor their Emperor. And others say it was the Romans, all right, but merely a band of bored soldiers from a nearby camp, with too little to do and quite possibly too much to drink. In any event, one thing today's spectator must admit: whoever carved the figure, they made his virility abundantly clear.

2. DORCHESTER AND THE LAND OF LAWRENCE AND HARDY

Dorchester

In all Dorset, Dorchester is the town most closely associated with Thomas Hardy. Here at nine he came to school. Here at sixteen he was apprenticed to the architect John Hicks. And here at forty-three he came from Sturminster Newton to build Max Gate, the house that was to be home for the rest of his life, where he wrote, among others, *Tess of the d'Urbervilles, Jude the Obscure, The Dynasts*—and the *Mayor of Casterbridge.* Dorchester *is* Casterbridge.

"Huddled all together," the novelist says of it, "compact as a box of dominoes." And, indeed, the town still is. Then and now a county and market center, it bestrides the A 35 twenty-seven miles west of Bournemouth and fifteen miles southwest of Sturminster Newton. Depending on his time, stamina, and appetite for Hardy, the visitor can spend anywhere from a day to weeks exploring the originals of the Dorchester streets and buildings, the fields, trees, and scenes that live again in the man's works. As one editor of Hardy put it, echoing a similar remark about *Ulysses* and Dublin, if all the maps of Dorchester were lost, *The Mayor of Casterbridge* alone would serve as well.

It was inevitable that Hardy should wind up there in 1883 to stay. His parents were still living in Higher Bockhampton, two and a half miles away, in the thatched cottage in which he'd been born. And, from his early architectural days on, he was forever returning to the area, wherever he might roam. He designed Max Gate himself, living at No. 7 Shire Hall Place off High West Street while building went on. He moved in, in June, 1885. A large, square-turreted red brick building now shielded by beeches and sycamores, and a mile out of town on the Wareham Road, the house then stood stark and bare on a rise of ground. But Hardy quickly planted trees, mainly Austrian pines—so many of them that later he wrote dourly of living "at the bottom of a dark green well."

It is now a good-sized house, easily twice its original modest proportions (only two rooms and a kitchen downstairs, three small bedrooms upstairs). For Hardy added much to it over the years, including the right hand turret, which now has a sundial with the dates he lived there: 1885–1928. Also, the place is much brighter than descriptions would have it, since most of the 2,000 pines he planted are gone.

Even before the house was finished, he was well along with the writing of

The Mayor of Casterbridge, and serial publication began in January of 1886. In the next forty years came *The Woodlanders* (1887), *Wessex Tales* (1888), *Tess of the d'Urbervilles* (1891), *The Well-Beloved* (1892), *Life's Little Ironies* (1894), *Jude the Obscure* (1895), other works of fiction, and several volumes of poems in addition to *The Dynasts* (1904, 1906, and 1908).

Hardy's study was a peripatetic affair, moving from place to place as the house grew. First he wrote in the room above the drawing room . . . then in a room looking west . . . and, finally, in a room with an opening to the east and Bockhampton. For her part, Emma's private hideaway was two tiny rooms in the attic, to which she would often retreat, especially when Hardy and a male guest settled down for a long gabfest. For though, like most writers, Hardy treasured—and needed—his privacy, a number of noteworthy visitors came to Max Gate to pay their respects, among them, in 1923, the Prince of Wales.

One of the sights of the 1890's was Hardy and Rudyard Kipling careening abreast on their bicycles, laughing perhaps at their recent adventure hunting for a house for Kipling. While Kipling inspected the house, Hardy had tried to impress the old lady who owned it: "My friend is no other than Mr. Rudyard Kipling." She had never heard of him. A bit later, while Hardy was out of the room, it was Kipling's turn: "My sponsor is Thomas Hardy himself." Her reply: "And who, pray, is he?" Another bicycling visitor was A. E. Housman.

Almost the first callers were Mr. and Mrs. Robert Louis Stevenson, who arrived little more than a month after the Hardys moved in. Fanny Stevenson's appraisal of Emma Hardy's odd behavior was as prescient as it was unkind: "What very strange marriages literary men seem to make." Later guests were to verify how right she was. When Irish poet and playwright W. B. Yeats came in 1912 to present Hardy with the Royal Society of Literature's gold medal, he found himself discussing the lives and habits of Emma's two cats—who at the time happened to be sitting on the table beside her plate. Similarly, both John Galsworthy and James M. Barrie developed an antipathy for the Hardys' dog Wessex. Galsworthy, who thought Hardy "a nice, dried up, alert old fellow," was bitten by the dog. And Barrie reported that the animal "proved a slight strain to the guests at dinner, by walking on the table and taking their food."

Robert Graves, Siegfried Sassoon, and T. E. Lawrence were others who visited Hardy in his later years. Lawrence, who was stationed at nearby Bovington Camp with the Tank Corps and had sought the novelist's advice about publishing *Seven Pillars of Wisdom,* was a particular favorite of the Hardys. He gives a memorable picture of Hardy at eighty-three: "There is an unbelievable dignity and ripeness about Hardy; he is waiting so tranquilly for death, without a desire or ambition left in his spirit as far as I can feel it."

Modern visitors to Dorchester cannot see Max Gate, for though it is owned by the National Trust, it is lived in by a private family, and neither home nor gardens are open to the public. Moreover, the house cannot be seen from the road. And even if it could, it would be suicide to try; traffic, especially in summer, is heavy on the Wareham Road, and cars whiz by at a perilous pace.

Fortunately there is no need to disturb Max Gate's privacy. For there is a perfect full-sized replica of Hardy's study in the Dorset County Museum on High West Street in Dorchester, conveniently near the Tourist Information Centre. And you can get a taste of "Casterbridge" from the start by staying at either the King's Arms, an eighteenth-century hotel on High East Street, or at the Antelope, a sixteenth-century coaching inn a few steps away on South Street. (Both hotels are two-star and near the Information Centre.) It was through the spacious box window of the King's Arms that Susan Henchard saw the mayor of Casterbridge—the husband who had sold her for five guineas eighteen years earlier. And it was at the Antelope, with its twin-bow-window front, that Lucetta le Seur arranged to meet Henchard to hand over her letters.

A detailed guide to all the Dorchester places and buildings that figure in Hardy's works need not be given here. You can get an abundance of material at the centre, or from the Thomas Hardy Society*, and shape your own tour to suit your personal desires and limitations. But, however much—or little—time you decide to allot add twenty percent to it: you'll find yourself stopping oftener, and longer, than you'd planned.

Weymouth

Eight miles south of Dorchester is Weymouth, a sea resort on the A 354. The population (with contiguous Melcombe Regis) is over 40,000. The novelist and poet Thomas Love Peacock was born there in 1785 but soon moved away. George III, however, who first came for a holiday in 1789, was so captivated he returned again and again. And Thomas Hardy was associated with Weymouth much of his life. Indeed, he wrote a good deal of his first published novel, *Desperate Remedies,* there in 1869–70. Not at all coincidentally, the book's heroine, Cytherea Graye, has lodgings in "Budmouth" (Weymouth) with a brother who works in an architect's office. At the time, Hardy had lodgings in Weymouth while working in an architect's office.

Twenty-nine years old and still a bachelor, Hardy enjoyed the town thoroughly. The curving, mile-long Esplanade along the shore especially

*The Vicarage, Haselbury Plucknett, Crewkerne, Somerset TA18 7PB

charmed him, as *Desperate Remedies* makes clear: "the long line of lamps on the sea-wall" seemed "to send long tap-roots of fire quivering down deep into the sea." Each morning at seven he would plunge into that sea to bathe, and most evenings after work he would row far out into the bay—often before joining the quadrille class that he later confessed was "a gay gathering for dances and love-making by adepts of both sexes."

Perhaps the place proved even too merry: after five months he moved back to Higher Bockhampton, his birthplace, so that he could concentrate on finishing his novel. But for the rest of his life he was in and out of Weymouth, and it was a favorite destination for bicycle jaunts after he settled down at Max Gate in Dorchester. The city and his experiences there figure in a number of his poems and novels.

Hardy's lodgings in Weymouth were in Wooperton Street—No. 3 of a row of narrow but pleasant three-storey terrace houses, each with its own upper storey bow window jutting out over the sidewalk. As for George III, he stayed at what is now the Gloucester Hotel (two stars) on the Esplanade, and you can stay there yourself if you like. It has a grand view of the sea.

Higher Bockhampton and Stinsford

About three miles northeast of Dorchester, and a short way off the A 35, is a narrow track with the merest scattering of houses on either side, hardly enough, really, to be called a village. This is Higher Bockhampton, and in the unassuming brick-faced dwelling at the end of the track—the picture postcard epitome of an English thatched cottage—Thomas Hardy was born on June 2, 1840. It was his home for the next thirty-four years, until his marriage, and it drew him back again and again almost until the day he died.

Upstairs, just off the room in which he was born, is the small bedroom he shared with his brother Henry. In its deep window seat, overlooking the garden, Hardy first tried his hand as a novelist with *The Poor Man and the Lady* (never published), went on to *Desperate Remedies* (1871) and *Under the Greenwood Tree* (1872), and became firmly established with *Far From the Madding Crowd* (1874).

The house itself appears in *Under the Greenwood Tree* as the home of the Dewy family, "a long, low cottage with a hipped roof of thatch, having dormer windows breaking up into the eaves, a chimney standing in the middle of the ridge and another at each end." Hardy's parents lived out their lives there, and after their mother's death in 1904, his brother and two sisters stayed on until 1912. Hardy often walked over from his home in Dorchester; and even after a bachelor friend took over the place, Hardy would still drop in from time to time, though the visits made him sad.

Today the house is owned by the National Trust and, in season (usually

Hardy's Cottage, Higher Bockhampton, Dorset

Robert M. Cooper

March to mid-October), the outside can be seen at any time, the inside, by appointment—by letter or telephone—with the tenant. Coming from Dorchester you take the *second* turning to the right marked "Higher Bockhampton." (You can take the first turning if you're the adventurous type who relishes bowling down a lane barely wide enough for your own car with a Leland lorry in that same lane heading toward you.) Signs will soon direct you to the Hardy Cottage carpark, from which it's a pleasant ten-minute walk through the woods to the house. On view inside is the sitting room with the low oak beam and stone-flagged floor of the Dewy's lively Christmas party . . . the tiny "office" where Hardy the elder paid off the help (he was a master mason) . . . and upstairs the two bedrooms. Return to the ground floor is made memorable by a trip down the very steep stairs—more nearly a ladder—that served as a back stairway for the Hardy boys to avoid disturbing their parents. A nice touch to wind up with: tea in Mellstock Tea Rooms, Bockhampton Lane.

Mellstock was Hardy's name for Stinsford, and its church quire—and their resistance to the new vicar's efforts to disband them in favor of an organ, forms the story of *Under the Greenwood Tree*. Hardy's own grandfather, father, and uncle had all been stalwarts of the Stinsford quire (i.e., "choir," a combination of instruments and singers), he himself had taught Sunday School, and the family burial plot was in the churchyard. Hardy's ashes, of course, are in the Poets' Corner of Westminster Abbey, but his heart was buried in Emma's Stinsford grave. (Nearby, incidentally, is the grave of C. Day Lewis, poet and devotee of Hardy.) Inside the church, in memorial to Hardy, is a stained glass window of Elijah the prophet. Stinsford—little more than the church, the vicarage, and a house or two—is just off the A 35, a bit more than a mile south west of Higher Brockhampton.

Clouds Hill

Eight miles east of Dorchester, and a couple of miles south of the A 35, on the wooded slope of a hill of the same name, is a tiny cottage called Clouds Hill (no apostrophe.) It's brick, two storeys—two rooms on each floor, but one of each little more than a closet. Even now it looks like the kind of place a lowly private in the Tank Corps at nearby Bovington Camp might rent as an inexpensive retreat from barracks life. And, indeed, a private did just that in 1923 for only two shillings, six pence a week—a Pvt. T.E. Shaw. But Shaw was no ordinary private. In reality, he was T. E. Lawrence . . . Lawrence of Arabia.

"T. E.," as his friends called him, had fled to the Tank Corps after the newspapers penetrated his disguise as "Aircraftsman Ross." He needed "a warm solitary place to hide in sometimes on a winter evening" while working on his endless revisions of *Seven Pillars of Wisdom* (1926). True, Clouds Hill,built in 1808, had long been neglected and was now practically a ruin. But he liked to work with his hands, and his needs were simple. With money from the sale of a gold dagger got in Mecca during the glamour days, he fixed the upstairs first and furnished it sparsely: a leather-covered settee, window seats, book shelves, an end table that doubled as a desk, a few tea things, and a gramophone with a huge horn. There was no plumbing.

"I don't sleep here," he wrote a friend, "but come out at 4:30 P.M. til 9 P.M. nearly every night, and dream, or write or read by the fire, or play Beethoven and Mozart to myself on the box." Over the door to the house he carved in Greek an inscription from Herodotus—loosely translated, "Why Worry?" Said he firmly, "Nothing in Clouds Hill is to be a care upon its inhabitant." Once, when a serviceman from the Arabian days offered himself to Lawrence as a valet when he should retire, T. E. replied gently, "No, Clouds Hill wouldn't look right with a valet."

In 1932 he translated the *Odyssey* of Homer—only to make money to improve Clouds Hill, he said—and proceeds were sufficient to make it livable enough to retire to, especially with the installation of a bathroom and a hot water plant. As the work progressed, he exulted to a friend: "Soon I shall have my very own bath! The first I have ever owned in exclusiveness. A milestone in my life."

Both at Bovington Camp and later when he rejoined the R.A.F., he was always generous in sharing Clouds Hill, letting friends like E. M. Forster, the novelist, use it with or without his presence, and bringing comrades from the camp back with him—assortments of two, three, four or more of all kinds—to share an evening. One of them, Alex Dixon, almost Lawrence's Tank Corps slavey, describes him on a typical night, "feeding the gramophone, making tea, stoking the fire and, by some magic of his own, managing without effort to keep everyone in good humor. There were many picnic meals (stuffed olives, salted almonds, and Heinz baked beans were regular features) washed down with T. E.'s own blends of China tea. Some of us used chairs, others the floor while T. E. always ate standing by the end of the wide oak mantelshelf which had been fitted at a height convenient to him." The mantel is about four feet from the floor. Lawrence was not a tall man.

In March of 1935, T. E. was discharged from the Air Force and looked forward to long, happy years of writing, music, and quiet content in his little cottage. "Wild mares," he wrote Lady Astor in May, "would not at present take me away from Clouds Hill." Five days later he was dead, victim of a crash when he swerved his motorcycle to avoid hitting two boys on bicycles.

Clouds Hill is owned by the National Trust and open to the public several days a week, April through September. Downstairs is the bookroom, dominated by the huge leather-covered divan and cushion Lawrence himself designed. Crammed into what little space remains are pictures and photographs, copies of T. E.'s books, and a duplicate of the Lawrence bust in St. Paul's Cathedral. Upstairs are the "Music Room" and tiny Bunk Room. The Music Room, a study in brown with massive exposed beams, has Lawrence's leather settee, folding table, the mantel he ate from, a coffin stool given him by Hardy's wife, and the gramophone.

Off this main room is the Bunk Room, with ship's bunk, small table, mirror, rugs—and an Arab robe with a glamorous history. It was given to the National Trust by Sir Alec Guiness, who explains its background thus: "It is a garment that (Sir Sidney) Cockerell bought from an Arab when he and Wilfred Blunt (I think) were wrecked off Sinai some time in the 1880's. He paid a sovereign for it—to protect himself against the sun. Later he gave it to T. E. as a dressing gown, and eventually T. E. left it to G. B. S. (George Bernard Shaw) who also used it as a dressing gown. It was finally sent back to Cockerell, who gave it to me."

Moreton and Wareham

Lawrence's grave is in the parish church (in the new cemetery) at Moreton, two miles west of Clouds Hill on a little unnumbered road. There is a statue of him in Arab robes at St. Martin's church in Wareham, an ancient little town seven miles southeast of Clouds Hill on the A 352.

Bere Regis—Puddletown—Lower Waterston

Visitors to Clouds Hill with a special yen for Thomas Hardy's novels will find scenes from *The Return of the Native, Tess of the d'Urbervilles,* and *Far From the Madding Crowd* all within easy distance.

A bit more than three miles to the northeast, right at the junction of the A 35 and A 31 is Bere Regis (Bere as in "beer" and "Regis" because King John—he of the Magna Carta—not only visited, but even built a royal residence there). In *Tess,* the town figures as "Kingsbere sub Greenhill." All around Bere Regis there are things to see, but the beautiful old parish church is a four-star must, even without its literary connections. But literary interest it has, for here in the chapel, now named after them, are buried the actual "knightly family" to whom, in Hardy's novel, Tess's father traces his ancestry with such tragic results.

Henry VIII granted the manor of Bere Regis to a Robert Turberville. A brass plate on the southeast wall and a large stone slab on the floor of the South Aisle attest to the death of Robert, 5 April 1559. The stone marks the entrance to the large vault below in which the Turberville lords of the manor had the right of burial. Over the slab is the colorful South Window with the arms of all those who held these memorial rights from King John down to recent days. This is the "beautifully traceried" window of Hardy's book, bearing the family crest which Tess's mother recognizes as she sets up the old four-post bedstead for the children under the south wall.

The church abounds with nonliterary delights as well, among them the curiously carved roof of the nave, with its four impressive bosses and the large wooden figures of the twelve Apostles peering down. Wonderfully amusing are the carvings on the capitals of the pillars on the south side, especially one depicting a man with a toothache and another of a monkey and dogs baiting a bull.

Puddletown Four miles northwest of Clouds Hill (and midway between Bere Regis and Dorchester) on the A 35 is Puddletown, the "Weatherbury" of Hardy in *Far from the Madding Crowd.* Here, with its "hideous gargoyles," is the church where Gabriel Oak and the others sing, and the dashing Troy spends a wretched night. Bathsheba's "fine old Jacobean house," fluted pilasters, paneled and columnar chimneys, and all, is at Waterston Manor in Lower Waterston, two miles away.

3. LYME REGIS AND RACEDOWN

At the very western edge of its coastline along the channel, just where Dorset is about to yield to Devon, is Lyme Regis. On Lyme Bay and the A 3052, Lyme Regis is still a favorite resort for those who shun such big commercial holiday spots as Bournemouth. Among its literary visitors of note were Jane Austen, Alfred Tennyson, and John Galsworthy.

Jane visited Lyme Regis several times in the early years of the nineteenth century, often staying for some weeks at a time, going to balls, and parading about to see—and be seen by—other visitors just like herself and to mock in her gentle way the prevailing "manners:" "It was absolutely necessary I should have the little fever and indisposition I had; it has been all the fashion this year in Lyme." She describes the town's attractions succinctly in *Persuasion* (1818): "As there is nothing to admire in the buildings themselves, the remarkable situation of the town, the principal street almost hurrying into the water, the walk to the Cobb itself, its old wonders and new improvements, with the very beautiful line of cliffs stretching out to the east of the town, are what the stranger's eye will seek."

The Cobb (literally "pier" or "breakwater") is the town's famous trademark, a stone wall protectively surrounding a circle of sailboats of all sorts, ideal for parading about in one's finery. And, atop this stone ring is an even higher level of wall for the more daring, such as *Persuasion's* Louisa Musgrove, who romantically flings herself from the upper wall into the arms of the dashing but unready Captain Wentworth—and nearly kills herself when her head hits the pavement.

Among those attracted to Lyme by reading this dramatic scene in the novel was Alfred Tennyson, who wrote his friend and fellow poet, William Allingham, in the summer of 1867 inviting him to join him there: "I have wanted to see the Cobb ever since I read *Persuasion.*" They walked to Lyme Regis from the Dorchester train station (Tennyson was a prodigious walker), and immediately after taking lodgings, the laureate insisted upon being shown the Cobb.

Exactly forty years later, just after publishing what was to be the first of the Forsyte Saga, *The Man of Property,* John Galsworthy came to this part of the Dorset coast in the spring of 1907 and was more charmed with its neighbors than he was with Lyme Regis: "We enjoy ourselves quite well here, and went a long walk on Thursday to Seaton along the cliffs; and then drove on to Beer—Seaton is rotten, but Beer is a jolly little old-world place. Charmouth we went to and found very nice. Lyme itself we don't care for—it's too *grey,* and the natives are so d——d ugly."

Poor Lyme Regis. It deserves much better.

Birdsmoor Gate Before he leaves Lyme Regis and Dorset, the true Wordsworth devotee may want to take a six mile run up the Crewkerne Road (the B 3165) to a handful of houses called Birdsmoor Gate. For on its outskirts, in 1795–97, in the squarely built, three-storey house called Racedown Lodge, the poet reached the mental, moral, and emotional nadir of his life:

> Sick, wearied out with contrarieties,
> [I] Yielded up moral questions in despair.
>
> This was the crisis of that strong disease,
> This the soul's last and lowest ebb; I drooped,
> Deeming our blessèd reason of least use
> Where wanted most. . . ."
>
> *The Prelude. Book XI*

Circumstances at Racedown hardly seemed propitious. Their neighbors were "miserable peasants," wrote sister Dorothy, his only companion, "with every vice that usually attends ignorance in that class." The nearest post office was miles away, and provisions had to come from Crewkerne. He lived, William said, mainly "upon air and the essence of carrots, cabbages, turnips."

Yet Wordsworth fought his way through to become one of England's great poets, thanks to Dorothy ("She, in the midst of all, preserved me still/ A Poet") . . . and thanks, too, to that very post office, however distant. For it brought him letters from the newfound friend he'd met in Bristol, Samuel Taylor Coleridge, filled with warmth and admiration (he'd already decided Wordsworth was a genius), and keen, creative criticism of the poems Wordsworth began to send him.

Best of all, in June 1797 came Coleridge himself, leaping over a gate and bounding down a pathless field. He stayed three weeks and was back in four days: the Wordsworths must come at once with him to Nether Stowey (Somerset) for a reciprocal visit. They did—and never returned to Racedown. (For details of this see pp. 269-270.)

As a private home, Racedown is not open to the public, but you can drive past it and have a look at the village, if you like.

LOWER AVON

Lower Avon

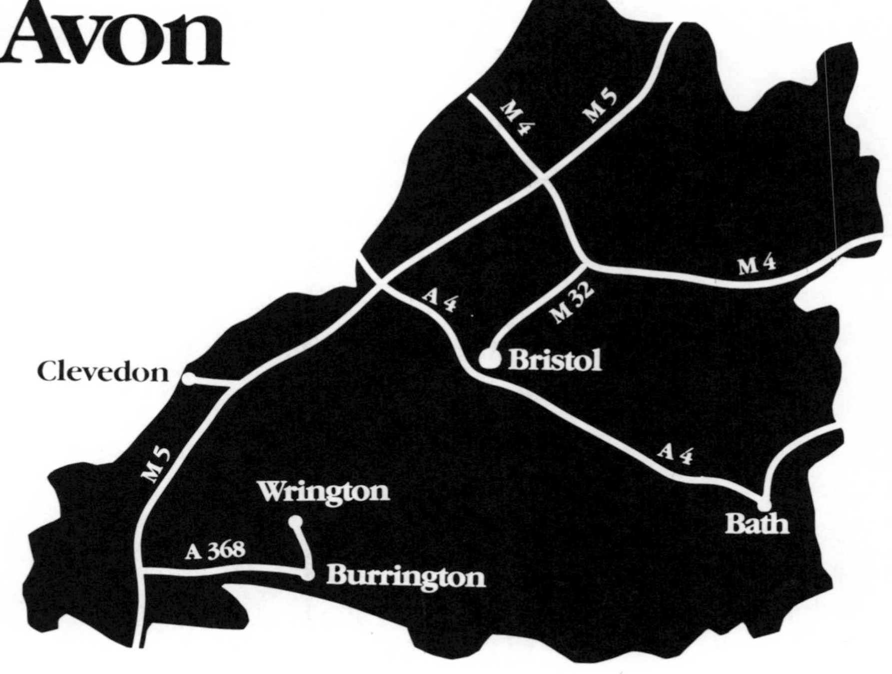

M 4
M 5
M 4
A 4
M 32
Bristol
Clevedon
A 4
M 5
Wrington
Bath
A 368
Burrington

> . . . there was the same noble country, the same broad expanse of hill and dale, the same beautiful channel stealing on, far away; the same lofty mountains which, like the troubles of life, viewed at a distance, and partially obscured by the bright mist of its morning, lose their ruggedness and asperity, and seem all ease and softness.
>
> Charles Dickens, *The Pickwick Papers*

Yes, this is Avon, though Dickens was speaking of Somerset. For Dickens was describing the country around Bath, and Bath was then Somerset. There are more than a few who live there now who wish it were Somerset still and decry the creation in 1972 of "Avonshire" out of Bath and Bristol and a few other odds and ends from Gloucestershire and Somerset.

Today Bath is served by a network of modern roads—the A 4, A 39, A 367, A 36, and A 46 all meet there—and the mighty M 4 is only eight miles to the north. But for all that, Bath and its surroundings remain essentially the same noble country, call it what you will. The same beautiful channel (the Severn) steals on, just seventeen miles to the northwest. And for us as for Dickens, the same lofty mountains (the glorious Cotswolds) stretch on for fifty miles or more to the northeast.

There is, too, the same literary history, going back to the Middle Ages and before. Chaucer's much-married "worthy wif" was from "biside Bath," after all, and Thomas Chatterton's fifteenth-century "Thomas Rowley" was a Bristol monk . . . and Chatterton himself was a Bristol Boy.

The Royal Crescent, Bath, Avon

By Courtesy of Bath City Council

1. BATH

In a literary name-dropping contest, Bath would lead all other cities save London by a wide margin and come close to matching that galaxy of ghosts described earlier as haunting the whole of Kent. For on the streets of Bath jostle—if ghosts can jostle—the wraiths of Fielding and Sheridan and Dr. Johnson and Jane Austen and Shelley and Dickens . . . of Tom Jones and Mrs. Malaprop, Catherine Morland and Mr. Pickwick, Matthew Bramble and the Wife of Bath . . . and dozens and dozens more, real and fictional.

You can almost feel their presence as you retrace their steps. It is pure magic, for instance, to enter the city on a wet afternoon, as Jane Austen's Lady Russell and Anne Elliot did, and find yourself "driving through the long course of streets from the Old Bridge of Camden Place" and catching "the first dim view of the extensive buildings, smoking in rain." Today, it takes a bit of imagination to make the buildings seem that extensive, true—or to hear "the dash of other carriages, the heavy rumble of carts and drays, the bawling of newsmen, muffin-men, and milk-men." But in Bath, imagination comes easy.

In his twelfth-century *Historia Regum Britanniae,* that most inventive of historians, Geoffrey of Monmouth, solemnly asserts that Bath was created by black magic in 863 B.C. by a king named Bladud, who made the healing springs by dumping a stone big as a tree in the water. Bladud went on to rule for twenty years, Geoffrey assures us, and was succeeded by a son named Lear. Lear in turn, it seems, had no sons, but three daughters—Goneril, Regan, and Cordelia—a circumstance that William Shakespeare made rather much of.

Somewhat more reliable as history is the fact that soon after the Romans came to Britain in 43 A.D., they pushed their way to Bath and erected an appreciable city around those same waters. Remains of their elaborate baths, to be seen today beside the Pump Room, are impressive proof of the high standard of living they enjoyed.

After the Romans left in the fifth century, nothing of great moment happened in Bath for thirteen hundred years. Oh, in the sixth century the Anglo-Saxons invaded and made a mess of the place, but did give it a new name: "Hoet Bathum," the hot baths. And in the eleventh century it bet on the wrong man to succeed William the Conqueror—Robert instead of his unpleasant younger brother William Rufus—and got sacked and burned for its error. Bath rose again, however, to flourish as a clothmaking center in the Middle Ages, as exemplified by Chaucer's Wife of Bath, whose skill at "cloothmayking" actually "passed hem [them] of Ypres and of Gaunt."

Map of Bath

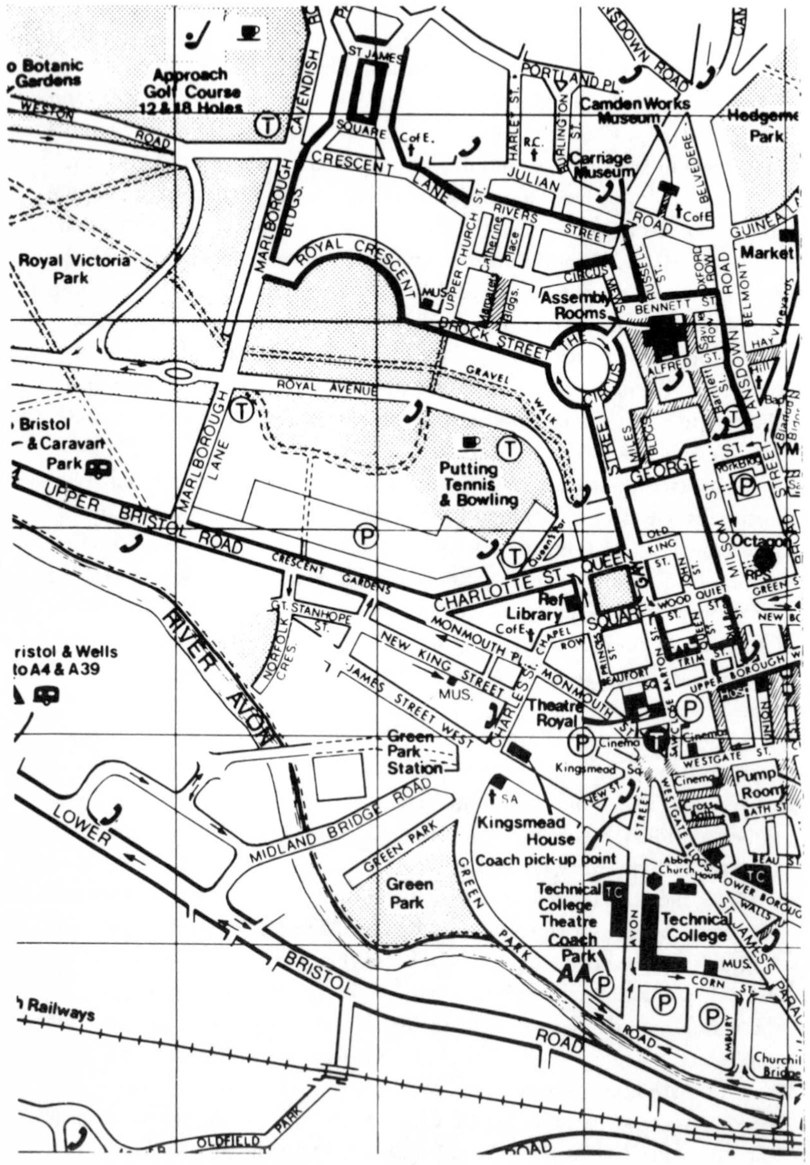
Botanic Gardens
Approach Golf Course 12 & 18 Holes
WESTON ROAD
CAVENDISH
ST JAMES'S SQUARE
CofE.
PORTLAND PL.
HARLEY ST.
R.C.
BURLINGTON ST.
Camden Works Museum
Hedgemead Park
BELVEDERE
Carriage Museum
CRESCENT LANE
JULIAN ROAD
CofE
MARLBOROUGH BLDGS.
RIVERS STREET
GUINEA LANE
Royal Victoria Park
ROYAL CRESCENT
UPPER CHURCH ST.
Catherine Place
MUS.
Margaret's Bldgs.
Assembly Rooms
CIRCUS
RUSSELL ST.
OXFORD ROW
ROAD
BELMONT
Market
Vineyards
BENNETT ST.
Saville Row
LANSDOWN
HAY HILL
BROCK STREET
THE CIRCUS
ALFRED ST.
Bartlett St.
GRAVEL WALK
ROYAL AVENUE
MARLBOROUGH LANE
Bristol & Caravan Park
Putting Tennis & Bowling
GAY STREET
MILES BLDGS.
GEORGE ST.
York Bldgs
UPPER BRISTOL ROAD
MILSOM ST.
Octagon
CRESCENT GARDENS
QUEEN
OLD KING ST.
JOHN ST.
CHARLOTTE ST.
Queen's Par.
Ref. Library
SQUARE
WOOD ST.
QUIET ST.
GREEN ST.
NEW BOND ST.
GT. STANHOPE ST.
NORFOLK CRES.
MONMOUTH PL.
CofE
CHAPEL ROW
PRINCES ST.
BARTON ST.
QUEEN ST.
TRIM ST.
RIVER AVON
NEW KING STREET
MONMOUTH
BEAUFORT
UPPER BOROUGH WALLS
Bristol & Wells to A4 & A39
JAMES STREET WEST
MUS.
CHARLES ST.
Theatre Royal
UNION ST.
Green Park Station
Cinema
Kingsmead Sq.
WESTGATE ST.
Cinema
Pump Room
NEW ST.
SA
BATH ST.
MIDLAND BRIDGE ROAD
Kingsmead House
Coach pick-up point
LOWER
GREEN PARK
Green Park
GREEN PARK
Abbey Church
TC
LOWER BOROUGH WALLS
Technical College Theatre
Coach Park
AA
AVON ST.
Technical College
MUS.
ST. JAMES'S PARADE
BRISTOL ROAD
CORN ST.
Railways
ROAD
AMBURY
Churchill Bridge
OLDFIELD PARK
ROAD

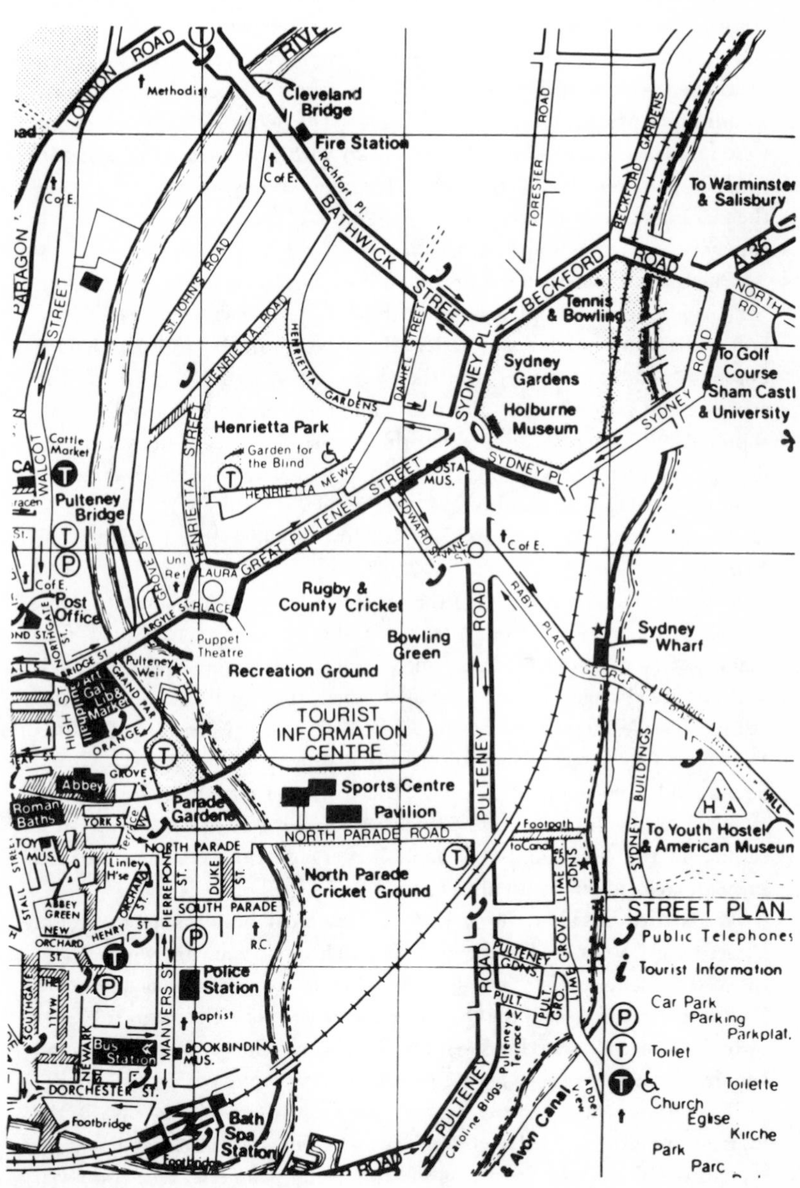
Cleveland Bridge
Fire Station
Methodist
To Warminster & Salisbury
Tennis & Bowling
Sydney Gardens
Holburne Museum
To Golf Course Sham Castl & University
Henrietta Park
Garden for the Blind
Pulteney Bridge
Post Office
Rugby & County Cricket
Bowling Green
Sydney Wharf
Puppet Theatre
Recreation Ground
TOURIST INFORMATION CENTRE
Sports Centre
Pavilion
Parade Gardens
Roman Baths
Abbey
To Youth Hostel & American Museum
North Parade Cricket Ground
Police Station
Baptist
BOOKBINDING MUS.
Bath Spa Station
STREET PLAN
Public Telephones
Tourist Information
Car Park
Parking
Parkplat.
Toilet
Toilette
Church
Eglise
Kirche
Park
Parc

By the seventeenth century, when both Pepys and Evelyn visited it, Bath had become a somewhat noisome and often dangerous stamping ground for drunken toughs, gamesters, and soldiers of fortune. Although Pepys said it had "a pretty good market-place, and many good streets, and very fair stone houses," other travellers complained that the streets were mean and narrow and the houses were jammed into the small area between the city walls. Even gentlemen who visited were quartered in rooms no better than garrets, according to Macaulay's *History of England:* "The floors of the dining rooms were uncarpeted, and were coloured brown with a wash made of soot and small beer in order to hide the dirt." Then came the eighteenth century and the making of the gem that is Bath—the work of four unusual men, with a timely boost or two from royalty.

Queen Anne provided the first royal boost, her visit in 1702 upgrading the city's reputation and making such visits fashionable. To handle the hordes that came in her wake, Bath built the North and South Parades, with dozens of handsome houses. But they were not enough. What to do? The answer came from the first and most important of the four pivotal men, Ralph Allen. Allen had the three things the city needed most: vision, daring, and money. As a bonus, he also had a quarry, from which came the stone that makes Bath's buildings so distinctive. It speaks well of Allen that he later served as the model for Squire Allworthy in Henry Fielding's *Tom Jones* (1749).

It was Allen who brought in the second of Bath's unique quartet, John Wood, Sr., an architect whom Allen retained to rebuild the city. Wood's first major achievement was Queen Square, northwest of the Upper Borough Wall, built between 1729 and 1735. The Square speedily became Bath's most fashionable address, the star tenant being the Prince of Wales himself. Wood then built Gay Street, which ultimately became the link between Queen Square and Wood's grandest work, The Circus, a stately circle of thirty attached houses in three arcs. Wood's last design was equally impressive, calling for the same number of noble homes, but this time arranged in a graceful crescent six hundred feet long.

Wood died in 1754, however, and the actual building of the Royal Crescent, as it was called, was bequeathed to his son, John, Jr., who had also finished the Circus. (The "Royal" again bespoke the patronage of a Prince of Wales, this one the son of the Queen Square benefactor.) The younger Wood's own chef d'oeuvre was the Assembly Rooms, which—as Jane Austen and Charles Dickens have shown—were the glittering center of Bath's social life.

The idea for the Assembly Rooms came from Richard "Beau" Nash, the fourth and most improbable of Bath's creators. For when Nash came to town soon after Queen Anne's visit, he was thirty and penniless, a ne'er-do-well dropout from the army and law school, a gambler and a dandy. Bath's ballroom and gaming halls were still cowering before the rudeness and violence of riffraff who mingled with their betters, muddying floors with their boots, tearing gowns with their spurs, insulting the women, and challenging the men. Nash, of all people, put a stop to that. When he was appointed to the honorary position of "Master of Ceremonies" of the Pump Room in 1705, by sheer audacity he proceeded to make himself undisputed master of Bath as well.

Nash cleaned up the Pump Room and posted a Code of Rules so strict that even a royal princess was refused her plea for one more dance after the decreed eleven o'clock closing. Nash banned swords—and duels—from Bath and caused streets to be paved and lighted. He had the Assembly Rooms built so that a gentleman could lose a fortune in elegant, comfortable, safe surroundings, and even by daylight if he liked.

In later years, sad to say, Nash fell from favor when a lawsuit revealed that he had taken a more than ceremonial interest in the profits from the gambling tables. But one person remained faithful to him till the end, and after—Julianna Popjoy, his mistress. For some reason, after his death she vowed never again to sleep in a bed. She must have kept her vow: she wound up living in a hollow tree in Wiltshire. Bath keeps her memory green. Beau Nash's home now houses one of the city's most elegant restaurants. Its name: Popjoy's.

Thanks, then, to the unlikely combination of one queen, two princes, a developer, two architects, and a gambler, Bath came to be the very embodiment of the eighteenth century. It is as if for this city there had been no Elizabethan Age before, no Victorian Age after. The modern visitor, when he sees Bath, is likely to have a sense of déjà vu. But so, possibly, did the eighteenth-century visitors when they came. And they came in legions.

It's been said that if you sat at a cafe table on Paris's Rue de la Paix long enough, you'd see everybody in the world who was anybody pass by. The same could have been said, and more truly, of eighteenth-century Bath's Pump Room. Well did *Persuasion's* Anne Elliot worry about Lady Russell's running into Captain Wentworth, "so liable as everybody was to meet everybody in Bath." Among the first "everybody's" of literary note to come to the revived Bath were comic playwrights Congreve and Gay, Pope and his friend Dr. Arbuthnot, Fielding and his rival Richardson, and Lord Chesterfield. Fielding came in 1748 and wrote some of *Tom Jones,* patterning Squire Western after a Bath neighbor as well as Allworthy after Ralph Allen. Lord Chesterfield arrived in 1738, and liked it so well he stayed until 1771, and wrote many of his famous *Letters* to his young illegitimate son from Bath.

In the fifties and sixties, visitors included Edward Gibbon, Laurence

Sterne, Horace Walpole, and Tobias Smollett. Smollett had already published *Roderick Random* (1748), but in Bath he made one last try to succeed as a doctor before turning to a writing career in that precarious new genre, the novel. *Humphry Clinker* (1771) as well as *Roderick Random* reflect his days in Bath. But if Matthew Bramble's opinions in the later novel are anything like his creator's, Smollett did not like the changes the Woods had wrought.

The approaches to Queen Square, Bramble declared, were mean, dirty, dangerous, and indirect. Gay Street was difficult, steep, and slippery. In Bath he finds nothing but noise, tumult, and hurry. "Every upstart of fortune, harnessed in the trappings of the mode, presents himself at Bath, filling the public rooms with a vile mob of noise and impertinence."

Nor did the flood of visitors abate in the seventies. With the completion of the Assembly Rooms in 1771, Bath was awash with VIPs. In that decade alone came such writers as Sheridan, Goldsmith, Scott, Southey, Dr. Johnson (and, of course, Boswell, his human tape recorder), Mrs. Thrale (Piozzi), and Fanny Burney. Sheridan's experiences in Bath were typically flamboyant. Soon after his family moved there in 1770, he eloped with a Bath girl, rescuing her from the clutches of a dastard who'd been hounding her . . . married her secretly in Calais . . . and returned to fight two duels with the bounder (outside the city limits, naturally). Sheridan's two best plays, *The Rivals* (1775) and *The School for Scandal* (1777) both have their roots in Bath.

Scott and Southey came to Bath as children, Scott to stay with his uncle on the South Parade, and Southey with his aunt in Walcot. But Dr. Johnson was the undisputed leader of English letters when he made a number of visits in the 1770's. One of his choicest quips came in defense of a woman of Bath. Told by scandal mongers that she used rouge, he replied "Better she should be reddening her own cheeks than blackening other people's characters."

Dr. Johnson was attracted to Bath by his intimate friend Mrs. Thrale, wife of a wealthy brewer who for years kept a house in Bath. It was the Thrales, too, who brought Fanny Burney there on several occasions. In later years the novelist came back to live in Bath, and both she and her French refugee husband are buried in the Walcot cemetery.

The woman writer most closely associated with Bath, however, is Jane Austen. The city seems overrun with plaques proclaiming her presence. Actually, two houses mark where she stayed on visits, and four others, where she lived at various times between 1801 and 1806. In addition, Bath figures prominently in both *Northanger Abbey* and *Persuasion*.

But the Austen family had ties with Bath even before Jane's birth in 1775. Her grandparents lived in retirement there; her parents were married there; and an uncle had settled at No. 1 Paragon, where Jane's family visited from time to time. In 1799, when Jane was twenty-four, they took quarters at No.

13 Queen Square. It's the last in the row of attached four-storey houses running west from today's Francis Hotel. Jane and her mother shared "two very nice-sized rooms, with dirty quilts and everything comfortable." Said Jane, "far more cheerful than Paragon."

In 1801, Jane's father retired as rector of Steventon in Hampshire, and the family took a lease on No. 4 Sydney Place in Bath, responding perhaps to a newspaper advertisement: "The situation is desirable, the Rent very low, and the Landlord is bound by contract to paint the first two floors this summer." The situation wasn't all that desirable—it was across the river from the heart of town—but it did overlook the Sydney Gardens, whose music, fireworks, watershows, and public breakfasts were great attractions. The Austens stayed in this house three years, and Jane revised and finished *Northanger Abbey.*

When the Sydney Place lease ran out, the Austens moved first to No. 27 Green Park Building (October, 1804–March, 1805), then to No. 25 Gay, near the Circus, and finally—after their usual summer holiday away—to Trim Street for the winter of 1805–06. This was their last stay in Bath.

It is not likely that Jane Austen would identify herself with the superficial and affected Isabella Thorpe of *Northanger Abbey,* who scornfully declared of Bath that "though it is vastly well to be here for a few weeks, we would not *live* here for millions." But Bath may well have begun to pall, and Jane seemed happy enough to leave it for Southampton.

In any case, with the beginning of the nineteenth century, Bath had begun to change drastically. Increasingly, it had become a retreat for the modest retired, with the fashionably rich more and more deserting its once-lustrous rendezvous for newer and more glittering resorts like Brighton, plaything of the latest Prince of Wales. But a number of writers still came to Bath to visit or stay, nonetheless. Their names are not inconsiderable, either: Landor, Shelley, Lamb, De Quincey, Coleridge, Wordsworth, Southey, Thackeray, Bulwer-Lytton, and Dickens.

Landor came to Bath in 1811, saw a beauty across the ballroom, fell in love on the spot—and married her. Twenty-seven years later he returned to live there, staying from 1838 to 1858. Some of his best-known *Imaginary Conversations* were written in Bath. And it was while visiting Landor, whom he came to see a number of times, that Charles Dickens conceived the idea of Little Nell for *The Old Curiosity Shop* (1841). It was Landor, too, who served as the model for Boythorn in *Bleak House.*

Shelley's stay in Bath was tumultuous even for so frenetic a man as he. He established himself in Queen Square in September, 1816, with Mary Godwin—though he was still married to Harriet Westbrook—and Mary's half sister, Clare Clairmont. In the next three months, another of Mary's half sisters committed suicide . . . Harriet drowned herself in London . . . and

Clare gave birth to an illegitimate daughter. The father? Gordon, Lord Byron.

Bath's fictional ghosts can in no way match in numbers this parade of figures from actual life. But among the imaginary characters are some of the most amusing ever created. There is Chaucer's Wife of Bath, burying husband number five even as her eyes search alertly from beneath that enormous hat for number six. And Smollett's self-proclaimed misanthrope, Matthew Bramble, fulminating against Bath as a national hospital where none but lunatics are admitted. Of thirteen guests in a coffee house, he counts seven lamed by gout, rheumatism, or palsy; three maimed by accident; and the rest either deaf or blind. To him the Circus looks like Vespasian's amphitheatre turned inside out, and the sprawl of new buildings like the disjointed remains of an earthquake.

The very essence of Bath's social life, with its regimented gaiety and glittering emptiness, is Sheridan's target in *The Rivals*. Fag, servant to the supposed "Ensign Beverly" comes upon Thomas, servant to Sir Anthony Absolute, newly come to Bath:

> Thomas: But pray, Mr. Fag, what kind of a place is this Bath? I ha' heard a deal of it—here's a mort o'merry-making, hey?
>
> Fag: Pretty well, Thomas, pretty well—'tis a good lounge; in the morning we go to the pump-room (though neither my master nor I drink the waters); after breakfast we saunter on the parades or play a game of billiards; at night we dance; but damn the place, I'm tired of it; their regular hours stupefy me—not a fiddle nor a card after eleven!

The incomparable Mrs. Malaprop, too, was at heart a leader of this same society, for Sheridan originally intended his *School for Scandal* to be laid in Bath, and the play is born of one of Nash's Rules: "that all repeaters of lies and scandals be shunned by all company, except such as have been guilty of the same crime."

In her own well-bred way, Jane Austen is no more sparing of Bath's preening peacocks. There is Isabella Thorpe in *Northanger Abbey*, for instance, fuming at being held up by traffic outside the Pump Room because young ladies like her are forever being detained, "however important their business, whether in quest of pastry, millinery, or even (as in the present case) of young men."

And in the same novel Jane parallels Sheridan's lampoon of the city's elaborately structured idleness, as Mr. Tilney gravely mocks Catherine's "busy" days in Bath:

"Were you never here before, madam?" he asks.
"Never, sir."
"Indeed! Have you yet honoured the Upper Rooms?"
"Yes, sir; I was there last Monday."
"Have you been to the theatre?"
"Yes, sir; I was at the play on Tuesday."
"To the concert?"
"Yes, sir; on Wednesday."
"And are you altogether pleased with Bath?"
"Yes; I like it very well."
"Now I must give one smirk," Tilney concludes, "and then we may be rational again."

Jane Austen's *Persuasion,* too, is largely set in Bath, but now the city is twenty years older and is beginning to seem dowdy, at least to those who hugged the superficial to their hearts. The Misses Musgrove yearn for a distinguished address—"none of your Queen Squares for us!" The Elliots spurn the Pump and Assembly Rooms, finding their evening amusements "solely in the elegant stupidity of private parties." And Sir Walter mourns the lack of beauties: in Bond Street once he watched eighty-seven women go by "without there being a tolerable face among them."

Even more déclassé is the Bath Charles Dickens presents in *The Pickwick Papers,* yet another twenty years later than *Persuasion.* The denizens of the Assembly Rooms are now the likes of Lord Mutanhed, Lady Snuphanuph, and Mrs. Colonel Wugsby. The once omnipotent Master of Ceremonies has shrunk to Angelo Cyrus Bantam, Esquire, a "charming young man of not more than fifty" with a perpetual smile, toadying to a vulgar and stupid clientele.

Mr. Pickwick and company ensconce themselves first at The White Hart Hotel, opposite the Pump Room, and then at the Royal Crescent, and proceed to a set of adventures rivaling anything in *Humphry Clinker,* for Dickens is a true son of Smollett. Most hilarious, perhaps, is Mr. Winkle's wild night at the Crescent, when he gets locked out, bolts into Mrs. Dowler's sedan, and winds up being madly pursued by Mr. Dowler with knife in hand.

The Pickwick Papers was published in 1836–1837, and by then Bath's heyday was long over. The city was already essentially as Arthur Waugh, father of Evelyn, described it in the first part of the twentieth century:

A city of the eighteenth century, bland and beautiful, dreaming with her grey stone eyes of the glories of an unforgettable past.

You'll find it so today. The throngs of literary ghosts still roam its streets, content in scenes unchanged since when they lived. Yes, on almost every street you'll feel their presence well-nigh palpable.

A Literary Tour of Bath

Because there are so many literary sites to see in Bath, it's best to follow a definite and detailed itinerary. The following will save you a lot of time, to say nothing of energy—the streets are steep! Of course you'll walk: there are few places to park a car along the way, and too much to see anyhow.

1. Begin at the **Tourist Information Centre,** at Cheap Street and Union. It has abundant maps and material and makes an excellent starting point.

2. Leave the Centre and go right across the way to the **Pump Room.** Rebuilt in 1795, it was the heart of fashionable Bath. Restoration after WW II damage made it much as it was in JANE AUSTEN and *The Pickwick Papers.* Open daily; morning coffee; luncheon on the terrace; tea.

3. Next to the Pump Room are the **Roman Baths,** dating from the first century. Water's still hot (120°); still medicinal.

4. Now walk east across the courtyard pausing to look west through the Colonnade and across the street at the flats and shops. There stood **The White Hart Hotel** where JANE AUSTEN's Musgroves and CHARLES DICKENS's Pickwick stayed.

5. At the end of the courtyard is the **Abbey,** where PEPYS slept through a sermon, and bell-ringers welcomed each new coachful of visitors.

6. Continue east to **Terrace Walk,** where SHERIDAN wrote some of *The Rivals* at No. 7, and then down to **North Parade.** As you go east along the Parade, note No. 9, where WORDSWORTH lived (1841) . . . and No. 11, home of both GOLDSMITH (1771) and EDMUND BURKE (1790's).

7. At the end of North Parade, go south on Duke to **South Parade** where FANNY BURNEY stayed with the THRALES (1778) at No. 14 and SIR WALTER SCOTT lived as a boy at No. 6.

8. At the west end of South Parade is **Pierrepont,** where LORD NELSON stayed at No. 2 . . . LORD CHESTERFIELD at No's. 3A and 4 (then one house) . . . SHERIDAN's rescued beauty, Elizabeth Linley, was born at No. 5.

9. At Linley House, take Old Orchard St. to Henry and continue west as Henry becomes New Orchard and Lower Borough before running into Westgate Buildings, where—in **Chapel Court**—HORACE WALPOLE lived (1765) . . . and *Persuasion*'s Anne Elliot visited her impoverished friend Mrs. Smith, much to her uncle's horror.

10. Running north from the junction of Westgate Buildings and West-

gate Street is **Sawclose**, where BEAU NASH lived in the house that's now **Popjoy's** restaurant; Nash's eagle-bedecked carved doorway and first floor salon survive.

11. West of this same junction is **Kingsmead Square,** with an enormous oak tree. SHERIDAN placed the last scene of *The Rivals* here.

12. From Kingsmead Square go down New Street, then right on James to where it meets Charles Street on the right and Green Park on the left. The eastern side of the **Green Park Buildings** was destroyed in WWII, but the western side was spared, and JANE AUSTEN lived at No. 27 for six months (1804–05) dampness and all.

13. Two other streets in this area have their interest. Historian EDWARD GIBBON often visited **No. 22 Charles Street** where his stepmother lived. And **No. 19 New King Street** offers its own footnote to KEATS. For there lived William Herschel, whose discovery of the planet Uranus inspired these lines in "On First Looking Into Chapman's Homer":

> Then felt I like some watcher of the skies
> When a new planet swims into his ken.

14. From Charles Street **Queen Square** is only a few steps northeast via Chapel. JANE AUSTEN's house (1799) is No. 13, on the southwest corner of the Square; No. 6, along this same row, was SHELLEY's during that hectic winter. The house was another victim of WWII, but a plaque marks the site.

15. At the southeast corner of the Square, Barton Street leads south to **Trim Street** where the AUSTENS spent their final months in Bath. On Trim, too, was the home at No. 5 that GEN. JAMES WOLFE left in 1759 for his little trip to Quebec.

16. From the east end of Trim the way goes south on **Old Bond** (where Sir Walter Elliot saw no beauties), then east on Upper Borough Walls and Bridge Street to **Pulteney Bridge.** The bridge, a picturesque Florentine affair lined with shops, was opened in 1771; and JANE AUSTEN trod it constantly coming and going from Sydney Place.

17. Sydney Place is about a third of a mile due northeast of the bridge, by way of Argyle, Laura Place, and Great Pulteney. **Laura Place** is where *Persuasion*'s Lady Darymple lived "in style" . . . and *Northanger Abbey*'s Catherine Morland stayed on **Great Pulteney,** as in real life did BULWER-LYTTON (at No. 2, then a hotel). The AUSTEN house on **Sydney Place** (she spelled it Sidney) was No. 4.

18. Back at the bridge, a right turn up Northgate takes you to the bottom of the "V" formed by Broad and Walcott Streets. Here is **St. Michael's** parish church—the parish of CHAUCER'S Wife of Bath, for she lived not *in* the

city, but "biside" Bath. The present church dates only from 1837, but a shop up the street houses a bit of the medieval church where she would have wed her husbands five "at chirche dore."

19. After about 700 feet, Broad becomes Landsdown Road, and at this point York Buildings runs off to the left, Paragon to the right. On **York Buildings** is the **Royal York Hotel** (three-star) where Queen Victoria stayed as a princess . . . DICKENS stopped to conceive Little Nell . . . and JANE AUSTEN scornfully depicts the young Thorpes of *Northanger Abbey* bolting down their lunch and dinner. And JANE herself would have visited **No. 1 Paragon** often to see her aunt and uncle.

20. A little further up Landsdown, also off to the left, is **Bennett Street.** On Bennett are the **Assembly Rooms,** redolent of JANE AUSTEN and CHARLES DICKENS, and still a major attraction. Here *Northanger Abbey*'s Catherine finds her Mr. Tilney . . . *Persuasion*'s Anne regains her Captain Wentworth . . . and *Pickwick Papers*' Mr. Pickwick is entrapped by Lady Snuphanuph. A "must see" at the Rooms today is the **Museum of Costumes** (open daily for a fee), where displays of fashions bring old Bath to life.

21. Fom the Assembly Rooms, St. James's Square—highest spot (topographically) on the tour—is reached via Russell Street, Rivers Street, and Crescent Lane. MRS. THRALE lived on **Russell** . . . and both LANDOR (at No. 3) and *Persuasion's* Lady Russell on **Rivers.**

22. In **St. James's Square,** LANDOR stayed (1837 to 1857) at both No. 1 and No. 35 where DICKENS visited him.

23. From St. James's it's mercifully down hill all the way. First stop, via Marlborough Buildings, is (halfway down on the left) the handsome **Royal Crescent,** where SHERIDAN snatched Elizabeth Linley away from No. 11 . . . CHRISTOPHER ANSTEY, Bath's own Poet Laureate, lived at No. 5 . . . and *Pickwick Papers*' Mr. Winkle found himself being chased all over the Crescent by an irate Mr. Dowler, carving knife in hand.

24. Directly east from the Crescent, Brock Street leads to **The Circus,** where commemorative plaques proliferate. Among them are those for THACKERAY, at No. 5 . . .PITT, No. 7 . . . LIVINGSTONE, No. 13 . . . and GAINSBOROUGH, No. 14.

25. Running south from The Circus and connecting it with Queen Square is **Gay Street,** where lived FANNY BURNEY (No. 41) . . . JANE AUSTEN (No. 25) . . . and *Persuasion*'s Admiral Croft.

26. From Gay Street it's only a zig (turn left halfway down Gay onto George Street) and a zag (then right on Milsom) back to the starting point. **Milsom** was JANE AUSTEN's favorite shopping place for bonnets, laces, and gowns. On Milsom Street, too, her Anne Elliot thrills inside a pastry

shop as Captain Wentworth enters . . . and laughs outside a printshop as Admiral Croft ponders the picture of a ship that never was.

With that the tour is over. For Milsom quickly yields to Union . . . and the Pump Room.

2. BRISTOL

Huddled in a four-mile hollow at the confluence of the Avon and Frome rivers, Bristol also sits athwart the intersection of two of England's great highways, the M 4 and the M 5.* Seven miles to the northwest is the sweep of the Severn, majestically parting England from Wales. Fourteen miles to the southeast is Bath, steeped in its Georgian nostalgia. Bristol, all big-city bustle and business, suffers by comparison with both. Little suggests to the casual visitor anything of literary consequence. Yet from Bristol's harbor sailed the hero of one of the greatest satires of all time, and in Bristol another sailor (this one real) planted the seed of a romance whose appeal proved worldwide and everlasting. From Bristol, too, came the most poignant of poetic prodigies, and full-blown, one of the loveliest and best-known of reflective poems. And in Bristol was printed what Ernest Bernbaum called "the most important poetical publication in the English language since the appearance of *Paradise Lost.*"

Still, the strictly "bustle and business" image of Bristol persists. For above all other English cities, Bristol owes its greatness almost wholly to trade, and for centuries visitors have seen little else to talk about. In the very decades when Bath was rising to grandeur, Horace Walpole, the gothic novelist (*Castle of Otranto,* 1764), was calling Bristol "the dirtiest great shop I ever saw;" satirist Richard Savage was lashing it with:

> Still spare the catamite and swing the whore,
> And be whate're Gommorrah was before;

and Alexander Pope was asserting with less than civil leer: "very, very unpleasant, and no civilized company in it." According to one tourist of the

---

*Great Britain has at least six "Avon" rivers, including this one, rising in the Cotswolds and emptying into the mouth of the Severn; one rising near Marlborough (Wilts.) and emptying into the English Channel; and Shakespeare's Avon, beginning in Northamptonshire, passing Rugby and Stratford, and joining the Severn at Tewkesbury (Glos.).

day, "the very parsons of Bristol talk of nothing but trade and how to turn a penny."

And even the talk of trade was not always edifying. There was, for instance, Bristol's preeminence for almost a millennium in the slave trading of the western world. Even before Canute and the completion of the first thousand years of Christianity, Bristol carried on a brisk traffic in slaves—native Englishmen at that! Even members of England's royal house openly engaged in slave trading. And, though William the Conquerer and his successors did their Norman best to stamp it out, as late as 1127 and the *Gesta Regum Anglorum* and its sequels, William of Malmesbury was lamenting the practice. A lively writer as well as an accurate historian, William vividly describes how, in the twelfth century, Bristol Harbor was crammed with ships from all parts of Europe. But elsewhere he deplores how English nobility are wont "to sell their female servants, when pregnant by them, after they have satisfied their lust, either to public prostitution or to foreign slavery." In later centuries, with the development of the New World, the slaves were predominantly blacks from Africa, as many as 100,000 in a single year. And on such trade Bristol continued to thrive, even to 1800.

Yet this same despised Bristol trade money subsidized both the discovery of the North American mainland and the launching of the Romantic Movement. From Bristol's harbor, financed by Bristol tradesmen and buttressed by the king's letters patent, Henry VII's "well-beloved John Cabot, citizen of Venice," sailed on May 2, 1497, ultimately to discover Newfoundland. And in the 1790's a Bristol family grown rich on the slave trade played a vital role as William Wordsworth and Samuel Taylor Coleridge talked themselves into *Lyrical Ballads*—about which more anon.

Before Wordsworth and Coleridge, there were other eighteenth-century visitors to Bristol of literary note, among them Daniel Defoe, Pope, Tobias Smollett, Richard Savage, Horace Walpole, Dr. Sam Johnson, and the fictional Lemuel Gulliver and Matthew Bramble. Thomas Chatterton and Robert Southey were born there. Indeed, Defore is generally thought to have learned the basis for his *Robinson Crusoe* (1719) from Alexander Selkirk, a Scottish sailor, at the home of a Bristol matron named Mrs. Damaris Daniel. In 1704 Selkirk had been abandoned on the Pacific island of Juan Fernandez and somehow managed to survive—without so much as a man Friday—for four years before being rescued. According to Mrs. Daniel, Selkirk gave Defoe his personal papers of the adventure.

Alexander Pope got to Bristol, like Horace Walpole and so many before and since, simply because it was near to Bath. Pope was a warm friend of Ralph Allen, mentioned earlier as a major developer of Georgian Bath and prototype of Fielding's Squire Allworthy. While visiting Allen in 1739, Pope followed his doctor's orders by "drinking the waters warm at Bristol"—quite possibly for the very reason that they were in no way as fashionable as those of Bath. In addition to finding Bristol "very unpleasant," Pope remarked that it was "much crowded with a strange mixture of Sea-men, women, children, loaded Horses, Asses, and Sledges," as well as "hundreds of Ships, their Masts as thick as they can stand by one another."

Pope is best known for the biting tongue that won him the title "Wasp of Twickenham." But during this same Bristol visit he displayed notable delicacy and kindness to a fellow writer. "There was," Pope wrote a friend, "Mr. Savage *to be* found, but indeed I could not *find* him, thinking it would have given him some Confusion." Confusion is putting it mildly. For at that very moment, the destitute Savage was living it up in the big city, while he was supposed to be living frugally in rural Wales on money provided by Pope and others.

But, as Dr. Johnson's *Life of Mr. Richard Savage* (1744) shows, such behavior was typical of the brilliant but wholly unreliable satirist, who claimed (with no shred of proof) to be the illegitimate son of the fourth Earl Rivers. This time, for a while, Savage ingratiated himself with Bristol's leading citizens. But his considerable charm wore thin. Early in 1743 he was jailed for debt in the city's Newgate Prison. There he died in August, bereft of all friends but one—the Wasp of Twickenham.* To the end, Pope sent him a yearly pension of £20. Savage's epitaph for Bristol was worthy of his name:

> Boast thy base Tolsey, and thy turn-spit dogs,
> Thy Halliers horses and thy human hogs;
> Upstarts and mushrooms, proud, relentless hearts;
> Thou blank of Sciences! Thou death of Arts!

A scant nine year's after Savage died was born a boy whose poetic gifts were more remarkable, whose life was more melancholy, whose fabrications were more fantastic—and who even came to see himself as the successor to the ill-starred debtor of Newgate:

> My prudent neighbors (who can read) can see
> Another Savage to be starv'd in me.

The boy was Thomas Chatterton.

The details of Chatterton's brief, pathetic life are all too quickly told. His very birth (November 20, 1752) foreboded ill. For his father, age thirty-nine

*Savage's grave is in the churchyard of St. Peter's, near where Newgate Prison stood.

and master of the Pine Street School of St. Mary Redcliffe Church, had been dead these three months since, and his mother, not yet twenty and remarkably nondescript, was utterly without means of making a living. As early as age five the boy was dismissed from this same school as a "dullard." And at age eight he was relegated to Colston's Hospital, a charity school where the routine was that of a reformatory, aptly dubbed "a prison for a hundred future apprentices," and the only curriculum was writing and accounts. At fourteen the boy's future seemed unalterably determined: he was apprenticed to John Lambert, attorney, to be trained as a clerk. What he was NOT to do was clearly spelled out to him: "Taverns he shall not frequent, at Dice he shall not play, Fornication he shall not commit, Matrimony he shall not contract."

What he did do instead the world now knows well. He mooned over manuscripts and old books from the muniment room of St. Mary Redcliffe, developing the background and skills that enabled him, at barely sixteen, to fabricate a group of poems by a supposed fifteenth-century Bristol monk named Thomas Rowley, whom he also invented.

Although the poems showed marks of genuine genius, from the start this "medieval find" of Chatterton's occasioned much controversy; worse yet, they did nothing to further his fortunes. At seventeen and five months, he abandoned Bristol for London, boasting that "Bristol's mercenary walls were never destined to hold me." Half-jokingly, perhaps, but prophetically too, he wrote a friend, "if [all] should fail me, my last and final resort is a pistol." All did fail him and within four months he was dead by his own hand. It wasn't a pistol, but arsenic.

Six years after his death, the authenticity of Chatterton's "Rowley Poems" was still being debated. It was that, plus an instinctive desire to prove things for himself, plus the fact that he happened to be visiting in Bath, that drew Dr. Johnson to Bristol in 1776, with Boswell in tow. Poor Bristol! Johnson was no more enchanted with it than most eighteenth-century visitors. Displeased with his inn, he managed to skewer it and two of his favorite targets—Boswell and Scotland—with a single thrust. Asked how he would describe the inn, he roared: "Describe it, Sir?—why, it is so bad Boswell wished to be in Scotland!"

He was more patient with two Bristolians who tried to convert him to a belief in Rowley, but no more yielding. For one, George Catcot, he obligingly read some of the verses aloud. And for another, William Barrett, he gravely examined some of the "original" manuscripts. He even huffed and puffed his way up the steep steps to St. Mary Redcliffe's tower to view "the very chest itself" that purportedly had hidden the manuscripts for three hundred years. But, as Boswell reported later in his *The Life of Samuel Johnson*

(1791), the "manuscripts" were executed very artificially, and the chest was but a chest. But with that keenness and fairness that mark the quintessential Johnson, he said of Chatterton himself: "This is the most extraordinary young man that has encountered my knowledge. It is wonderful how the whelp has written such things."

And now for details of Bristol's part in the birth of the Romantic Movement—a role that even in hindsight smacks of improbability. Consider the odds against Wordsworth and Coleridge ever meeting at all, let alone getting along. In 1794, at twenty-four, there was Wordsworth in the Lake District, behind him a serene upbringing in those same peaceful surroundings and an undistinguished three years at Cambridge . . . and ahead of him, he hoped, a tranquil retreat somewhere in rural England.

And 230 miles away, at twenty-one, there was Coleridge at Cambridge (he entered just after Wordsworth left). Behind him was a turbulent Devon childhood, eight years in a London charity school, a dropout from Cambridge to join the army (as a private!), and a dropout from the army to rejoin Cambridge. Ahead of him? Who knew?

One thing these apparently mismated souls had in common: neither had the slightest notion of stepping foot in Bristol. Yet before 1795 was out, that was precisely where they were to meet for the first time.

The unwitting catalyst was John Pinney, scion of a Bristol family grown rich on slave trading before turning to the sugar trade. His handsome new house on Great George Street was becoming a meeting ground for literary people, and it was there in the late summer of 1795 the two poets met. Coleridge got there through a friend he'd recently acquired while passing through Oxford—Robert Southey, young Bristol poet destined one day to be poet laureate. And Wordsworth got there because a Cambridge classmate had suggested he go talk to Pinney about the latter's country home in Dorset.

What followed was spectacular. Wordsworth got the home, Racedown Lodge, rent free, and lived there for two wonderfully restorative years. Coleridge got a Bristol maiden for a wife (Southey married her sister). And both poets got a valuable new friend, a Bristol publisher named Joseph Cottle, who assisted them in countless ways from 1795 on. Meanwhile their own Bristol-born friendship flourished. Coleridge visited the Wordsworths at Racedown, and when that wondrous windfall came to an end in 1797, Wordsworth rented Alfoxden House in Somerset to be within easy walking distance of Coleridge, who had moved to Nether Stowey. Thereafter, their visits became almost daily. As their heretical ideas burgeoned, they began to write the poems that were to become *Lyrical Ballads* (1798). When publication time came, to whom did they turn? Joseph Cottle, of course.

Not only that, but it was on Cottle's dining room table that one of the crowning pieces of the book, "Lines Composed Above Tintern Abbey," was first set down. Wordsworth tells the story of the poem's creation:

> I began it upon leaving Tintern, after crossing the Wye, and concluded it just as I was entering Bristol in the evening. . . . Not a line of it was altered, and not any part of it written down until I reached Bristol.

Alexander Pope called the medicinal waters of Bristol "full as warm as new milk from the cow." Tobias Smollett, however, said they contained "nothing but a little salt and calcareous earth," so that a man ought to be "fitted with a cap and bells" who for so paltry an advantage would expose himself "to the dirt, the stench, the chilling blasts, and perpetual rains, that render this place to me intolerable." Or at least, so Smollett has Matthew Bramble say about "The Hot Wells" in *Humphry Clinker* (1771).

Bramble had come to Bristol to rescue his niece from the too persistent attentions of Jack Wilson and put his party up in Clifton, a fashionable suburb on the city's western edge. Similarly, Fanny Burney, writing in the same decade, has the heroine of *Evelina* (1778) and Lord Orville stay in an elegant Clifton mansion and frequent the Hot Wells while discovering: a) they love each other; b) he never wrote that nasty letter anyway; and c) she is really the daughter of wealthy Sir John Belmont!

The most comic use of Bristol as a setting, however, may be that of Dickens in *The Pickwick Papers* (1837), when he has Mr. Winkle, who has fled Bath to escape death in a duel at the hands of the ferocious Mr. Dowler, suddenly encounter in Bristol's Bush Hotel none other than Mr. Dowler, who has fled Bath to escape death in a duel at the hands of the ferocious Mr. Winkle. Dickens himself had stayed at the Bush on several occasions, notably in 1837 while covering the by-election of Lord Russell, and in 1842 while seeing Longfellow off at the conclusion of the American's tour of England.

Obviously, Bristol cannot provide any such extended literary tour as Bath. It never had anything like that number of literary landmarks. But even if it had had, odds are today's visitors would have seen few of them. For probably no other English city was so cruelly savaged by World War II bombing. But some sites remain, especially those connected with Chatterton. On Redcliffe Way (formerly Pile St.) is the compact little four-room house where he was born. It's open to the public several times a week (but check for days and hours). And just beyond is St. Mary Redcliffe, which Queen Elizabeth I called "the fairest, the goodliest, the most famous parish church in England." Here Coleridge and Southey were married to the Fricker sisters; and in the muniment room, of course, Chatterton "found" those Rowley manuscripts. On the green outside the church is a statue of Chatterton as a Colston bluecoat boy.

There are several sites within easy driving distance of Bristol worth mentioning. At Clevedon, ten miles to the west, is the tomb of Arthur Hallam, Tennyson's beloved Cambridge schoolmate, whom he eulogized in "In Memoriam A.H.H." (1850). Although Tennyson poetically describes the grave as

> Where he in English earth is laid,
> And from his ashes may be made
> The violet of his native land,

Hallam actually is buried in a vault inside St. Andrews Church. Tennyson had not attended Hallam's funeral and didn't visit Clevedon until sixteen years later, while on his honeymoon.

Biggest tourist attraction in Clevedon, though, is the home of Hallam's maternal grandparents, Clevedon Park, a thirteenth-century manor house on eleven and a half acres with additions made every century since. The novelist Thackeray stayed there several times, once while working on *Vanity Fair* (1847); and "Castlewood" in his *Esmond* (1852) is modeled on it, though transplanted to Hampshire. It is now owned by the National Trust and open to the public. Out on Old Church Road is a site of another sort, "Myrtle Cottage" with a plaque that proclaims it's the "pretty cot" covered with jasmine and myrtle to which Coleridge brought his new bride in 1795. You don't *have* to believe the plaque, but there *is* the myrtle.

Wrington, ten miles southwest of Bristol, rates two minor footnotes. John Locke, who was to have such influence on the writing and thinking of the eighteenth century and whose *Essay Concerning Human Understanding* (1690) was a landmark, was born there in 1632. And Hannah More, now largely forgotten but prominent in the eighteenth century as dramatist, novelist, and Tractarian, was buried in its churchyard in 1833. She had lived for thirty years in nearby "Barleywood."

One final word before leaving Avon. A couple of miles south of Wrington is Burrington. And six miles out of Burrington (actually just over the border in Somerset) is a cave whose merits are celebrated Sunday after Sunday in England and America alike: it's the "Rock of Ages" that cleft for Augustus Toplady during a thunderstorm in 1775.

SOMERSET

Somerset

Western Somerset

Nether Stowey to Porlock

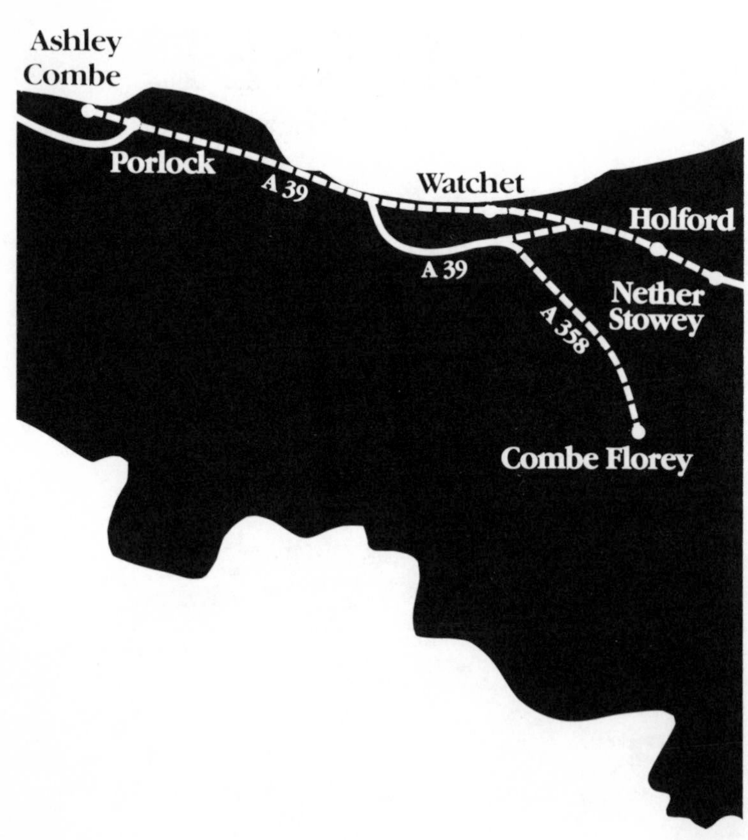

Eastern Somerset
In and About Wells

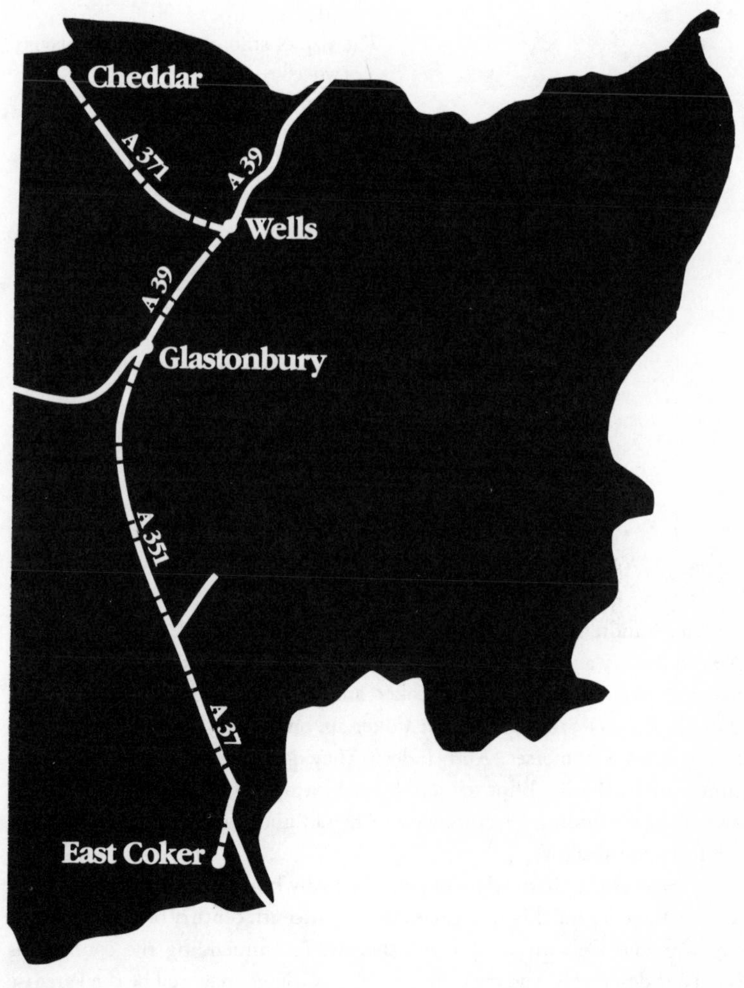

The many-steepled tract magnificent
Of hilly fields, and meadows and the
sea,
With some fair bark, perhaps, whose
sails light up
The slip of smooth clear blue betwixt
two isles
Of purple shadow!

S. T. Coleridge, "This Lime Tree
Bower My Prison"

Whisper of running streams, and
winter lightning.
The wild thyme unseen and the wild
strawberry
The laughter in the garden, echoed
ecstasy
Not lost, but requiring, pointing to
the agony
Of death and birth.

T. S. Eliot, "East Coker"

One hundred forty-five years separate Coleridge and his lime tree in Nether Stowey and *The Rime of the Ancient Mariner* (1798) from T. S. Eliot and his wild strawberries in East Coker and *Four Quartets* (1943). In space, though, Nether Stowey and East Coker are only thirty miles apart—thirty lovely miles of Somerset. And, indeed, they don't seem all that far apart in time, either. (Eerily, Eliot felt a distinct kinship with the earlier poet, once even abruptly ending a lecture with "The sad ghost of Coleridge beckons to me from the shadows.")

The fact is the sharp edges of time are easily blurred in most of Somerset. Today's traveller quickly recognizes the seventeenth century of Pepys, "where my wife and Deb mightily joyed thereat, I commending the country, as indeed it deserves." And over the next rise as you go may well be the Paradise Hall of eighteenth-century Squire Allworthy, "as commodious within as venerable without" in Fielding's *Tom Jones* . . . or a country manor with the "hospitality and ancient dignity" of nineteenth-century Sir Walter Elliot's Kellynel Hall in Jane Austen's *Persuasion* . . . or a "tawny-coloured, well-built rural church" out of a Trollope novel.

A good-sized county, Somerset is, running from Bristol Channel at the top nearly to the English Channel at the bottom. But its handful of significant literary sites, now that it has lost Bath, can be pretty much discussed (and visited) in two clusters: the Wells-Glastonbury area of the northeast and the striking stretch from Nether Stowey to Porlock, much of it skirting the northern coast.

1. IN AND ABOUT WELLS

Wells

Wells is a mere twenty-one miles south of Bristol on the A 39, but it might as well be in another world. It gives one the impression of having largely ignored history. Its cathedral, with admirable impartiality, shrugged off the despoilations of Henry VIII and Cromwell alike. Ducks and swans swim in the moat outside the Bishop's Palace as they always have, and when the quaint old clock in the north transept strikes the quarter hour, little mounted knights come out to knock their comrades off their horses, as they have been doing every fifteen minutes since the fourteenth century.

One immediate convert to Wells was T. E. Lawrence who, in 1923—he was then masquerading as Pvt. Shaw in the Tank Corps at Bovington Camp in Dorset—drove up to Wells on his motorbike. He describes the city's charm succinctly: "Very beautiful it was:—a grey and sober town, stiffly built of prim houses, but with nothing of the artificial about it."

Loyal Wellsians—and there are 9,000 of them—will tell you that *their* Cathedral was truly-truly-truly the model for Barchester Cathedral in Trollope's first successful novel, *The Warden* (1855). They buttress this with the parallel between the old charity maintained for Wells's woolcarders and the novel's Hiram Hospital's charitable foundation maintained for those thirteen old bedesmen. Alas for Wells! When a historian friend pointed all this out to Trollope while they were tramping about Somersetshire, he snorted that this was utter nonsense. He had had Winchester in mind and had never even heard of the Wells woolcarders. But Trollope enjoyed being testy and even perverse. Another time, when questioned about Barchester, he avowed he detected "a touch or two of Salisbury" here and there, and "sometimes perhaps of Winchester, but no more than that." So, when you're in Wells, looking at those lovely twin towers, go ahead and think "Barchester." (When you are in Winchester, of course ______!)

Glastonbury

Only six miles southwest of Wells on the A 39, but both infinitely older and infinitely more modern, is Glastonbury. Traditionally, it's called "the holyest earthe in England" and with good reason. Here St. Joseph of Arimathea, who buried Christ, came to build the first Christian sanctuary in the British Isles. With him he brought, the story continues, the Holy Grail, the chalice used by Jesus for the Last Supper, later hidden by Joseph in a well by the sanctuary to protect it from marauding Saxons. This same soil was later enriched, if not hallowed, in the fifth (sixth?) century when King Arthur and his Queen Guinevere were buried there.

For Glastonbury claims to be the Isle of Avalon to which the mortally wounded Arthur was mysteriously conveyed. (Well, Glastonbury once WAS an island.). Anyway, what were reputed to be the bones of Arthur and his errant mate were uncovered outside the Lady Chapel of Glastonbury's Abbey in 1191 and finally translated to their present grave in front of what was then the High Altar in 1276, with Edward I present to give the royal stamp of approval.

Today Glastonbury handles both its Arimathean and Arthurian legends with consummate twentieth-century efficiency, whisking the daily deluge of cars and tour buses in and out of carparks and their occupants in and out of the excellently marked Abbey grounds. There are talk boxes for hire, too, giving briskly canned accounts of the glamorous doings of yore, lest you miss the royal graves, or the Chalice Well, or the "Glastonbury Thorn" said to have sprung from St. Joseph's staff.

The ruins of the Abbey are on the skimpy side, having been plundered for centuries after Henry VIII's dissolution to build roads and houses. But the pilgrims continue to come, drawn by the lure of Arthur that continues to grow, fed by the literally countless poems, chronicles, romances, plays, and novels written since twelfth-century Geoffrey of Monmouth turned his inventive mind to transforming a Celtic chieftain of murky myth into an historical figure. To mention but a few, Arthur and his knights have been celebrated from the great cycles of medieval romance, Chaucer's "Wife of Bath's Tale," and the anonymous "Gawain and the Green Knight" of the fourteenth century through Malory's *Morte Darthur* (1485) and Spenser's *The Faerie Queene* (1590) to Tennyson's *Idylls of the King* (1859–1885). Tennyson was so enamoured of Arthur he came to Glastonbury in 1850 to spend part of his honeymoon.

Noteworthy among treatments since Tennyson are Mark Twain's burlesque, *A Connecticut Yankee in King Arthur's Court* (1889); E. A. Robinson's *Merlin* (1917); T. H. White's three novels, published collectively as *The Once and Future King* (1958); and the hit musical that was based on them, *Camelot,* first produced in 1951 and still staged here and there. Earlier memorable musical versions of the Arthurian material include the opera, *King Arthur* (1691) by Henry Purcell, with libretto by John Dryden, and Richard Wagner's *Tristran und Isolde* (1865), *Parsifal* (1882), and that earlier opera about Parsifal's (Sir Perceval) son, *Lohengrin* (1850).

Just outside Glastonbury, incidentally, is Sharpham Park, where was born about 1543 Edward Dyer, poet and friend of Sir Philip Sidney, and best known for "My Mind to Me a Kingdom Is." By coincidence, eighteenth-century novelist Henry Fielding was born in that very house some 165 years later.

Cheddar

If you have a suppressed passion for caves—the kind with stalactites which to the fanciful become "underground countries of natural cathedrals reflected in clear bottomless lakes," and attract endless tourists and wall-to-wall souvenir stalls—Cheddar is only eight miles northwest of Wells on the A 371. And what's grand about the Cheddar caves is that you can indulge yourself under the guise of a literary pilgrimage. For Coleridge visited them, and they may (*may,* that is) have contributed their tiny bit to the exotic imagery of "Kubla Khan." Anyway, Coleridge walked to Cheddar on a number of occasions during his stay at Nether Stowey (1796–1799), several times with William Wordsworth and his sister Dorothy.

In 1794 Coleridge had visited Cheddar with Robert Southey, and the latter's description of the cliffs in which the caves are located is truly graphic. "Never," he wrote, "did I see a grander scene—immense rocks rising perpendicularly from the glen to such a height as pained the neck of the spectator, and terminating in the most bold and fantastic manner." It's a good thing Southey liked the cliffs so much. The only lodging the two poets could find was a garret room in a "poor pothouse," Coleridge proved "a vile bedfellow," and when they awoke in the morning, they found the landlord "took us for footpads and had bolted the door on the outside."

East Coker

Twenty miles south of Wells, beloved of T. S. Eliot and still largely unspoiled, is the hamlet of East Coker. (Actually it's just outside Yeovil and off the A 37.) The American poet was forty-nine when, in 1937, he first saw the village his ancestors had left in the seventeenth century to join the new colony in Massachusetts. Eliot was enchanted with stone cottages and farmhouses, golden with age, and

> . . . the deep lane
> Shuttered with branches, dark in the afternoon
> Where you lean against a bank while a van passes,

and with the thirteenth-century church of St. Michael, where "old stones that cannot be deciphered" bespeak "a lifetime burning in every moment."

He put them all into the "East Coker" section of *Four Quartets*. And when it came time for him to die, St. Michael supplied his resting place, and the poem provided his epitaph. You'll find it on an oval stone tablet set into the west wall of the church: "In my beginning is my end. Of your kindness pray for the soul of Thomas Sterns Eliot, poet. In my end is my beginning."

2. ALONG THE TOP: NETHER STOWEY TO PORLOCK (THE A 39)

After carrying one southward through Wells and Glastonbury, the A 39 abruptly turns west and northward for forty-five tortuous, tempting, and teasing miles before it leaves Somerset and crosses over into Devon. As you twist and turn, climb and drop, you feel with Dorothy Wordsworth "there is everything here." But she walked. In a car, the vistas flash and disappear, tantalizingly snatched away by a bend in the road or a gauntlet of hedgerows that forbid seeing or stopping.

It is the same route the twenty-two-year-old Charles Lamb took in 1797 in the Bridgwater day coach, bound for a week's holiday with dear friend and boyhood schoolmate, S. T. Coleridge, and his first meeting ever with William Wordsworth. Bridgwater is a city of goodly size, as Somerset cities go, fifteen miles west of Glastonbury. Eight miles further west, just off the highway, is Nether Stowey, Lamb's destination.

Nether Stowey

Nether Stowey consists chiefly of one avenue, St. Mary Street, that spreads like a "Y" into two arms. At the end of the left arm, Lime Street, on the left side, is the house Lamb was looking for. Neither house nor town was designed to impress the visitor. It's a small, dark structure of mustard-colored stucco and, with its hanging sign dangling over the walkway to the narrow doorway, suggests a second-rate pub. With a shock you realize the "sign" is actually a painting of Samuel Taylor Coleridge. For here the author of "The Rime of the Ancient Mariner" came to live at Christmastide of 1796.

Although the house is much changed since then, and the present rust-colored tile roof was originally an appealing thatch, the poet's first glimpse could hardly have been more prepossessing than ours. He had been warned by his friend, Tom Poole, a Nether Stowey tanner, that the house was tiny, ugly, and inconvenient. But "its vicinity to you," Coleridge had insisted to Poole, "shall overbalance its defects."

Defects there were. His "study" was dark (it still is), the window wouldn't open, and quarters were severely cramped. There were only two rooms downstairs, plus a kitchen with an open fireplace, and three bedrooms above to serve a considerable household—Coleridge, wife Sara, and son Hartley; an epileptic paying guest-pupil named Charles Lloyd; and a maid. Coleridge's first report to Joseph Cottle, his Bristol printer-benefactor, is what one might have surmised: "On the Saturday, the Sunday and ten days after my arrival at Stowey, I felt a depression too dreadful to be described."

But much of this might have been ill health and desperate finances. For soon he was writing friends, "our house is better than we expected. There is a comfortable bedroom and sitting room for C. Lloyd and another room for us, a room for Nanny, a kitchen and outhouse." He gardened and took care of his ducks, geese, and two pigs; he read and wrote. And there were diversions: "a number of pretty young women in Stowey, all musical . . . for [whom] I pun, conundrumize, *listen,* and dance." Sundays he preached at the Unitarian Chapel in Bridgwater or Taunton. "So joggs the day," he wrote, "and I am happy."

Today only four of the original rooms remain: the kitchen (now the room on the *right* as you enter) and the sitting room (on the left) downstairs . . . and two bedrooms above. Only the sitting room is open to the public (it's a National Trust house), and the memorabilia are few. But among them is the sword Coleridge wore when, as "Silas Tomkyn Comberbacke," he was a trooper in the King's Light Dragoons. The absurd alias was born of panic, so some say. Overwhelmed by debts and disconsolate at not winning a coveted scholarship, he had dropped out of Cambridge and, on impulse, applied for admission to the Dragoons.

"Your name, Sir?" demanded the reviewing officer. S. T. Coleridge groped desperately for one to fit his initials. "Com . . . Comberbacke," he stuttered.

"And the rest of it?"

"S-Silas. Silas Tomkyn Comberbacke, Sir." And so, though he couldn't stay on a horse, he became a cavalry man.

Coleridge Cottage, Nether Stowey, Somerset

By Courtesy of The National Trust

Though he was at Nether Stowey less than three years, they were his most productive in poetry, highlighted by the "Ancient Mariner," "Kubla Khan," and "Christabel." They may well have been his happiest, too. For his beloved Wordsworths—William and his sister Dorothy—became his neighbors, just three miles down the road. It happened with a suddenness hard to believe.

Coleridge had visited them at Racedown in Dorset the summer of 1797, tearing himself away June 28.* On July 2 he was back, in Tom Poole's one-horse chaise. Dorothy must ride it, and the two men walk, the forty miles to Nether Stowey for a return visit. The Wordsworths did and fell in love with the country side. That Charles Lamb showed up for *his* holiday made it all the jollier, though the little house must have bulged. Utterly enchanted, the Wordsworths looked about for a cottage and lucked into a real find: Alfoxden (or Alfoxton) House outside the village of Holford. They never did get back to Racedown. On July 13 they were in their new quarters. "We are three people," said Coleridge, "but only one soul." Ahead of them lay, though they knew it not, *Lyrical Ballads*.

Alfoxden (Alfoxton) House

From Coleridge's drab little house on Lime Street in Nether Stowey, you get back on A 39, follow it about three miles through the village of Holford, and come upon a road sign that beckons you to a house of quite another sort. Following the sign, you drive down a long lane, cool, tree-lined, inviting. And at its end sits a large, elegant mansion with white-columned entrance bidding you welcome: Alfoxton Park Hotel.** Yes, this is the very Alfoxden House where William Wordsworth and his sister Dorothy spent a year—from summer 1797 to summer 1798. No wonder Dorothy wrote so delightedly of the place: 'Here we are in a large mansion, in a large park with seventy head of deer around us. . . . There is furniture enough for a dozen families like ours. There is a very excellent garden, well stocked with vegetables and fruit. . . . The front of the house is to the south; but it is screened from the sun by a high hill. . . . From the end of the house we have a view of the sea." All this—furniture, gardens, stables, and coach house—for £23 a year!

One thinks of Wordsworth as the "Lake Poet" and his inspiration as the magic names of the Lake District: Grasmere, Rydal, Ambleside, Windermere. Yet in fact his most influential single effort, *Lyrical Ballads,* belongs to Alfoxden. Here, in almost unbroken interchange with Coleridge, were

---

*For details of this visit, see p. 234.

**Wordsworth spelled it "Alfoxden," or, at times, following the local pronunciation, "Allfoxen."

hammered out the ideas about poetry that Wordsworth expressed so forcefully in the famous *Preface* of 1800. And the lovely Quantock Hills swelling above their Alfoxden door gave rise to much of the book's verse—"We are Seven," "Her Eyes Are Wild," "Expostulation and Reply," "The Tables Turned," "The Thorn," "Idiot Boy," and others.

This brief but climactic interval in Somerset might even lay a small claim to "Lines Composed above Tintern Abbey." For it was written only days after Wordsworth had left Alfoxden and while he was still under the spell of the Quantocks. How powerfully this spell worked not only upon him but upon Coleridge he makes clear in these lines from *The Prelude* (completed 1805) addressed to that same "beloved Friend":

> That Summer, under whose indulgent skies,
> Upon smooth Quantock's airy ridge we roved
> Unchecked, or loitered 'mid her sylvan combs,
> Thou in bewitching words, with happy heart
> Didst chaunt the vision of that Ancient Man,
> The bright-eyed Mariner, and rueful woes
> Didst utter of the Lady Christabel. . . .

The Alfoxden idyll came to an end in an incongruous, almost comic-opera way. Their neighbors from the first had suspected the oddly behaving unmarried northerner and that sister with the darting eyes with whom he lived, rambling about the hills with that equally strange Samuel Coleridge. Wasn't *he* a Unitarian minister? And weren't both men poets? Worst of all, hadn't this Wordsworth chap actually entertained John Thelwall, a notorious agitator who had been jailed for his revolutionary beliefs? (That Thelwall had gone seeking Coleridge and had no connection with Wordsworth apparently was irrelevant.) All this seems to have upset the St. Albyns, owners of the place. In June, 1798, their first year was up, and the Wordsworths left Alfoxden.

As a thriving hotel now, "Alfoxton" is, of course, open to the public (at last listing, March to December). It still boasts of fifty acres of parkland, and the views over the Quantock Hills to the Bristol Channel are still unsurpassed.

Holford has one other claim to literary notice. Virginia and Leonard Woolf stayed there at the Plough Inn on their honeymoon in August, 1912 (and came back the following summer). She was ecstatic about the place itself: "If you ever want a most comfortable Inn, delicious food, cream for every meal, quite cheap, come here." But she did record one reservation on a postcard sent to her friend Lytton Strachey, the eminent biographer and critic: "Divine country, literary associations, cream for every meal, but cold as Christmas and steady rain." The front of the card was a picture of Alfoxton House, and to her message Virginia added an afterthought: "P. S., Who lived at Alfoxton?"

Watchet—Ashley Combe—and the Man from Porlock

One of Coleridge's favorite parts of Somerset was the rocky coastal stretch between Nether Stowey and Lynmouth (in neighboring Devonshire). And, twice, a visit to this area was to result in one of his best-known poems—though neither turned out as first expected.

On a dour November day in 1797, he and William and Dorothy Wordsworth set out from Alfoxden on a walk to Lynmouth and Lynton, thirty-five miles to the east.* They didn't get started until 4:30 in the afternoon, typical of the bizarre behavior that had made their neighbors think they were spies. As they walked, they began sketching the outlines of a poem, for they had decided they would collaborate on one and sell it for £5 to pay for the trip's expenses. Coleridge laid the foundation, basing it on a friend's dream of a "skeleton ship" with a crew of phantoms. An "Old Navigator" would be the chief character. Wordsworth added details: the Navigator shoots an albatross (Wordsworth had just been reading about albatrosses) and is persecuted by avenging spirits. The dead crew is "reanimated" to work the ship.

The walkers stopped for the night at Watchet, a fishing village eight miles from home, and, over dinner and into the night, the poem grew—but largely on Coleridge's part. For as Wordsworth later admitted, "the style of Coleridge and myself would not assimilate." And so the scheme of collaboration was dropped, and "The Rime of the Ancient Mariner," save for a few lines, became Coleridge's, to be finished at Stowey.

Watchet and the church of St. Decuman on a hill at the edge of town may well have been in Coleridge's mind as he wrote:

> The ship was cheered, the harbour cleared
> Merrily did we drop
> Below the kirk, below the hill,

as the Mariner sails off on his momentous voyage. (If you want to see Watchet and the church, you'll have to leave A 39 and take a "B" road to the coast.)

Coleridge was in the same area the following summer for a brief stay at Ash Farm, a couple of miles out of Porlock. It was a lonely farmhouse high

---

*In a note written years later, Wordsworth indicates that they actually went to Dulverton instead.

above Ashley Combe, with the sea dashing on the rocks below a fitting setting for what happened. For Coleridge, after taking opium prescribed for an attack of dysentery, fell asleep in his chair and while unconscious composed an entire poem of two or three hundred lines in his head.

When he awoke, so he insisted, the whole thing was absolutely clear to him, and he began "instantly and eagerly to write it down." But, after fifty-four lines, came a knock on the door. Enter the best-known unknown in literature, "a person on business from Porlock." Who he was, what his business was, Coleridge doesn't say. But when he left, an hour later, the poet could recall only a few scattered lines and images of the rest of the poem. "Kubla Khan" remains the most haunting of fragments.*

Running off the A 39 at the top of Porlock Hill there is today a little road with a place that is still called Ash Farm—though nearby Broomstreet Farm disputes its claim to being "the" farm in question. Be that as it may, Porlock Hill, with its steep, lowest gear descent, provides a truly spectacular view of the sea far below. And at its bottom is a first rate pub, Ship Inn, where they'll show you "Southey's Corner," the fireplace nook where the laureate-to-be dashed off some verses while stopping there. Sad to say, the fireplace now boasts a space heater.

Porlock Hill also figures in R. D. Blackmore's novel, *Lorna Doone* (1869), especially as the scene of the Doones's murder of John Ridd's father. Blackmore's grandfather was rector of nearby Oare, and in 1925 the church there installed a centennial tablet in the writer's honor. It was in this very church that Lorna, even as she exchanged marriage vows with John Ridd, was fatally shot by Carver Doone.

Combe Florey

One final note on Somerset. Among twentieth-century converts to the Quantock Hills area, beloved by Coleridge and Wordsworth, was Margaret, favorite daughter of Evelyn Waugh, the novelist. On a holiday with a school friend in 1956 she fell in love with Combe Florey, five miles southwest of Nether Stowey, and especially with the handsome manor house in the park. "O please do get Combe Florey," she wrote her father. "I like it so much . . . and perhaps we could keep a horse."

It is pleasing to report that Waugh, whose satire could be so biting, was as indulgent as any father ought to be. Besides, he said, it "was cosy, sequestered, with great possibilities." So he bought it. He lived there until his

*Modern researchers tend to doubt that the poem was so purely an "unconscious creation" as Coleridge later described.

death in 1966 and wrote the last volume of his war trilogy, *Unconditional Surrender* (1961) there.

The house must have been fascinating to visit, for Waugh filled it with a wild mixture of Victorian furniture and decorations, what he called "atrocities" of Ethiopian art (including a large, "macabre" carving of a squatting camel), and a many-colored monstrosity of a carpet based on one that had won the high prize of the Great Exhibition of 1851.

Combe Florey was also the home of another famous satirist, Sydney Smith, who was rector from 1829 until he died in 1845, even though from 1831 on he had to reside in London three months of the year as canon residentiary at St. Paul's. The Georgian house he had in Combe Florey is now called "the old Rectory."

DEVON

Devon

1. The Northern Arc

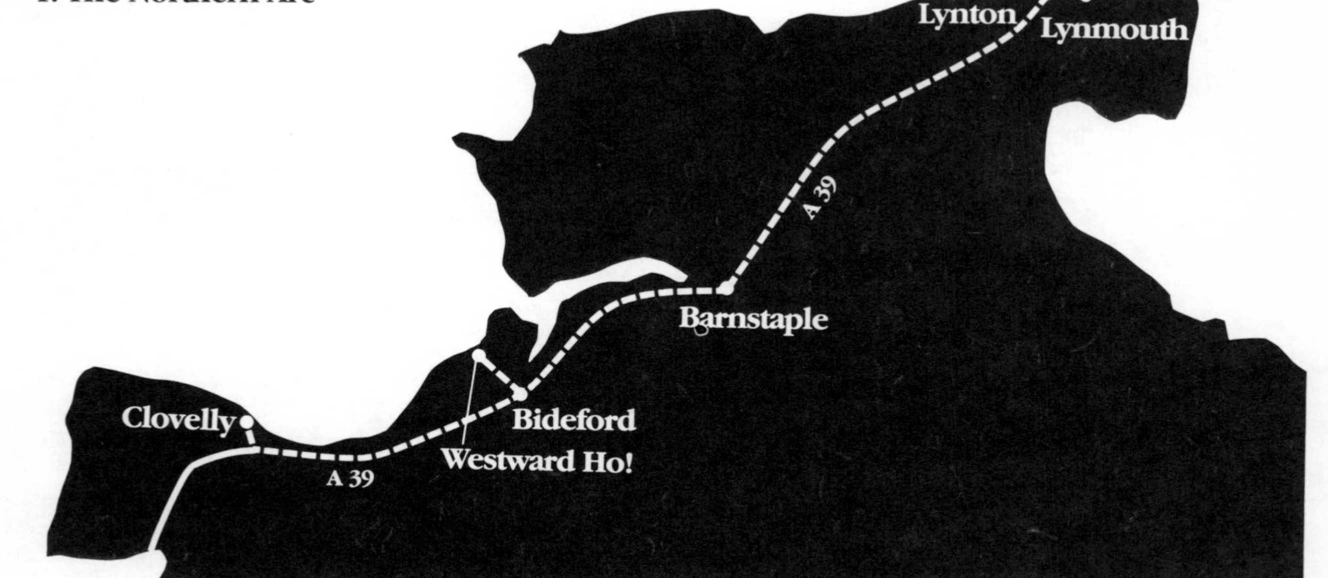

Where the salt sea innocuously breaks,
And the sea breeze as innocently breathes
On Devon's leafy shores; a sheltered hold,
In a soft clime encouraging the soil
To a luxuriant bounty!

William Wordsworth, *The Excursion*

The road in front of us grew bleaker and wilder over the huge russet and olive slopes, sprinkled with giant boulders. Now and then we passed a moorland cottage, walled and roofed with stone, with no creeper to break its harsh outline. Suddenly we looked down into a cuplike depression, patched with stunted oaks and firs which had been bent by the fury of years of storm.

Sir Arthur Conan Doyle,
"The Hound of the Baskervilles"

If it strikes you that Wordsworth and Conan Doyle are talking about two entirely different Devons, you're right. They are. But Devon is large (only Yorkshire and Lincolnshire are larger) and the traveller can find any number of Devons as he traverses its more than 2600 square miles. Along its northern edge are the jagged gray cliffs plunging to the waters of the Bristol Channel. At its bottom are the red cliffs that as often drop abruptly into the English Channel. And in between are all manner of hills and valleys and moors and combes and quaint little villages, filled in summer with shoulder to shoulder Englishmen on holiday. There are even cities—a few—if you MUST have them, especially the Pilgrim Fathers' Plymouth, now swollen to a quarter of a million people, and Exeter (100,000) with its brutally bombed Cathedral now restored.

Like other people, English writers have found their own Devon to enjoy or disdain, each in his own way. In the seventeenth century, the poet Robert Herrick sometimes liked it and, as these lines indicate, sometimes decidedly did not:

> More discontents I never had
> Since I was born, then [sic] here;
> Where I have been, and still am sad
> In this dull *Devon*-shire.
>
> "Discontents in Devon"

But then, Herrick was stuck as vicar in a tiny Devon village when he'd much rather have been in London.

On the other hand, Wordsworth and Coleridge loved it. Coleridge, indeed, was born there, and while in Nether Stowey thought back fondly of his Devon boyhood, and dreamt

> Of my sweet birth-place, and the old church tower,
> Whose bells, the poor man's only music, rang
> From morn to evening. . . .
>
> "Frost at Midnight"

And Shelley was so taken with one little Devon village, while merely passing through, that he stayed for nine weeks, his wife Harriet rhapsodizing, "it seems more like a fairy scene than anything in reality." But Keats grumped, "I shall never be able to relish entirely any Devonshire scenery."

In short, the Devon you find depends on WHO you are—WHERE you are.

Visitors to the farthest reaches of the "West Countree" who want to see all of it usually cover Devon and Cornwall together in one great circle. It makes sense and saves time, effort, and petrol. And even while adhering to the general plan of treating one county at a time, a discussion of their literary sites can take advantage of the same circular scheme: dividing Devon into great arcs at top and bottom and then doing Cornwall as one elongated loop. (Drivers are invited to join arcs to loop as suits them best.)

1. THE NORTHERN ARC

When William Wordsworth, his sister Dorothy, and Coleridge took the famous walk in 1797 that led to the writing of "The Rime of the Ancient Mariner," their avowed destination was Lynmouth and Lynton, the twin cities at the eastern edge of Devon and its breathtaking northern coast. There follows, as one moves westward, a string of other seaside resorts—Ilfracombe, Barnstaple, Westward Ho!, Bideford, Clovelly—all so popular that in season natives are said to disappear indoors or into their gardens in self defense, not to be seen for weeks on end. It's probably little comfort to them to know that today's invaders are retracing the steps of not only Wordsworth, Coleridge, and Shelley but of Tennyson, Dickens, and Kipling as well.

Lynmouth and Lynton

If you approach Lynmouth and Lynton from Northern Somerset, you will be retracing the steps of Wordsworth and Coleridge quite literally, for you'll be taking the A 39, a highway that skirts their homes at Nether Stowey and Holford (Alfoxden House) in Somerset and largely follows the route they took on their frequent walks to Lynton, in Devon.

They're small, these two villages, and lovely: Lynmouth on the shore, where the waters of the East and West Lyn meet to form the single river that empties into the Bristol Channel . . . and Lynton at the edge of the steep cliff 450 feet above. It was Lynmouth that Harriet Shelley was referring to when she wrote, "It seems more like a fairy scene than anything in reality."

What particularly drew Wordsworth and Coleridge to Lynton was the overwhelming Valley of Rocks, which they insisted on calling Valley of Stones. Coleridge, apparently, took almost everyone who came to see him at Nether Stowey on a walk there, though Lynton was thirty-odd miles away. (To Coleridge this was nothing. He once walked it alone in a single day, returning the next.) One such guest was Robert Southey, fellow poet and brother-in-law, whose description of the spot explains its appeal:

> Ascending half a mile from [Lynmouth] up a road perpendicular almost, you turn into the Valley of Stones—a miraculous place. The range of hills here next the sea are completely stripped of their soil and only the bones of the earth are left—stone upon stone—I conceive [it] therefore to be the remains of some work erected by the Devils who came to intrigue with the fifty daughters of Diocletian, for I can trace no other inhabitants of our island who possessed power enough for the work.

Wordsworth himself had hardly settled down at Alfoxden near Coleridge when he was taken off to see the sight. And it was at the valley that the two first planned to collaborate on a poem, "The Wanderings of Cain,": each was to write a canto, and whoever finished first was to do the third. But when Coleridge brought Wordsworth his completed section, he found his friend with "a look of despondency fixed on an almost blank sheet of paper." No wonder their attempt to write "The Ancient Mariner" together failed. Wordsworth did, however, weave hints of the Valley of Rocks into his own "Peter Bell."

Shelley and his wife Harriet stumbled upon Lynmouth and the Valley for themselves. They had only planned to pass through the town in the summer of 1812, on their way to Ilfracombe. Instead, they found themselves taking the only vacant cottage in town and staying two months. Harriet tells why: "It combines all the beauties of our late residence with the addition of a fine bold sea. . . . We have roses and myrtles creeping up the sides of the house, which is thatched at top."

Shelley was equally enthusiastic. "Mountains certainly of not less perpendicular elevation than 1000 feet are broken abruptly into vallies [sic] of indescribable fertility & grandeur. . . . In addition to these is the sea, which dashes against a rocky & caverned shore, presenting an ever-changing view."

But it was the sea that betrayed Shelley. He was seen throwing dark green bottles into the water—containing seditious pamphlets. Barely in time, the Shelleys fled to Ilfracombe with authorities from Barnstaple baying at their heels.

R. D. Blackmore, whose novel *Lorna Doone* centers on this section of the country, makes good use of the Valley of Rocks and its atmosphere. Here's his description:

> On the right hand is an upward crag, called by some the "Castle," easy enough to scale, and giving great view of the Channel. Facing this, from the inland side and the elbow of the valley, a queer old pile of rocks arises, bold behind one another, and quite enough to affright a man. . . . This is called the "Devil's Cheese-ring," or the Devil's "Cheese-Knife," which means the same thing."

Blackmore's hero, John Ridd, meets the mysterious "wise woman," Mother Meldrum, at Castle Rock but is afraid to visit her winter home under the Devil's Cheese-ring, as were all the natives, especially after dark or on a gloomy day.

You can stay at "Shelley's Cottage" if you like, for it's now a pleasant looking hotel. But it's a far cry from the rather tiny place the poet knew, having been much built upon and altered, especially since a fire in 1907. However, Harriet's view of the "fine bold sea remains."

Barnstaple—Bideford—Westward Ho!—Clovelly

Travellers going from Lynmouth-Lynton to Cornwall pass through Barnstaple, Bideford, and Clovelly—all on the A 39—and narrowly miss Westward Ho! Each is worth a nod, however cursory.

Barnstaple With 18,000 people, Barnstaple is the largest of the four but rates the briefest nod. If you're driving through, though, you might want to dazzle a companion by casually mentioning that John Gay, author of *Beggar's Opera* (1728), was born here in 1685 and that Shelley's manservant got jailed here in 1812 for distributing the poet's inflammatory "Declaration of Rights."

Bideford Pronounced "Biddyford," Bideford is nine miles southwest of Barnstaple. Charles Kingsley stayed there at North Down House in 1854, and opens his best-known novel, *Westward Ho!* (1855) with a description of it:

> All who have travelled through the delicious scenery of North Devon must needs know the little white town of Bideford, which slopes upward from its broad tideriver paved with yellow sands, and many arched old bridge where salmon wait for autumn floods, toward the pleasant upland on the west.

Kingsley's hero, Amyas Leigh, lives at Burrough Court, two miles out of Bideford, and all of this part of North Devon, native country for Kingsley, is featured in the book.

Shortly after Kingsley's stay, Charles Dickens and his friend, Wilkie Collins, author of *The Moonstone,* came to Bideford in November of 1860 while gathering material for their collaboration, "A Message from the Sea." They stayed at "a beastly hotel," Dickens said. "We had stinking fish for dinner, and have been able to drink nothing, though we have ordered wine, beer, and brandy-and-water."

Westward Ho! This is a small resort just outside Bideford, and yes indeed, it was named for Kingsley's novel. In Victorian days it was known for its United Services College, a sort of cram shop for boys preparing for military exams and careers. Rudyard Kipling was a student there from age twelve to seventeen (1878–1882), and he describes both the school and its environs in his *Stalky & Co.* (1899). The headmaster, Cormell Price, had been a schoolmate of Kipling's uncle, the painter Burne-Jones, and was a friend of William Morris, Swinburne, and Browning.

Clovelly Eleven miles west of Bideford, Clovelly is the best known of these North Devon resorts and the most scenic. Its one main street is a narrow cobblestoned slit in the cliffs that drops 400 feet so precipitately that not only are cars or carts impossible, but even walking can be hazardous for those without a touch of mountain goat in their veins. At 2:30 A.M. in the winter the town's population is 531. But at high noon in summer it appears to be 100,000—10,000 of them a solid river of demon-driven flesh tumbling

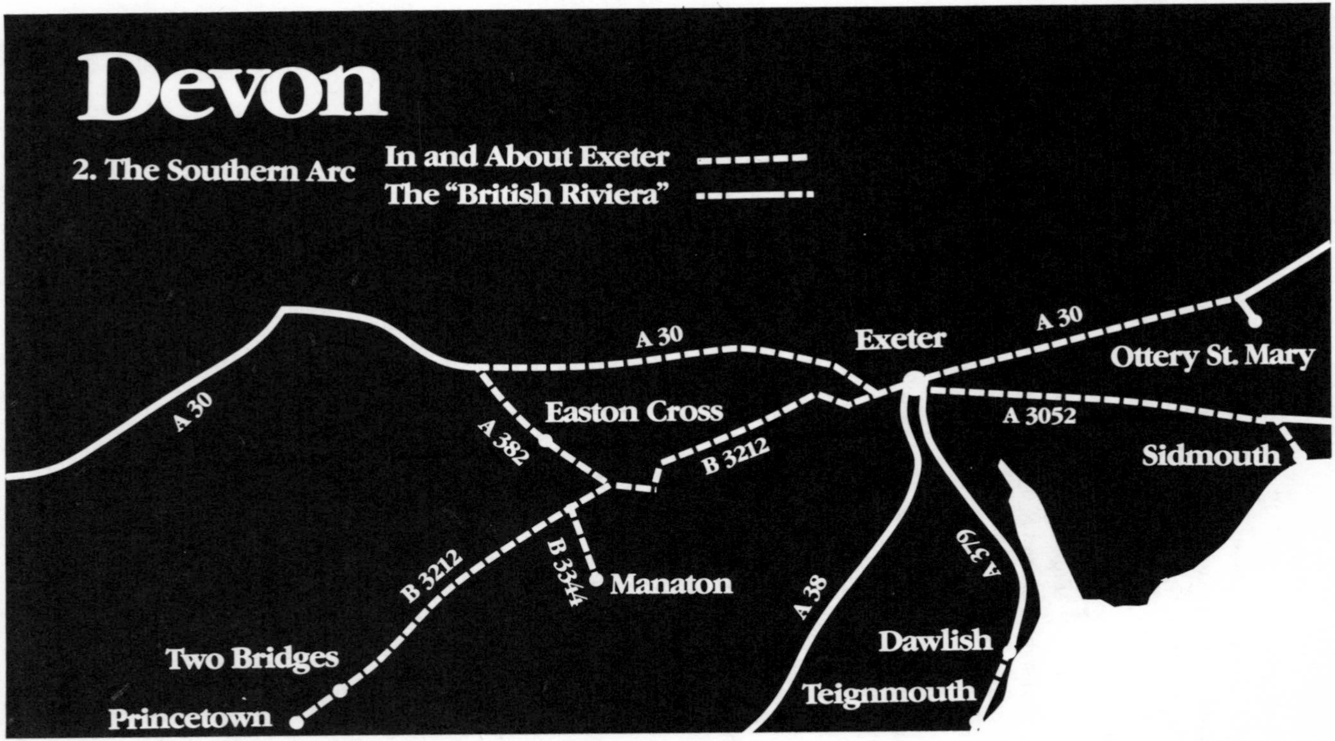

Devon

2. The Southern Arc

In and About Exeter

The "British Riviera"

A 30
A 30
A 30
Exeter
Ottery St. Mary
Easton Cross
A 3052
A 382
B 3212
Sidmouth
B 3212
B 3344
Manaton
A 38
A 379
Dawlish
Two Bridges
Teignmouth
Princetown

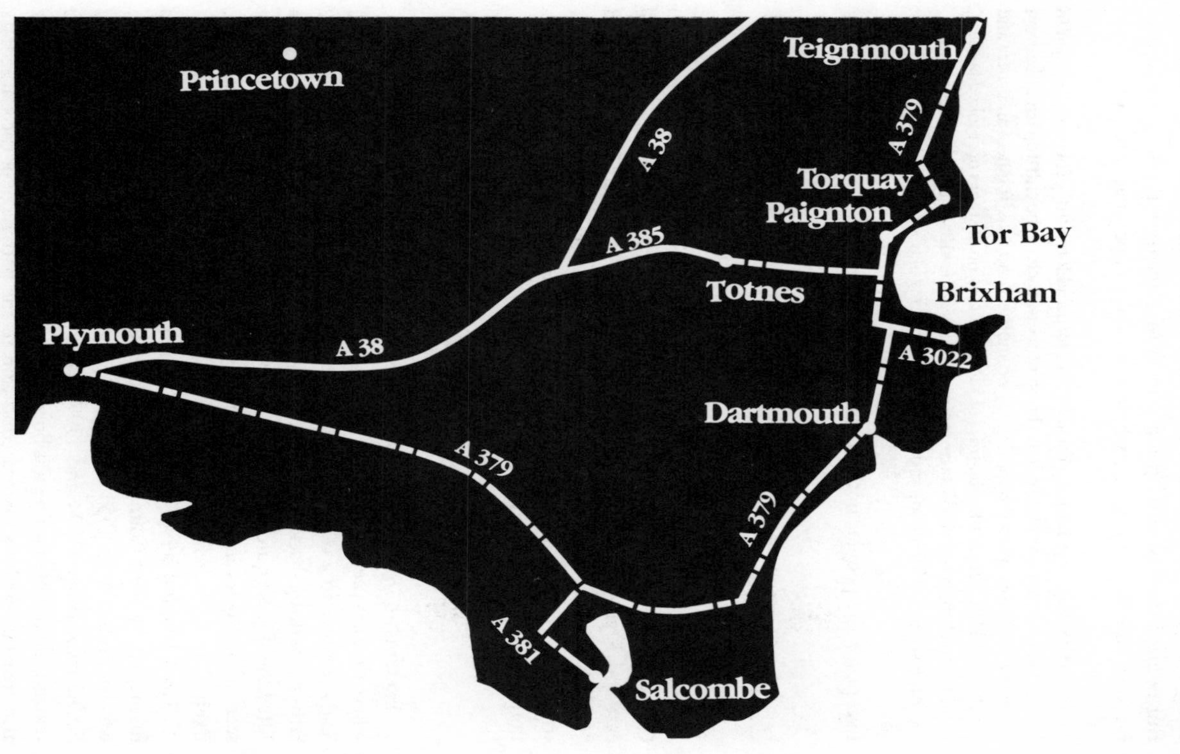
Princetown
Teignmouth
A 379
A 38
Torquay
Paignton
Tor Bay
A 385
Totnes
Brixham
Plymouth
A 38
A 3022
Dartmouth
A 379
A 379
A 381
Salcombe

down to the sea . . . the other 90,000 crammed into the tiny pocket at the bottom, clamoring to be rescued by a Land Rover.

Clovelly has been described by a number of writers, including Charles Kingsley, who lived there as a boy while his father was rector, in *Westward Ho!* But perhaps the best description is in "A Message from the Sea," by Charles Dickens and Wilkie Collins, where the village appears as "Steepways":

> . . . the village was built up the face of a steep and lofty cliff. There was no road in it, there was not a level yard in it. From the sea-beach to the cliff-top irregular rows of white houses, placed opposite to one another, and twisting here and there and there and here, rose, like the sides of a long succession of stages of crooked ladders, and you climbed up the village or climbed down the village by the staves between, some six feet wide or so, and made of sharp irregular stones.

Except for the people, nothing has changed much.

2. THE SOUTHERN ARC

The arc that runs roughly along Devon's southern coast from Dorset to Cornwall has two great anchors—Devon's two largest cities, Exeter in the east and Plymouth in the west. In between lies the heart of the so-called "British Riviera," an infinitely elastic hyperbole beloved by travel agents, stretchable to the uttermost reaches of Cornwall if need be, even unto Polperro, Penzance, and Land's End itself.

In and About Exeter

Exeter is an impressive and at times surprisingly modern city of 100,000, where the ages blend and merge. A late twentieth-century mall, for instance, leads the way to a cathedral that dates from the twelfth century. The city fathers, harking back to that bitter May of 1942 when German bombers filled the sky, are quick to explain: "The many handsome buildings now to be seen in the streets are reminders not only of a resurgent, but also of a blazing, Exeter."

The Cathedral serves as a symbol of Exeter's leading role in the religious history of the West Country. Miles Coverdale, famed translator of the Bible, was its bishop from 1551 to 1553. Richard Hooker, author of *The Laws of Ecclesiastical Politie* (1594 and 1597) has a statue in the Cathedral close, to remind us not only that he was born in Heavitree, now an Exeter suburb, but also that he owed his Oxford education to the patronage of the Cathedral's

Bishop Jewel. And Thomas Fuller, author of *Worthies of England* (posthumously published in 1662), preached there often from 1642 to 1647 and served as chaplain to Charles I's daughter, Henrietta, who was born in Exeter.

The Cathedral houses two books of incalculable value: The Exon Domesday Book, the western half of William the Conquerer's historic eleventh-century survey, and the Exeter Book of about 975, containing among others the world's only manuscripts of such notable Old English works as "The Wanderer," "The Seafarer," "Widsith," and "Deor."

In the very shadow of the Cathedral, quite a different sort of building recalls Devon's naval history, especially those glorious days under Elizabeth I when England was exploring the New World, smashing the Spanish Armada, and establishing itself as a sea power. Leading the way were the great sea captains of Devon—Drake, Hawkins, Frobisher, Gilbert, and that patron of Edmund Spenser and no mean poet himself, Sir Walter Raleigh. When they were in Essex, Mol's, in the Cathedral close and England's first coffee house (1596), was a favorite rendezvous. Another was the Ship Inn, still standing and still serving, of which Drake said, "next to mine own shippe, I do most love that old Shippe in Exon, a tavern in Fyssh Street, as the people call it, or as the Clergie will have it, St. Martin's Lane."

During the nineteenth century, a number of writers came to Exeter for one reason or another, among them Southey, Dickens, Thackeray, Tennyson, Robert Louis Stevenson, and George Gissing. But not all of them were as happy to be there as Drake. Not Robert Southey, for example, who, in the last year of the eighteenth century, actually took lodgings at a place challengingly named "Hobson's Choice" and had Coleridge as a house guest. Wrote Southey: "My remarks upon the city are that it stinks—and that on public rejoicings they ring *two* bells at one church and *one* at another, which makes excellent ding dong music."

In contrast, Charles Dickens loved Exeter and visited it several times. In March, 1839, he came to find a home for his parents sufficiently remote from London, he hoped, to curb his ever-improvident father from his expensive borrow-and-spend habits. The novelist found "a jewel of a place" in Alphington (now part of Exeter), called Mile End Cottage, with "the one-mile stone from Exeter opposite the door." "The neighborhood," he wrote, "I suppose the most beautiful in this most beautiful of English counties."

He was equally delighted with the room he had at Exeter's New London Inn while house hunting: "My quarters," he said, "are excellent, and the head-waiter is *such* a waiter!" He had an amusing encounter there, too. He was outside the water closet when he heard a man's voice (of "tragic quality") crying within, "There is somebody here!" Alarmed, Dickens burst in—and

The Exeter Book's Exeter Cathedral, Devon

By Courtesy of The Exeter Tourist Office and Nicholas Toyne

found, more than a little startled by the intrusion, Charles Kean, the famous actor.

It was also in Exeter that Dickens had found the model for his "Fat Boy," Joe in *Pickwick Papers* (1837), at The Turks Head, a restaurant dating from the thirteenth century and still proudly announces, "Dickens wrote here, and his corner is preserved."

That fellow Victorian and novelist, Dickens's sometime friend William Makepeace Thackeray, knew Exeter well, for his stepfather retired from the army in 1825 and took over a mansion in nearby Ottery St. Mary. The teenage Thackeray relished his holidays there away from Charterhouse School and was often in Exeter.

In his novel *Pendennis* (1848–50) Exeter appears as "Chatteris." To it teenage Arthur "Pen" Pendennis rides from his nearby home of "Clavering St. Mary," for the "purpose of carrying to the *County Chronicle* a tremendous and thrilling poem for the next week's paper." Exeter had a theatrical company, and so does Chatteris, where Pen falls in love with the ravishing (but stupid) actress Miss Fotheringay, née Emily Costigan.

In the summer of 1867 Alfred Tennyson used Exeter as a base for an extensive walking tour of Devon with a friend, Francis Palgrave, who reported he had never seen the poet enjoy himself so brilliantly as among the beautiful combes and on the lonely beaches of Devonshire. Robert Louis Stevenson, however, who suffered from tuberculosis, was hardly as fortunate. When he came in August of 1885 to see the West Country after visiting Thomas Hardy in Dorchester, he wound up stranded in his Exeter hotel room until mid-September, following a nearly fatal fit of hemorrhaging.

For yet another Victorian author, Exeter must have provided some rare moments of pleasure in a life wracked by poverty and misery. George Gissing lived in Exeter from 1891 to 1893, and included Exeter scenes in *Born in Exile* (1892), which he wrote while there, and depicted the countryside in the semiautobiographical novel, *The Private Papers of Henry Ryecroft* (1903), in which books and memories help the hero blot out the harshness of real life.

For a walking tour of Exeter, the Cathedral in the center of town is a convenient place to start. You'll want to see it anyway, and sites of literary interest are all near by. The Exeter Book is in the Cathedral library in the adjoining Bishop's Palace (open Monday–Friday afternoons, but you'd better check). In the close, to the north of the Cathedral, is the statue of Richard Hooker, and at the north corner of the close is St. Martin's Church, next to which you'll find Raleigh's favorite rendezvous, Mol's Coffee House (now an art and gift shop). Just off the close is Martin's Lane and The Ship Inn, so dear to Drake's heart.

After you leave the close, a few steps to the northwest is High Street, down which you'll quickly spot the pillared front of the twelfth-century Guildhall (the oldest municipal building in England). On its left is Dickens's Turks Head restaurant. (The Turk's *head* sticks out from the middle of the little ledge that separates the ground floor from the one above it.)

Final Exeter note: just for fun, while you're strolling down the High Street, keep your eyes open for two stores: Pitts and Ratners. Between them is the narrowest street in the kingdom—Parliament Street—varying from twenty-five to forty-five inches in width.

Sidmouth

Regency houses, red cliffs, a sand and pebble beach, and resort hotels—that's Sidmouth, a pleasant fifteen mile drive from Exeter, southeast along the A 3052. In *Pendennis* Thackeray calls it "Baymouth," where young Pen, smitten by Miss Fotheringay's charms, goes to learn more about her from his school chum, Foker. Finding Foker gone, he sits and bites his nails by "the much-sounding sea . . . . bright and immeasurable," as the "blue waters came rolling into the bay, foaming and roaring."

In real life, Sidmouth was the scene for unrealized love involving two of England's best known women writers. The first didn't get her man. The second didn't want hers. Jane Austen holidayed there in the summer of 1801 and met a young gentleman named Mr. Blackall, who, it seems, was so attractive that years later Jane's sister Cassandra confessed that she herself had "thought him worthy to possess and likely to win her sister's love." But, alas, soon after, Mr. Blackall suddenly died.

In August of 1832, Elizabeth Barrett's father brought the family to live in Sidmouth, hoping the warmer climate would improve her health. They stayed until 1835 and her health did indeed improve, for she became able to ride her donkey along the shore and on the cliffs and to wade "up to her waist in the wet grass or weeds." She also enjoyed the company of a Rev. George Hunter, but in no way responded to the ardor of his affection. Even so, he persisted for thirteen years, right up to the time of her marriage to Robert Browning.

Ottery St. Mary

Twelve miles almost due east of Exeter, off the A 30 and five miles north of Sidmouth, is Ottery St. Mary, the "sweet birthplace," as he called it in his "Frost at Midnight," of S.T. Coleridge. He was the last of a brood of thirteen children born to the vicar and headmaster of Ottery St. Mary's King's School. The vicar was an amiable, absentminded fellow, quite capable of showing up for breakfast with the bishop without his wig. Young Coleridge adored his father, whom he called "a perfect Parson Adams," after the character in Fielding's *Joseph Andrews*. The father's sudden death followed by the son's exile to Christ's Hospital in London may well have laid the foundation for the restless, undisciplined poet to come.

Coleridge returned to Ottery St. Mary several times, but not too happily. Once he came back on a vacation from school and was delighted to find the initials he had carved in a cave, but his mother refused to let him in the house while he was wearing his blue Christ's Hospital charity coat. And after he grew up, he didn't get along well with his brothers, who disapproved of his ideas and his way of life. There is a commemorative plaque to Coleridge—showing a bust and an albatross—on the Ottery St. Mary churchyard wall.

Another writer with a lasting love for Ottery St. Mary was William Makepeace Thackeray, whose army-major stepfather bought the imposing stone mansion of Larkbeare, a mile and a half out, when Thackeray was fourteen. A student at Charterhouse, Thackeray would count down the days before each holiday then go racing off in glee to Larkbeare. And when he finished at Charterhouse he lived at Larkbeare from May to the following February while the major prepped him for Cambridge.

In *Pendennis,* the most autobiographical of his novels, "Clavering St. Mary's" is, of course, Ottery St. Mary, and Larkbeare becomes "Fairoaks." Thackeray's affection for both shines in the book's description of their fictional counterparts:

> At sunset, from the lawn of Fairoaks, there was a pretty sight: it and the opposite park of Clavering were in the habit of putting on a rich golden tinge, which became them both wonderfully. The upper windows of the great house flamed so as to make your eyes wink; the little river ran off noisily westward, and was lost in a sombre wood, behind which the towers of the old abbey church of Clavering (whereby that town is called Clavering St. Mary's to the present day) rose up in purple splendor.

Dartmoor—Easton Cross—Manaton—Two Bridges-Princetown

Of the two huge national parks of Southwest England—Exmoor mainly in northern Somerset, and Dartmoor in southern Devonshire—Dartmoor is the larger (over 200 square miles versus 120), the wilder, the more rugged, and the more romantic. Conan Doyle's description in *The Hound of The Baskervilles* (page 277 above) does it justice.

The Exeter-based traveller who has a day to spare would do well to use it for an exploration of the moorlands, including spots that attracted Tennyson, Galsworthy, and Evelyn Waugh. But if you plan to leave your car at any time and tramp about on foot, the following from a guide book of fifty years ago still makes charming sense:

> The pedestrian is advised to provide himself with a good map and compass; to refrain from attempting to cross swampy spots; to make for a valley if overtaken by a mist; and to remember that recent heavy rain is apt to make the streams impassable.

Easton Cross A village only fourteen miles west of Exeter, puts one well into the northeast corner of Dartmoor. To plunge quickly into the moorlands you take the narrow B 3212 and then turn right when you come to the A 382. Or, to ease in, there's the more comfortable A 30 skirting Dartmoor's northern edge, with a left turn at the A 382. In any event, about half way down, or up, the latter is Easton Cross—and Easton Court hotel.

Easton Court is a thatched fifteenth-century house with oak beams and open fireplaces. It's of special interest because fifty years ago it was run by a sturdily independent American woman named "Nannie" Cobb, who had a soft spot for writers. She provided them with a place that felt like a country house rather than a hotel and encouraged but never intruded on them. Among those who came back a number of times were Alec Waugh and his more famous brother, Evelyn.

Evelyn was especially taken with Easton Court and Nannie and helped support her in her later years (she died in 1960) with gifts of money. Among things he worked on there, at least in part, were *Remote People* (1931), *Black Mischief* (1932), *Ninety-Two Days* (1934), *Mr. Loveday's Little Outing* (1936), *Handful of Dust* (1934), and *Brideshead Revisited* (1944). Early on he penned a description of Easton Court that is vintage Waugh:

> . . . it is very odd. Kept by a deserter from the Foreign Legion and an American lady called Mrs. Postlethwaite Cobb who mixes menthol with her cigarettes. And we drink rye whiskey in her bedroom, and there are heaps of New York magazines and rather good, sophisticated food. I think it is a distributing centre for white slaves and cocaine or something like that. They never give one a bill.

Manaton Manaton is the kind of place it's almost impossible to get to accidentally. Although it's only a dozen miles southwest of Exeter and is on a B road (the 3344), it is not on the way to anything. And though it has charming views, its handful of houses and small post office and store hardly clamor for attention. Yet for nearly twenty years it was one of John Galsworthy's most favorite spots on earth.

Here he worked on many of his most successful novels and plays. And here, in fact, occurred in July of 1918 what he called "the happiest day of my writing life," when "it suddenly came to me that I could go on with my Forsytes and complete their history in two more volumes with a link between." The completed *Forsyte Saga,* he said, "will be my passport . . . to the shores of permanence." He plunged at once into a "Second Part of the Forsyte Saga," to be called *The Second Flowering.*

In a story called "Buttercup Night," Galsworthy describes how he first came to this remote bit of moorland:

> I had walked with my napsack twenty miles, and there being no room at the tiny inn of the very little village, they directed me to a wicket gate, through which, by a path leading down a field, I would come to a farmhouse where I might find lodging.
>
> . . . The moment I got into that field I felt within me a special contentment, and sat down on a rock to let that feeling grow. . . . Leaving the rock at last, I went toward the house. It was long and low and rather sad, standing in a garden all mossy grass and buttercups, with a few rhododendrons and flowery shrubs below a row of fine old Irish yews.

Supposedly Galsworthy discovered Manaton and this old stone farmhouse called Wingstone in early 1904. But it may well have been a year earlier, for there is evidence that in truth he and Ada had clandestinely stayed there the Easters of both 1903 and 1904 while she was still married to his cousin, Major Arthur Galsworthy (who becomes Soames in *The Man of Property* [1906] as Ada becomes Irene). Anyway, after his father's death freed him of filial compunction, John brought Ada with him openly to holiday together the Christmas of 1904. The major then had no choice but to divorce Ada, as she had wanted him to do for nine years.

After their marriage the following September, John and Ada came to Wingstone regularly for the next several years to stay as paying guests. But in 1908 they took a long lease on the front part of the house—the whole of the guest portion—while the farmer and his family continued to live in the back. For the next fifteen years, this was the Galsworthys' second home, often for long stretches at a time.

Their part of Wingstone was attractive and ample. From the lane in back a private drive curved 'round to the front of the house where flower beds, a long stone veranda, the main door, and tall French windows greeted such guests as G. B. Shaw. In addition to sleeping quarters, the Galsworthys had two front rooms opening on the veranda: one a dining room-study, and the other a sitting room with Ada's piano.

But Ada was far from happy at Wingstone. It was too isolated, the climate did not suit her, and living was rough and primitive. There was no electricity, only oil lamps and candles. And no bathroom, not even plumbing—baths were a hip bath in front of the fire, with water carried up from the kitchen below. Besides, Ada was often bored. Typical was a comment she made while Galsworthy toiled away happily, in April of 1908, on what ultimately became *Fraternity* (1909), "This is no holiday for me: housekeeping and people and ordering rubbish from shops."

For Galsworthy, however, Wingstone was always a precious place. When, in June of 1923, he learned he could no longer renew the lease, he was heartbroken: "Alas for us!—or for me, rather, because I think Ada is almost glad to be quit of Devonshire damp—Wingstone will be reft from us next month . . . to me it's a blow."

Two Bridges-Princetown The hamlet of Two Bridges, twenty miles southwest of Exeter, owes the bulk of the outsiders who pass through to two things: mainly to its location at the junction of the two major roads that cut through the heart of Dartmoor (if slender ribbons like the B 3212 and the B 3357 can be called "major"), making it an excellent center for walking tours . . . and to its proximity to Princetown, little more than a mile southwest, home of the famous and dreaded Dartmoor Prison, which drew the attention of Alfred Tennyson and John Galsworthy.

Tennyson came through en route from Exeter to Dartmouth on his 1867 walking tour of Devon with Francis Palgrave. Palgrave recorded how they walked through "Dartmoor, desolate and eerie even under the brightest sun, to Princetown: a village gloomy in itself from its high, wind-exposed site, and more so from the great convict-prison."

Palgrave goes on to give an amusing and human picture of the poet laureate: "The inn," he wrote, "rough and small but clean was in accord with our surroundings. One bedroom with two huge four-posters was allotted us: and Tennyson lay with a candle, reading hard at [a] book." As it turned out, he kept poor Palgrave awake far into the night, for he was engrossed by the big question of the book: the delayed confirmation of its grown-up hero. Finally Tennyson announced, "I see land. Harry may be going to be confirmed at last." With a happy sigh, he blew out the candle and fell fast asleep. (The book? *The Daisy Chain* by Charlotte M. Yonge.)

Galsworthy's interest in Dartmoor Prison was more than casual. Prison reform had become a prime concern, and he stayed in Two Bridges for three days in 1907 while he did research in Princetown. His investigation of the British prison system culminated in *Justice* (1910), one of his truly notable plays. But the theme appears in several other works, including this chilling picture of a prisoner in solitary, from "The House of Silence":

> . . . in the small white-washed space, with a black floor whence he has cleaned all dirt, he spends only fourteen out of the twenty-four hours alone, except on Sunday, when he spends twenty-one, because it is God's day. He spends them walking up and down, muttering to himself, listening for sounds, with his eyes on the little peephole in the door, through which he can be seen but cannot see.

Galsworthy's horror at this must have been all the greater for its contrast with the "glorious air, cliffs, sands, and skies" of the Cornish coast he had left just before reaching Princetown. Happily, among those impressed by *Justice* was Winston Churchill, who speedily effected some prison reforms, including diminution of solitary confinement.

The "British Riviera"

From Exeter, the A 379 runs south along Devon's coastline for thirty-five miles before leaving the sea and heading westward for Plymouth. Threading the highway are resorts and accommodations for all tastes and coffers; for unlike its Continental counterpart, Devon's Riviera beckons to rich and poor alike. At the one extreme are unpretentious places where hotels run to two, one, or no stars, and where a London clerk and his family can lie along the blackened-sand beach behind their self-erected windbreaks for a full week at bargain rates. At the other is Torquay, with its four and even five-star palaces where a London banker and his family can enjoy sauna baths and heated outdoor pools—and never go near the sea.

Dawlish—Teignmouth

Only a couple of miles apart, thirteen and fifteen miles south of Exeter, Dawlish and Teignmouth (TIN-muth) belong to the poor man's Riviera. That ubiquitous nineteenth-century duo, Jane Austen and Charles Dickens, both passed through Dawlish and gave it brief mention in their works. In Jane's *Sense and Sensibility* (1811), that priceless coxcomb, Mr. Robert Ferrars, insists that the heroine, whose home was actually four miles north of Exeter, lived in a cottage near Dawlish; for—as Jane wryly remarks—"it seemed rather surprising to him that anybody could live in Devonshire without living near Dawlish."

Oddly enough, Dickens's Nicholas Nickleby *was* born on a small farm near Dawlish, which his father soon "spec-u-lates" away, leaving the family destitute. But at the end of the novel, happily, Nicholas—now rich and prosperous—is able to buy it back and produce "gradually about him a group of lovely children."

And in real life John Keats spent several months of 1818 in Teignmouth which, indeed, is near Dawlish. His visit to the Dawlish Fair resulted in a frolicsome, bawdy little poem that might astonish those who know only his great odes and "The Eve of St. Agnes." It begins:

> Over the Hill and over the Dale,
> And over the Bourne to Dawlish,
> Where ginger-bread wives have a scanty sale,
> And ginger-bread nuts are smallish

proceeds through:

> Rantipole Betty she ran down a hill
> And kick'd up her petticoats fairly:
> Says I, I'll be Jack if you will be Gill
> So she lay on the grass debonnairly

and ends deliciously several stanzas later with:

> O who wouldn't hie to a Dawlish fair,
> O who wouldn't stop in a Meadow,
> O who wouldn't rumple the daisies there,
> And make the wild fern for a bed do?

Keats also shows his comic bent with an account of John Milton at Teignmouth in 1651, girding himself for his blistering reply to Salmasius, the French defender of Charles I: "I have heard that Milton ere he wrote his Answer to Salmasius came into these parts, and for one whole month, rolled himself for three whole hours a day, in a certain meadow hard by us—where the mark of his nose at equi-distances is still shown. The exhibitor of said Meadow further saith that after these rollings, not a nettle sprang up in all the seven acres for seven years."

Keats's own stay in Teignmouth (to care for his tubercular brother Tom) began in April of 1818 and lasted into May. He didn't like it one bit. For example:

> . . . you may say what you will of Devonshire: the truth is, it is a splashy, rainy, misty, snowy, foggy, haily, floody, muddy, slipshod county. . . .

and:

> Had England been a large Devonshire, we should not have won the Battle of Waterloo.

Torbay: Torquay

In the spring of 1968, three resorts on Tor Bay, just below Teignmouth—Torquay, Paignton, and Brixham—joined to form the County Borough of Torbay, which they hoped would become one of England's greatest holiday havens. They had much to offer: twenty-two miles of pebbly inlets and sandy beaches, a backstop of striking red cliffs, a generally benign climate, and attractions that ran the gamut from quaint to sophisticated, with enough of the garish in between to satisfy the most bourgeois of hearts.

There has been a settlement at Paignton since the Bronze Age. And Brixham was old when Sir Francis Drake sailed into its harbor with the first prize ship captured from the Spanish Armada. But it was Torquay that established the area when the wives of English naval officers stationed there in the early nineteenth century discovered its delights while their husbands went about their blockade duties against Napoleon.

When boasting about the hordes of visitors who have flocked there ever since, Torbay can drop almost as many literary names as Bath could in the eighteenth century. It won the hearts of writers as different as Alfred Tennyson and Henry James and broke the hearts of Elizabeth Barrett and Sean O'Casey. It charmed and then frightened Rudyard Kipling, and it harbored George Bernard Shaw while he prepared for battle against the whole British government. It gave birth to a swashbuckler with a deft hand for pornography and inspired a dying clergyman to write one of the world's most beloved hymns.

The swashbuckler was Sir Richard Burton, born at Torquay in 1821. Adventurer, explorer, diplomat, and writer of over eighty books on his travels, he is best remembered today for his translations of *The Arabian Nights* (1885–88) and of *Kama Sutra* (1883), *The Perfumed Garden* (1886), and other works delicately described as "Arabian erotology."

The clergyman was Henry Francis Lyte, who came to Brixham as curate-at-large in 1823. The faith and serenity with which he faced his imminent death from tuberculosis in 1847 shine through the immortal lines of "Abide with me," written on the afternoon after he had given his final sermon, as he sat on some rocks and watched the sun set over the fishing boats in Tor Bay:

> Abide with me; fast falls the eventide
> The darkness deepens; Lord, with me abide!
> When other helpers fail, and comforts flee
> Help of the helpless, O abide with me.

Alfred Tennyson was another whom the view of this harbor inspired to write. He had come to Torquay on a visit in 1838 and ecstatically dubbed it "the loveliest sea-village in England." In particular he was entranced, as he made his way in gathering gloom from the hill to the harbor below, by the sight of a buoy appearing and disappearing phosphorescently in the darkening sea. He captures the scene charmingly in that happy and serene pastoral, "Audley Court":

> . . . as we sank
> From rock to rock upon the glooming quay
> The town was hush'd beneath us; lower down
> The bay was oily calm; the harbor-buoy,
> Sole star of phosphorescence in the calm.
> With one green sparkle ever and anon
> Dipt by itself, and we were glad at heart.

Elizabeth Barrett (she hadn't even met Robert Browning then) came to Torquay that same summer of 1838 and stayed for three years, the last of which proved the bitterest of her life.* In poor health from adolescence on, she had been brought there, along with her numerous brothers and sisters, in hopes she would improve. At first she was happy. Her first collection of verses, *The Seraphim and Other Poems,* was published that year; and though sales were on the slender side, the reviews were good.

But in 1840, while sailing in nearby Babbacombe Bay, her brother Edward's boat was caught in a sudden squall, and he drowned. It took Elizabeth months to gain control of herself; for of all her brothers, he was her favorite, her "best beloved." Even in the following summer, the event still haunted her "like the oppression of a perpetual nightmare." Her perilous health seemed to make moving from Torquay impossible, yet, she said, she "could not face remaining another year in this miserable place." And so, in September of 1841, she was carried into a carriage equipped with a bed, and "drawn out of the carriage like a drawer out of a table, and deposited [with a shawl over her face] in a bedroom at the different inns" along the way back to London.

To Sean O'Casey, the dramatist, Torquay brought even greater heartbreak, if that were possible. Forced to leave the house in Totnes that he had come to love, despite initial grumbling that "even a miracle couldn't make [it] comfortable," he came to Torquay in 1955 with equal reluctance. His wife, Eileen, had found a flat in the St. Marychurch suburb, part of a white, stone,

*Bath House, where she stayed, is at 1 Beacon Terrace and is now the Hotel Regina.

two-storey house at 40 Trumlands Road. Its four rooms, plus kitchen and bath, were adequate but no more than that.

But O'Casey soon settled into it. The large front room looking across the Downs was for the rest of his life, in his view, "home." He not only slept and dressed there; but he lived there with his remarkably wide-ranging assortment of books surrounding him and his beloved armchair snuggled against the gas fire. On the two ancient typewriters he had brought with him from Dublin nearly thirty years before, he resumed the writing that to many had long since stamped him the greatest living Irish playwright.

He was seventy-six. But, said he, "I am not waiting for Godot to bring me life; I am out after life myself." Then, as 1956 neared its end, came the cruelest of blows. Niall, the younger son—at twenty, bright and handsome as only a young Irishman can be, arrived home for the Christmas holidays pale and a bit weary. Run down and needing a good rest, said his parents. Leukemia, said the doctor. Two weeks later he was gone. "To go so young, and life so much within you and around you," the father wrote as he grieved. "Oh, where was the Lord's deliverance?'"

O'Casey struggled on. There were even a few plays: *The Drums of Father Ned* (1960), and, in 1961, *Behind the Green Curtains* , *Figuro in the Night,* and *The Moon Shines on Kylenamoe.*

At last, in a Torquay nursing home in September of 1964, the end came mercifully. As drama critic Brooks Atkinson put it: "His heart stopped beating. In eighty-four years of unselfish living it was the first time his heart had failed him." His ashes were scattered where Niall's had been seven years before, in London's Garden of Rememberance, between the Shelley and Tennyson rose beds.

Three of Victorian fiction's most successful moonlighter novelists were a feisty clergyman and a pair of dudish politicians. Charles Kingsley, vicar of Eversley in Hampshire, was the clergyman, an archetypal "muscular Christian" who dared take on the great Cardinal Newman himself—with disastrous results. And Edward Bulwer-Lytton and Benjamin Disraeli, prototypical dandies and friends, were the politicians. Both achieved high office and both were rewarded with titles by Queen Victoria—the former ultimately becoming Secretary of the Colonies and Baron Lytton, and the latter, twice Prime Minister and Earl of Beaconsfield.

A disparate trio, these three. But in addition to enjoying unusual success as part-time novelists, they shared one thing more: a love of Torquay. Indeed, Torquay might well have figured as a key setting in Kingsley's best known novel, *Westward Ho!* (1855). Kingsley, though he grew up in north Devon, had been born at Holne vicarage, Dartmoor, barely a dozen miles from

Torquay. In 1854 he happily repaired to Livermead on that city's outskirts while his Hampshire rectory was being refurbished.

From his window in Livermead, Kingsley could look across Tor Bay to Compton Castle, ancestral home of Sir Walter Raleigh's half brother, Sir Humphrey Gilbert. There is no doubt that this view stirred in Kingsley thoughts of the great naval days of Queen Elizabeth that he brings to life in his book. In fact, he recalls in the novel "the terrible and glorious pageant which passed by [the bay] in the bright July days of 1588, when the Spanish Armada ventured slowly past Berryhead with Elizabeth's gallant pack of Devon's captains following fast in its wake." But, at his wife's urging, Kingsley left Torquay for the North Devon coast to complete his wait. There he began to write *Westward Ho!,* and there he placed the home of Amyas Leigh, his hero.

Bulwer-Lytton came to Torquay, as had so many before him, seeking refuge from "the cold and gloom" of London. That was in 1864, and thereafter it was his usual winter retreat, especially after he bought Argyll House on Warren Road in 1867. He liked to pretend that the place was a wondrous breeder of idleness. Typical are these comments over the years: "I am laboriously idle (1867). . . . I like Torquay much in a lazy way (1868). . . . I am not only idle, but all literary exertion is repugnant to me (1871)." Actually, however, as these very years will attest, at Torquay his literary career went on apace. He worked there on the proofs of his *Miscellaneous Prose Works* in 1867, wrote much of his striking satirical novel, *The Coming Race* in 1871, and even in the last year of his life (the winter of 1872), though sick and often in pain, finished *Kenelm Chillingly.*

Benjamin Disraeli, a welcome visitor at Argyll House, himself became attached to Torquay in the oddest way of all. By mid-century, as the sometimes audacious author of novels like *Vivian Grey* (1826–27), *Coningsby* (1844), *Sybil* (1845), and *Tancred* (1847) and as a dazzling if controversial politician, he was accustomed to receiving letters of all kinds. But none startled him quite as much as one he got one day in 1851 from a Mrs. Brydges Willyams. She was, it turned out, a wealthy widow, lived in Torquay, and was well over eighty. Would Disraeli, she asked, be the executor of her will? In return, she promised, though they had never met, she would make him primary beneficiary. Her reasons were—to her—well, reasonable. She liked his novels and besides she was, like him, a Christian but intensely proud of her Jewish ancestry.

Mindful of the possibly damaging effects such a bizarre arrangement might have on his reputation and political fortunes, Disraeli replied with extreme caution, promising only to look her up next time he was in Torquay. He did, and they became fast friends. She came to call him "dear Dizz," sent him Tor Bay's best turbot and prawns, and advised him he could live to be a hundred if he stayed away from doctors. In exchange, he sent her trout and partridge, and charming, detailed letters about his activities, sometimes as many as thirty in a single year.

He also came to Torquay at least once a year to visit her, driving her out to see the local sights, holding little dinner parties, and staying up late to play écarté with her. But he was always careful to stay at the Royal Hotel rather than at Mount Braddon, her home. When Mrs. Willyams died, in 1863, she was as good as her word: she left him well over £30,000, a great fortune then.

On his way to St. Ives in Cornwall the summer of 1894, Henry James stopped off in Torquay to see W. E. Norris, a prolific writer of well-wrought novels in the Trollopean manner, who lived there. His three days there, James wrote, "were rendered charming by the urbanity of my host and the peerless beauty of Torquay, with which I fell quite in love." How deep this love was is proved by his returning the next July and—after a London hiatus—September and October. He stayed at the Osborne Hotel, which still flourishes on Hesketh Crescent, elegant now (four stars) as then. James, though forever complaining to friends how little money he made from his novels, always managed to go first class. The Osborne was no exception. There, as he worked on *The Spoils of Poynton* (1897) and a short story that later bloomed as *The Ambassadors* (1903), he enjoyed a fine suite with large living room and balcony, plus a six-foot chambermaid who fixed a hot tub for him each morning.

Despite such luxury, the very next year James was using his "poverty" as one of two compelling reasons why he could not vacation in Torquay yet a third time, much as he wished to: "I must take a house this time—a small and cheap one." Besides, he added, "I must (deride me not) be somewhere where I can, without disaster, bicycle."

Had Henry James ridden a bicycle in Torquay, he might well have been waved to as he wobbled past by a little girl of five with yellow sausage curls and a solemn face, who was to grow up to write books with a popularity and sales beyond James's wildest dreams. For Agatha Christie was born in Torquay in 1891 and grew up there in a big, rambling, loose-jointed house called Ashfield. It was in the Tor Mohun area, which she later described as the nonfashionable, older part of town. Maybe it was, but her father's labors, as she reports them, were hardly Herculean: "He left our house in Torquay every morning and went to his club. He returned in a cab, for lunch, and in the afternoon went back to the club, played whist all afternoon, and returned to the house in time to dress for dinner."

Torquay still has houses that evoke memories of those days of idyllic leisure, but Ashfield itself is gone. When she learned, in 1962, that it was to be torn down to make way for a housing development, Agatha Christie tried to buy it. But the developers refused. Bitterly, she recounts her visit a year and a half later to the spot where it had stood: "There was nothing that could even stir a memory. They were the meanest, shoddiest little houses I had ever seen."

Oddly enough, the five-year-old Agatha might also have waved at yet another bicycling writer perhaps even more unsteady on his mount than Henry James. In 1896 Rudyard Kipling came to live in Maidencombe on the eastern edge of Torquay. He rented Rock House and jubilantly compared it to the beloved house in Brattleboro, Vermont, he had so recently been forced to give up:

> . . . a big stone and stucco [house], long, low, with two stories, stuck on the side of a steep hill falling away almost as sharply as the lower slopes of Wantastiquet [in Vermont] to a hundred-foot cliff of pure red soil. Below that is the sea, about two hundred yards from the window.

From the work table where he wrote he could look directly down on the fishing craft tending their lobster pots.

Besides working at what was eventually to become *Stalky & Co.* (1899), Kipling, along with his wife, started "learning to ride things called 'bicycles'." Each thought the other delighted with both the house and their new hobby. But they were wrong on both counts. One "fortunate day," as Kipling termed it, their bikes skidded and dumped them rudely on the roadway. Getting dazedly to their feet, Kipling recounts in *Something of Myself,* "we made mutual confession of our common loathing of wheels." The house, too, palled, producing "a growing depression which enveloped us both . . . the Feng-Shui—the spirit of the house itself." So, using "a doubtful cistern for a stalking horse, we paid forfeit and fled," only nine months after moving in.

Today's traveller, if he bothers to turn off the highway at Maidencombe and drive up Rock House Lane, will find the solid, imposing house still there, still surrounded by lovely gardens and still guarding the same lovely view—and wonder what in the world got into the Kiplings.

If Rudyard Kipling came to Torquay seeking peace and quiet, George Bernard Shaw came there to do battle. He was never reluctant to take on anyone found "drivelling in slack-jawed blackguardism." But the battle he waged in 1914 from Torquay's Hydro Hotel was astounding, even for him. For his adversaries were little short of the entire British nation, and his target was England's involvement in World War I. Actually, he had no patience with either side in the war: "I felt as if I were witnessing an engagement between two pirate fleets." But, since he and his family and friends were, as he put it, aboard the British ships, he didn't want the latter defeated.

This touch of self-interest, however, in no way lessened his anger at what he felt were the diplomatic and military blunders and disasters of his adopted country. Sweeping together all the pertinent documents he could lay his hands on, he descended on Torquay in August, 1914. With the rooftop of the Hydro as his personal Command Headquarters, he spent the next several months writing the blistering indictment he called "Common Sense about the War." Predictably, its major effect was to stamp him in the public eye as disloyally pro-German. The effort did have one notable result, however: thanks to his lofty perch, he acquired the sun tan of his life.

While at Torquay Shaw took time off to run up to Manaton, fifteen miles to the northwest, with the dramatist-actor Harley Granville-Barker, to help John Galsworthy celebrate his forty-seventh birthday. But Galsworthy himself was an old Torbay visitor. For his mother lived there, and during the winter of 1914–15 the novelist was there almost constantly, staying at the Torbay hotel* while attending her in what proved to be her final illness. What is more, one of Galsworthy's earliest pieces, the title story of *The Man of Devon* (1910), published under the pseudonym John Sinjohn, featured the Devon countryside and the sea, "wonderful under the black wild cliff," just four miles below Brixham.

After this parade of famous writers who graced Torquay with their presence, the name of our final luminary may seem not only anticlimactic, but improbable as well—Eden Phillpotts. But there was indeed an Eden Phillpotts, and he lived from 1901 to 1928 at Eltham, Oak Hill Road where, year after year, he turned out novels and plays too many to mention. He looked upon his prodigious output in the most modest of lights, however, saying: "I do very little except write. I am not robust, and I detest society in any shape or form."

Even so, in his day, Phillpotts was likened to Thomas Hardy; moreover, Torquay was impressed enough to award him the "freedom of the town." And Torquay, one must admit, had known a writer or two in its time.

Totnes

Stretching westward from Torquay are about seven miles of unsullied Devonshire engagingly called the South Hams. And just at their edge, on the A 385, is Totnes ("tot-NESS"), where charming Elizabethan houses and courtyards still stand as they did in Daniel Defoe's day. So, for that matter,

*The Torbay hotel, a large four-storey stone-faced building fronting the sea, is still pleasantly in business (three stars) on Torbay Road.

does the Royal Seven Stars Hotel, the "great inn next the bridge" where he stayed. Defoe liked Totnes, recommending it in his *Tour Through the Whole Island of Great Britain* (1724–27) "especially for such as have large families and but small estates." S. T. Coleridge and Robert Southey, those fellow Romantic poets and brothers-in-law, were impressed with Totnes, too, on their Devon walking tour in 1799.

A more modern booster of Totnes was George Bernard Shaw, simply because it was only two miles southeast of Dartington where, he insisted, Sean O'Casey must send his sons to school as day students. In *Sunset and Evening Star* (1954) O'Casey wryly describes how it happened:

> Dartington Hall is the place for your boys, said Shaw.
>
> It's going to cost a lot, murmured Sean anxiously.
>
> No more than others, said Shaw, shutting up Sean.

So the O'Caseys quit London for Totnes in 1938. For the next seventeen happy years they lived in an old Victorian house named Tingrith on Station Road. It had large rooms: Sean's had a coal fire big enough to take logs. It also had both a garage and stables, and gardens front and rear—all for only £85 a year. Sean quickly came to love it, as his autobiography makes clear:

> Apart from the quiet hurry of market day, gentleness is the first quality to give it; gentleness in its buildings, and in the coming and going of its people; and in the slow, winding, winding of the River Dart from the moor to the sea. Oh, lord, the natural lie of it is lovely.

O'Casey's genius flourished in Totnes. Beginning with *The Star Turns Red* (1940) there came a steady flow of plays including *Red Roses for Me* (1942), *Oak Leaves and Lavender* (1946), and *Cock-a-doodle Dandy* (1949). And all six volumes of his beautiful autobiography were written in that same Tingrith study, from the initial *I Knock at the Door* (1939) to the final *Sunset and Evening Star*.

In 1955, when their landlord abruptly told them he wanted the house for his relatives, O'Casey was, in his wife's words, "lost and disconsolate. . . . 'So it's goodby to Tingrith,' sighed Sean. It was."

Dartmouth and Salcombe

If one chooses to meander along the Devon coast from Tor Bay to Plymouth, rather than striking inland and straight across, Dartmouth and Salcombe are two stops of some literary interest. Dartmouth comes first, five miles south of Torbay, on the A 379. Chaucer gives it its claim to fame in the Prologue to *The Canterbury Tales,* but in typical tongue-in-cheek fashion:

> A Shipman was ther, wonynge fer by weste;
> For aught I woot, he was of Dertemouth.

For all I know, that is, he was of Dartmouth. Nevertheless, Chaucer's sly hesitancy has hardly hindered some scholars from running down the original "Shipman" and claiming with fetching assurance he was a John Hawley, who died in 1408. There's even a brass of this John Hawley in the chancel of Dartmouth's St. Saviour's church. What boots it that the real John Hawley was a wealthy ship *owner* and Chaucer's man, only a sailor?

Salcombe lies at the very tip of Devon's most southern thrust into the English Channel, twelve miles below Dartmouth. It has ties to both Tennyson and John Galsworthy.

Tennyson is supposed to have gained the descriptive details of "Crossing the Bar" while on a friend's yacht in Salcombe Harbor in 1889, especially the "hollow moan" of the waves as they crossed the sand bar and the picture of

> Twilight and evening bell,
> And after that the dark

as he sat on the deck at sunset listening to the bells of Salcombe church ringing for evensong. The poem itself, however, as we've said, flashed into his mind whole the next year, during the twenty minute ferry ride from Lymington to Yarmouth en route to his winter home on the Isle of Wight.

For John Galsworthy, Salcombe proved more important by far. Mainly for his wife's health he spent the winter of 1905–06 at Salcombe's Bolt Head Hotel, built like a Swiss chalet 140 feet above the sea.* And what an astounding winter it proved to be. For not only did Galsworthy spend his time correcting the proofs of *The Man of Property,* which was to lift him once and for all from the common herd of writers to the position of a ranking novelist, but he also wrote his very first play, *The Silver Box* (originally *The Cigarette Box*).

He had scant hope for its success. "All actor managers get about 40 plays a week to look at," he wrote a friend, "and I have no reason to believe I can write a play better than anybody else." Almost apologetically, he sent it off to Harley Granville-Barker, London's newest and most exciting actor-manager. What happened next was incredible. It got to town Saturday; Granville-

*Still a hotel and rated four stars.

Barker and G. B. Shaw read it Sunday; and Barker accepted on Monday. In one fell swoop Galsworthy had arrived as a dramatist, too.

Plymouth

Plymouth, standing on the A 38 at the very southwestern edge of Devon, is by all odds Devon's largest city. In a number of ways, it reminds the visitor of Bristol: in its great bustling port, for instance, and grand naval history; its brisk no-nonsense air; and its pockets of strikingly modern buildings, like the civic center on the Royal Parade. This modernity, subject of some controversy, came about just as Bristol's did, too—because of the appalling devastation of World War II bombing, when 75,000 buildings of greater Plymouth were destroyed.

Americans know Plymouth, of course, because the Pilgrims sailed from there to establish their colony in Massachusetts. But few realize how accidental this distinction was. Our founding fathers disconsolately put into Plymouth only to allow those in their second ship, the Speedwell, which was leaking, to crowd in with those already jammed aboard the Mayflower.

Although Plymouth has produced no great writer of its own, from time to time visitors of literary bent wandered by. In the eighteenth century, for instance, both Dr. Sam Johnson and his good friend Fanny Burney, the novelist, found their way there. In the 1760's, Johnson came to Plymouth to stay with the noted artist, Sir Joshua Reynolds, who was born there. Once Johnson even jokingly took part in a quarrel then raging between the old town of Plymouth and The Dock, or Newtown section. When Newtowners petitioned for some of Plymouth's fresh water supply, Johnson replied with mock zeal: "No, No! I am against the dockers. I am a Plymouth-man. Rogues! let them die of thirst. They shall not have a drop."

Fanny Burney visited Plymouth in 1789 and raved about Saltram House, built about 1750 around the remnants of an old Tudor mansion. "One of the most magnificent in the Kingdom," she said. "Its view is noble." It now belongs to the National Trust and remains an outstanding tourist attraction, with among other treasures fourteen portraits by Reynolds, who was often a guest at Saltram.

In the next century, Plymouth did beget a poet who, if not among the literary giants, possessed considerable charm and wit—Austin Dobson, born there in 1840. And among notable visitors were Thackeray in 1832 and Tennyson in 1848. Thackeray stayed at the Wheatley Hotel, with less than happy results: "I eat at least 2 pounds of boiled beef & suffered for my beastly voracity all night," he complained. What was more, "I was almost sacrificed to the bugs."

Tennyson's stopover was the last leg of his tour of the West Country, chiefly Cornwall, and was breathlessly recorded by a twenty-year-old would-be writer named Elizabeth Rundle, who showed him her poems. He visited at her uncle's country house at Upland and told Elizabeth, "Do not publish too early, you cannot retract." But he approved her knowing Greek, saying he only disliked *pedantry* in women. When Elizabeth did get around to publishing, she managed over fifty books and sold briskly in the United States as well as England.

In the twentieth century, Plymouth visitors included Thomas Hardy and Sean O'Casey. Hardy's first wife was born there, and in his poem "West-of-Wessex Girl" he mourns the fact that they had never been there together—his first visit coming four months after her death. O'Casey came to Plymouth now and again between 1938 and 1954 from his home in Totnes, and in *Sunset and Evening Star* he sensitively sums up the city of today:

> Away to the west is Plymouth, a fair part of it bloodily scooped away by war; but definite still and as alive as ever; where Drake set foot on his rocking ship to sail out to shatter the bombastic shadow and substance of Spain's Armada, and so disperse the glowing dream of John of Austria. . . .

From Plymouth, one crosses westward over the county line into Cornwall. You can hardly do better than to leave to O'Casey the final word: "Oh, the Devon people have a beautiful carpet under their feet."

CORNWALL

Cornwall

1. The Channel Coast: Polperro to Penzance

2. The Ocean Coast: St. Ives to Morwenstowe

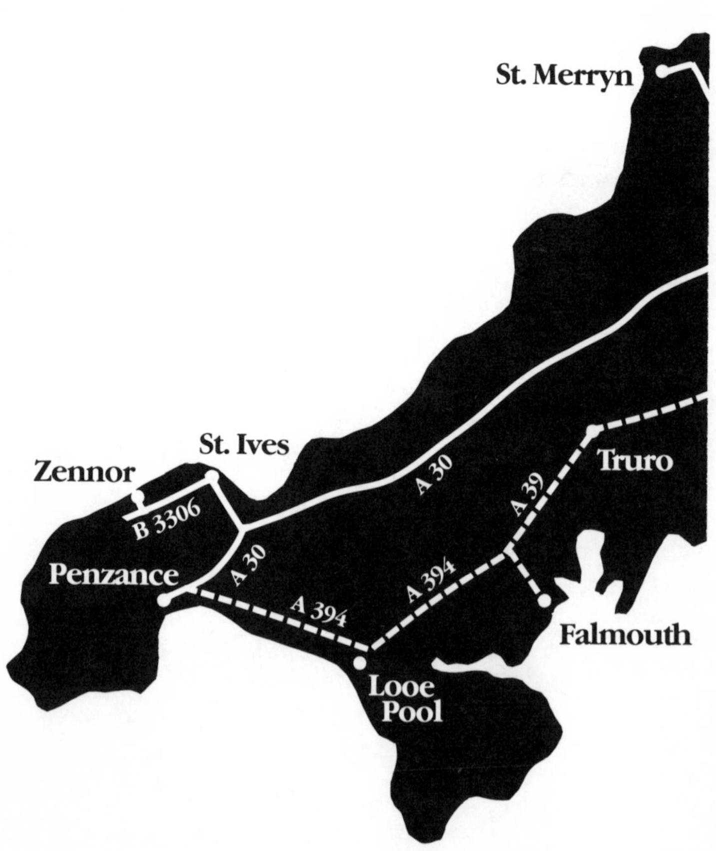

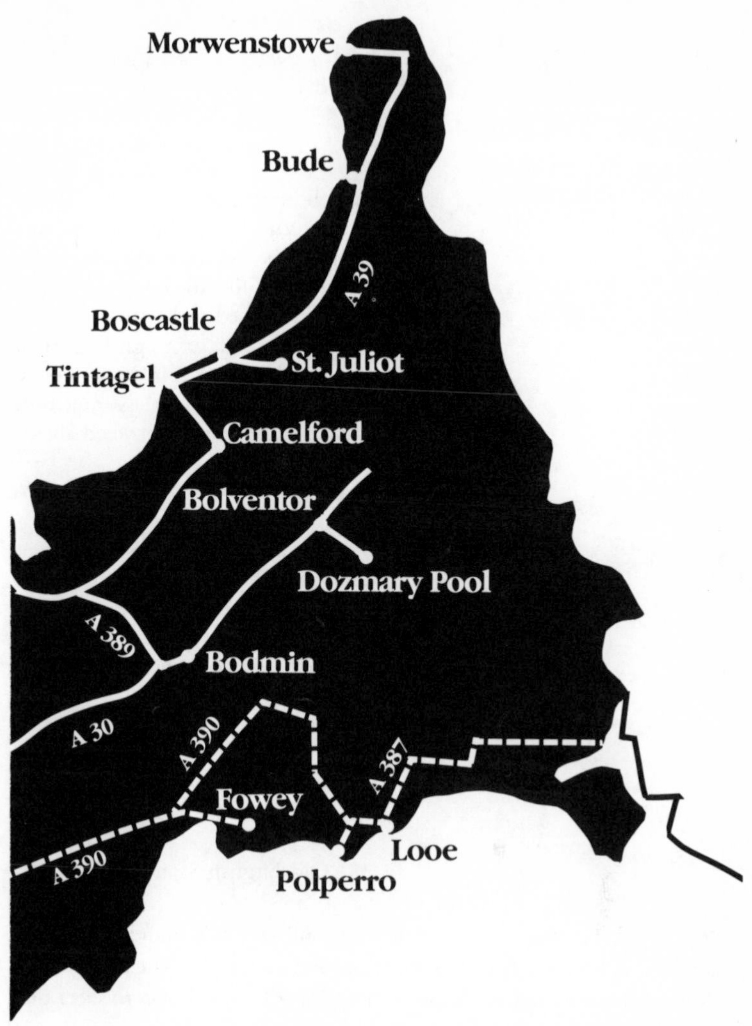
Morwenstowe
Bude
A 39
Boscastle
St. Juliot
Tintagel
Camelford
Bolventor
Dozmary Pool
A 389
Bodmin
A 30
A 390
A 387
Fowey
Looe
A 390
Polperro

. . . the serene impassive sea, visible to a width of half the horizon, and meeting the eye with the effect of a vast concave, like the interior of a blue vessel. Detached rocks stood upright afar, a collar of foam girding their bases, and repeating in its whiteness the plumage of a countless multitude of gulls that restlessly hovered about.

Thomas Hardy, *A Pair of Blue Eyes*

On the high tors the slabs of stone leant against one another in strange shapes and forms, massive sentinels who had stood there since the hand of God first fashioned them.

Daphne du Maurier, *Jamaica Inn*

By Tre, Pol, and Pen
You shall know the Cornishmen.

Old English Saying

If it cared to, which is doubtful, Cornwall couldn't round up enough inhabitants to fill the city of Toledo, Ohio; and its 1,357 square miles would rattle around in the state of Delaware. The rest of England likes to sneer that "Cornwall does not grow wood enough to make a coffin" and certainly not enough writers to fill an anthology, even if one included luminaries like Silas Hocking and his brother Joseph.

But your true Cornishman—usually darker and shorter than other Britons—will tell you fiercely that Cornwall is a duchy, not a shire, and that its dukes have run the gamut from Regan's husband to Princess Diana's* . . . that Spenser's Knight of all Virtue, King Arthur, was actually a Cornishman himself, born (or at least *found*) at Tintagel and slain near Dozmary Pool . . . and that even as late as the mid-1800's Cornwall had its own language, hence

*Yes, it's true: the Prince of Wales is also the Duke of Cornwall.

"Tre" (house), "Pol" (pool), and "Pen" (headland). Cornwall also has perhaps the most spectacular of all England's spectacular coastlines, providing at Land's End the American traveller with his first thrilling glimpse of England as his plane wings eastward through the dawn. (It must be said that Land's End looks a whole lot better from the air than on the ground.)

With a few exceptions, the literary sightseer who goes by car can see everything on his list by making a loop of the highways that roughly parallel Cornwall's Atlantic and Channel coastlines—in the south westward from Plymouth to Penzance, then northeastward from Penzance to where the A 39 crosses into Devon, heading for Clovelly.

1. THE CHANNEL COAST: POLPERRO TO PENZANCE

Polperro

A bit more than fifteen miles west of Plymouth, on the English Channel and the A 387, Polperro in season is almost as crowded as Clovelly. It's more charming, however, and looks much more like the quaint little English fishing village of your imagination. And it has far more the air of a place where people actually live. They fight desperately to keep it so. Only residents are allowed automobiles. The visitor must leave his in the ample carpark, which appears to be Polperro's most prosperous enterprise.

The town's chief street runs along the water, where the natives can fish from their balconies and even—so one said—from the "loo." The tiny picture-book harbor has its full quota of mysterious-looking caves, including one called inevitably The Smugglers'. From these rocks shone the final beacon warning Sir Francis Drake the Spanish Armada was coming. Out of the harbor a street climbs sharply up a craggy cliff. There, among the line of houses peering over its edge, is The Cobbles, a thin little three-storey cottage of white-painted stones, built smack against the rock so that the back of the top floor seems to open on to the ground. "Absolutely my dream place," novelist Hugh Walpole declared the moment he saw it. In March of 1913 he moved in with a year's lease. At first all was chaos: the ceiling fell in, the fireplace smoked, the oven wouldn't work. But Henry James sent not only his blessing but "a very pleasant and convenient and solid old desk" (though they had to remove the windows to get it into the house).

Best of all, Walpole found an idyllic workshop in a tiny hut on a ledge directly above his own rooftop, with an incredible view of the ocean and an inaccessibility most writers only dream of. From this hut, in whole or in part, poured an astounding deluge of books, among them *The Green Mirror,* begun in 1914 (published in 1918); *The Dark Forest* (1916), perhaps his best; *The Captives* (1918); *The Secret City* (1919); *The Young Enchanted* (1921); and *The Cathedral* (1922).

Walpole's prolificity was truly amazing. Once, when eager to change publishers, but still in debt to his current firm for one more book, he wrote a complete novel and managed to get it published just six months after the first word was written. Most wondrous of all, one critic found in it "the deep encompassing swell of a divine overtone." And though Rebecca West said, "It's certainly true that I don't like your work, I think it facile and without artistic impulse." Joseph Conrad, Henry James, Virginia Woolf, and Arnold Bennett all had kind words to say of Walpole.

Besides, it is hard to belabor a writer so disarming about his own success. Witness the ingenuousness with which he described a dinner conversation with Virginia Woolf: "I was diffident but Virginia encouraged me, talking about writing as if we were on a level." After her *Orlando* was published, he observed: "This marks the difference between genius and talent. *Orlando* is *all* genius. I have only a good talent."

Walpole kept The Cobbles until 1921 and gave it up then, most reluctantly, only because Polperro was getting to be too well-known and too visited, and because he had become quite entrenched in his London quarters. The house remains in private hands, and at last report was owned by a prominent member of Polperro's considerable colony of artists.

And on to Penzance

As the sea gull flies, it's about fifty miles from Polperro to Penzance, but it's much further by car. There's nothing of literary importance that makes the trip imperative, and even the places worth a brief mention are out of the way. Still, if you've got the time, it's a pleasant meander; and if you don't care to leave the main highways (the A 390, A 39, and A 394), at least you'll know what lies behind some of the road markers you'll pass.

Fowey (pronounced FOY.) First of these markers you'll meet along the A 390 points the way to Fowey, five miles west of Polperro. Fowey is a charming assortment of narrow streets and whitewashed houses, and is one of the West country's oldest seaports. It was a thriving harbor as far back as Edward I, furnished over forty ships for the siege of Cadiz in 1346, and contributed more than London did to Drake's thrashing of the Spanish Armada. Its contributions to literature are Sir Arthur Quiller-Couch and, through him, Daphne du Maurier and Kenneth Grahame.

Quiller-Couch—novelist, essayist, and poet, but perhaps best known as the editor of *The Oxford Book of English Verse*—came to live in Fowey in 1892, and died there in 1944. A native of Cornwall, "Q," as he was known, often drew on what he called the "Delectable Duchy" for his material. He served as Fowey's mayor, 1937-38, and there's a memorial in his honor in Hall Walk.

Quiller-Couch and Fowey both contributed to two of this country's most successful thriller novels. For among Q's friends was the popular actor Gerald du Maurier, who bought a cottage in Fowey as a summer place. Their daughters became devoted friends, and it was with Foy Quiller-Couch that young Daphne du Maurier first visited the hostel she was to make world famous: Jamaica Inn.

Moreover, the Quiller-Couch tales of the strange owner of Menabilly—an empty, neglected old mansion above Pridmouth Bay—planted the seeds that were to grow into *Rebecca*. As Miss du Maurier's *The Rebecca Notebook* indicates, Menabilly utterly captivated her from her first childish glimpse of it. Inevitably, it became the Manderley of her novel. And as a final fillip, she wound up renting, rehabilitating, and living in Menabilly itself.

Kenneth Grahame too got to Fowey on his visits to his friend Quiller-Couch. During these holidays he wrote a number of those delightful letters to his son that came to be *The Wind in the Willows* (1908) and even got married in Fowey's St. Fimbarrus's Church.

Golant Also off the A390, and just two miles above Fowey, Golant is by tradition the setting of the Tristram and Iseult love story. And there is even the mound of Castle Dore—said to be the palace of King Mark of Cornwall (uncle to Tristram and husband to "La Beale Isoud")—to prove it.

Falmouth At the eastern end of the A 394, and on a little peninsula that juts out into the English Channel twenty three miles southwest of Fowey, Falmouth has got to be as beautiful a harbor as all England can boast. On the wall of its Green Bank Hotel (three stars), a three-storey eighteenth-century inn at the water's edge, are reproductions of two letters to "My Darling Mouse" from "Your Loving Daddy," describing the "horrid, low trick" of one Mr. Toad, "a bad, low animal." This is the only hint the visitor will get that Kenneth Grahame was a guest here in 1907 and in one of these very rooms wrote the bulk of the *Wind in the Willows* letters.

Mylor A couple of miles north of Falmouth, the village of Mylor briefly housed short story writer Katherine Mansfield and author and editor John Middleton Murry in 1916, two years before their long-delayed marriage.

Twenty-three years later, a late-blooming, self-educated novelist with a decided Dickensian bent, Howard Spring, finally achieved popular (and financial) success, enabling him, he said, "to buy a home where I had long desired to be: on the sea's edge in Cornwall." At Mylor, of course. The book was *O Absolom!* (in America, called *My Son, My Son!*), translated into seven languages and made into a hit movie. Nor was this triumph a onetime fluke, for in Mylor he continued his success with *Fame Is The Spur* (1940); part II of his autobiography, *In the Meantime* (1942); and *Hard Facts* (1944).

Looe Pool Only a mile and a half below the A 394 at Helston, is Loop Pool, the place to go if you're heading for Penzance, are dying to see a spot where Sir Bedivere finally disposed of King Arthur's sword Excalibur, and haven't got time to go to Dozmary Pool. To accept Looe as *the* pool of Arthurian legend, of course, you'll have to wink at the fact that it's a good fifty miles from Slaughterbridge, where Arthur reputedly fought his last and fatal battle. But then, Slaughterbridge's credentials are hardly impeccable either.

Penzance As he drives down its busy, traffic-jammed streets, the visitor may well wonder, "where is the romantic little Penzance of Gilbert and Sullivan's pirates?" For with over 19,000 residents plus swarms of tourists in summer, Penzance is a considerable city. Situated on the A 30 and on the Channel coast ten miles east of Land's End, it is, in fact, Cornwall's largest.

The narrow side streets, many with little houses on raised terraces overlooking the harbor, and the subtropical plants including palm trees do give the place a certain charm. As for real literary significance, it has none. In the early part of this century, it was the home of John Davidson, a Scottish poet. But even there, there's a bit of the comic opera, however macabre. When seized one day with a moment of melancholia, he walked out into the sea and drowned himself. Whereupon the good people of Penzance solicitously went out searching for him. And when they found his body, they ceremoniously buried it with full honors—back in the sea.

2. THE OCEAN COAST: ST. IVES TO MORWENSTOW

St. Ives

St. Ives sits at the top of the A 3074, which from June to September seems like one gigantic funnel for half the tourist coaches in Southern England. In August especially, St. Ives's major street, plunging from 300 feet above the sea to the Guild-hall and Town Centre, becomes an obstacle course daring the visiting driver to thread its intricacies.

How different it was nearly a hundred years ago when, according to her nephew Quentin Bell, to Virginia Woolf it was "the Eden of her youth, an unforgettable paradise." Her father, Sir Leslie Stephen, had discovered the town "at the very toenail of England," as he said, on a walking tour in 1881, the year before Virginia was born. The following spring he took Talland House on Talland Road, high above St. Ives Bay, and for the next fourteen years it was the Stephens's summer home. It was a large house, and it needed to be. To start with there was the Stephens ménage, twelve strong; Virginia, her parents, her sister and two brothers, her half sister and *her* two brothers, the cook, the maid, and the Swiss governess. And always there were countless guests, uncles and aunts, nephews and nieces, and people of every description, among them notables from the world of literature.

Sir Leslie was no mean literary figure himself. The model for Vernon Whitford in George Meredith's *The Egoist*, and, by his first wife, son-in-law to William Makepeace Thackeray, Stephen was a noted critic and magazine editor; biographer of Pope, Swift, Johnson, and George Eliot; and major editor of the monumental *Dictionary of National Biography.* Talland House was admittedly untidy, even shabby, but there was no resisting its easygoing liveliness. Meredith loved to sit under the trees, reading his poetry to the women. American humorist, critic, and poet James Russell Lowell would chase little Virginia (his goddaughter) up and down the sloping garden. And Henry James would stalk about, bemused by it all.

There is no record of what the ten-year-old Virginia thought of Henry James, but there is no doubt of her reaction fifteen years later, when she visited him at Rye. Her account is wickedly hilarious:

> . . . Henry James fixed me with his staring blank eye, it is like a child's marble, and said, "My dear Virginia they tell me, they tell me, they tell me, that you—as indeed being your father's daughter, nay your grandfather's grandchild, the descendant I may say of a century, of a century, of quill pen and ink, ink, inkpots, yes, yes, yes, they tell me, a h m m m, that you, that you, that you *write* in short."

Focal point for the children at Talland House was the cricket pitch, where Virginia, the "demon bowler" as her brother called her, and her playmates cavorted so late into the night they had their ball covered with luminous paint. In the summer of 1893, one of the most avid of these participants was a strikingly handsome six-year-old boy who, like Virginia, was to win fame as a writer, and, like her, come to tragic end: Rupert Brooke.

Virginia Woolfs love for St. Ives is reflected in *Jacob's Room* (1922), the novel that signaled that she had arrived at artistic maturity and was on the threshold of fame; in *To the Lighthouse* (1927); and in *The Waves* (1931). Although *To the Lighthouse* is purportedly about the "Ramsays" on holiday at their summer home in Skye, the family is in truth the Leslie Stephens, their home is Talland House, and the lighthouse is the one called Godrevy, still to be seen in St. Ives Bay.

With heavy hearts, the Stephens gave up Talland House in 1895, unable to bear the thought of seeing it again following the rather sudden death of Virginia's mother in May. Today it is just another big old house divided into flats and catering to the holiday hordes.

Just around the corner from Talland House, in sharply contrasting elegance, is Tregenna Castle, an imposing eighteenth-century stone-built castle in 100 acres of grounds, a four-star hotel with amenities and prices to match. Here in 1894 stayed Henry James, less than charmed with it all:

> I sit here looking out at *my* nice, domestic, inexpensive English rain, in *my* nice bad stuffy insular inn. . . . Here I go out for long walks on wet moors. . . . In the morning I improve the alas not shining hours, in a little black sitting-room which looks out into the strange area—like unto that of the London milkman—with which this cidevant castle is encompassed and which sends up strange scullery odours into my nose.

James went on to complain, "my 'holiday' is no holiday and I must drive the mechanic pen." Those last two words may well be the key to his disgruntlement. For he was in the fifth and, as it turned out, last year of a project his heart was no longer in: the discouraging and abortive effort to turn himself from a novelist into a dramatist. If so, it would have cheered him no end had he known that within five months he would begin toying with the germ of what ultimately became the best-known short story he ever wrote, "The Turn of the Screw."

Zennor

The rocky hills outside the village of Zennor, five miles southeast of St. Ives, are notable for two things: an unusually fine and large cromlech*—and the cottage in which D. H. Lawrence suffered an experience so devastating that at the mere memory of it five years later, he "trembled helplessly."

Lawrence was already a harried, almost hunted man when he came to Zennor in March of 1916, looking for a place to live. He was still recovering

*a circle of stone "legs" supporting a "tabletop" slab of rock, built as a tomb in times that predate history.

from the shock of having his new novel, *The Rainbow,* prosecuted—and destroyed—as obscene. Now, hooted from London and penniless, he and his wife Frieda, while alighting briefly at Zennor's drab Tinner's Arms, heard of a cottage called Higher Tregerthen. It was a cold, dreary, dirty little "granite hole," two storeyed, but with only one room per storey. But it met the Lawrences' sole criterion—at £5 per year it was cheap! Resolutely, they moved in and set to work to make it liveable.

By the first week in April, Lawrence could write to a friend, with a satisfaction that is touching:

> Our cottage is practically done. At last I am in my own home and feel content. I feel I have a place here. The cottage looks *very nice*. I made a dresser, with cupboard below, and shelves for plates above, also bookshelves. These are painted royal blue, and the walls are pale pink, and the ceiling with its beams is white. This is downstairs, a rather low, square room with thick walls. Upstairs looks really beautiful: a good-sized room with a large deep window looking at the sea, and another window opposite looking at the hill-slope of gorse and granite. Your embroidery hangs on the slanting wall of the big window, and the countrypair on the bed is brilliant and gay: it is very nice.

By this time Lawrence had lured their friends, the novelist Katherine Mansfield and her critic husband, John Middleton Murry, into joining them in the cottage next door. But Katherine found this proclaimed Eden less than paradise:

> Today I can't see a yard, thick mist and rain and a tearing wind with it. Everything is faintly damp. The floor of the tower is studded with Cornish pitchers catching the drops.

The last straw was when Lawrence demanded that Murry join him in "Bludbrüderschaft" (blood-brothership), bloodletting ritual and all. By mid-June the Murrys were gone, and, as it turned out, so was the friendship. But the episode was hardly forgotten. Lawrence had begun to work on what was to become *Women in Love* (1920). In it, as the somehwat tartly drawn Gerald and Gudrun, Katherine and Murry appear, Bludbrüderschaft and all.

The Lawrences stayed on at Higher Tregerthen for a total of eighteen months, but toward the end of 1916 things assumed an increasingly threatening air. As Germany's submarines took an ever-growing toll of British shipping, English authorities hunted for espionage along their own coastline. A prime area of suspicion was the northern (Atlantic) coast of Cornwall. And prime suspects became the Lawrences, whose cottage overlooked the very sealanes along which allied ships plied their way to the major port of

Bristol. After all, wasn't Frieda Lawrence not only German, but actually a cousin of THE Baron von Richtofen, Germany's most feared flying ace? And didn't Lawrence go about, brazenly opposing the war and singing German songs?

First a constable called at the cottage to check their identification papers. Then, once or twice, the Lawrences were stopped when returning from shopping and their bundles were searched. At Christmas, two Americans who had come to visit had their papers examined; and one of them, when he went on to London, was arrested, taken to Scotland yard, stripped, and searched.

The climax came the following October. One night while the Lawrences were at the home of a nearby friend, there came a banging at the door, and in burst "a lieutenant with three sordid men." Who, they demanded, had been signaling from the uncurtained upper window? Actually, it was only the housekeeper finding her way to bed with a lighted candle, but no one listened. Here was proof at last that the Lawrences were spies!

The sad, incredible aftermath is reported in the writer's own words in a letter to a friend:

> Now comes another nasty blow. The police have suddenly descended on the house, searched it, and delivered us a notice to leave the area of Cornwall, by Monday next. . . .
>
> This bolt from the blue has fallen this morning: why I know not, any more than you do. I cannot even conceive how I have incurred suspicion—have not the faintest notion. We are as innocent even of pacifist activities, let alone spying of any sort as the rabbits in the field outside. And we must leave Cornwall, and live in an unprohibited area, and report to the police. It is *very* vile. We have practically no money at all—I don't know what we shall do.

To find Higher Tregerthen today takes an intrepid soul and luck akin to a miracle. From St. Ives you take the B 3306 about four miles east and begin asking for the Tinner's Arms. Once there, you start asking anybody on either side of the bar if they'd ever heard of D. H. Lawrence or his cottage. Pure luck will determine whether you get a "yes" and firm, accurate directions . . . or a vague wave of the hand . . . or absolutely blank looks. If you *do* get good directions, you'll find yourself on the narrowest of rocky lanes, barely one car wide, that runs down to the sea. And shortly before you run into the water, you'll spot a cluster of three forlorn stone cottages. One is the "granite hole" you're looking for. If there's washing on the line, it's occupied.*

*In 1919, Virginia Woolf heard about the Lawrence cottage and its two neighbors from Katherine Mansfield and rented them. But apparently she never went there.

Bodmin—Bolventor—Dozmary Pool—St. Merryn

The heading for this section, "THE OCEAN COAST: ST. IVES TO MORWENSTOW," tests the elasticity of truth. For in actuality, when you drive the fifty miles or so between the two towns, you see the ocean only at the very beginning and very end of your trip. And at that, you have to leave the main highway to get to Morwenstow itself. Furthermore, there is nothing of overwhelming literary importance along the way. But if you're heading east anyway, there are a few points you may want to note as you pass by or near them: Bodmin, Bolventor (Jamaica Inn), Dozmary Pool, and St. Merryn.

Bodmin This is the county seat of Cornwall and lies on the A 30, forty miles northeast of St. Ives. Sir Arthur Quiller-Couch was born there in 1863. And D. H. Lawrence twice went there during World War I to be examined for military service. Both occasions proved to be nightmares.

Lawrence was called there from Zennor in July, 1916. He found the food revolting, the barracks so prisonlike he thought of Oscar Wilde, and he cringed at displaying his tattered underwear as he undressed. To his intense relief, he was given complete exemption from all military service because of his lung condition.

The following June he was again summoned there, with the same result: "I got myself rejected again at Bodmin on Saturday: cursed the loathsome performance."

Bolventor A tiny village ten miles northeast of Bodmin on the A 30, Bolventor is the site of Jamaica Inn, immortalized by Daphne du Maurier in her best-selling novel of the same name (1936). Although she placed her story back in 1815, the inn still looks suitably stark and forbidding, with its cold stone, gray slate, and tall chimneys conjuring up the "wild and lonely spot where the giant, wolf-faced Joss Merlyn" held forth, and "respectable folk whip the horses past." Then, writes du Maurier, the coaches avoided the inn, "for its name was evil, and no man knew what horrors its dark shutters hid." Today, they stop there in droves, and you have to fight your way to the bar through tourist hordes queuing up to buy sleazy souvenirs. Alas for one's romantic visions!

Dozmary Pool Across the street from the Inn, a simple road sign points off to the right, directing you down a narrow road to Dozmary Pool. This is where, indeed, Sir Bedivere may well have thrown Excalibur, sword of the dying King Arthur (on the third reluctant try, 'tis true), to the hand that rose mysteriously from the water to grasp it.*

---

*Looe Pool near Penzance, of course, disputes Dozmary for this honor. (see p. 314).

St. Merryn On the coast a dozen miles north of Bodmin, St. Merryn has some interest for fans of D. H. Lawrence. For it furnished him his first refuge from London late in 1915, following the shocking court order for the destruction of his *The Rainbow,* as obscene. The cottage was lent to Lawrence by a friend, the novelist J. D. Beresford, and for a little over two months gave him a rare interval of tranquility during this traumatic period of his life.

"We came here tonight," he wrote the evening of December 30, "—a nice old house with large clear rooms, and such wonderful silence—only a faint sound of the sea and wind. It is like being at the window and looking out of England to the beyond."

Camelford—Slaughterbridge—Tintagel

This is King Arthur's country, or—in the words of Richard Burton's song in *Camelot*—"so they say." In fact, the hamlet of Camelford (on the A 39, ten miles due north of Bodmin, but sixteen by car) *was* Camelot, according to tradition. And Slaughterbridge, a mile beyond, claims to be the scene of Arthur's final, fatal battle. Be that as it may: there's nothing to see at either spot today, though Tennyson records finding "King Arthur's stone . . . by a rock under two Sycamores" in 1848.

Tintagel, however, three miles further northwest, is another matter. You get to Tintagel over the B 3263, a better road than you might expect. It has to be, for in summer a veritable chain belt of buses crawl along it, dumping their contents endlessly into what must be the tawdriest tourist trap in all England.

The town's main street is not without a number of charming old houses, including The Old Post Office, a fantastic little building that dates back to the fourteenth century and has an undulating roof of stone (that's right, *stone*). From this street a Land Rover plunges you down a rocky chute to the sea, to the base of the massive cliff and "Merlin's Cave" from which, you are told, Merlin fished the infant Arthur out of the water. And half way up the rock are the very ruins of "Arthur's Castle."

Briefly you forget that the Arthur of legend is about as authentic as Peter Pan and that the castle ruins you're staring at in actuality housed nothing more ancient or romantic than the twelfth to fourteenth century Earls of Cornwall. For one wonderful moment, you let the wild, craggy beauty of the great slate cliffs rising starkly out of the water and the white pounding waves win you over to awe in spite of yourself. No wonder Tennyson loved it and visited it repeatedly.

Arthur's Tintagel, Cornwall

Robert M. Cooper

St. Juliot

Three miles to the north of Tintagel, on the B 3263, is Boscastle. And two miles east of Boscastle, on a little side road, is St. Juliot. Here in March, 1870, came a young architect and would-be writer named Thomas Hardy, summoned from Dorset to advise on the restoration of the tower of the church of St. Juliot. He stayed for a week at the rectory, where pretty young Emma Lavinia Gifford filled in as hostess for her ailing sister, the vicar's wife. The seven days proved plenty of time for Hardy to fall in love, though it took four more years, frequent visits, and much correspondence before Emma finally became Mrs. Hardy.

By that time, Hardy had already capitalized on the romance by turning it into the novel, *A Pair of Blue Eyes,* published in 1873. Although he changed the topography somewhat and altered some place names—the church, for instance, becomes St. Agnes—the modern visitor can easily find the sites of key events in the book.* The "serene impressive sea" is still there in a vast concave at Pentargon Bay near Beeny; the old Rectory (now a private home) is still a "little paradise of flowers and trees;" and St. Juliot's churchyard still seems "a delightful place to be buried in." Within the church are plaques denoting Hardy's restoration work and honoring Emma and the Reverend Caddell Holder, her vicar brother-in-law, as well as some of Hardy's architectural sketches.

Bude and Morwenstow

The last two places of any literary importance the visitor to Cornwall passes before he—and the A 39—head northward into Devon for the trek east are Bude and Morwenstow. It is fitting that both are associated with Alfred Lord Tennyson, for the poet dearly loved Cornwall and gave its legendary Arthur new luster in his *Idylls of the King* (1859–1885). He first visited both in 1848 while on a tour of the West Country.

Bude

It is hard to conceive of anyone so dignified as Tennyson—and so aware of that dignity—taking a pratfall. But take one he did at Bude, and of monumental proportions. He arrived there just at dusk, burst into the house where he was to stay, and raced down the hall shouting to the girl who let him

*An inexpensive tour pamphlet (No. 9) with excellent directions and a map is available from The Thomas Hardy Society, Ltd., Dorchester, Dorset.

in: "The sea, the sea! Where is the sea? Show me the sea!" Oblingingly, she opened the back door, and Tennyson shot through it—and crashed six feet to the gravel beach below. It took six weeks for his injuries to mend sufficiently for him to move on. Bude is a pleasant little city (5,600 people), has a number of attractive hotels, and the view of the ocean *is* delightful. One could do worse than choose Bude for his last night in Cornwall. John Galsworthy did that in 1906 and wrote: "It's *glorious* here."

Morwenstow

Morwenstow is some seven miles north of Bude (on a narrow unnumbered road about three miles west of the A 39) and a little more than a mile below the Devon county line. The village is quaintly hidden in a wooded combe. Above, rising to 450 feet, is Eagle's Crag, with a last spectacular view of the wild Cornish coast. In 1848, when Tennyson went there after leaving Bude, Morwenstow housed one of the strangest of all the weird and wonderful men that Cornwall ever produced: the Reverend Stephen Hawker, vicar of Morwenstow for the past fourteen years and poet in his own right.

What a pair these two made as they met! Tennyson, with his great targe of a hat and dark Spanish cloak, "a tall swarthy man," in Hawker's words, "with an eye like a sword." And Hawker himself, in claret-colored coat with tails, blue fisherman's jersey, and flesh-colored beaver hat without a brim . . . a man who preached sermons accompanied by nine cats and once sat several nights on the cold wet rocks of Bude's beach, stark naked save for a seaweed wig and oilskin tail, impersonating a mermaid.

Innately shy, Tennyson at first hid his identity, but when Hawker innocently quoted at length from *Morte d'Arthur* and "Locksley Hall," and announced that their author was not only his own favorite poet, "but all of England's," Tennyson confessed that he was that author. Thereafter, the two got on famously, chattering on about Arthur and other Cornish legends, and savage tales of smuggling and storm-dashed ships, and spouting Shakespeare and Byron.

"Indeed a day to be remembered," said Tennyson as they parted.

Leaving Cornwall and England, one remembers many such.

INDEX

Key to the Index

1. AUTHORS: are in all capital letters.
2. *Titles:* are in italics.
3. Churches: are included if they are
   a. actual (not fictional)
   b. extant
   c. of enough literary interest to warrant a visit
4. Hotels—Inns—Restaurants—Pubs: are included only if they are
   a. actual (not fictional)
   b. of literary interest
   c. still serving the public.

   A separate listing of such places also appears at the end of this index, arranged by cities and with the page numbers where they are discussed.

Hotels, Inns, Restaurants, and Pubs